# ENCYCLOPEDIA OF
# MODEL AIRCRAFT

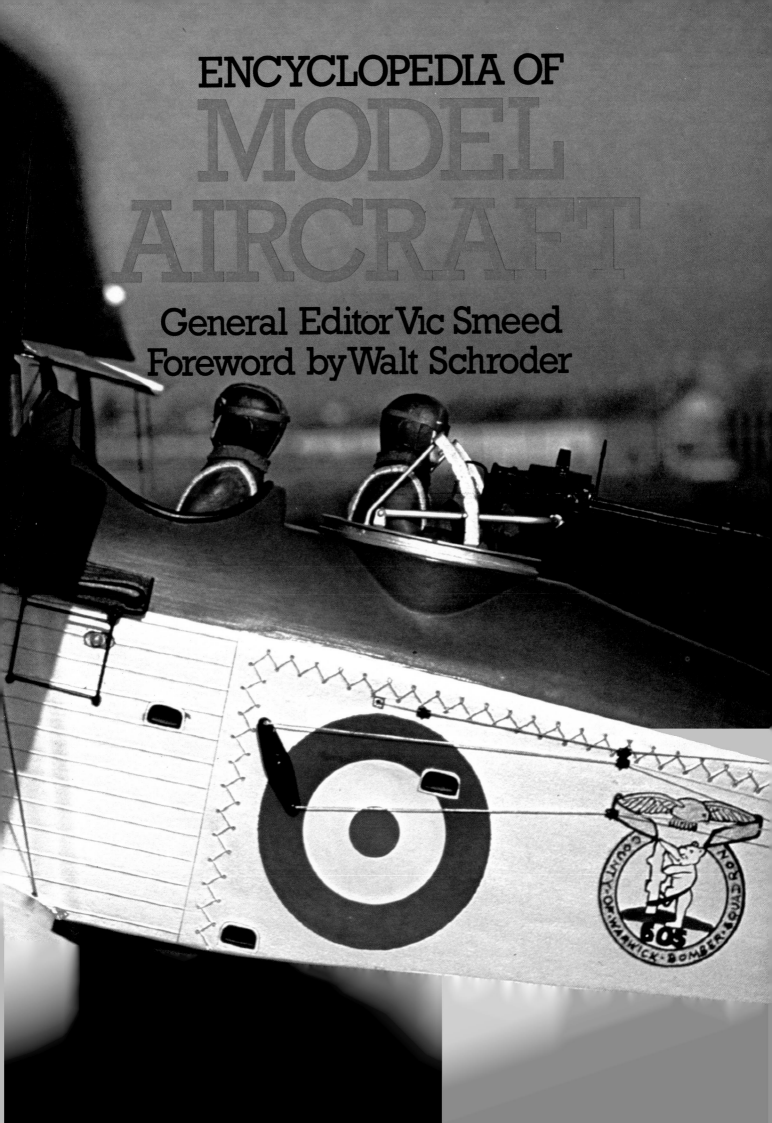

# ENCYCLOPEDIA OF
# MODEL
# AIRCRAFT

## General Editor Vic Smeed
## Foreword by Walt Schroder

First published 1979 by
Octopus Books Limited
59 Grosvenor Street
London W1

© 1979 Octopus Books Limited

ISBN 0 7064 0988 4

Manufactured in United States of America

# Contents

# Foreword

I would not believe it possible, after more than forty active years in the model aircraft hobby and having read most every book written on the subject, that I could find another that could hold my interest for any reasonable period of time. I did however, with the *Encyclopedia of Model Aircraft*.

It covers every major facet of the model aircraft field of endeavors in good, even great depth and is compiled in such an interesting manner as to hold your attention right to the very end. Even on such subjects that may have never drawn your interest before!

In my more than thirty years of editing model aircraft material of many categories, it is difficult to work up

enthusiasm, but I found something in each of the chapters that held my attention to its finish, and holding an editor's attention is a real challenge for any publication.

Vic Smeed is to be complimented on the selection and organization of the varied contributions of those selected to add their expertise to this volume.

It should do much to continue the upward movement of this very complex hobby sport which requires the expertise and knowledge incorporated in this encyclopedia. It will find a very important place in this always growing and ever more sophisticated aircraft modeling hobby!

Walter L. Schroder
Publisher Model Builder Magazine

# History of Model Aircraft

Reproductions of contemporary engravings on opposite page show, *top*, William Henson's 'Aerial Steam Carriage', a full-size project based on the successful Henson/Stringfellow model of 1848, *left*, Alphonse Penaud's 'planophore' rubber-powered model of 1871 and, *right*, a practical ornithopter, also by Penaud, which flew in 1872. The photograph *below* shows a meeting of the Bristol Model Aircraft Club in 1913. Models are mostly twin pusher propeller A-frames, but one tractor type is visible at extreme left.

Man has always been fascinated by flight, as is evidenced by the mythology of early civilizations and the work of artists through the centuries. The remarkable Leonardo da Vinci, who is believed to have made a successful model helicopter, was the first to leave a record of possible designs for flying machines, one or two of which could well have proved sufficiently successful to have encouraged further development. Other figures of history were less practical, for example Roger Bacon, who wrote a specification in 1250; he was convinced that air had an upper surface, on which a sufficiently light vessel would float. In 1670, Francesco de Lana wrote of experiments he had made with balloons, but he did not proceed because he felt that attempts to navigate the air might be regarded as impious and he also foresaw, with astonishing clarity, the effects of air raids.

Successful flight was achieved in 1783 by the Montgolfier brothers, using a hot air balloon, and balloons flew extensively for the next hundred years or so. Navigable balloons proved something of a problem, however, until the practical development of semi-rigid balloons and power units of moderate weight for the amount of power developed. Before this, balloon flights relied on wind direction, and it is of interest to mention that the first aerial crossing of the English Channel was achieved by Blanchard and Jefferies as early as January, 1785.

Heavier-than-air machines were inhibited to a large extent by the

conviction that flapping wings (ornithopters) were necessary, and the inability of a man's muscles to provide adequate power. The first successful heavier-than-air flight was by a 3m (10ft) wingspan steam-powered model weighing a little under 4kg (9lb) built by Englishman John Stringfellow in 1848. This model was the fruit of cooperation between Stringfellow and William Henson, and the latter's patent of 1842 covers virtually all the elements of a present-day aeroplane.

The next successful pioneer was Alphonse Penaud, a Frenchman who produced a number of model designs employing rubber motors. His 'planophore' covered a distance of 60m in 13sec in 1871, and he built a successful ornithopter in 1872, the principles of which are identical with those used by such models today.

Successful man-carrying flight is normally ascribed to the work of Otto Lilienthal, who was the first person to study gliding flight scientifically, and whose machines would not look too out of place at a modern hang-gliding gathering Lilienthal's actual flights began in 1893 and he died following a gliding accident in 1896. Percy Pilcher had travelled from England to Germany and made flights on Lilienthal's machines; his first design flew in 1895 and he was readying a machine for power installation in 1899 when he too sustained fatal injuries in a gliding accident.

One other 19th century pioneer should be mentioned, Sir George Cayley, known as the Father of British Aeronautics, and who is considered by many authorities as the true inventor of the aeroplane. He built the first of a series of model gliders in 1804, and recent experiments, which included the building and flying of a man-carrying glider from sketches and details in his notebooks, lend substance to the claims that he had built and flown (with his chauffeur as pilot) a successful man-carrying glider some sixty years before Lilienthal. Cayley conducted aerodynamic research years ahead of its time and is credited with early discoveries on airscrews, cambered wings, stability, and even streamlining.

The first outdoor free flight by a power model (Stringfellow's having flown in a disused lace factory) was made in 1896 by Professor S. P. Langley in the USA; Langley then scaled the machine up and in 1903 two unsuccessful attempts were made to fly it with C. M. Manly at the controls. Although the failures were clearly due to the launching gear, Langley's backers refused further financial help and the project stopped. In 1914 Glenn Curtis borrowed the machine from the Smithsonian Institute, replaced the fabric, mounted it on floats, and flew it without difficulty.

Orville and Wilbur Wright became interested in, particularly, Lilienthal's work and built a glider in 1900. Their experiences with it led to construction of a wind tunnel, and a second glider was made in 1902, incorporating lessons learned with the aid of models in the tunnel. It was this machine, fitted with a four-cylinder petrol engine chain-driving two own-designed propellers, with which the first man-carrying power flights were made at Kitty Hawk, North Carolina, in December 1903.

Interest in aviation spread rapidly, and many models were made and flown in the early 1900s. Among the modellers in Britain were de Havilland, Sopwith, Fairey, Handley Page, A. V. Roe, and Camm, all to become household names in full-size aircraft manufacture. Most of the models were rubber-powered and of the A-frame twin-pusher configuration, though there were some 'spar monoplanes', or what would nowadays be called stick models. One or two clever model engineers produced successful small petrol engines in the 1908–1914 period, notably, for aircraft models, the Stanger and Bonn–Mayer engines, but apart from one or two individuals, gliders seemed to hold little interest. There was sufficient activity for a semi-national body, the Kite and Model Aircraft Association, to run competitions, and the first Wakefield Cup was presented in 1911 by Sir Charles Wakefield. There was even a short-lived magazine, the *Amateur Aviator*, which first appeared in 1912, though the model sections of *Aero* and *Flight* magazines and the *Model Engineer* were the widest-read sources of information.

The materials used in model construction then were usually birch

strip and veneer, spruce, sometimes piano wire or bamboo, and oiled silk covering. Wings were usually single-surfaced, with ribs steamed in a jig, and propellers were 'bent-wood', i.e. steamed to shape from fairly thick veneer. If the propeller was at the front, it was a tractor, if behind, a pusher. Flights were most frequently hand-launched, but ROG (rise off ground) records were separately categorized, covering duration or distance for any model, 'hydro off water', and 'single tractor screw spar model'.

In France in 1911 the Godfroy brothers flew a model with a V-twin petrol engine for five laps, tethered to a pole, and in 1914 D. Stanger set a free-flight petrol-engined model record (51sec!) in front of Royal Aero Club observers at Hendon; this record stood till 1932. The model was a 2135mm (7ft) span tail-first biplane weighing 5kg (10¾lb) with a V-twin engine weighing about 1250g (2lb 12oz).

One other form of power became available before the 1914–18 war, and this was the compressed-air engine. A small, usually three-cylinder radial engine was fed with air from a large but very light brass foil tank, which was usually wire-wound for strength and often com-

prised the fuselage itself. Air was pumped into the tank with a motor-cycle tyre pump. A record flight of 67.6sec was set with one of these engines as late as 1929.

The Great War, while interrupting model development, created much greater air-mindedness, and the London Model Aeroplane Society, revived from pre-war, changed its name in 1922 to the Society of Model Aeronautical Engineers and succeeded the K. and M.A.A. as the national governing body. One of the early Presidents was Air Vice Marshal Sir Sefton Brancker, the Minister for Civil Aviation, and it was he who approached Sir Charles (later Lord) Wakefield in 1927 on the matter of an international trophy. The earlier cup, last competed for in 1914, had been lost, and an international trophy was sought following the visit of a small British team to Philadelphia in 1926. Sir Charles presented a splendid cup, which became the most prestigious international award for some thirty years, and is still competed for today.

At this time, materials for modelling had remained almost unchanged, though ply and cellulose-doped Japanese silk had joined the list; geared rubber motors, usually using small clock gears, were being used by experts, and the first kits for flying models were becoming established. Gears had first been introduced in 1914, the year in which covered fuselages began to be noticed, but the progression to

geared, fuselage models was very slow. In terms of durations, flights had crept from about 40sec in 1914 to 60sec in the late 1920s; the first competition for the Wakefield Cup in 1928 was won with a flight of 52.6sec (T. H. Newell) and the 1929 event with 70.4sec (R. N. Bullock).

A revolution was about to occur, however. Records of early activities in other countries are difficult to trace, but aeromodelling was gaining ground in most European countries and all English-speaking countries, especially the USA. In the late 1920s, balsa structure and tissue covering appeared in America, and someone discovered stretch-winding of rubber motors. These techniques were used by Joe Earhart to win the 1930 Wakefield Cup event for America with a best flight of 2min 35sec, using a straightforward model of balsa/tissue construction which weighed only 70g (2½oz) against the 230–280g (8–10 oz) of the other competitors. Conditions were blustery and so relatively flimsy a machine had been given little chance, so the shock can be imagined!

Conversion to balsa, tissue, and ungeared single-skein motors turning large propellers was rapid and almost total, but America again won the Cup in 1931 (4min 24.8sec). The competition was declared null in 1932, won by Britain in 1933, 1934, and 1936, America in 1935, 1938, and 1939, and France in 1937.

Petrol engines began to reappear in 1932/3, mostly large by today's standards (15–30cc) until the intro-

Meeting of the Air League in the London area in 1909. Models are Twining type with double stick fuselages.

Compressed-air models on Wimbledon Common in 1924. Air tank size is noticeable. Rarely seen today.

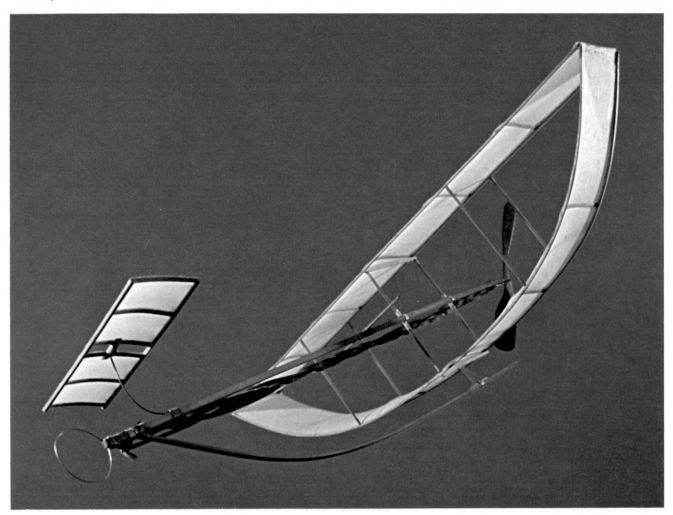

duction in 1934 of the famous Brown Junior 9cc motor, in America, followed soon after by the 6cc Baby Cyclone, also American, and the then tiny 2.3cc Elf, which originated in Canada. They caused a rapid tightening of rules, since on both sides of the Atlantic there was initially nothing to prevent such engines entering the established rubber powered events!

Gliders, or sailplanes as they began to be called, also returned in the early 1930s, a leading influence being the German, Horst Winkler. Rubber-powered free-flight speed models enjoyed a vogue, and there were experiments with autogiros, indoor models, steam power, flying boats, and many other slightly off-beat types of model, as well as the first steps into accurate scale flying models.

Increasing numbers of kits became available; in Britain a 500mm (20in) model kit could be bought for 9d (4p) and a 1270mm (50in) rubber model kit for 5/– (25p). Equivalent kits in the USA were 15 cents and $1. Engines were more expensive, from about £10 in Britain and $20 or so in the USA. Specialist model shops began to appear, often relying on mail order, and manufacturers proliferated. A majority of

these were one or two-man businesses, established by enthusiasts, and many of today's major model firms stem from such small beginnings. Regular monthly magazines devoted solely or primarily to model aircraft began publication in several countries, and model flying clubs by the score came into existence. Sunday flying became a regular summertime pastime.

Successful radio controlled flights were made in 1936/7, though they were not the first ever, since in the 1920s a radio controlled airship was used as a music-hall turn. This

*Above:* Well-known in its day was the Bragg-Smith single pusher of 1912. This model is a faithful replica.

*Below:* An early commercial model, sold ready to fly, was the 'Skysail' spar tractor of 1927–8.

*Opposite top:* the original A-frame built by D. A. Paveley in 1926 which won national trophies in 1926, 1927 and 1928 and was the first model sent to America for proxy flying.

*Opposite bottom:* Stanger V4 petrol engine built in 1906 and flown successfully in 1908.

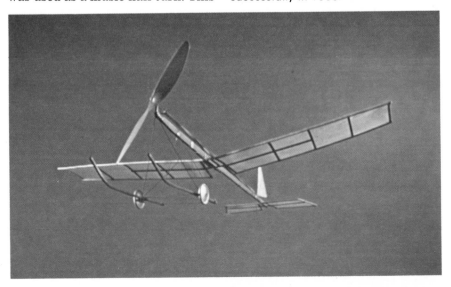

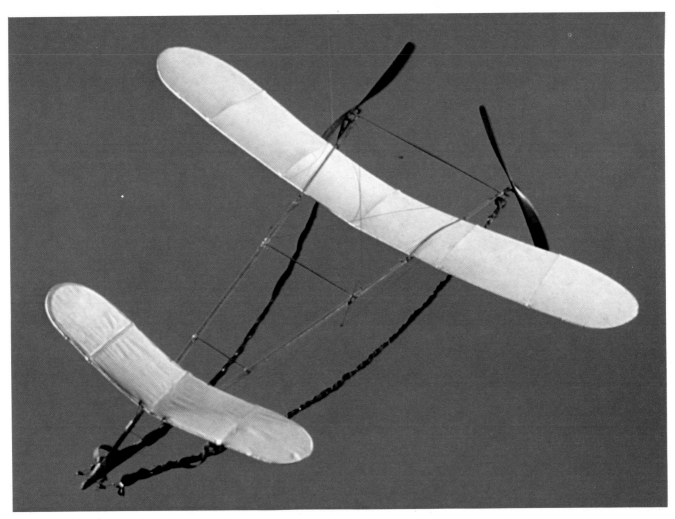

model used a spark transmitter and coherer receiver and dropped sweets and occasional bank notes on the audience! The 1936 aircraft used valve (tube) equipment which was heavy and at times temperamental, but these pioneer attempts led ultimately to the marketing, fifteen years later, of reliable commercial radio control equipment and today's miniature sets.

International competitions were getting into their stride, with as many as eight nations attending and others sending models to be flown by proxy, when World War 2 broke out. All large models, and any with petrol engines, were banned in England, and competitive activity virtually ceased here and in Europe. The war, however, made many more people conscious of the air, particularly the younger age groups, and with the need for aircraft recognition and the help afforded by scale models for this purpose, the number of modellers actually increased during the years between 1939 and 1945, despite shortages of ideal materials.

America was more fortunately placed and two major developments occurred there during the war years, the introduction of control-line flying, which opened up a vast new area of model operation, and the invention of the glowplug, which removed the need for heavy and sometimes unreliable ignition equipment for model engines. At the same time, the so-called 'diesel', or compression-ignition engine, was developed in Switzerland, achieving the same purpose.

The immediate post-war years saw an enormous surge of interest in model flying. Though rubber power maintained its following, it was soon equalled and surpassed by towline gliders, free-flight power models, and control-liners. The die-sel engine, which never really caught on in America, reigned supreme in Europe for several years, with innumerable examples flowing from small manufacturers in, particularly, Italy, France and Britain. Another form of power plant made a brief appearance – the pulse jet, which produced a blast of noise audible for some 5km on a still evening, and control-line speeds of some 250kmh (160 + mph). In contrast, RTP (round the pole) rubber models, flown tethered indoors, enjoyed a brief vogue. These were developed late in the war, and flights of three or four minutes were possible. International meetings restarted, with 20–25 nations participating.

Commercial radio control equipment started to appear in 1950, and immediately another whole new dimension was added to the hobby. Initially, only one model could operate at a time, due to mutual interference, and the sets were heavy and sometimes temperamental. Transistors were virtually unknown to most people at the time, but within three or four years they were being incorporated in model gear, and technology advanced at an ever-accelerating pace.

The last, and very recent, innovation is electric power. A model

13

powered by an electric motor made a short hop seventy years ago, and electric RTP models were demonstrated in 1946. There were electric free-flight kits on sale in 1948, but practical and consistent electric flying for the average modeller, tethered, free-flight, or radio-controlled, has only been developed over the last ten years.

Nowadays the intending modeller can be bewildered by the number of avenues to explore in the world of aeromodelling, and it may therefore be helpful at this juncture to categorize the various aspects. There is one immediate division, flying or non-flying. The latter is now dominated by the injection-moulded plastic kit, but there are devotees of traditional wood and metal construction, vacuum-formed plastic kit modellers, and a growing number who build from plastic card and strip. Almost all non-flying models are scale representations of full-size aircraft, but occasionally a builder will experiment with a 'dream machine', or build a replica of only part of an aircraft – perhaps a section of a wing showing the structure with the installation of cannon and necessary ancillaries. Most models fall into one or other of the recognized standard scales, but occasionally large and detailed non-flying aircraft are seen.

Flying models are basically separated into three main groups:
  (i) Free-flight – rubber, glider, power, scale or functional.
  (ii) Control-line – stunt, speed, team-racing, combat, scale.
  (iii) Radio control – power or glider, scale or functional.

Unfortunately it is not quite as simple as this, as each broad group sub-divides. Thus a glider, either free-flight or radio, may be intended for slope-soaring or thermal flying; it can be for either if it is a scale model. There are sport models in each category as well as competition models, and the latter are divided into various classes for different contests. These classes are set out in the following chapters, and it is perhaps therefore sufficient at this point to define the term 'sport model'.

Serious competitive flying appeals to a relatively limited proportion of aeromodellers – 5% is a figure which has been suggested – and thus compares with, say, yacht racing, which is indulged in by only a small number of those who enjoy pottering with boats. Competitions normally produce the advances in design and the new materials and

techniques which create progress and which filter down to improve all models, but regular participation in competitions demands dedication and expenditures in time and money (not least in travelling to the events) beyond the average modeller, whose pleasure comes from a weekly trip to the nearest flying field and who, if persuaded, may have a go at the local club's spot landing event as the limit of his competitive ambition. This enthusiast flies for fun, and in many cases prefers a simply-maintained, rugged and long-lived model of moderate performance to

a highly-tuned, sensitive, and possibly more expensive contest model. A sport model may therefore be a model designed specifically for fun flying, or possibly training, or it may be, effectively, a detuned version of a competition model.

What sort of person constitutes the average modeller? Surveys over a number of years indicate that the average age is 23, and this is an indication of the number of older people who retain an interest, since about a quarter of all aeromodellers are still at school or college, even omitting plastic kit builders. Flying

*Above:* Accurate replica of T. H. Newell's *Falcon*, winner of the first Wakefield Cup competition in 1928, built by Lt Cdr Alwyn Greenhalgh, official historian to the SMAE.

*Below:* A modern non-rigid airship model, radio-controlled but usually flown in a large hangar.

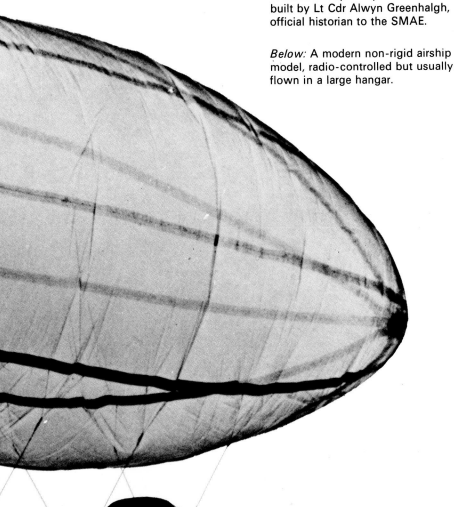

models can be exciting and offer a challenge to young people; furthermore, the number of tools required is very small, and reasonably quick results can be obtained. Increasing numbers of schools are encouraging modelling as part of practical work or as an extra-curricular activity.

There is a gap in the 20–30 age group, the decline in active modellers being attributed to marriage and home-making, but considerable numbers return to building and flying in their 30s and many pursue their interest into their 60s and 70s. Modellers come from all walks of life, but a noticeably high proportion are professional men, doctors, dentists, architects, solicitors and so on, who find relaxation from the stress of everyday life in model construction and operation. As would be expected, a lot of engineers, particularly from the aeronautical and electronics industries, are enthusiasts, but the butcher and the baker derive as much enjoyment, and can be just as competent, as their scientifically qualified clubmates.

Aeromodelling offers a challenge and the opportunity to develop manual dexterity, planning and foresight, powers of observation and mental calculation, and patience. It teaches simple aerodynamics, how to read a plan, the use, advantages and limitations of various materials, even simple stress laws and meteorology. As a pastime it is healthy, exciting and satisfying (if at times frustrating!) and it has therapeutic qualities; it encourages craftsmanship and the appreciation of skill. It can be regarded as a hobby or as a serious sport, and it can be enjoyed on an outlay of a few pennies a week or on a millionaire level. Not an unimpressive catalogue for an amateur pursuit!

Professionally, models are extensively used in scientific investigation, from solid wind-tunnel models to accurate radio-controlled scale machines used to establish, for example, the safest technique for ditching a particular full-size design. Models played a large part in solving the Comet disasters and in correcting a particular spinning characteristic of the Javelin fighter; they are used militarily as R/C targets and visual range R/C missiles, and quite extensive use is now being made of them for meteorological and monitoring purposes. Non-flying models play a major part in livery design for airlines, as publicity and sales aids, and of course, for record purposes, as in museums.

# Plastic Kits

## World War 1
## Between the Wars
## 1939 to the Present

Despite the fact that most plastic kits are easy to assemble, there are still several basic rules that may prove useful, and it is hoped that the following suggestions will help improve modellers' skills. Before attempting to build any plastic model aeroplane kit, one should first wash all parts in soapy water, which serves to remove the mould release oil from the components. The cleaning is important because it reduces static, found on most plastics, and aids adhesion of paint and cement. Once dried the components should be cut from the 'trees' that hold them together in the box. Never be tempted to break pieces off, as they are easily damaged and will demand unnecessary filling or repair later.

### Assembly

Fuselage halves are usually the first major item to be assembled and all interior detail is best added and painted beforehand. Most aircraft kits now include interior parts, although there will be room for improvements. How much detail should be included depends on the

Typifying the colourful biplane fighter, this Bristol Bulldog is made from a $\frac{1}{48}$ scale plastic kit originally produced by Inpact but more recently available from Life-Like. Kits in $\frac{1}{72}$ scale for this aeroplane are also made. *Model by F. Henderson.*

skill of the modeller and the degree of reference material available.

When cementing fuselage halves together, always apply glue to the mating edge of one or both sides and bind the parts together with tape until the adhesive dries. Usually this takes about 24hr before the joint is really firm. The joint line must then be completely removed by scraping with a knife blade, or alternatively filed, but always finishing up with wet and dry paper liberally lubricated with soapy water.

During the building of the model it will become obvious that some parts fit badly, leaving gaps that will require filling and smoothing if a neat job is the aim. There are a number of proprietary brands of modelling filler on the market and most work reasonably well if carefully applied. Many modellers have found, however, that interior Ready-Mixed Polyfilla (a plaster filler for home decorators) is a more suitable alternative. It is easily applied and sanded and does not melt or attack plastic as some other fillers do if applied too liberally.

Always follow the manufacturers' instruction sheets carefully; only when experience grows can one proceed to assemble the model in-dependently. Test fit each component before actually glueing and never rush a stage, but work carefully and thoroughly. It is worth bearing in mind that polystyrene adhesive fails to work on painted areas. When pre-painted parts are ready to install, scrape off any paint that might have strayed onto the glueing area.

It is a common 'fault' of aircraft models that items are moulded too heavily, undercarriage doors and wing trailing edges usually being the first to suffer. The latter can be filed and sanded down, but under-carriage doors are best replaced by cutting replacements from thin plastic sheet. The original kit part can be used as a template before it is discarded.

Biplane subjects can be a cause of headaches during assembly, but care and common sense can render construction of these types no more difficult than a sleek jet fighter. The most important point to consider is whether wings and fuselages should be finished, painted, and decals (transfers) added before assembly. There is nothing more difficult than trying to wield a paint brush around the inside of engine cowls or apply-ing decals to a fragile structure supported merely by fine struts. On most model aircraft, important de-tails (including aerials, wheels, un-dercarriage doors) need not be attached until the aircraft is almost finished. Again it is advisable for small parts to be prepainted before assembly.

Undercarriages are all import-ant. If the model is to be represented on the ground, oleo legs should be reduced in height and tyre bases flattened. The latter is easily ac-complished by heating gently then pressing onto a flat hard surface. The walls of the 'tyre' should bulge quite realistically as a result.

**Painting and finishing**
Before attempting to paint the model, major components should be more or less completely assembled (except as above) but with all detail parts left unfitted and clear parts masked, if spraying. Paints – always enamels – should be rigorously stirred and thinned too. Aim for a consistency akin to milk and ensure the paint is devoid of lumps and dust. Always work the brush (choose a fine sable) in one direc-tion at a time and avoid the desire to cover in one coat. At least 12 hours should elapse before a second coat is applied, in case the first moves. Brushes should be washed

carefully and diligently in white spirit before storing in a light-proof box. Hairs should be protected at all costs and lengths of tube can be slipped over the shanks to achieve this.

One of the biggest problems is painting the framelines of cockpit canopies and gun turrets, and a method of achieving a realistic appearance is the use of painted stripes. Thin lines of adhesive tape or decal sheet can be made by careful slicing with a sharp knife, using a steel rule as a guide. These should be prepainted in the surrounding base colour and left to dry, after which they are simply cut to length and applied with tweezers.

If handpainting the frames is considered, at least ensure that a firm and comfortable grip of both canopy and brush is possible. To achieve this the canopy should be mounted onto a small length of wood serving as a handhold. Double-sided tape can be used for 'adhesion' and serves another purpose in that the glueing areas are kept free of paint. With the canopy easier to handle, painting should be made correspondingly so, and the result will show.

Decals are perhaps the simplest of operations and usually are the last. They should always be carefully trimmed to remove backing film and then applied to their correct positions on to the model. Forceps or tweezers are essential to transfer the smaller items, and they can be eased into final location by a soft sable brush, after which a soft lint-free cloth is used to absorb excess moisture around the decals. It is imperative that decals should never be *soaked* in water, because if this is done, the adhesive qualities will be seriously reduced and they can subsequently fall off the model. Smooth gloss finishes provide the best base for decals and many modellers varnish their creations before adding markings, regardless of the intended finish. When the decals have dried they are further fixed by more clear varnish, matt, satin or gloss dependent on the subject. Such a procedure usually results in removing all traces of untrimmed carrier film.

In order to produce really fine models and include correct details and colouring, the modeller will have to become more than just a modeller, but an amateur historian as well. It should be important to collate photographs, magazine features and books to create a useful reference library; luckily there is a vast amount on the market.

Local libraries are rarely considered but really are a great source of reference and most volumes can be made available through them. One should always manage to collect as many references as can be afforded and subsequently file them under a sensible indexing system. But in the final analysis, photographs remain the only viable source of reference and these should be studied whenever possible. Only then will the modeller really appreciate the aircraft in question and this will reflect in the model as he strives to capture its character in miniature.

## World War 1 Models

To many modellers the character and appeal of a vintage aircraft is difficult to resist, particularly of those colourful warplanes produced during the 1914–18 war period. There was a time when the range of World War 1 plastic aircraft kits offered a healthy selection of prototypes. Recently, however, the number has regrettably dwindled as moderate sales result in moulds being 'rested' for a few years. Any hope of new WW1 subjects is really now in the hands of the vacform manufacturers.

For anyone wishing to construct some of these early types, very few subjects provide so much enjoyment in their creation – not that they are the easiest to build, but by demanding more skill from the modellers they represent a greater challenge. This is especially true when considering that many kits of WW1 aircraft are inaccurate and below current standards.

The following suggestions will be more or less applicable to any WW1 aircraft kit because there are several important and common factors to consider while building. The thickly moulded trailing edges of wings, for example, should always be refined by sanding until they are wafer thin, and the same procedure applies to wing tips, which also need reducing. Obviously this will destroy some of the wing rib detail which might as well be eradicated anyway, for few manufacturers have really captured the character of a fabric doped flying surface properly or convincingly.

Basically, new rib positions can be applied by heat stretching plas-

*Left:* $\frac{1}{48}$ scale Fokker DRI in authentic markings of von Richthofen.
*Right:* Albatros DVa, $\frac{1}{72}$ scale, also in Richthofen markings, with sprue struts and rolled wire rigging. *Both models by R. Rimell.*

tic sheet strips to make fine 'ribbons' which can be cut up and applied to the upper surfaces of wings and tailplanes with careful amounts of liquid polystyrene cement. This also gives the modeller the chance to reposition the rib tapes correctly, for often they are moulded at the wrong angle or unequally spaced. Under the wings, the corresponding positions are marked by scribing closely spaced parallel lines for each rib with a metal point and then sanding down afterwards. Additionally, it is essential to separate ailerons, elevators and rudders and recement them at different – albeit realistic – angles.

Tail surfaces are rarely moulded thin enough in section and in most cases complete replacements should be considered; these can be easily cut from thin plastic sheet suitably shaped with rib tapes added and scored as described above.

Cockpit detailing is limited only by personal skill and the amount of reference material available. The character of these early types is always enhanced by interior fittings, and at the very minimum these should include a floor, seat, harness, control panel, control column and rudder bar. It is left to the real enthusiast to add more, such as internal structure, throttle quadrant, and pressure pump, all of which can be built up from stretched plastic sprue, and plastic sheet. Seats should also be replaced by scratch building, since few supplied in kits

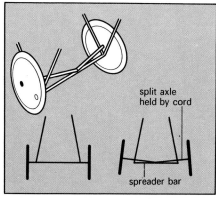

split axle held by cord

spreader bar

softening plastic wheel to create tyre flattening

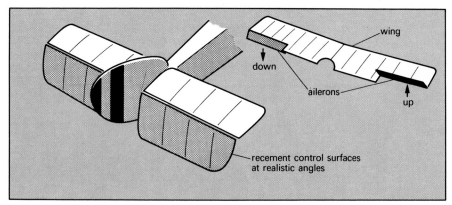

wing

down

ailerons

up

recement control surfaces at realistic angles

ever look realistic, usually misshapen, always oversized.

Interiors should of course be painted before and during the addition of cockpit detail, and care should be exercised to keep all colours muted. A neutral shade such as light buff or dull grey is suggested and these should always be matt. Attach each small additional component with small dabs of PVA wood glue, which dries invisibly and will not melt fine plastic, and

*Above:* Some of the simple modifications which can turn a lifeless plastic model into a convincing representation of an aeroplane as it actually appeared.

*Below:* This BE2c used a combination of DH4 wings and other components from a $\frac{1}{72}$ Airfix kit with a fuselage built up from plastic sheet, incorporating a fully furnished cockpit. The model represents the machine flown by Lt Leefe Robinson, VC. *Built by R. Rimell.*

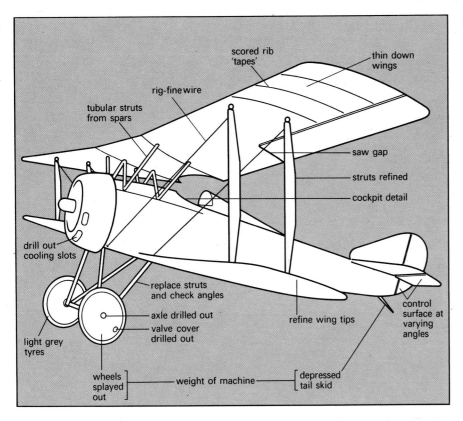

Labels on diagram:
scored rib 'tapes'
thin down wings
rig-fine wire
tubular struts from spars
saw gap
struts refined
cockpit detail
drill out cooling slots
replace struts and check angles
axle drilled out
valve cover drilled out
refine wing tips
control surface at varying angles
light grey tyres
wheels splayed out
weight of machine
depressed tail skid

the use of tweezers and a stand magnifying glass should be seriously considered when undertaking such fine work. The most important point to remember when modelling vintage subjects, whatever their physical dimensions, is to keep each component as *near to scale* as possible. If small details cannot be reproduced small enough they are best disregarded altogether, although there are several important components that should be attempted, such as control horns on elevators, rudders and ailerons. These can be cut from thin plastic sheet or stretched plastic sprue, depending on the shape and section of the original. Also tubular gun sights and tail struts should be replaced with rod of finer section, but little details such as these are best left aside and attached only after the model has been painted. Windscreens are rarely provided in kits and are grossly oversized when they are. Obtain thin sheets of clear plastic or stiff cellophane which can be easily cut, folded to shape and attached with PVA adhesive. Where bombs are included these simply plug into wings and fuselages, usually with complete disregard for a bomb rack. The latter can be built up with care and the bombs themselves improved by the addition of finer fins and reshaping.

The importance of thinning wings has already been mentioned, and now struts too, must come in for the same treatment. Invariably these are moulded oversize, which is a problem few tool-makers are able to prevent.

Tubular struts can be fabricated from stretched plastic sprue, which are the 'trees' that retain all the parts in a kit. The procedure is simple, for the sprue is merely held over a mild heat source such as a candle and when the plastic becomes floppy, both ends are pulled quickly apart to produce a fine strand. If the sprue is carved beforehand to streamlined shape, thin streamlined section struts will be formed, and the same process can be used for forming louvres and air scoops of varying sections. Several aircraft types feature large-chord struts that are usually more or less accurate in most kits as far as the outline goes, nevertheless they still need reducing in thickness with leading and trailing edges carefully thinned down by sanding. At first sight sprue struts may appear weak and liable to collapse, but once the model has been rigged it is surprising just how rigid the structure can become. Just like its full-size counterpart, of course.

Exhaust pipes, gun barrels and split axles should always have their ends drilled out or replaced with fine tube which can be fashioned in the same way as sprue, though a different material is used. On many ball-point pens the ink-carrying tube, when emptied, can be heat pulled and produces quite fine tubes to create exhausts, intakes, and gun muzzles.

Always check carefully with photographs and drawings when assembling a particular aircraft, for angles of undercarriages, wings and struts are surprisingly difficult to represent, and time taken measuring lengths, angles – even setting up a jig – is well spent. Most WW1 undercarriage axles were split in the centre and flanked by spreader bars; when aircraft were at rest this resulted in the wheels splaying outwards, a feature readily apparent in many Sopwith types, for example.

One major failing with WW1 aircraft kit subjects is some manufacturers' insistence on treating main components to an 'authentic fabric finish'. This usually takes the form of a coarse stippled effect overall and is of course, pure nonsense. Fabric weave is practically invisible on the actual aircraft, filled as it is with several layers of dope, and so there is *no* excuse for representing it on any model and it should always be removed completely by gentle sanding.

Painting these early types often presents problems due to the amount of conflicting references available. In practical terms, a little careful pre-planning is essential. For instance, it is advisable to paint completely all the sub-assemblies and major parts and add decals before final assembly takes place.

Apart from the sprayed camouflage on certain German aircraft of the period, there will be little use for an airbrush when painting WW1 models. Since most will be quite small, masking off appropriate areas could be rather tricky anyway. Brush painting is usual.

The overall 'khaki' finish coded PC10 and applicable to most British aircraft is perhaps the easiest of all to apply. But it should be noted that there was a common practice for the upper colour to wrap around the lower clear doped surfaces, giving an outlined appearance when viewed from underneath. Draughting tape can be utilized to achieve a hard line during painting this feature.

Repair patches and 'recovered' control surfaces can add extra touches and are simply applied by using a slightly paler mix of the main surrounding colour. Patches may take the form of small circles or squares but one should resist the temptation to add a great number.

In the majority of cases, two- or multi-colour disruptive patterns such as used by Germany and France were applied by hand brushing at the factory. Therefore demarcation lines separating the colours should be hard and not soft. Lozenge patterns on German and Austrian aircraft are the most difficult to achieve, especially in $\frac{1}{72}$ scale, for there were several variations in colours and patterns, and their application should be carefully researched. At least one decal manufacturer supplies a four-colour German pattern in strip form, but one must resort to handpainting the other styles. One method is to cut stencils and spray the colours through, or alternatively hand paint by number – a laborious process, to say the least!

The aluminium finishes used by French and German manufacturers can cause problems when trying to reproduce them accurately. Mixing matt pale blue with 'silver' enamel makes for easier application and certainly looks more authentic if several thin coats are carefully applied. Aim for a semi-gloss finish for WW1 models – never a *high* gloss sheen as this would be totally out of place and disastrous on small scale aircraft. Admittedly, most WW1 dopes were glossy when fresh, but toned down considerably in service use.

Engines and machine guns were very often exposed on early aircraft and so special attention must be paid when modelling and painting these items. The correct colouring of engines involves quite a lot of thought – do not be satisfied with a mere coat of matt black. Cylinders and crankcases should be painted a dull silver grey with push rods in aluminium, and manifold pipes a dull copper. Tone down each metallic colour and when dry wash the engine with thinned deep brown enamel, to provide an 'oily' appearance. Paint machine guns in a dark grey colour with just a touch of dull silver.

A close study of photographs shows that rarely, if ever, were aircraft tyres coloured black; use dark grey instead, and very pale grey in many cases would be more accurate.

Propellers and struts, often clear varnished, pose other problems in trying to reproduce them by painting. Many more experienced modellers even carve these components from wood, alleviating the chore of careful brushwork. Where differing woods were used for laminations, a really steady hand is needed when lining in the appropriate colours. The propeller hubs are invariably a dull metal colour and don't forget that these appear on both sides – or should. Brass leading edges, sheaths and fabric covered propeller tips are easily painted on if the subject demands it.

The model's appearance, even if painted properly in the correct markings, fully detailed and corrected during construction, still needs the final touch – rigging. A daunting task to many but one that is essential if the character of these early types is to be captured.

For $\frac{1}{72}$ scale models, fine copper wire (44swg) is the ideal material and can be bought in rolls from suppliers of radio and electrical equipment. It needs to be straightened out by rolling on a flat hard surface under a steel rule or by cold drawing. The latter technique involves clamping one end of a length into the jaws of a vice and gripping the other with a pair of pliers. Gentle pulling should cause the wire to stretch and remain taut.

The distance between pick-up points on the model is transferred to the wire using a pair of dividers for direct measurement. A small dab of PVA wood glue is applied to each point on the model and the wire dropped into place with tweezers. Start with the centre section struts and work outwards, care-

*Below:* Rumpler CIV using $\frac{1}{72}$ Airfix Hanover CLIII wings and plastic card fuselage. Airfix Roland CII behind. *Right:* $\frac{1}{72}$ Handley Page 0/400 with full internal detail, from Airfix kit. *All built by R. Rimell.*

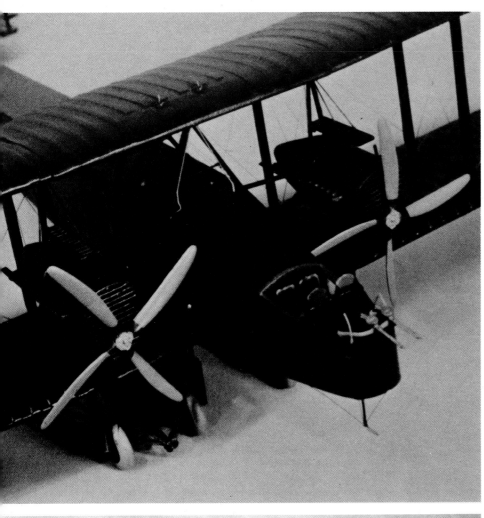

fully applying one wire at a time. PVA adhesive is really superb for the purpose for it is quite resilient, and holds even on painted surfaces.

For larger subjects and scales, cables can be made from stretched sprue instead, but the process of application is just the same. Never, ever, use fine thread of any kind.

'Weathering' the model should be done carefully and restraint exercised with reference sources constantly being consulted. From the adjacent areas beyond the ends of exterior exhaust pipes, light stains over wings and fuselages should be applied using dark grey paint. An airbrush is really essential for this but not for the residue streaked on lower fuselages of rotary engined powered aircraft. Careful mixing of browns and ochres to represent mud also adds realism. Dry brushing the mix by careful stippling of wheels, tail skid and lower portion of the rudders looks exceptionally characteristic if not applied too liberally. But do not cake the model in mud, subtlety is the key for a convincing result.

Most WW1 aircraft kits lend themselves to conversion and even semi-scratch-building, for many components provided are common to many other types. Indeed it is perfectly possible to make almost the entire Albatros fighter family based entirely on the two versions kitted. Yet others yield wings and fuselages that are simply adapted to suit the most varied of subjects. The Revell Nieuport 17 for example (now hard to find) can be changed into many types in its family, the 11, 16, 24, 27 and triplane plus of course the German copies, Siemens Schuckert and Euler D fighters. With such potential it is surprising that WW1 types are now infrequently available, but in the fickle world of plastic kits, the trend may well be reversed in the future.

Displaying WW1 models can be an even more enjoyable pastime if you lack neither space nor imagination. Even simple dioramas can enhance the completed model considerably and section of stubble field, a few wheel chocks, oil cans etc., scattered about plus a few figures is often more than sufficient. Taking it further, ambitious projects could involve whole squadrons, complete with staff cars, trucks, tents, hangars, and adjacent farm buildings.

The scope is unlimited, for once the techniques of building WW1 types have been mastered, the modeller is usually hooked for life . . .

# Between the Wars

### Defining the era

A clear definition of the machines of the between-wars era does not come easily because its extremities are decidedly indistinct. For four or five years after the armistice of November, 1918, for both military and the emerging civil purposes, First-War machines continued in service, while new types of aircraft appearing from 1935 onwards were mostly those which were to find fame, or failure, serving the warring nations in the conflict of 1939–45.

The appellation 'biplane-era' is often given to the period, but that is clearly a misnomer for, although biplanes predominated, monoplanes were very much in evidence and by 1932–3, notably in the USA, where the Martin B-10 bomber and Boeing 247D and Douglas DC-2 transports were pointing the way to the future, the biplane's ultimate eclipse was becoming evident.

### The model approach

It is a sad but true fact that the model kit manufacturers have not regarded the between-wars years as a lucrative source of subjects for their kits. There have been a number of forays of varying enthusiasm, notable among them the production, some years ago, by Inpact, of four outstandingly good kits, in $\frac{1}{48}$ scale, depicting the Bulldog, Fury, Flycatcher and Gladiator; the kits were superb but were obviously not a commercial success and the firm soon went out of the plastic kit business, the moulds passing to Life-Like from whom the kits are

still available. Airfix, Frog, Matchbox, Revell, Monogram, Heller and others have all tested the water and, apparently, achieved some degree of success with their limited ventures but not sufficient, it seems, to tempt them into wider coverage. On the other hand, the Williams Brothers, one of the smaller American companies, have made a speciality of the period and cater for the real enthusiast modeller. One of the most ambitious projects so far has come from Hasegawa who produced, a few years back, four American fighters of the early 1930s, the Boeing P-12E, F4B-4 and P-26A and the Curtiss BF2C-1 and all in $\frac{1}{32}$ scale.

The following among modellers for the twenties' and thirties' aircraft is enthusiastic but limited and thus the mass of the kits produced is angled towards the periods in greatest demand, World War 2 and the modern jets. Fortunately the vacuum-formed kit makers can remedy this, for they are involved in much smaller expenditure on their moulds and thus can undertake limited production runs. Concerns such as Contrail, Rareplanes and By-Planes produce many types of aircraft never likely to appear commercially from any other source. These kits are a vital part of the coverage of the more neglected periods of aviation. Despite the obvious neglect, it is still possible, by using all $\frac{1}{72}$ scale kits, injection moulded and vacuum-formed, so far issued. plus some simple conversions, to build more than a hundred between-wars types.

The dire need for economy in the stringent days of the early 1930s meant that the designers tended to make the maximum use of a proven design, adapting it to various tasks, and this means that the aircraft concerned are particularly suitable for conversion subjects. The De Havilland Moths are dealt with later in this chapter but others come readily to mind, such as the Hawker Hart, two-seat day-bomber, which spawned the Audax, Demon, Hardy, Hart Trainer, Hector, Hind and Osprey, all convertible, with varying degrees of difficulty, from the Airfix Demon kit. Other good examples are the Boeing P-12/F4B series and the variants of the Curtiss biplane fighters of which several can be modelled using parts from existing kits. The ultimate in satisfying an urge to possess a model which is never likely to be produced as a kit is to build it completely from scratch and the aeroplanes of the twenties and thirties lend themselves well to this advanced branch of modelling.

### Adding that characteristic touch

In the days when around 192km/h (120mph) was considered a respectable speed, the need for streamlining was not of prime importance and external appendages such as bomb racks, camera guns, radiators, oil coolers and even spare wheels and propellers were attached to the

The Handley Page Heyford of 1933, last of the RAF's heavy biplane bombers. From plastic card, $\frac{1}{48}$ scale.

exterior of aeroplanes, adding to the built-in drag of the rigging, control horns and wires, fixed undercarriages and, frequently, uncowled engines. It is important, in order to give a model the true period character, to incorporate such features and, for a biplane, rigging is mandatory for any modeller truly aiming at realism; nor does it have to be too difficult, provided that it is tackled in the right way and the most suitable materials used. For very small models, probably the easiest method is to use finely stretched plastic sprue which can be cemented into place without the need for drilling holes, but it is less durable than fine nylon thread which requires holes for fixing but will better withstand handling. For larger models, fine brass wire, cut accurately to length and then stuck into place using cyanoacrylate or quick-setting epoxy glues, looks very well and is not affected by changes of temperature or humidity which can cause thread to sag. The vital thing is to choose a thickness of rigging material compatible with the scale of the model, for overscale rigging can look worse than no rigging at all.

## Colourful finishes

Compared with the drabness of the war years immediately preceding and succeeding it, the inter-war period was, by and large, a colourful one and provides excellent opportunities for the modeller with an aptitude for painting. Undoubtedly the most common basic finish was aluminium, either as polished panels or painted on fabric or wood. The polished metal areas can be well represented by a rub-on silver finish such as 'Rub-'n-Buff', but it is difficult to get a really satisfactory dull aluminium appearance for, if a brush is used, the paint tends to appear streaky and, if sprayed, too shiny. For a smooth finish, spraying is virtually essential and the brightness can be reduced by adding a little compatible matt light grey paint to the silver. There are, in fact, household types of aluminium paint available from department stores which can give excellent results and cost only a fraction of the price of specially prepared model paints; a word of caution, however, test first on a piece of scrap plastic to ensure compatibility.

In the Royal Air Force, the night-bombers were painted a dull green, known as 'Nivo', but most other types wore brighter hues and the gay unit markings of the fighters are a model painter's delight, or nightmare, depending upon his ability at hand painting! There are few commercially available transfers (decals) available for planes of our period, although Modeldecal have produced one useful sheet (Number 31) with attractive $\frac{1}{72}$ scale markings for the Bristol Bulldog, Hawker Fury, Gloster Gladiator and Armstrong Whitworth Siskin, all of which are available as kits. Numbers and letters for serials can usually be obtained from Letraset and other rub-down transfers.

## Diorama settings

A pre-World War 2 airfield can give inspiration for many diorama settings, with simple ground equipment and aircraft of generally moderate size. Control towers, crew-rooms and even small hangars are a practicable proposition in $\frac{1}{72}$ scale and some OO/HO model railway buildings can be utilized. Typical of the period are such items as the Hucks Aero-Engine Starter which was mounted on a modified Model T Ford chassis and the 'wind stocking', always present on the old grass aerodromes to indicate the wind direction. Road vehicles of various sorts can be adapted from military or railway accessory kits.

## References

Books specifically referring to the inter-war years are not too plentiful, but there is much information in the histories of individual aircraft companies, air forces and airlines. The aeronautical periodicals publish a great deal of useful material and many plan-packs are available of types suitable for modelling. If you should be so fortunate as to live within easy travelling distance of any of the great museums with aeronautical collections, you can find many preserved aircraft on display; the Royal Air Force Museum at Hendon, London, is a fine example, while at the Shuttleworth Collection at Old Warden, Bedfordshire, the many historical aircraft are kept in flying condition. Other countries also have their collections and visits to them can be of inestimable value to the modeller.

*Below left* is a Boeing P-26A 'Peashooter' and, *right*, a Boeing F4B-4, (a Monogram kit), famous US Army and Navy fighter aircraft of the early 1930s. These models are both to $\frac{1}{72}$ scale, but $\frac{1}{32}$ kits are produced by Hasegawa. *Models built by F. Henderson.*

Record-breaking aircraft; $\frac{1}{72}$ models of a Northrop Gamma (Williams Brothers' kit) and the Fairey Long-range Monoplane (Airframe kit).

### The Moths: spirit of the era

When, in February, 1925, Captain Geoffrey de Havilland first demonstrated the prototype of his DH60 Moth biplane, towing it behind a car with its wings folded to a width of only 2.95m (9ft 8in) so as almost to fit into a family garage, he started what was to become a virtual revolution in the design of the light plane, suitable for instruction and for flyers of moderate means; few indeed are the aircraft which more truly convey the spirit of the inter-war period. The family of small biplanes which evolved from the basic, 60hp Cirrus I engined Moth appeared over more than a decade and many examples will still be flying well into the 1980s.

Far and away the most prolific, principally because of the mass-production undertaken to supply the need for primary trainers in World War 2, was the DH82a Tiger Moth, many being transferred to the Civil Register in the post-war years. The variants of the original DH60 Moth mostly took their names from the type of engine fitted, Cirrus, Gipsy and Genet Moth among them so, because the air-frame varied only in detail, it is possible, from only two $\frac{1}{72}$ scale

French Armee de l'Air fighters, the dainty 1935 Dewoitine D501 and the parasol-wing Morane Saulnier MS225 of 1932, both from $\frac{1}{72}$ scale Heller kits.

kits, the Gipsy Moth by Frog, now marketed by Novo, and the Tiger Moth by Airfix, to build a series of models, employing only quite elementary conversion techniques. The four different Moths shown can all be built from the two basic kits and the following notes cover the main conversion features.

### DH60G Gipsy Moth G-AAAH

The famous *Jason* which was used by Amy Johnson for her record flight from England to Australia in 1930 is now on permanent exhibition at the Science Museum in London; the engine is a 120hp Gipsy II. The Frog/Novo kit is made for this machine and no conversion is required although some improvements can be effected by thinning down the various struts, which all tend to be oversize in section.

### DH60 Genet Moth J8820

The Royal Air Force used, among other Moths, a version fitted with the 75hp Armstrong Siddeley Genet I five-cylinder radial engine which gave a very different appearance, although the basic airframe remained unaltered. This example was one of a batch of six used by the Central Flying School around 1927, some taking part, as an aerobatic team, in the Hendon Air Display of that year. The conversion follows similar lines to that for the Cirrus Moth, but the overall length was slightly greater and the cylinders of the radial engine can be made as described in Chapter 4. The exhaust pipes are separate curved stubs for each cylinder and can be made from wire.

### DH60GIII Moth Major G-ADAT

Inverting the in-line, four-cylinder Gipsy engine, uprating it to 130hp and completely enclosing it with a neat cowling resulted in a totally different outline, but it still fitted neatly into the Moth's slim fuselage. This conversion calls for rather more work than the others and involves cross-kitting parts from both the Gipsy Moth and Tiger Moth. From the Airfix Tiger Moth kit take the nose section of the fuselage and the complete landing gear, for this version had a split-axle undercarriage and, more often than not, low-pressure wheels. After cutting the nose from the Gipsy Moth fuselage, as with the other conversions, mate the Tiger Moth nose section to it, re-shape to get a smooth contour

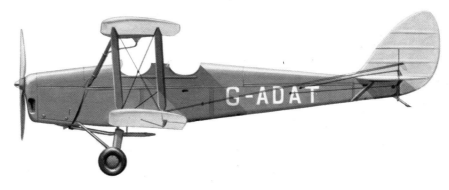

and fill any gaps. Also from the Gipsy Moth kit take the wings, tail surfaces, interplane and centre-section struts and propeller. Finally, a long exhaust pipe, made from brass or nickel silver wire, is fitted between the landing gear legs.

### DH82a Tiger Moth G-ARAZ

Many Tiger Moths were made surplus by the Royal Air Force and found their way on on the Civil Register: this example is

one. The model can be built directly from the Airfix kit.

All of these types had a petrol pipe leading from the centre-section gravity tank to the top of the fuselage; it can be made from wire, shaped to suit each individual aircraft. Where new wooden nose sections are required for these conversions, reference can be made to Chapter 4 for tips on shaping balsa wood components and bonding them to plastic.

# 1939 to the Present

The tremendous growth in the hobby of model making owes a great deal to the modern injection moulded plastic kit. Since its introduction some 25 years ago, the basic kit has been refined to a degree which makes comparison between the offerings of the early 1950s with those of today a worthwhile and informative exercise.

The modern trend is to include more and more detail, both internal and external, as well as optional parts to enable the constructor to produce a variant of his own choice from the basic kit subject.

This trend does not have the effect, as many suppose, of reducing skill levels; on the contrary, it tends to create a necessity for extra dexterity in handling the many components and fitting them correctly. But when the model has been completed there is a common factor which, in many ways, is a great leveller, and this is in the finish achieved by the individual modeller concerned. Many of the early plastic kits which are still available in their original form have provided the basic material from which really experienced modellers have produced models capable of holding their own against the very latest releases. Apart from the obvious modification work necessary to

achieve such acceptable comparisons, the common denominator is, more often than not, the final paint finish. A new model assembled skilfully, but poorly painted, will not stand comparison with an old model which has been worked on carefully in both the construction and painting stages.

With all modelling there is no substitute for patience and practice, and these two important factors must be cultivated to the full, especially when it comes to achieving authentic and acceptable finishes. But before going on to look at some of the techniques which will enable such finishes to be obtained, let us first consider some of the basic differences and factors controlling the reasons for applying either a new-look factory fresh finish, or a worn and weathered one.

The variety of kits now available is such that even the most fastidious modeller is able to be very selective in his choice of subject matter, a choice often governed by circumstances not directly associated with model making. The most restrictive element is often the space available to the modeller, not so far as the actual modelling is concerned, but where to display the fruits of his labours when they are complete. Because of this, scales small enough to enable a reasonably representative selection, but large enough to enable every skill to be practised to its full, are the most popular.

Almost since the start of aircraft modelling as a serious hobby, the two scales which fit the defined parameters have been universally adopted, these are $\frac{1}{72}$ and $\frac{1}{48}$ scales. Within these two there are enough kits available to satisfy practically every requirement for what can be termed a 'theme' collection.

There are many modellers who derive enormous pleasure from constructing perhaps one large scale kit on an occasional basis, and, in contrast, there are those who rush through every phase of construction and painting, producing maybe four or five models every month. Between these two extremes are those who form the backbone of the hobby and are its most serious devotees. These modellers will eventually decide on a particular period in history, a certain type of aircraft,

The nose of a $\frac{1}{48}$ scale Vought A7D model, considerably greater than life size. Slight variation in colour on the noseleg is the only obvious lack in a very convincing model.

or the aircraft used by a chosen squadron, and concentrate their efforts towards constructing models with such a common bond. In such a collection, it is important that all models are the same scale and finished to a common standard; deviation from the former might become necessary and is very much a personal matter, but every effort should be made to adhere to the latter by finding a standard one is capable of achieving on a regular basis, and then sticking to it.

During World War 2 aircraft were mechanically maintained to a very high standard, but in many cases their paintwork weathered very badly due to the outside environment in which many of them were kept, as well as the continual attention from ground crews servicing and rearming them. Although standard camouflage colours and patterns were laid down by officialdom, it was not always possible for the rules to be strictly observed. On many occasions paint of the specific colour was not readily available, or other more pressing operational commitments took priority over painting. Even new aircraft tend to show evidence of wear, especially around panel fastenings, so it is very rare to see any aircraft in the sort of pristine finish obtained if no effort is made towards authenticity. The basic difference can be summed up by asking the question, 'Are we making a model or a replica?' A model is, for example, a perfect scale reproduction of a particular aircraft in authentic markings and correct camouflage as it *should* have appeared; a replica is a perfect model of a particular aircraft as it *did* appear. Once again personal choice is very much the deciding factor and the reader should not be influenced by something he does not agree with.

In addition to wear caused by exposure to the elements, paint also faded or was a different tone when produced by a variety of makers over a period of time. Whether or not such tonal differences should be allowed for in modelling is well outside the scope of this particular chapter. Many people, and the writer is inclined to agree with them, feel that this really is trying to carry scale modelling too far, especially as colour viewed by several people is rarely exactly the same to any two of them. But if you wish to tone down camouflage colours by all means do so by judicious use of paler shades than those

originally specified.

Immediately after the War, air forces were run down and for a long period of time operated old aircraft with fewer people. In many cases the aircraft concerned did not show signs of wear as quickly as they had done when they were engaged in warlike activities, the reasons being that there was more time to tend to them and paints used gradually became more durable. As peacetime air forces took delivery of new equipment and the jet-age was born, aircraft became more colourful and their natural aluminium or high gloss camouflaged paintwork tended not to show as much wear and tear. The hey-day of immaculate aircraft and gaudy squadron markings started to draw to a close in the mid-1960s; since then there has been a definite move towards more sombre tactical schemes and camouflage patterns, which are only broken by yellow stencilling and perhaps the colours of national markings, although of late even the latter have been toned down. So, before deciding just how any model is to be completed, it is a good idea to collect as many photographs as possible and form a mental picture of just how you want the model to look when it is finished.

Weathering and wear must be kept within acceptable proportions and relative to the scale of the model being worked on. It would, for example, be quite wrong to reproduce a scrape 12.5mm ($\frac{1}{2}$in) on the fuselage of a $\frac{1}{72}$ scale Spitfire where it would represent a mark of nearly 1 metre (3ft), but acceptable for such a blemish to be included on a $\frac{1}{24}$ scale model. The best guide is to remember that the model should only show suggestions of detail that would be seen if the real aircraft were to be viewed from a distance where it appears the same size as the model.

There is no substitute for looking at the real thing whenever possible, and this can be achieved by visiting museums and air displays and making sure that a careful note is taken of every small detail that will come in useful when modelling. Those who like making models of airliners have the advantage of being able to visit the public viewing areas of major airports and seeing their subjects at fairly close range. Airliners are extremely expensive and represent a big investment on the part of the company owning them; they are therefore looked after most carefully, and generally speaking do not show as many signs of wear

29

as their military cousins. However, if a really close look is taken at an airliner, it will quickly be seen that panels are chipped, oil has seeped through on to some surfaces, and what seems to be pristine white paint is slightly streaked in places. With care such blemishes can be reproduced, but in the small scales often used for airliner kits, extra care, and knowing precisely when enough is enough, are essential.

There are many ways any model can be weathered and all of them should be tried on a scrap model or perhaps even one built for such a purpose. To represent paint chips it is entirely wrong to take a brush with silver paint on it and spot one or two blemishes in appropriate places. All aircraft have a primer applied to their natural finish over which is applied the final paint scheme, and when the paint is

*Top:* Four-engined bombers of World War 2 are more frequently found in $\frac{1}{72}$ scale, due to sheer physical size. Slightly out-of-focus background enhances realism on this B-17 Flying Fortress.

*Above:* Particular aircraft can often be modelled, when detailed references sources are not difficult to find. The Handley Page Halifax *Friday the Thirteenth* is mounted on a simulated concrete hard standing.

*Above right:* Republic F-84s were supplied to many NATO countries; this one is in French colours. Early kits tended to over-emphasize panel lines, as is evident in this picture.

*Right:* One of the first supersonic fighters in service was the North American F-100, which can make a colourful subject. A history of fighter development is entirely possible, using available plastic kits.

chipped, the primer or the natural metal shows through. So on a model the same procedure will produce convincing results. Spray or paint small areas of silver before any other finishing is carried out, then take some masking fluid or tape and apply this in the areas which will eventually be exposed. Now paint the model in its final scheme then remove the masking, the result will be areas of exposed silver which look like wear rather than daubed-on silver paint.

Any national markings must be applied before any weathering is carried out, since these are just as prone to wear as the rest of the airframe. Scuffs on the wing surfaces or around inspection panels and crew entry hatches are produced by using an ear bud to apply gently a minute portion of 'rub 'n buff' to the engraved panel lines. This must

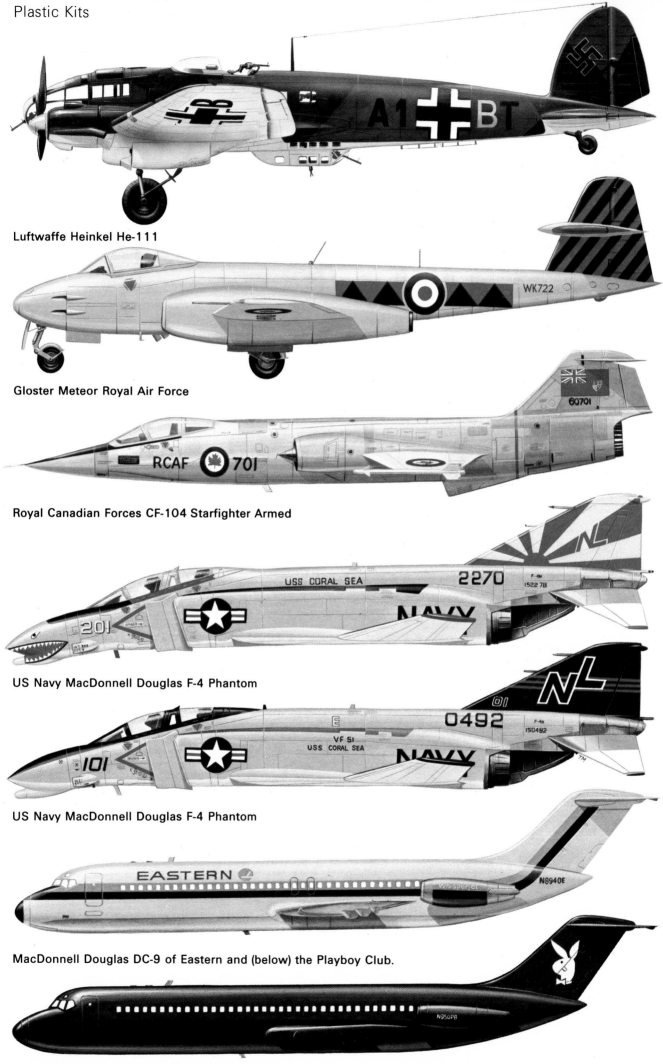

Luftwaffe Heinkel He-111

Gloster Meteor Royal Air Force

Royal Canadian Forces CF-104 Starfighter Armed

US Navy MacDonnell Douglas F-4 Phantom

US Navy MacDonnell Douglas F-4 Phantom

MacDonnell Douglas DC-9 of Eastern and (below) the Playboy Club.

be done very carefully, but if it is overdone, it is not too difficult to repaint or spray the exaggerated area after cleaning off the paste.

Engraved panel and control surface hinge lines should be accentuated by running a very diluted mix of dark grey or black paint and thinners along them. This is easily done by dipping a size 00 or 000 brush into the mix and gently touching it at the base of the line; capillary action will do the rest. Similarly graphite dust, obtained by rubbing the lead of a soft pencil on glasspaper, can be used to highlight matt black painted gun barrels or bombs or other areas on the model. The dust is simply rubbed into the component or area and the degree of sheen arrived at is governed by the amount of time spent working it in. Moving parts such as undercarriage oleo legs should never be painted in silver; the paint should be toned down with a touch of grey or better still steel, and then dry highlighted or toned down even more by the dry brushing technique. This is a very useful skill to master, especially when it comes to weathering.

Basically all that is done is that a brush is dipped in silver, black or grey paint which is then brushed off on a piece of card or scrap plastic. The brush is then worked over the area concerned and small particles of the original colour are worked into it. This is one of those tasks which sounds hard, but is in fact quickly mastered once it is tried; the effect is well worth it.

Attention must be paid to every part of the model, since it is pointless to make the airframe look worn but ignore, say, the wheels, which may have tyres in a new and immaculate finish. It is best to use a

American aircraft often offer a variety of attractive colour schemes, the F-4 Phantom being a case in point. Landbased aircraft are tending to become more sober, since bright colours render concealment difficult.

very dark grey paint for tyres and highlight the treads with a mix of black or brown, depending on the aircraft and where it is likely to have operated from.

Indian ink is a very useful addition to the modeller's paint box. Diluted with water and allowed to run from filler caps, panels, wheel wells, and vents, it will produce very authentic looking stains.

The watchword in weathering is moderation: don't overdo it, for nothing looks worse than a model which looks ready for the scrap heap. Always stop one step ahead of where you planned to, and, if you have an air brush, make the final step an overall light spray with a very diluted wash of grey or black. This tends to tone in all the areas weathered with those not touched, and avoids a patchwork quilt effect. Always remember there is no substitute for practice, and weathering skills will come if you try hard enough and use imagination.

Displaying completed models in a glass case or on a shelf is the method favoured by most modellers. It is fun occasionally to make a change and try other modelling skills by creating a diorama. This is a method of using the model to tell a story, which can be complex or simple, fact or fiction.

A Phantom standing on a concrete hardstanding with all its weapons carrying 'remove-before-flight-tags', the nose wheel tethered, and the pilot's ladder in place, creates a simple scene which attracts attention. Similarly, a Lancaster bomber at the end of a wheels-up landing can be shown with its crew having scrambled clear looking at the furrows carved by their aircraft and the path it followed strewn with pieces of wreckage. A poignant scene, but a familiar WW2 one captured in miniature for all time.

There is nothing difficult about creating a diorama providing some basic rules are observed. Always

try to make the base big enough; at least twice as long as the subject matter is a reasonable guide. Use Polyfilla, papier mâché, or plaster-of-Paris to form the landscape, and remember that all objects have weight and must be shown to be resting in the terrain rather than on it. It seems obvious that all components must be to the same scale, but quite often one will see a $\frac{1}{32}$ scale aircraft with $\frac{1}{48}$ scale people or vehicles. The scene must also be a realistic one. Do not, for example, make a superb job of creating a desert oasis then insert into it a piece of equipment only associated with the Arctic!

The base should be made of wood which is thick enough to look right, too thin and it might warp, too thick and the model looks unbalanced; it should also have as much attention paid to its finish as the rest of the model. Far too often good dioramas are spoiled by the base having exposed edges which appear to have been chewed off a tree trunk by the modeller's teeth. A smooth regular border painted or edged with veneer adds that essential touch of class. Almost any material used by model railway enthusiasts can be employed in creating an aircraft diorama, and finishes can be achieved with water paints, oils, enamels or a combination of all three. Plants, shrubs and trees can be bought or scratch-built, but when laying these out remember that unlike man, Mother Nature does not build in regular rows and patterns, but follows a random order.

Ideas for dioramas can come from books, films, television, newspapers, magazines and a fertile imagination: it is another aspect of modelling which is worth trying, for perhaps not only will that loved Spitfire look better in a genuine reproduction of a 1940 blast-proof pen, but in constructing the pen another useful skill will be mastered and turned to many other uses.

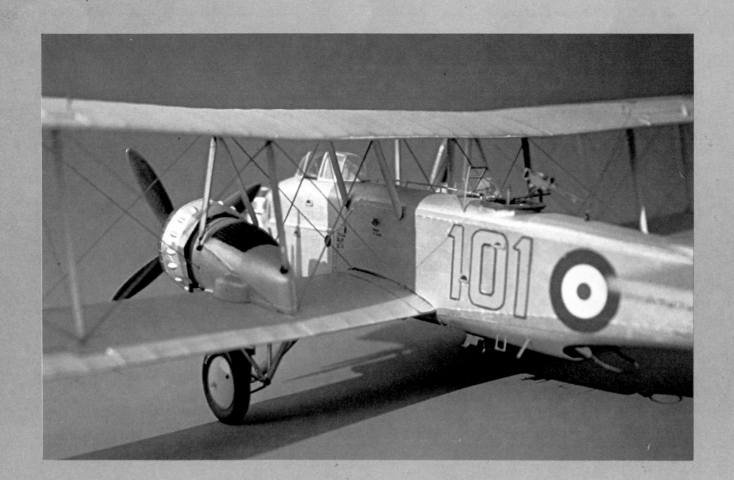

# Building in Plastic
## Plastic Card
## Vacuum-formed Models

### Plastic Card Modelling

The title of this section may seem less familiar than the overused 'scratch building' but, in fact, it is the only correct description of this area of modelling for it describes exactly what it is and indicates quite clearly that it is derived from card or paper modelling. Plastic card modelling, therefore, is an extension of the old art of card modelling utilizing the versatile medium of polystyrene plastic sheet, which resembles fine quality card. It owes almost everything to card modelling and nothing to plastic kit construction and it is important to appreciate this from the start.

In plastic card modelling, a three-dimensional form is created from flat sheets of plastic card by the modeller using his skills and know-

*Below:* An unusual subject, an Avia BH33 built in plastic card to $\frac{1}{48}$ scale by H. Woodman. *Left:* A Boulton Paul Overstrand to the same scale which was awarded a Championship Cup at a recent Model Engineer Exhibition.

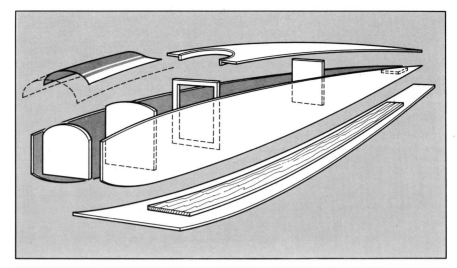

*Top:* A simple square-type fuselage typical of early aircraft offers few difficulties especially when the front decking curves only one way.

*Centre:* A slightly more elaborate turtle-backed fuselage, though still straightforward and built on a basic box.

*Bottom:* Stages in shaping a plug for a moulded fuselage with, beneath, the female half of the mould.

ledge of the material. If the terms 'wood' or 'metal' are substituted for 'plastic card' the definition can apply to all areas of modelling activity.

## Materials

Plastic card is polystyrene formed into convenient flat sheets in varying thicknesses; the thinnest available is five thousandths (5 thou) of an inch (an eighth of a millimetre) which is about the same as the pages of this book. It is also available in 10, 20, 40 and 60 thou (0.25, 0.5, 1.0 and 1.5mm) and greater thicknesses. It is white, which is the best for modelling; colour has no advantage. (Transparent card is a different material, its only advantage is that it can be fixed with plastic cement, and acetate sheet is often of more use.)

In appearance the material is rather like extremely good quality Bristol board used by commercial artists for mounting. It has all the board's qualities and more besides, including the most valuable one of softening slowly when a gentle heat is applied, so that it can be moulded by simple techniques.

It can be cut easily with a sharp blade and indeed it is not necessary with the thicker card to cut all the way through, for a firm initial cut will allow the card to be broken cleanly. Cutting with scissors should be avoided as the action of the scissor blades tends to warp the card. It can also be scored, laminated and sanded.

Plastic card is available from many model shops and is usually supplied in sheets about 25 × 30cm (10 × 12in). The disadvantage of this is that should a larger unit be required the modeller has to find another source, probably a specialist plastics supplier.

The best adhesive is plastic cement, which 'sticks' by dissolving the plastic card slightly and forming a weld when it is dry. This method of adhesion should be remembered, for if it is not understood disasters can occur. Cement

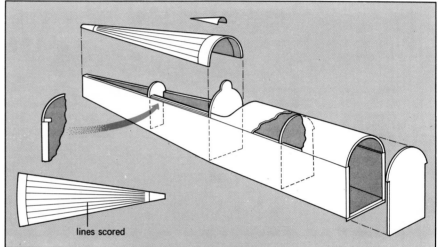

lines scored

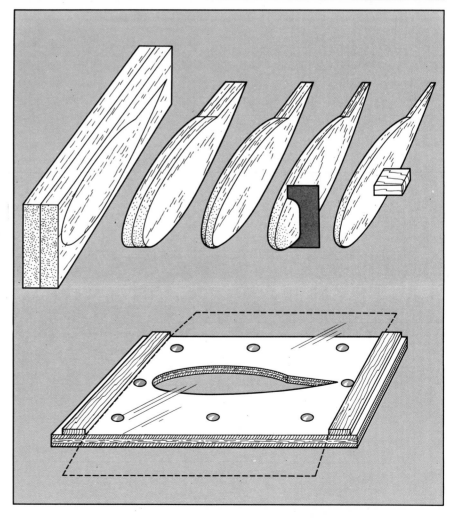

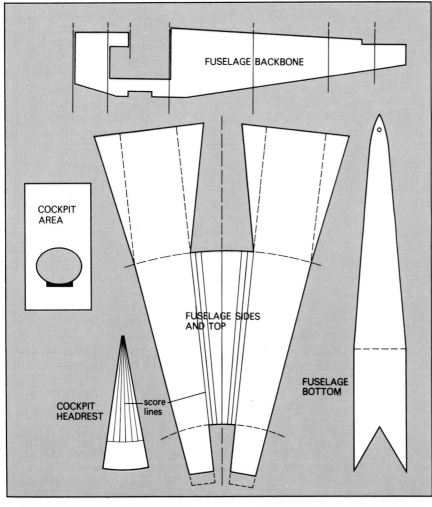

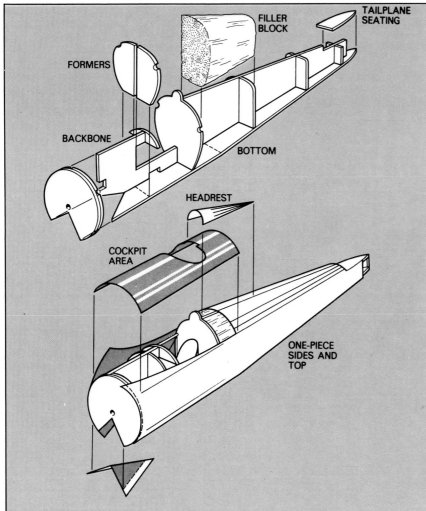

is available in two forms, thin, in bottles, and thick, in tubes. If a quantity of thick cement is deposited on a palette it can be thinned as required by the addition of thin cement. A good guide is to use just enough cement to do the job; avoid excessive amounts, for the work can be ruined. For very thin card matt varnish can also be used.

**Tools**
There are few essential tools, but one is obviously a cutting knife. The best is one with easily replaceable blades and a long narrow wedge shape which can be used equally well for long straight cuts, involved angles or curves. The most useful is the type which consists of a handle and a pack of snap-off blades. With a knife a straight-edge is needed, and a steel rule is ideal. For curves, some inexpensive French curves can be used and, with care, it is easy to learn the technique of using the curve as a guide without damaging it. Cutting circles and discs is even easier, for all that is required is a set of dividers of the type found in children's geometry sets. The circle is scribed on to the card and it can be pushed out with no difficulty.

Probably the most expensive items are a set of fine files and a set of miniature drills with a pin vice to hold them. As the drills and files are used on a soft material they never wear out and with care will last a lifetime.

Occasionally a fine saw is needed, mainly for cutting up a balsa block when making a male mould. (It is best not to use the saw on plastic as the friction melts the plastic and clogs the saw teeth.) A balsa plane which uses a razor blade is useful for trimming down balsa when making wing cores etc. and forming male moulds. The ideal sanding material is 'wet and dry' paper as used in the motor trade. When used wet with soap it gives a very fine finish on plastic card. It is available in varying grades of coarseness, the most useful being the two finest grades.

*Top:* The various parts of a fuselage laid out on flat plastic card.

*Below:* The assembly of the cut out parts; note the use of filler block. Accurate alignment is essential to ensure that the tailplane sits squarely on its seating so that it is parallel with the mean line of the wing(s).

Other useful items include such things as cocktail sticks, bulldog clips, household pins, elastic bands and Scotch tape, masking tape (which is easier to remove), and double-sided tape.

Finally, some drawing instruments are essential, not only for drawing (for it may be necessary to create one's own plans) but for marking out the plastic card for cutting. The necessity for accuracy when doing this cannot be over-emphasized.

Fillers are used to conceal a crack, a space or a junction, and so in plastic card modelling they are used very little. Plastic kit modellers use fillers a great deal to create different shapes and structures, but in plastic card modelling this is all done by moulding or shaping lami-

*Below:* Stages in forming wings. Balsa cores prevent sag and add to overall stiffness, and are secured with double-sided adhesive tape. Undercambered wings need a temporary packing piece beneath to produce the correct section. *Below right:* Modern wings are thicker and bi-convex. Cut-outs are made for landing and navigation lights, and ailerons should always be cut away, detailed, and replaced, as shown.

nated card and filler is unnecessary. 'Plastic fillers' available commercially can damage the plastic, so if making a shape which requires the use of a filler (such as the building of a wing fillet) a cheap and harmless water-softening wood filler, such as Brummer Stopping, is ideal. It dries hard and attaches itself to plastic card provided that the base is firm; it can be sanded and shaped to quite a fine edge without crumbling and is used by carpenters and cabinetmakers.

## Techniques

The first fundamental is to realize that a three-dimensional model is to be created from pieces of flat plastic card and the second is to gain a thorough knowledge of the properties of that material. Waste some material in experiments in cutting, scribing, scoring and moulding to get the feel of it. Try applying cement to see how far it is possible to go before damage occurs. Practise scoring using a not too sharp point for fine lines and, say, an empty ball-point pen for thicker ones. Like cardboard, the material can be folded, but only up to 10 thou (0.25mm) thickness, over this it will crack.

A cornflake box starts out as a series of flat rectangles, and a machine cuts, scores and folds the flat design into the final shape; this is termed a 'flat cut out', and is useful when building the fuselages of aircraft of WW1 vintage and earlier. Another method is to cut out the top, bottom and sides and attach them to a central keel or core of thicker card, which gives greater strength and helps with alignment and shape. This is called a 'simple box'. A further refinement is to attach to the box a series of additional structures such as a curved turtle back or side panels and this becomes a 'built-up box'.

If the shape contains a great deal of double curvature, such as the fish-shaped fuselage of an Albatros DV, it becomes necessary to mould it in two half shells. Some fuselages can be built up with a mixture of all the above; the modeller must decide for himself how to go about it.

To make a moulded shape two moulds are necessary, male and female. The male is made slightly undersize to allow for the thickness of the plastic card, and the female mould is an aperture through which the male is inserted, with heated plastic card in between. It is a very

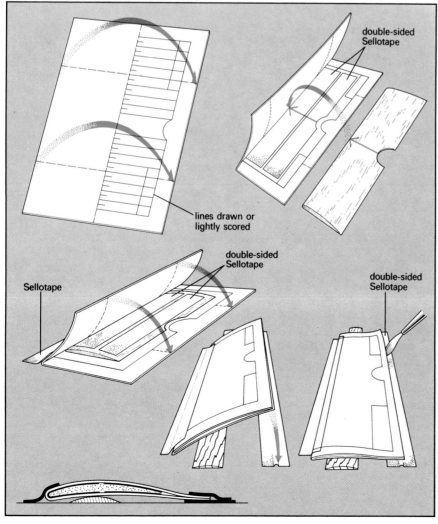

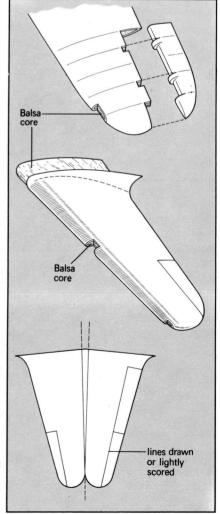

simple procedure and in some small items, the female mould is not needed at all. To heat the plastic use a small spirit lamp, or for a large area use an electric fire. The plastic card will soften visibly after only a small degree of heat is supplied. When it starts to go very shiny and discolours it is too soft and only practice will indicate when the right moment occurs.

To make fuselage moulds, two pieces of balsa are lightly stuck together into a block, using minimal balsa cement. The shape is then carved and sanded using the joint line as the central guide; the two halves are then gently prised apart and the two male moulds are ready. The female mould is merely an appropriately shaped hole cut in a piece of balsa sheet. Do not use too thin a sheet as it may split and spoil the mould. For very small items, such as gun or cylinder blisters, the male mould is best made from hard wood (a tooth pick is often ideal) and merely pressed into a piece of plastic card immediately after heating. In this way, using acetate sheet, tiny transparent shapes for navigation light covers can be made without difficulty. Such small items are stuck

*Top:* A $\frac{1}{48}$ Travel Air 2000 painted to represent a Fokker DVII for the 1938 film 'Men With Wings'.

*Right:* A 1909 Voisin biplane flown by Moore-Brabazon, holder of the first British pilot's licence.

*Below:* Supermarine Walrus amphibian on a ship's catapult. This model won the Championship Cup in the 1978 Model Engineer Exhibition.

*Above:* An Armstrong Whitworth Siskin, now included as part of the RAF Fighter Command memorial.

*Right:* A Curtis BFC-2, a US 'pursuit ship' of the early 1930s.

in place with matt varnish.

The interiors of fuselages can be strengthened in various ways, depending on shape and size; for example, the male mould can be used as a fuselage filler, appropriately cut away at the cockpit area. Apart from bulkheads made from heavier card, expanded polystyrene, being virtually weightless and easy to come by, is ideal for internal support as long as varnish is used to stick it in place.

A final refinement is to 'skin' the fuselage partially or totally with 5 thou (0.125mm) card or metal foil, adding external detail (rivet heads, stitching, panel lines etc.).

Matt varnish is used to attach the skin, both surfaces being painted and allowed to become tacky. The very thin plastic card can be attached with cement but only with very great care and after some experience.

**Wings and tails**
The whole basis of wing and tail surface construction consists of folding a piece of the thinner plastic card; the fold becomes the leading edge and the two edges joined together become the trailing edge. The trailing edges of aircraft of all periods must be sharp, and in the smallest scales, razor sharp. For the narrow leading edges of early aircraft it is necessary to form a tight fold and without using some heat this is not possible without cracking the plastic. To obtain the fold using card up to 20 thou (0.5mm) thickness a balsa sandwich must be used.

The beginner is again encouraged to experiment with some card, say a piece of 10 thou material. First, fold the card carefully; it will be noted that the fold does not stay tight but slowly opens up. To keep it tight the folded card should be inserted between two pieces of balsa plank to form a sandwich with the folded edge not protruding beyond the edges of the balsa. If this sandwich is held firmly and in front of an electric fire, the plastic will soften at the only part which is exposed, the fold. At the same time squeeze the two pieces of balsa together between the fingers and then take the work away from the heat. Allow about 10 seconds to cool and it will be seen that the plastic has formed a very tight and permanent fold. Another advantage of the sandwich is that when modelling wings of fabric-covered aircraft, the wing ribs are represented by scoring and during the heating and folding process the scoring is covered and so protected from the heat, for the scored lines will flatten out if subjected to heat.

To give internal support a 'core' of sheet balsa is used, which not only prevents warping but also acts as a base to support struts. The core is roughly shaped to the correct aerofoil section and planform, somewhat smaller than the correct size of the wing, inserted between the folded plastic card wing, and help in place with double sided Scotch tape, which is more effective than adhesives. Any camber required is achieved by supporting the wing as necessary during the formation stage. The same basic principles apply when modelling the wings of modern aircraft. The balsa core is shaped from a plank of appropriate thickness using the razor blade plane and glasspaper. It is a good idea to paint the finished balsa core with plastic cement to seal it and provide a firm surface for the Scotch tape.

Ailerons and where necessary, flaps, *must* be cut away from the wing, the leading edges rounded and then replaced and held with pieces of fuse wire. The same principle applies to rudders and elevators, although in some cases it is best to make the items separately, depending on the design of the original. Vertical fins and tailplanes are made in the same way as wings, but to achieve the very thin appearance of such appendages appropriate to early aircraft, the balsa core can be dispensed with.

Waste sprue from plastic kits can be used for many details, as described elsewhere; delicate parts should be stuck in place with matt varnish. Plastic sheet can also be used to make sprue, for by carefully cutting a narrow strip of 40 thou (1.00mm) card and heating it, a very fine flat (or shaped) strip of plastic can be obtained. Many ink containers in ball-point pens are made from a soft and flexible translucent plastic tube which if carefully heated will soften and can be drawn like plastic sprue. The result is a fine hollow tube which is most useful for exhausts and guns. The best adhesive is again matt varnish.

### Spare parts from kits

Engines, propellers, exhausts, wheels and engines and in some items can be made from plastic card and other plastic materials. Scrap plastic kits also provide quite a good selection of items, such as wheels and engines and in some cases, propellers, which may require remodelling or refining. A tread on the wheel of a DH9a, for example, is not acceptable. Early aircraft wheels can be made using plastic curtain rings or plastic 'O' rings, used by engineers.

Radial engines fitted to early aircraft were often fully exposed and so require much detail. Kit engines can be used, but such clumsy practices as moulding the pushrods as a solid wedge integral with the cylinders means that much reworking is necessary; such measures as disguising this with paint are unacceptable; one of the most enjoyable things about scale modelling is the addition of such small items.

Another material which has many uses is the range of tough plastic components produced in Britain by Plastruct. Primarily for architectural modellers, the range includes a good range of plastic tubing which can be used for cylinders ('bound' with fine sprue to emulate cylinder fins) and the smallest tubing is supplied with a wire core which can be removed with stripping pliers, leaving a fine tubing which can be further modelled and shaped for exhaust pipes and guns.

### Choice of subject and scale

The techniques outlined can apply to aircraft models of all periods: indeed, the rather stark lines of modern jet aircraft provide easier subjects than their more curvaceous forebears. A model of an antique aircraft always seems to attract more attention than that of a jet, partly because it possesses more character and has the same romantic appeal as vintage cars, period ships and steam locomotives. Perhaps it is the closer association of man with its levers, wires, copper tubing, brass radiators, wire wheels, plywood and fabric than the modern computer-built, computer-flown mass of internationally standardized equipment. The reader must make his own choice of subject.

The subject of scale is one of degree. The smallest general scale is the universally popular $\frac{1}{72}$; building in larger scales entails a considerable increase in the amount of detail, which in turn requires more research and reference. A scale of $\frac{1}{48}$ allows a model of sufficient size to include a great deal of detail without being too big. It is a matter of personal choice, but the reader is advised not to embark upon a large scale model without all the available reference material collected together and handy.

### Research

There is not enough space to do more than touch on the very important subject of research, except to give a few hints. The traditional modeller starts with an idea, an urge to build a model of something that takes his fancy, and is not intimidated by the fact that the model is not available in kit form. He will collect material, photos, pictures from magazines, data on the dimensions and construction of the original. This involves a great deal of work and time sifting through the vast amount of material published on aviation subjects. A basic guideline is that all pictures (i.e. photos or photographic reproductions) are useful and the true researcher collects these and pastes them in some form of book to be studied closely. Historical societies' journals contain vast amounts of material at a fraction of the cost of some books and is of far greater accuracy. Research also means visiting reference libraries and museums (with camera or sketchbook) or state archives.

A good set of drawings is essential, and the modeller may have to create his own if accurate ones are not available. Check a published drawing with all the detail available on the subject, from basic dimensions to overall shape.

In a few cases original aircraft can be seen in museums, and sketches and photographs are useful adjuncts to studying the machine at close hand, though to get the true feel the sight of the real thing must be supplemented by pictures of it in service.

Total coverage in research is rarely possible, so that guile and knowledge must bridge the gaps. This is accepted procedure in restoration work everywhere.

A true model is a reconstruction of a fragment of history in miniature, to as high a degree of accuracy as possible. This means the whole model, not just the colour scheme and markings. The reader should regard the art in that light.

In these days of mass production and labour-saving devices it is the original creation brought into existence through hard work, determination and skill that is valuable; there is no short cut.

### References

*Scale Model Aircraft in Plastic Card* by Harry Woodman published by Argus Books Ltd., Argus House, 14 St James Road, Watford, Herts at £2.95.

# Vacuum-formed Kits

Despite the enormous number of injection moulded aircraft kits available to modellers the world over, there are still many fascinating subjects that will never be kitted. The reason is pure economics. While Spitfires and Messerschmitts sell rapidly to youngsters who make up the bulk of the market, rarer types will just not have mass appeal. With the staggering costs of even small moulds, one can hardly blame manufacturers for shunning less saleable products.

But several years ago when the plastic aircraft hobby really began to be taken seriously, it was realized there was also a market for more individualistic models – albeit a small one. The answer was the vac-form kit, components moulded directly to sheets of plastic card, economically produced and generally of short duration runs. The child grew up swiftly and now there are many brand names being produced in the UK, Canada, USA, Germany and even Czechoslovakia.

It would be irresponsible to recommend vac-form kits to the complete novice, but after plenty of practice, and experience of making more complex kits, a good vac-form is a natural and obvious progression. We use the term 'good' advisedly for it has to be said that many vac-forms require a lot of improving, but in most cases the effort expended is completely repaid by the results that can be achieved by a careful modeller.

## What is a vac-form?

In their most basic forms vac-form kits contain one or more (depending on the subject) plastic sheets that carry the major – sometimes all – components required to build the model. If relevant a sheet of transparent plastic, not usually polystyrene, is included for cockpit canopies, windows, etc. Recent and welcome innovations by a few of the better-established manufacturers are the inclusion of injection moulded or diecast detail components such as wheels and propellers. Even more welcome are decal sheets – a rare item in such kits.

In several cases production runs are limited to around 1000 and as might be expected, overall quality can vary within the available models and out of a dozen or so manufacturers, only a few really approach the finesse of an injection moulded equivalent.

Nevertheless, the advantage and real purpose of vac-forms is the provision of aircraft subjects of appeal to enthusiasts which are unlimited in size, as they are in scope. Another advantage of vac-forms is the very thin sections of fuselage and engine cowlings. Detailing of cockpit areas is made simpler and can be more realistic by having a thin wall to work on. Cockpit widths are more to scale and there are no lugs, location tabs, steps etc. to remove and fill. Careful application of internal structure can be more easily carried out as a result and if a cockpit door

is to be cut open, it too looks better for being of finer section. Really large models can and have been produced including $\frac{1}{72}$ scale airliners, and huge modern bombers. The larger models demand even more skills and should not be tackled unless the modeller is confident of the result. Much of the hard work is alleviated on many kits by the supply of the aforementioned smaller parts in a different material. Nevertheless, most manufacturers continue to mould wheels, undercarriage legs etc., integrally with the formed sheets. Such small components are rarely usable and are unconvincing if they are, so the modeller will have to resort either to manufacturing his own or robbing the spares box.

## Techniques

Due to the fact that vac-form sheets are generally of thin plastic, choice and use of adhesives should be considered carefully. Liquid polystyrene cement such as Slater's Mek Pak, Humbrol Poly 70, and the American Weld On No. 3 are to be preferred to tube cement. The latter can all too easily melt vac-form components but, then, so too can the liquids if used carelessly.

Before assembly can commence each major item needs to be removed from the plastic sheets and

A 1914–15 Etrich-Taube modelled at $\frac{1}{72}$ scale from an Airframe vacuum-formed kit. Wheels and propeller left-overs from another plastic kit.

this can be a tricky procedure. To undertake the task without risk of damaging the components, no attempt should be made to cut the part out in one operation. Instead carefully score around the edges of the component using a sharp craft knife. Repeat this several times and go lightly. All too often a heavy handed approach at this stage can make the knife slip and damage the moulded sections – often almost beyond repair. The next operation is to flex the sheet and the component gently until the part more or less separates by itself, and this process should be repeated until all components are released. It might be a good idea to retain the scraps of backing sheet for use as strengthening tabs later in the construction.

Before joining together the two halves of the fuselage, the edges that require glueing must be sanded perfectly flat. To do this efficiently one requires a really flat cutting/sanding board. This need be no more sophisticated than a sheet of glass or a block of chipboard of reasonable dimensions. On to one side of this should be mounted a sheet of wet and dry paper, fixed with strips of double sided tape.

The paper should be liberally dampened and the component carefully rubbed to and fro until the surfaces to be glued are flat. It is essential that a check is constantly made on the progress of the sanding. A common error is to remove too much plastic, which results in a skinny ill-fitting fuselage, for only the true thickness of the carrier sheet ought to be eradicated. One useful tip is to run a fine pencil along the edge of the lip formed by removal from the sheet. This easily indicates the depth to which the plastic should finish.

As regards to wings and tails, it is of extreme importance that all trailing and leading edges are kept as thin as possible. Nothing is more harmful to realism than a wing trailing edges which if scaled up would resemble a large plank. Wings can be difficult to grip when sanding, especially if they are very small, and to overcome this, handholds should be manufactured from tape folded back to back.

Even on the more delicate World War 1 types or later biplanes, most vac-form kits supply wings and tails in two halves. This provides problems in endeavouring to obtain fine sections and it is probably better to discard the lower section, refine the upper half, and score in rib positions underneath with a

metal scriber. These operations are really essential for many early aircraft tail units, where even a single thickness of plastic may look clumsy. On larger aircraft wings, a balsa core may also be considered to avoid sag, although several kits supply material for strengthening spars. Don't forget to separate ailerons, elevators and rudders where feasible and re-cement at desired angles – so much more realistic for display.

The newcomer to vacuum-formed kits or even plain plastic card must accustom himself to new techniques. Even cutting parts out is quite different from cutting wood or metal; the card tends to be stiff and slippery, making light cuts and good control of the knife essential. Some of the more useful pointers are illustrated in these sketches.

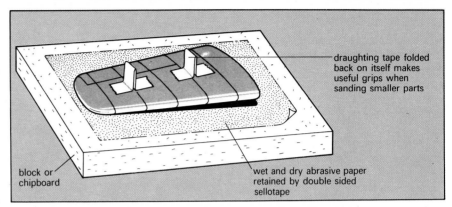

score around edge of parts lightly and do not attempt to cut right through plastic

bend parts up and down until both components part along scored the line

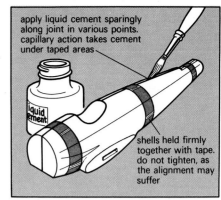

apply liquid cement sparingly along joint in various points. capillary action takes cement under taped areas

shells held firmly together with tape. do not tighten, as the alignment may suffer

draughting tape folded back on itself makes useful grips when sanding smaller parts

block or chipboard

wet and dry abrasive paper retained by double sided sellotape

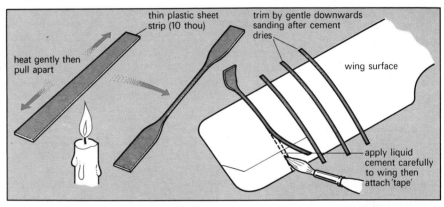

thin plastic sheet strip (10 thou)

heat gently then pull apart

trim by gentle downwards sanding after cement dries

wing surface

apply liquid cement carefully to wing then attach 'tape'

these parts can be cut by gradually cutting until knife penetrates and separates parts completely

gradual cuts

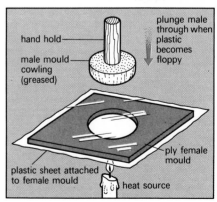

plunge male through when plastic becomes floppy

hand hold

male mould cowling (greased)

plastic sheet attached to female mould

ply female mould

heat source

## Construction

Having removed and cleaned up the various components, now is the time to really study the kit instruction sheets and go to work. It is logical to commence with the fuselage and before joining the two halves all internal detail is added along with bulkheads, stiffeners and location tabs. Prepainting must also take place in the interior before gently taping the fuselage parts together.

Ensure that the parts mate accurately before any attempt is made to glue them. Then apply liquid cement to the joint lines in various positions around the fuselage. If carefully applied with a soft sable brush, capillary action will take the solvent along the joint and under the tape. Repeat the operation several times and leave to dry. If the model is an extremely large one, further careful applications may be required, but ensure the first has hardened.

When firmly dry, remove the tape and clean up the joint with wet and dry paper. Carry this through until all sign of the joint has vanished and although moulded detail will be lost this can be restored with careful re-scribing. On longer fuselages location tabs are really vital to keep the sides located. On many of the larger models, especially those of lesser quality, several areas will require filling and smoothing. Commercial and proprietary brands of model putty should never be used on vac-forms as they too can easily melt the plastic. Even more so for vac-forms, ready mixed interior Polyfilla is, again, just the right medium. Easy to apply, it dries out quickly, sands easily and only requires one undercoat, perhaps two, before final painting. Subsequent assembly of the vac-form more or less follows the traditional methods of kit construction. Most manufacturers provide full size drawings along with detailed instructions and building tips for newcomers to the hobby.

## Improvements

There are a great many vac-form kits whose fidelity of detail falls way behind that of their contemporaries. In these cases the accent seems to be on quantity not quality, and several models fall foul of this policy. The lack of ribs on biplane wings and panels on fuselages – all have to be reinstated by the enthusiast. Happily it is not at all difficult.

Already mentioned has been the scoring of rib tapes on smaller 'fabric' covered wings but for the bigger subjects the upper surfaces at least need more drastic treatment. The tapes can be represented by stretching thin plastic strips over a heat source in the same manner for producing fine sprue. With care ultrathin plastic 'tapes' can be produced and then carefully daubed into place with a cement charged brush. Small panels can be represented either by scribing outlines with a metal scriber or the addition of 0.125mm (0.005in) plastic sheet rectangles glued into the correct positions. Stretched sprue can double for small door hinges, louvres and even cockpit padding.

It would be quite wrong to assume that the addition of extra detail on vac-forms is greater than injection moulded kits. Vac-forms may lack detail and require extra work but so do many of their more numerous brethren. The trouble with plastic kits is that the moulding process usually results in over-emphasis. Rarely are items like control horns, mass balances and aerial masts to scale, and they have to be replaced, just as the vac-form needs them to be added.

Very often, the vac-form has dis-

*Top:* A Fairey Swordfish at $\frac{1}{72}$ scale.

*Above:* Handley Page 0/400 and Sopwith Camel fighter, both at $\frac{1}{72}$ scale.

*Right:* $\frac{1}{72}$ Morane L. Saulnier as flown by S/Lt Warneford, VC from an Airframe vacuum-formed kit. *Models by R. Rimell.*

tinct advantages over the more traditional and numerous injection kits. For small WW1 biplanes, the thin sectioned wings are easily modelled and with care can even look translucent, for on clear doped fabric aircraft the structure was often visible through the covering. Vac-form plastic is so thin that this can be simulated by painting or lining the rib positions in midbrown paint and leaving to dry. Then using an airbrush or spray unit, dust a thin coat of pale buff over the wings. When the part is held up to a light source the effect is astonishing, but for it to work properly, only very light coats of paint should be applied.

## Conversions

Vac-forms can be converted just as easily as any other type of kit and perhaps a little more so. In fact there are even several manufacturers offering vac-form conversion kits designed to mate with existing plastics, thus enabling modellers to create yet more variations. These can take the form of new canopies, nacelles, cowlings – even complete fuselage shells – but care should be exercised when fitting them. The problem is that unless the vac-form components are very well moulded, the mating of injection parts is very difficult. They just look so obvious. The only solution is that if the vac-form parts carry scant detail, re-move moulded-line panels from all components and re-apply by scrib-

ing. At least that way the model will look consistent and not just an obvious jumble of parts.

Liquid cement only should be used to cement vac-form parts to injection moulded parts, and again use a soft filler such as Polyfilla. Conversion kits demand a lot of careful thought and one should always follow the manufacturer's instructions very carefully. In a few cases some vac-forms even include a choice of parts themselves, allowing further variants to be built. This is good, as most enthusiasts will wish to buy at least two kits.

### Moulding

Of course modellers can mould their own cowlings, fuselages, fairings, to extend the range of subjects even further. But this is into the realms of scratch-building, which is the natural progression from vac-form modelling.

Suffice it to say that moulding thin plastic sheet is not at all difficult and may be used in conjunction with vac-forms quite easily. Cowlings are natural subjects, especially those circular ones that enclose radial or rotary engines on vintage aircraft. Often these are ill formed

or split in two lateral halves on vac-formed sheets, making them unconvincing and difficult to model. A suitably shaped wooden dowel smoothed and greased is the ideal male mould. The female is merely a sheet of thin plywood with a circular hole cut into it which should have its edges rounded off and be slightly larger in diameter to allow the male mould to push plastic through it without jamming. A sheet of 0.5mm (0.02in) plastic sheet is pinned to the plywood and heated over an electric ring, plastic uppermost. When the latter begins to ripple, plunge the male mould

through. Leave to cool then remove and a perfectly shaped scale thickness cowling should have resulted – but it is advisable to make several in case of accidents. The advantages are obvious, with just one mould the number of cowlings that can be manufactured is unlimited.

The front of the cowling can be removed by gentle scribing with a pair of dividers in order to remove a circle of plastic. It is best to do this with the male mould in place.

With practice moulding will prove simple and effective and can be used to mould cockpit canopies, even quite complex shapes.

### Presentation

Vac-form kits if carefully made and painted should appear indistinguishable from injection moulded kits if placed alongside in a collection. Being so much lighter in weight they are surprisingly more resilient. If both types of models are accidentally dropped the vac-form (if it is a small one) will always sustain less damage.

Most vac-forms lack decals and one must be prepared to search out appropriate transfers. Luckily

there are a great many commercial ranges available to the enthusiast and these are recommended. Nevertheless, most are designed only for specific injection moulded kits – not vac-forms. A decal spares box therefore is to be seriously considered and as most kits nowadays provide optional decals, these should be saved whenever possible.

One should have access to reference sources, too, as there are several vac-form manufacturers that leave modellers in the dark as far as colour schemes and markings are concerned. True, the most sophisticated manufacturers supply drawings, schemes and most important, a list of reference works, but modellers should never shirk in their quest for detail.

### Unusual subjects

Vac-forms really score by filling as they do gaps in manufacturers' ranges. Some really interesting types have appeared, especially those of early civil and inter-war subjects. Also there are now more vac-form WW1 types from one manufacturer than there are available injection moulded versions, a difference from a few years ago, when the opposite was the case. For biplane enthusiasts, it is the vac-forms that serve them well.

As has been mentioned, early aircraft lend themselves to the process, where the delicate lightness of the original can be carefully matched. Nevertheless, it is surprising that several more modern types which one would consider to have real selling potential are only available as vac-forms, types such as the late Seafire, DH Rapide biplane, Douglas DC4, Avro Manchester, Pfalz DIII, Avro Vulcan, Victor K2, Focke Wulf Ta 154 and many others. Still, vac-forms create their own trends on occasion, for more than one has been closely followed onto the market by an injection moulded duplicate.

In summary, vac-forms demand a lot of care in construction, and considerable experience, but they fulfil an important role in plastic modelling. As more and more sophisticated kits match and sometimes even surpass injection-moulded models they should take on even greater significance. In providing a whole range of rare and unusual subjects, hitherto considered only by scratch builders, new avenues are opened to a wider market. For modellers wishing to improve their skills they can be unreservedly recommended.

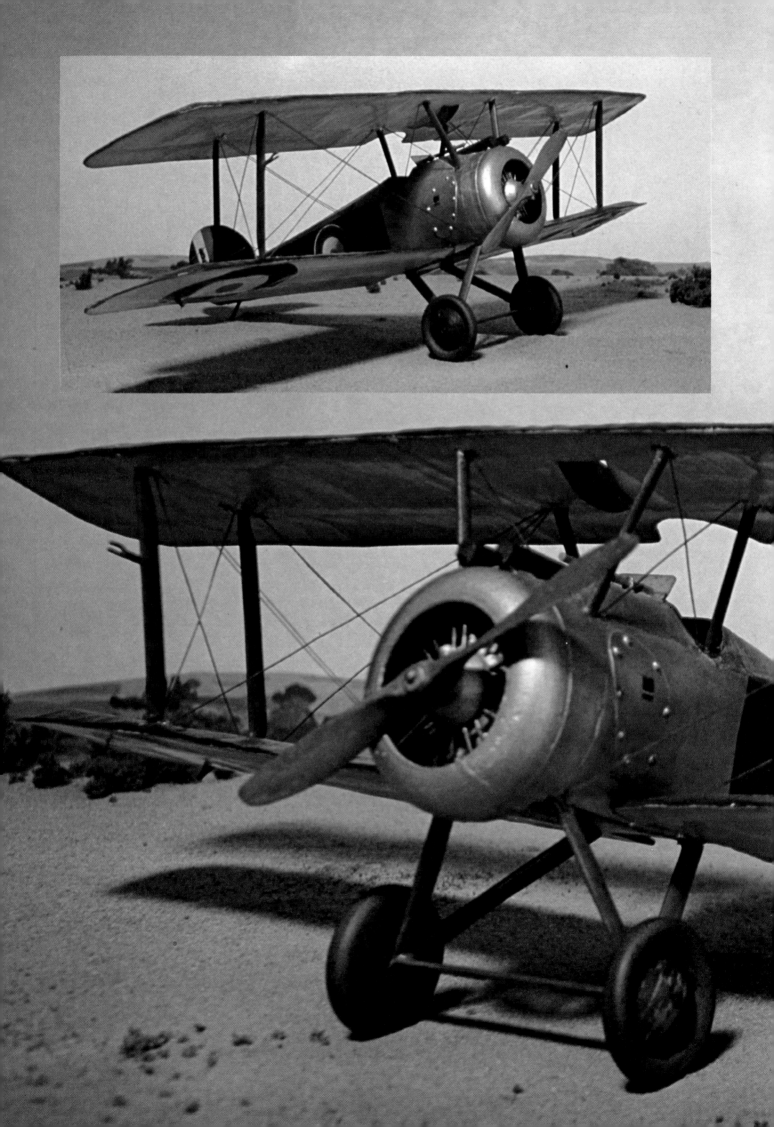

# Models in Other Materials
## Wood and Metal
## Industrial Models

**The heritage of wood models**
Before the age of plastics a wide selection of kits of non-flying scale models was available in wood, usually either balsa or obechi but sometimes hardwood, and in what are still the two most popular scales, $\frac{1}{72}$ and $\frac{1}{48}$. In many cases, the work involved was almost tantamount to scratch-building, for the wooden parts were usually only formed to approximate outlines, leaving the bulk of the shaping to be done by the modeller. The main advantage of the kits was that they provided items such as engines, airscrews and wheels, sometimes die-cast in metal, also scale drawings which were by no means as easy to obtain as they are nowadays. Pre-eminent in their respective fields were such makes as Skybirds in the UK and Hawk in the USA, the former containing hardwood fuselages and wings, as well as metal, fibre and celluloid

One of the finest fighting scouts of World War 1, the Sopwith Camel has appeared in various scales in plastic kit form. This $\frac{1}{24}$ example is, however, built of card, with wood struts, wheels and propeller. *Model by F. Henderson*.

components, the latter featuring mainly balsa wood and die-cast metal parts.

There are still some modellers who regret the passing of the wood kits and the special skills which went with them, so perhaps it is apposite to revive some of those skills and apply them to currently available materials.

## Planning the model

The first consideration is the choice of a suitable subject and clearly there is little point in picking one which is already available as a plastic kit, so the opportunity will normally be taken to make a model of a favourite aircraft which is not likely to be produced as a kit. Having decided upon the type to be built, the next step is to find the necessary drawings and as much information to supplement them as possible, principally photos in books and magazines.

## Working with wood

It is possible to carve virtually any shape from wood but the basic method is simple enough; first take a medium-hard balsa block with its three dimensions slightly larger than those of the part to be model-

led, then draw the outline on the two sides, always allowing about 0.75mm ($\frac{1}{32}$in) oversize all round to allow for sanding. Carve the block first to profile and then mark out and carve it in plan. Next make templates from plastic sheet to give the correct section (half templates will usually suffice) at stations covering each major change of section, and carve the wood carefully to fit the templates, remembering always that it is much easier to take a little more off than to put it back! A rub over with fine glass-paper reduces the component to its final size and shape and several coats of filler (sanding sealer or, alternatively, clear dope mixed with talcum powder) will be required to obtain a smooth, firm, blemish-free surface; after each coat has dried the wood should be rubbed down with flour-paper. This procedure is followed similarly for the wings, tail surfaces and, where applicable, engine nacelles.

## The smaller parts

Modelling a radial engine may seem to be a daunting prospect and yet, if tackled methodically and with patience, it is not too difficult. The crankcase and reduction-gear

housing are best built up from laminations of plastic sheet and then carved to shape, after which the centres of each cylinder are marked, a hole drilled and a small wire dowel inserted as a locator. The cylinders can be either plastic rod or wooden dowel, of suitable diameter, bound with thread to simulate the cooling fins, coated with thinned cement and, when dry, cut to length; a hole is then drilled in each cylinder to fit over the locating pin. Push-rods are cut from wire and rocker box housings and other small items made from plastic or wood. Cowlings can be made by wrapping thin plastic sheet around wooden dowel rod of suitable diameter, building up the required thickness in half-circles, laid alternately with the joints 180° apart; the dowel should be waxed to aid separation. Wooden-type propellers can be carved from wood blocks in the same manner as the larger components. Struts are best made from plastic sheet, reinforced with wire, and wheels, if not available in a suitable size from the spares box, can be made by laminating discs and rings cut from plastic sheet and then carved and sanded down, or turned if possible.

*Above:* This De Havilland DH89a Rapide was built recently from an original Skybirds $\frac{1}{72}$ wood kit, produced over 40 years earlier. The Rapide was a highly successful 'feeder liner' and later saw war service as a navigational trainer, the 'Dominite'.

*Below:* The Cierva C30A, also known as the Avro Rota, built in $\frac{1}{48}$ scale from an LDM cast white metal kit and finished as one of the original batch of 12 supplied to the RAF in 1934. The rotor of an autogiro is not engine-driven but rotates due to aerodynamic forces.

## Making the most of materials

The wisest approach to any kind of scratch-building of aircraft models is to study the available materials and then use them in whatever combination will give the best results. There is no need to try for production line methods, nor to be commercial, for the aim is a one-off model, built entirely for the modeller's own satisfaction and the time taken to achieve the desired result should be of only minor concern. The combination of wood, metal and plastic parts does not constitute a problem in assembly, because modern adhesives can cope with virtually anything, but a tip here about the sticking of polystyrene plastic to wood is appropriate. If the wood is first coated, in the area to be joined, with at least one thin layer of plastic cement which is then allowed to dry, polystyrene parts can easily be bonded to it with the same type of cement; wood glues will not bond to plastic.

## Going into details

Representing rib and stringer effects on the wooden parts can be done by cementing narrow strips of paper, or thin plastic sheet, in place; thread can be used for this purpose but is more difficult to place accurately and to fix securely. Small appendages, such as radio antennae and pitot tubes, are best made from wire, soldered where necessary – soldering can be very useful at times – for they need to be durable to withstand handling and possible knocks; plastic or wood can be used for these parts but are easily broken, whereas wire just bends and can be straightened.

The forming of cockpits and cabins is achieved by cutting away the appropriate area of the fuselage and, after fitting out the interior, inserting new side panels with windows formed and shaping and filling, where necessary, to blend into the fuselage lines; the amount of interior detail to be incorporated is at the discretion of the modeller. Once the wood has been completely sealed, surface detail can be marked, with a knife or scriber, against a metal edge or, for curved surfaces, a piece of plastic sheet. The painting of wooden or metallic surfaces has one useful advantage over plastics in that cellulose lacquer-based finishes can be used. Transfers (decals) are available, in great profusion, from a number of commercial sources.

## Tools of the trade

Only a simple tool kit is necessary, much of which will be in the hands of the plastic modeller already. Essential items are a modelling knife with a selection of blades of various shapes, small fine-nosed and square-nosed pliers, wire cutters, small drills with a pin-vice to hold them, a razor saw, a few small files including ones of flat, round, square and triangular sections and fine grades of glasspaper, including flour-paper. Additionally a metal set-square and straight-edge will prove of great value when setting out the wood blocks.

## Metal – a new approach

Kits in $\frac{1}{48}$ scale composed almost entirely of white metal components have recently begun to appear. The feel and weight of the completed models is distinctly odd to the modeller accustomed to working in plastic or balsa, but the appearance is undoubtedly good and the detail comparable with most plastic kits. The casting method has the advantage of being viable for relatively short production runs, totally uneconomic for plastic kits for which the mould cost would be vastly greater, so types of aircraft can be produced which have a limited appeal and might never appear in any other form. Two notable examples are the Pitts S2a Special and the Cierva C30a Autogiro.

Apart from the unaccustomed weight, there are other features of the die-cast model which are strange, although it is not really difficult to adapt plastic kit building techniques to suit. Most of the requisite tools will be to hand, files, pliers, wire cutters and 'wet and dry' carborundum paper being the main ones. Some cleaning up of the castings is necessary and possibly bending carefully in places to obtain an accurate fit of the parts, but assembly is not difficult, using quick-setting epoxy glue (low melting point soldering can be employed but only by the practised user). For spot-fixing the smaller parts the most effective adhesive is cyanoacrylate glue which has the useful property of setting positively in about ten seconds. Where any filling is necessary, auto-body fillers are suitable, but not those normally used for plastic kits.

Painting calls for a different approach. After thoroughly cleaning the metal, a primer needs to be applied, preferably by air-brush or aerosol spray, to prepare the surface for finishing. After that painting can proceed in the normal manner.

## Modelling in card

Undoubtedly the cheapest, although certainly not the easiest, material with which to work is

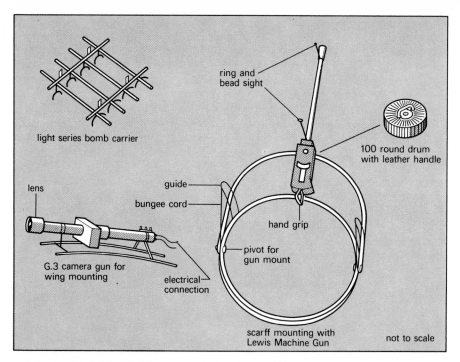

light series bomb carrier

ring and bead sight

100 round drum with leather handle

lens

guide

bungee cord

hand grip

G.3 camera gun for wing mounting

electrical connection

pivot for gun mount

scarff mounting with Lewis Machine Gun

not to scale

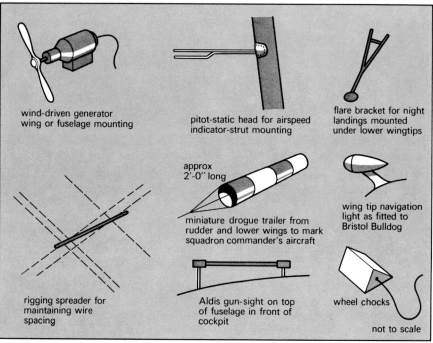

wind-driven generator wing or fuselage mounting

pitot-static head for airspeed indicator-strut mounting

flare bracket for night landings mounted under lower wingtips

approx 2'-0" long

miniature drogue trailer from rudder and lower wings to mark squadron commander's aircraft

wing tip navigation light as fitted to Bristol Bulldog

rigging spreader for maintaining wire spacing

Aldis gun-sight on top of fuselage in front of cockpit

wheel chocks

not to scale

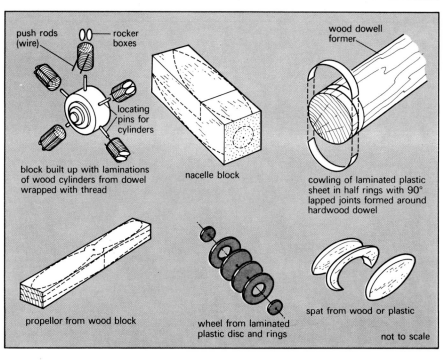

push rods (wire)

rocker boxes

wood dowell former

locating pins for cylinders

block built up with laminations of wood cylinders from dowel wrapped with thread

nacelle block

cowling of laminated plastic sheet in half rings with 90° lapped joints formed around hardwood dowel

propellor from wood block

wheel from laminated plastic disc and rings

spat from wood or plastic

not to scale

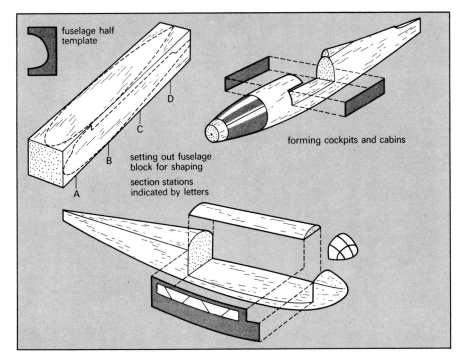

fuselage half template

setting out fuselage block for shaping

section stations indicated by letters

forming cockpits and cabins

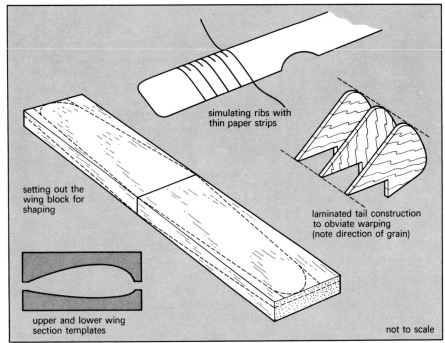

setting out the wing block for shaping

simulating ribs with thin paper strips

laminated tail construction to obviate warping (note direction of grain)

upper and lower wing section templates

not to scale

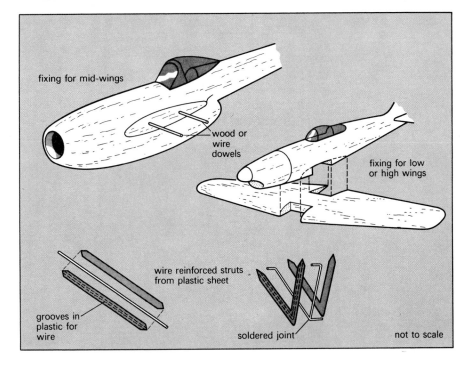

fixing for mid-wings

wood or wire dowels

fixing for low or high wings

grooves in plastic for wire

wire reinforced struts from plastic sheet

soldered joint

not to scale

The amount of visible detail on, particularly, military aircraft provides endless scope for a modeller's ingenuity. Some of those details, and standard methods of work with wood models, are illustrated here.

card, or board as it is sometimes termed. Nowadays the readily available, and easily worked, plastic sheet has largely superseded ordinary card and paper modelling as far as aircraft are concerned, but they are still popular for model railway buildings.

The history of the card model, as far as the UK is concerned, goes back at least to the late 1920s when a firm called Appleby produced pre-coloured cut-out sheets which purported to be for flying scale models. Although quite acceptable, for their time, as models, their performance was disappointing. A high point in the state of the art was reached in the mid-1930s when a large range of $\frac{1}{24}$ and $\frac{1}{48}$ scale models was made by Aeromodels, a Liverpool firm. These were printed in black lines on white card, so required painting by the modeller after assembly. The models were truly remarkable for their accuracy and completeness, the $\frac{1}{24}$ scale kits, featuring fully-fitted cabins, opening doors and even folding wings! Cork was used as reinforcement internally and there were some hardwood parts, and the resultant model was far more durable than were the built-up balsa wood models of the period.

For practical purposes, $\frac{1}{50}$ is the smallest advisable scale and the present-day cut-out card sheets, produced by such firms as Wilhelm-shavener Modellbaubogen, of West Germany, are mostly to that scale; such models are not comparable with the late-lamented Aeromodels series but can, with care and patience, be made into realistic miniatures, and they are pre-coloured.

Building from scratch in card involves techniques similar to those employed for plastic sheet, described in another chapter, but white PVA glue takes the place of polystyrene cement. However, card is more difficult to work with than plastic sheet and the latter material does most jobs better so, unless cost is the main consideration, scratch-building is best done in plastic card.

For card and paper modelling the tool kit required amounts to little more than a modelling knife, straight-edge, pencil and a pair of household scissors, plus suitable glue.

# Industrial Models

The value of research and test models is inestimable. They are used for every stage of aerodynamic development, to prove the feasibility and performance potential of new projects, but they must not in any way be confused with the sport flyer's scale model, no matter how closely related is the appearance to the full size. In fact, the model enthusiast generally produces a much more easily recognized replica. Drop test, wind tunnel and structural test models are normally very simple in detail; they do not need embellishment, for the primary requirement is accuracy.

Tunnel models have been used to prove aerodynamic factors ever since the first experiments by the Wright Brothers. Machined from close-grained timber, or in recent years steel and plastic resins, wind tunnel models are made to extremely close tolerances. When designed to break down so that changes in configuration can be checked, the tunnel model gives results relatively quickly.

The free-flying test model has become a valuable supplementary tool in research and development. Typical is work on the Anglo-French Concorde supersonic jet airliner. Prior to construction of the actual prototypes, the one time world speed record-holding Fairey FD2 was converted with an 'ogival' wing (curved leading edge delta) of the same shape as Concorde. Before the FD2 could air test the wing, a free-flight model of this airframe had to be drop tested.

The sophistication of the task created changes in model construction techniques, for the fuselage shell had to carry equipment weighing up to 25% of the total weight, and the wings, by virtue of their supersonic intent and desired ground impact resistance, had to achieve a strength/weight ratio well in excess of previous experience.

The answer came with moulded epoxy resin and glass cloth assemblies. First, a wooden mould pattern of extreme accuracy was carved to tolerances of 0.025mm (0.001in) including French polish finish. Next,

*Below:* A high standard is needed for commercial production of epoxy-cast models for airline publicity use. This type of modelling is close to mass production, with assembly line techniques and methods.

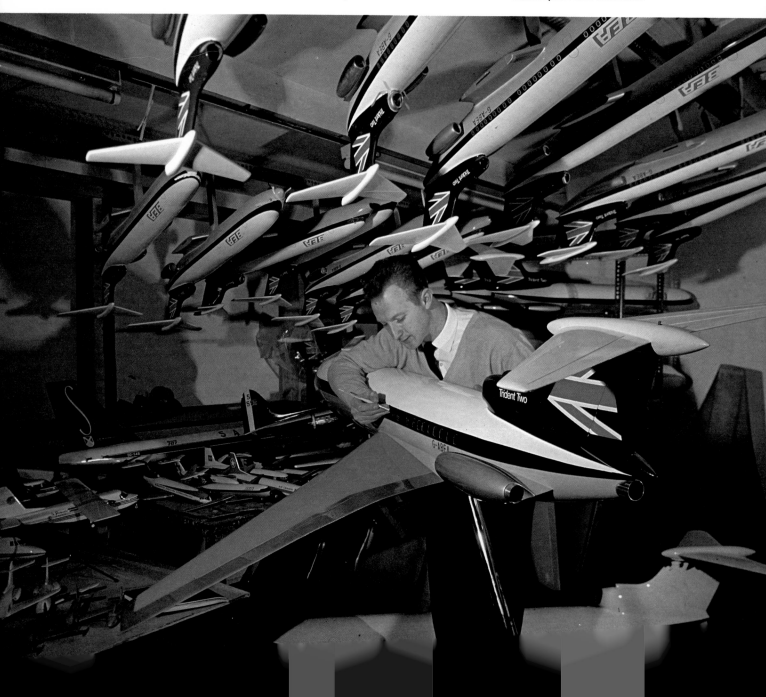

'Titanite' exothermic setting (heat generating) cement moulds were made, braced into steel frames. Into the moulds, layers of glass cloth and resin (Araldite) coupled with a calcium carbonate filler formed a shell for the eventual model, which had cavity areas cold urethane foam-filled for rigidity. Components were then assembled in a precision jig, where metal fittings were added, and final work on the exterior executed to bring the wings to limits of 0.125mm (0.005in) and the fuselage to 0.25mm (0.01in). One set of moulds in yellow pine could thus be used to produce repeated test models fairly quickly.

These drop test experiments employed a helicopter release. A very close approximation of the Concorde flight envelope, especially at extremely slow speeds, was accumulated long before the prototypes were first flown.

High speed research employs models of a different calibre. Made to much smaller scales and propelled by solid fuel rockets the velocity is in the order of 1600km/h (1000mph). At such speeds, visual observation is impossible, so the small model is equipped to telemeter measurements of pressures and accelerations from up to 20 stations. During the cruise (power-off) stage, a series of kine-theodolite survey cameras record azimuth and elevation, and velocity is determined by Doppler ratio. Such tests are used to discover pitching motions, divergences at speed, and stability. Scientists are concerned only with the aerodynamic shape, so the weight problem does not arise. Machined in steel and sometimes carrying further small rockets to fire at intervals to provide an oscillatory motion, these supersonic free-flight test bodies are

beyond the concept of general modelling.

Standard aeromodelling techniques have long been employed at NASA in drop tests. Models as heavy as 104kg (230lb) have been dropped from a helicopter at 1200m (4000ft), prior to deployment of a Rogallo type para-wing, for space recovery research. Precision was such that landings were positioned within a 6m (20ft) circle.

Robert Reed, then Head of Advance Planning, Re-entry Vehicles, at NASA Edwards Field, reported most favourably on the use of aeromodelling methods to an Astronautics Conference in Los Angeles. He revealed the use of a 7kg (15lb) 'carrier' model, of 3.2m (10ft 6in) span and 2.5m (8ft 3in) length, which was designed to air-launch up to 9kg (20lb) payloads which could be any of six re-entry bodies ranging from a 150gm (6oz) light-

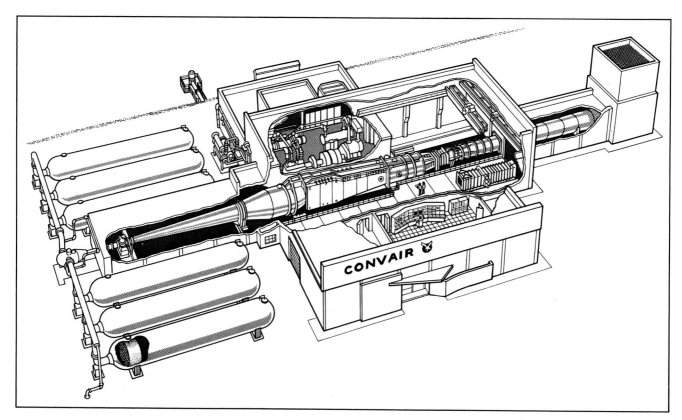

weight fixed control slender lifting body to a 1m (40in) long 4.5kg (10lb) fibreglass scale M2-F2 with a pop-out para-wing. Such studies offer low-cost, minimum risk examination of basic problems in research and are by no means limited to government establishments.

The Sandia Corporation of Albuquerque, New Mexico, saved itself much time and money thanks to sport modelling experience. Dan Parsons, a Scandia supervisor engaged with the company's tracking telescopes, conceived the idea of using radio-controlled (R/C) models for telescope tracking practice to accustom the operators to the skilful task of observing high flying jets. Drop tests of dummy bomb shapes, involving a study of target colours, were another aspect of

their experiments with the 1.8m (6ft) 3kg (7lb) models, which use 0.60 engines. A development was carriage of telemetry equipment to relay model-borne instrument readings as the small plane was guided 450m (1500ft) above an explosion. Blast pressure readings would be difficult to obtain by any other method.

Consolidated Vultee and Dornier have tested flying boats in radio-controlled model form. The object of these tests was primarily to ascertain hydrodynamic characteristics so that changes to the planing hull could quickly resolve problems. A colossal $\frac{1}{10}$ scale Convair XP5Y-1 of 4.46m (14ft 8in) span with four 2hp horizontally opposed twin-cylinder engines was flown at San Diego and a similar though

smaller Dornier Do24 at Bremen.

Convair became famous for their model department; another aspect of their research involved mechanically actuated models in a wind tunnel for filmed observation of crew escape systems. The rocket propelled shuttlecock action ejection seat which tilted the pilot back in his seat before leaving the cockpit in emergency was first tested with scale models before full-size experiments at Edwards.

Lockheed's model department is also famous for its achievements. The solution to the early problems of the Electra's disastrous wing failures was discovered through models with scale elasticity designed into their structure.

### Films

In the 'special effects' departments of the film companies, the model comes into its own for crash scenes. Gone are the days when model 'planes slid jerkily along stressed wires in a studio. Crash shots with all the blast in the wrong direction and obvious studio break-ups are past. So successful is the use of R/C scale aeroplanes before the cameras that the film makers maintain a deception that it is the real stuff they are flying. All that can be said

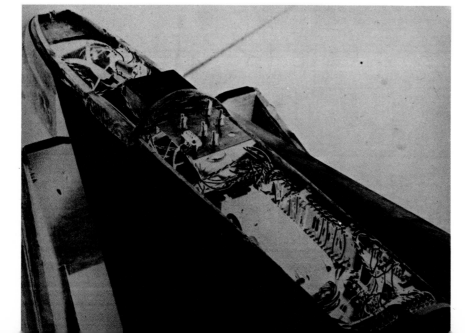

*Left and above right:* Dynamic drop-test model of the type released from a helicopter or captive balloon to give invaluable information on performance characteristics relatively cheaply. Radio control can be used to produce special situations on the way down.

is that when the screen shows two Ju 87s in spectacular mid-air collision, filmed in 1968 when there has not been a single example flying anywhere in the world for 20 years, what else could one possibly imagine has provided the spectacle? As art directors develop the techniques whole new fields open up for action scenes of extreme realism.

## Airline models

In the airline world the need for visual impressions of new aeroplanes and their colour schemes has created an industry of professional model makers engaged in production of sleek mini-liners for travel agencies of every nation. Pride of the trade are the $\frac{1}{4}$ scale 'sectionals' where a transparent plastic fuselage is left only partly painted to show the cabin interior. When re-equipment of an airline involves an entirely new type, such as the A300 Airbus and Boeing 767, the model suppliers have a boom on their hands.

Plastics feature largely in this business. Wings are of epoxy-fibreglass, with styrene mouldings with transparencies for the fuselage and, often, solid wooden tail surfaces. The smaller models are all styrene, vacuum formed or injection moulded in a one-piece assembly and decorated with special livery decals. It is not entirely unknown for an airline to adopt the livery created by a modeller for a prototype design.

When a full-scale aviation show is planned, such as the Paris or Farnborough Air Shows, these modellers come into the most interesting side of the job, for they alone have the responsibility of conveying to the public and their customer's opposition companies how good are the future projects. Models appear up to three years before an actual aircraft makes a first flight, and their surface finish, shape, cleanliness and presentation are critically important at Le Bourget or Farnborough.

There is a place for modelling in every manufacturing establishment, and although formal training courses are virtually non-existent, opportunity abounds for the hobbyist who is genuinely skilled in his craftmanship, adaptable in his interests and adventurous in his techniques.

*Right:* This radio-controlled flying scale Dornier Do24 was part of a research study on the feasibility of new production of this 40-year-old flying boat for commercial purposes such as water-bombing of fires and the like.

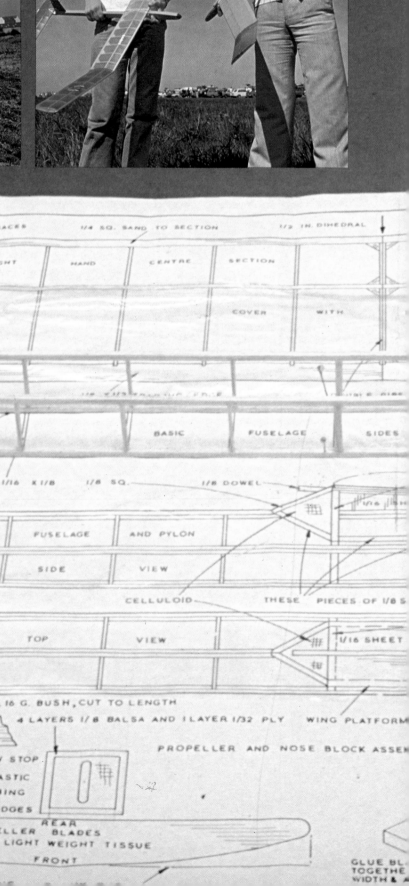

DOUBLE RIBS
ANGLE SLIGHTLY

PLY BRACES          1/4 SQ. SAND TO SECTION          1/2 IN. DIHEDRAL

RIGHT      HAND      CENTRE      SECTION

COVER      WITH

BASIC      FUSELAGE      SIDES

1/16 SHEET      1/8 SQ.      1/16 X 1/8      1/8 SQ.      1/8 DOWEL

FUSELAGE      AND      PYLON

SIDE      VIEW

BINDING      CELLULOID      THESE      PIECES OF 1/8 S

TOP      VIEW      1/16 SHEET

SPRING      WASHER      16 G. BUSH, CUT TO LENGTH

1/16 PLY SIDES
SIDES, FRONT
AND REAR      4 LAYERS 1/8 BALSA AND 1 LAYER 1/32 PLY      WING PLATFORM

3/8 SQ.      PROPELLER  AND  NOSE BLOCK ASSEM

16 G. WIRE      SCREW STOP

PLASTIC
TUBING

1/8 DOWEL
HINGES      ROUND EDGES
GLUED
IN BLADES      REAR
3/16      PROPELLER      BLADES      GLUE BL
TOGETHE
3/16      COVER WITH LIGHT WEIGHT TISSUE      WIDTH &

FRONT

PINS AND BANDS TO ASSIST FOLDING

# First Steps in Flight

## First Flying Models
## Building a Simple Kit

*Far left:* Young beginners with three examples of kitted novice models, a C/L stunt trainer, R/C trainer power model, and a towline glider trainer.

*Left:* A1 class gliders in the hands of young fliers have many advantages – they are inexpensive, straightforward to build, and have a satisfying performance.

**Why build a flying model?**

When Stringfellow and Penaud created the first powered flying model aircraft over 100 years ago, the answer to that question was the same as it is now – to achieve flight, to master the forces of nature and defy the laws of gravity is a natural desire of mankind. We have always wanted to fly, from the days of Icarus to the Wright brothers. If you can't actually go flying in a full-size aircraft, then there is no thrill quite like that of seeing your own model creation take flight! Since the times of Penaud, there have been many design refinements that enable even the neophyte to achieve initial success. In the USA, over half a million small rubber-powered 'Delta Darts' have been built and flown by beginners. Some of them are incredibly crude (built by youngsters who have never used a hobby knife or balsa glue) but the satisfying part is that they all fly. This act of flight is the thrill and stimulus to the imagination that bonds all the aeromodellers of many nations. You can feel that thrill for yourself!

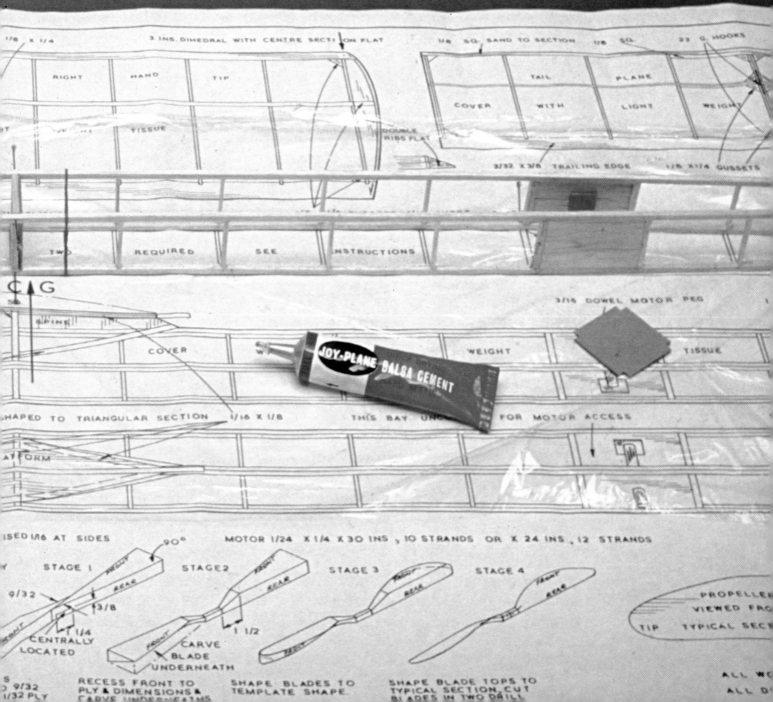

## Choosing the right model

There is such a great choice of aircraft types and model designs that it is difficult for the beginner to pick one that will give him initial success rather than crashes and frustration – or worse still, an incomplete and thus unflyable model. The natural tendency is to look for models that are very realistic, that have true scale appearance. The more complex or stylish these are the better – everyone would like to have a flying model of the Lindbergh *Spirit of St. Louis*, or the Wright Flyer, or the famous gull-wing F4U Corsair. However, even expert modellers have great difficulty in getting those particular examples to fly at all, let alone well.

If you must have a scale type model, choose one of the pioneer types or a home-built aircraft design. Generally these have the characteristics that make for easy construction and good flying. They have squarish outlines, box fuselages, long noses and tails, and large tail surfaces, relatively speaking. There are no complex curves to impede construction, and their proportions give them a built-in stability that is essential to 'pilotless' model flight.

Simplicity cannot be over-emphasized in choosing your first model, if you ever expect it to fly. If it has so many parts that you may tire of building before that exciting first flight, then avoid it. Seek instead a creation of few parts, perhaps all sheet balsa with no covering material. Covering is an essential skill for the high performance lightweight modeller to master, but it can be sidestepped. The great success of the AMA *Delta Dart* and the sister ship BBC *Hawk* is that the airframe is glued right to the covering. This covering is the actual plan for the model, so construction is rapid and almost foolproof. The triangular flying surfaces, while not very realistic in terms of full-scale appearance, are easy to make and warp-proof. Twisted warps in a first model can often spell disaster in flying.

Strength is another factor in choosing your flying model design. Look for structures that have thick balsa parts or sheet wood, rather than flimsy small strips. Reinforcement at critical points that take flight stress is important, such as the wing centre, propeller mounting and landing gear. All-balsa structures are generally very strong and have the added attraction of being able to be repaired easily in the event of a crash. Profile or stick bodies, while not realistic, are very good and quite sturdy.

Strength and simplicity are important, but probably the most critical factors in success are proportions and built-in stability. Models with long bodies and relatively large tails usually are the outstanding flyers. The dihedral (or 'bent' wing) angle of wing panels is important in providing built-in spiral stability, since most models fly in circles. Low wing models are more difficult to fly than shoulder wing or high wing designs, and biplanes are especially difficult. While a biplane has glamour, it also has potential for misalignment of wings, and the tail is usually small for the wing surface.

Power is another factor to consider. Gliders, either handlaunch or tow, are the simplest flying models. More thrills can be had by adding a propeller powered by rubber strands, a $CO_2$ motor, electric motor or internal combustion engine. Each of these have advantages, but the rubber model is the most universally popular.

## Indoor model flying

Newcomers to flying models should keep in mind that many good indoor flying sites abound in their communities, and indoor flying can provide all-weather fun day and night. Indoor models are generally much lighter in weight and seldom powered by anything other than

*Above far left:* the P30 class rubber model is a good introduction to rubber-powered competition flying.

*Above left:* This 7-year-old's 'Metric Penny' flew for 5m 12secs on his first visit to a 15m (50ft) high gymnasium.

*Left:* An indoor hand-launched glider, 610mm (24in) span and 27g (0.9oz) weight. British record-holder at 78secs.

rubber or $CO_2$, since oily, noisy internal combustion engines are unwelcome in school gyms and auditoriums. The heavy batteries required by electric powered models also make them very unlikely for indoor use. Towline gliders, which must be kited up to launch altitude, are also unsuited to flying indoors.

Nevertheless, a lot of enjoyment can be had from indoor flying. One of the most popular of internationally flown scale model classes, Peanut Scale, is flown indoors. These models are restricted to 330mm (13 in) wingspan and must be rubber powered. They take off from the floor in a realistic way and can often put in flights exceeding one minute. Normal endurance indoor models can be flown for up to ten minutes in small halls by beginners. The professionals can achieve half-hour flights with ease in larger sites. Such models are covered elsewhere in this book, but for the novice, we recommend that the first indoor model be a Pennyplane. This class was developed in the USA when it was found that the lightweight 'Easy B' (or EZB) was actually too difficult! Pennyplanes can be built with heavier grades of balsa to withstand flying and handling knocks. Many full size plans and a few kits are available for Pennyplanes. Try the MAP Plans Service *Penny Wise* or Vintage Aero kit *Metric Penny*.

### The best beginner models

Earlier on advice was given on how to choose a model that will fly well. The simple chuck glider, profile towline glider and basic engine-power models in this book are all good flyers and worth building if you do not choose to try a kit your first time out. However, there is a lot to be said for using a kit. They have all the materials, sometimes cut to shape, and the plans are usually full of building and flying advice. Often they are developed from a long line of prototypes before being mass produced. Feedback from builders helps to ensure that they fly well, especially if they are used in large school beginner classes. Good flying kits are a key part of these classes.

The two types of models that will give you the most satisfaction and good flying for your investment of time and materials are the small hand-launch glider (or chuck glider) and the Simple Rubber Power Stick Model (SRPSM). They are available in many varieties. The Humbrol *Ladybird* HLG and *Wasp* SRPSM are excellent choices. USA counterparts are M & P *Miniflash* and Jasco *Flash X-18* SRPSM. These 'top choices' are available in most hobby shops and have had extensive consumer testing. While the AMA *Delta Dart* and British BBC *Hawk* are excellent first flying models, they are not always on the dealer shelves. They are more often seen in class work or promotion of model aviation by aeroclubs.

The *Ladybird* and *Miniflash* gliders, while produced in different nations (UK and USA) are similar in approach. They are small, require less than an hour to assemble, and trim out easily. The former has vee dihedral and the latter tip dihedral, but this does not affect performance. Note that such chuck gliders can be flown indoors as well as out, and teach all the basic principles of flight (except power thrust) with minimum effort.

The Humbrol *Wasp* is actually a small ROG (Rise Off Ground) type but can be flown without wheels if you wish a true SRPSM. A 'stick model' is one where the rubber motor is hung from a bearing/shaft and a rear hook mounted on a motor stick, completely exposed. The use of a stick allows the wing to be moved fore and aft for trimming and motor can be wound easily from rear. Alternatively, you can wind up by simply turning the prop.

The Jasco *Flash X-18* is very simply the best SRPSM ever kitted. Years of development went into the design and kit instructions, and it is a very high performance model. The *X-18* is completely prefabri-

National German adhesive manufacturers run a nation-wide beginners' glider competition. The 1978 winner at Buhl was Stephanie Scholz, one of the relatively few lady competitors.

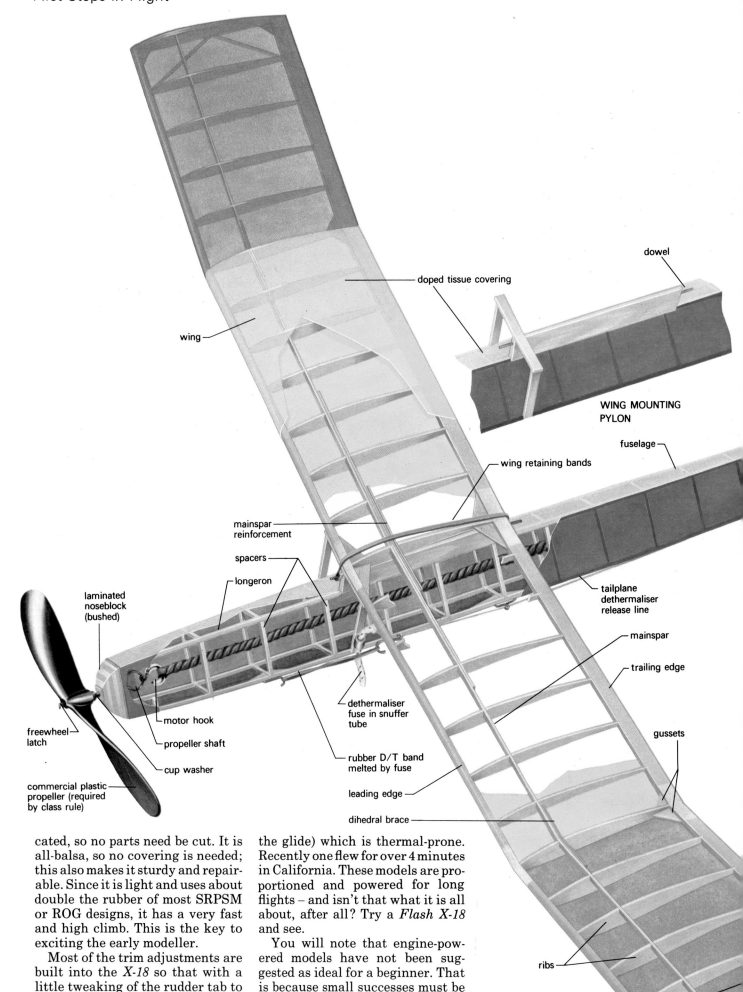

dowel

doped tissue covering

wing

WING MOUNTING
PYLON

fuselage

wing retaining bands

mainspar
reinforcement

tailplane
dethermaliser
release line

spacers

longeron

mainspar

laminated
noseblock
(bushed)

trailing edge

dethermaliser
fuse in snuffer
tube

gussets

freewheel
latch

motor hook

propeller shaft

rubber D/T band
melted by fuse

cup washer

commercial plastic
propeller (required
by class rule)

leading edge

dihedral brace

ribs

cated, so no parts need be cut. It is all-balsa, so no covering is needed; this also makes it sturdy and repairable. Since it is light and uses about double the rubber of most SRPSM or ROG designs, it has a very fast and high climb. This is the key to exciting the early modeller.

Most of the trim adjustments are built into the *X-18* so that with a little tweaking of the rudder tab to the right, a swift spiral climb results followed by a smooth right glide (the plastic prop freewheels in the glide) which is thermal-prone. Recently one flew for over 4 minutes in California. These models are proportioned and powered for long flights – and isn't that what it is all about, after all? Try a *Flash X-18* and see.

You will note that engine-powered models have not been suggested as ideal for a beginner. That is because small successes must be the groundwork for later happy flying. Chuck gliders and rubber models can be flown almost any-

## P30 CLASS RUBBER MODEL
## (for small-field flying)

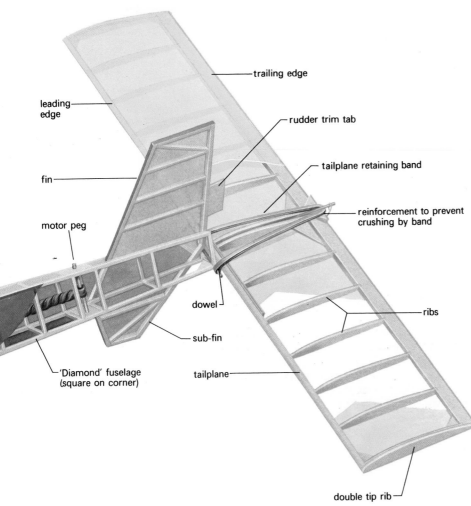

leading edge

trailing edge

fin

rudder trim tab

tailplane retaining band

motor peg

reinforcement to prevent crushing by band

dowel

ribs

sub-fin

'Diamond' fuselage (square on corner)

tailplane

double tip rib

tip braces

where, with no engine starting problems or equipment. A crash with an engine-powered craft will almost certainly result in damage, while lightweight HLGs and SRPSMs can bounce back for more after most prangs. Also there are limits on cost – almost any young enthusiast can afford the simple models, but power can become costly. Even the $CO_2$ motor can be expensive in initial cost and operation. But because it is adaptable to most small rubber power models (even fitted to SRPSM!) it is a good compromise; also it can be flown

anywhere, including your local school gym on rainy days.

Sooner or later, many flyers will want to advance to engine power and the noisy thrill of an internal combustion engine. Since control-line models are universally powered by engines, they are dealt with in a separate section near the end of this chapter. Free-flight models with 0.049 engine power are the best for beginners. Often a reed-valve engine from a demolished and discarded plastic control-liner can be adapted to free-flight sport use. If simple sport free-flight is desired, then a largish (900mm (36in) or so) cabin model can give many hours of flying fun. No timer is needed to control motor run; simply limit the amount of fuel used in the integral tank on the 0.049 engine. There are a number of kits that can be seen in the hobby shop; one good one is the KeilKraft *Wizard*. If you enjoy building from scratch, the *Tomboy*

(PET 398) and *Mandy* (PET 861) are good choices from the MAP Aeromodeller Plans Service (see 'Resources' at end of chapter).

If simple flight thrills you and motive power is optional, then the towline glider is second only to the chuck glider for most pleasure for the investment. Such models can be flown to a good altitude by kiting on tow, and launched into warm thermals for long flights. A slight variation on the towline glider is the 0.049 engine powered RC thermal soaring glider. For the same reasons that power models are not suggested for the complete beginner (crashes and cost), thermal RC flying seems best left for later. However, the new Cox *Sport-Avia* ready-to-fly model (requires only component assembly and simple radio installation) is a very good way to start in the sophisticated and expensive ($200 or £100 to get flying) world of radio control. It is a first-rate, quality kit.

### Control-line aircraft

Control-line models (or U-Control as they are sometimes called) are a special type of powered model aircraft that may be most familiar to beginners because of the mass marketing of small engine-powered, plastic devices. While these tiny scale and semi-scale designs have a great deal of consumer appeal, they are not the best way to get started in control-line flying. The potential for trouble in operation and flying is great and the opportunity to get advice from a salesperson is non-existent. The vast majority of these ready-to-fly plastic models end up in the rubbish or the back of the cupboard, a monument to disappointment.

Back in the days before injection-moulded plastics made such things possible, the novice had to create his own model from balsa sheet and strip, then cover it and paint it himself. This is still a very good approach, as it gives some understanding of the mechanics of the U-Control system and the airframe components. Building your own model also tends to make you more careful on the flying field and more likely to repair accidental damage so that you can go flying again. There are a great many good kits on the market and an equal number of plans available along with instructive articles on U-Control trainers.

The U-Control system itself is actually a patented invention of a man with a brilliant creative gen-

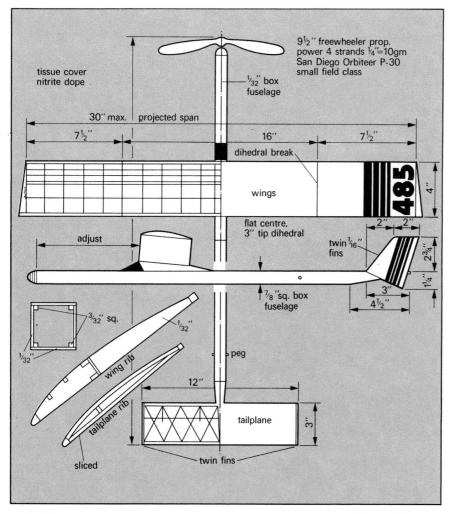

9½″ freewheeler prop.
power 4 strands ¼″=10gm
San Diego Orbiteer P-30
small field class

tissue cover
nitrite dope

1/32 box
fuselage

30″ max. projected span

7½″

16″

7½″

4″

dihedral break

wings

485

adjust

flat centre,
3″ tip dihedral

twin 1/16″
fins

2″ 2″

2¾″

1¼″

3″

4½″

3/32″ sq.

1/32″

1/32″

wing rib

7/8″sq. box
fuselage

peg

12″

tailplane rib

tailplane

3″

sliced

twin fins

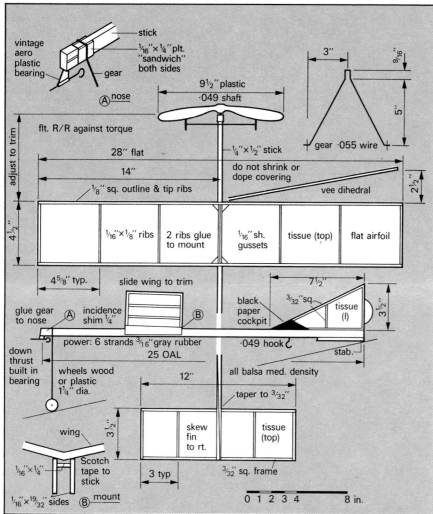

stick

vintage
aero
plastic
bearing

1/16″×¼″ plt.
"sandwich"
both sides

gear

Ⓐ nose

flt. R/R against torque

9½″ plastic
·049 shaft

3″

9/16″

¼″×½″ stick

gear ·055 wire

5″

adjust to trim

28″ flat

14″

do not shrink or
dope covering

4½″

1/8″ sq. outline & tip ribs

vee dihedral

2½″

1/16″×1/8″ ribs

2 ribs glue
to mount

1/16″ sh.
gussets

tissue (top)

flat airfoil

4 5/8″ typ.

slide wing to trim

Ⓑ

7½″

3/32″sq.

black
paper
cockpit

tissue
(I)

3½″

glue gear
to nose

Ⓐ

incidence
shim ¼″

·049 hook

down
thrust
built in
bearing

power: 6 strands 3/16″gray rubber
25 OAL

stab.

wheels wood
or plastic
1¼″ dia.

12″

all balsa med. density

taper to 3/32″

wing

3½″

skew
fin
to rt.

tissue
(top)

1/16″×¼″

Scotch
tape to
stick

3 typ

3/32″ sq.
frame

1/16″×19/32″ sides

Ⓑ mount

0 1 2 3 4       8 in.

ius, Jim Walker of the USA. In the early 1940s, Walker developed a control device for models which allowed them to be flown in a circle on two lines (wires) attached to a wingtip. These lines were affixed to a U-shape control handle at the pilot end and to wire leadouts inside the wing. These leadouts in turn controlled a small bellcrank in the wing root which moved a wire pushrod back to the hinged elevator surfaces, where a control horn transmitted 'push-pull' to 'up-down' motion. Simple wrist action by the pilot on the handle resulted in a tug on the up or down line and a resultant up or down elevator action. This enabled the pilot to loop, fly inverted, change altitude at will, and make precision landings, all within the bounds of the circle. This U-Control system has remained unchanged in principle to this day in worldwide use.

With this common control system, there are many varieties of models flown, often with subtle variations. The early models tended to be mostly aerobatic, since it was such an innovation to be able to loop the loop or fly inverted. The natural desire for power and speed led to higher speed performance craft, racing against the stopwatch. Then the brilliant idea of multiple pilots in the same circle struck, and team racing was born. Models of this class tended to look alike due to specifications laid down for the competition class. Meanwhile, aerobatic enthusiasts, bored with the loop, came up with the idea of aerial combat, as described in Chapter 7.

The modellers who preferred more scale realism still had many chances to show their skill, with true-scale replicas which merely took off and flew in circles, or with military types which took off and landed on small aircraft carrier decks with arresting gear. These scale replicas were also judged on appearance and scale fidelity as well as flight performance.

There developed, along with the above competition classes of flying, a great interest in sport control line. The models could be flown in the local schoolyard or park with no risk of flyaway, and the pace was easy. While competition classes

Two excellent beginner-type rubber models, a P-30 design and a 'stick R.O.G.' (rise-off-ground). Since both are all straight lines, scaling up to the dimensions given is simple if you fancy building one of them.

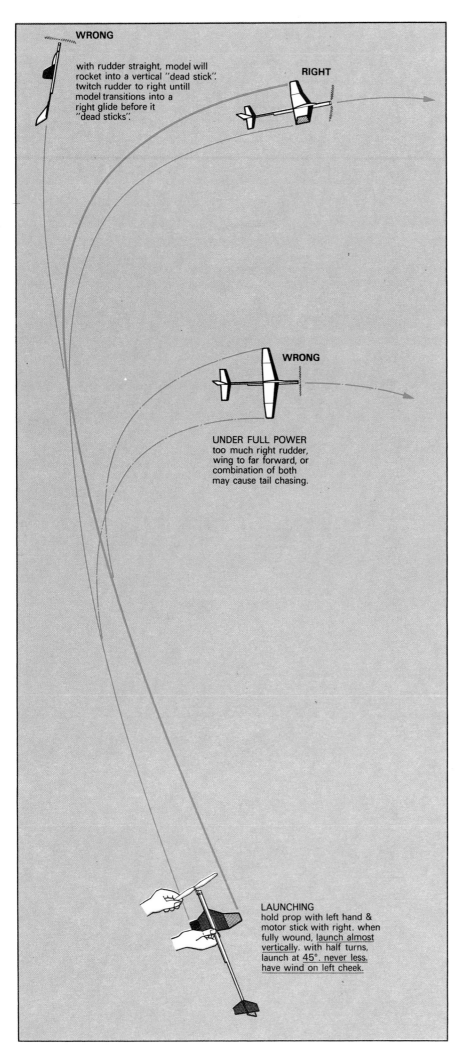

**WRONG**

with rudder straight, model will rocket into a vertical "dead stick". twitch rudder to right untill model transitions into a right glide before it "dead sticks".

**RIGHT**

**WRONG**

**UNDER FULL POWER**
too much right rudder, wing to far forward, or combination of both may cause tail chasing.

**LAUNCHING**
hold prop with left hand & motor stick with right. when fully wound, launch almost vertically. with half turns, launch at 45°. never less. have wind on left cheek.

could be emulated, there was no pressure to win and the skills of flying (and repairing after the inevitable prangs) could be mastered. Even plastic models contribute – the power plants are excellent and can often be recycled in another built-up model with success. These engines are all relatively easy to start and economical to run. They can also be muffled easily, an important point to remember if you fly in inhabited areas. The buzzing noise of a control-line model is often enough for a citizen to complain to the local authorities, and a flying site can be lost.

Another word of caution – never fly a control-line model near electrical transmission lines, which can be lethal. High tension current can kill you.

**Choosing a Beginner Control Liner**

The 0.049cu.in engine powered model design included in this book is an excellent way to get started, as it is a reasonable size and can be adapted to many powerplants, including the ones available from scrapped plastic models. However, you may wish to purchase a kit or try a design with a different flavour. You may also want to design your own, or at least modify an existing design to fit your concept and styling ideas.

The best thing to look for in a trainer aircraft is simplicity and strength. It should be easy to build and hard to destroy, with a lot of solid wood! A profile fuselage of solid wood is better than a box of sheet, and solid wings and tail surfaces are desirable. The problem with plastic models is that when they break, they cannot easily be repaired. However, a solid wood model can be pieced together with the magic of 5-minute epoxy glue or the rapid curing cyanoacrylate adhesives and made to fly again. Often these repairs can be made on the flying field, avoiding a trip home to the workshop. Covered, built-up wings need more time to repair.

There is no reason why a trainer has to be crude looking; in fact, it can be fairly realistic and scale-like, painted nicely and with a pilot in a simulated cockpit. Squarish lines

Part of the instruction material of the Jasco Flash X-18 shows the flight pattern at which to aim. Too little or too much rudder will reduce flight times; most models prefer a gentle turn to the right under power.

and a fairly long body are good design characteristics. A short coupled model is more sensitive to control and thus more likely to crash due to over-controlling. The new flyer has a natural tendency to overdo on control – actually very little wrist action is needed. An adjustable control horn on the elevator can also help. Try a very short throw on the pushrod for the first few flights, so the model almost flies by itself. A stunter or combat ship can be such a trainer.

Most model shops carry a selection of trainers or can order them from a manufacturer. The following is a brief list of some possible kits: KeilKraft *Champ*, *Phantom*, *Phantom Mite*, *Firefly*; Veron *Colt*; Cambria *Scout*; Quest *Imp*; Goldberg *Shoestring*, *Flitestreak*, *Stuntman*; Topflite *P-40*; Midwest *King Cobra*; Sterling *Ringmaster*, *Mustang*, *Spitfire*, *P-40*; Dumas *Tom-Tom* and *Little Tom-Tom*. There are many more from manufacturers in the UK, USA and Germany. MAP Plans Range *Deerfly*, *Shoestring* and *Little Brother* are good. There is no reason why selection has to be limited to the small 0.049 powered craft. A good 0.19 engine in a larger trainer, or a profile stunter with the control horn throw limited, can be an excellent first choice. The larger model can be flown in the wind and is often more docile on the controls. Such a model should always be flown with a muffler if near housing.

Another approach to a trainer aircraft is to try a model designed more for speed than aerobatics. The Rat Racer and Mouse Racer fall in this class, the former usually powered by 0.40 engines and the latter by 0.049. Reed valve 0.049 (again from surplus plastic crashes) engines can power very competitive Mouse Racers. One of the best Mousers we know of is the *Cat's Paw* which is available only as full size plans for construction – no kit – from Model Airplane News, One N. Broadway, White Plains, N.Y.

Once the beginner has developed skills in controlling his craft and running the engine, he can advance to more exciting flying such as stunt, combat or racing. That is why we suggest that a dual-purpose model can be useful, especially the racing type. There are many combat kits available in the shops, sometimes in pairs so you have one to fly while the other is under repair. The attrition rate is high!

Accessories and making a first flight are described later.

**Resources for further flying fun**
If aeromodelling interests you and you want to progress to more complex models and perhaps to competition flying, you will need to do two things to expand your horizons and increase your skills. One is to join a club and the other is to read the other books and magazines available on model aircraft. Your local hobby shop can give advice on how to join a club, or you may wish to write your national aero club for information. In the UK this is the Society of Model Aeronautical Engineers (Kimberley House, Vaughan Way, Leicester) and in the USA the Academy of Model Aeronautics (815 Fifteenth St. NW, Washington D.C.) which has a good club programme that helps beginners. Sweden is another country where the aeroclubs help the fledgling – contact SMFF, Box 10022, 60010 Norrkoping. Addresses of aeroclubs in other countries are available from the Federation Aeronautique Internationale offices at 6 Rue Gallilee, Paris, France.

Current model magazines often have beginner articles or features. The UK magazine *Aeromodeller* (MAP Publications) has a regular section to help fledgling flyers. In the USA, *Model Airplane News*, *Model Aviation* and *Flying Models* will sometimes have articles of interest to newcomers. Sadly, the magazines that are published in other countries seem to cater to the experts.

General interest books that can stimulate interest and impart knowhow can be seen at bookstores or library. Among the best are: *This is Model Flying* by Martin Dilly (Hamish Hamilton, London); *Basic Aeromodelling* by R. H. Warring (Argus Books, Hemel Hempstead); *Model Aircraft Aerodynamics* by Martin Simons (Argus Books); *Flying Hand Launch Gliders* by John Kaufman (William Morrow, New York); and *Indoor Model Flying* by Ron Williams (Simon & Schuster, New York).

While we are advising on the best kits, we must mention the Humbrol line of 'Five Stages of Modelling'. This graded, progressive approach starts with a simple HLG, goes to a SRPSM/ROG, then a cabin rubber model, then to a pair of towline gliders (the *Dragonfly* is the best). Similar graded sets are not available from others, but good kits are. For HLG we suggest trying the St. Leonard's *Atom 12* or *Atom 18*, the Cambria *Bandit* and *Lucifer*, the Sig *Flip* and *Pigeon*. For SRPSM, build the Sig *Thermal Dart*, *Uncle Sam* or *Cub*. The Peck Polymers *Peck ROG* and *Stringless Wonder* are great flyers, while the Vintage Aero *Mini-Square Thing* and *Square Thing* are outstanding. Look for these on the hobby shop shelf, or ask for them. Happy landings!

*Above far left:* An all-balsa beginners' control-line model available in kit form. All-sheet models are tough.

*Above left:* 'Peanut' class models are popular for indoor flying. This is a Pietenpol Air Camper from a kit.

*Left:* Three rubber-powered scale models; that on the right would be by far the best choice for a beginner. A big, high-wing boxy model is easier to build and to fly.

# Asteroid

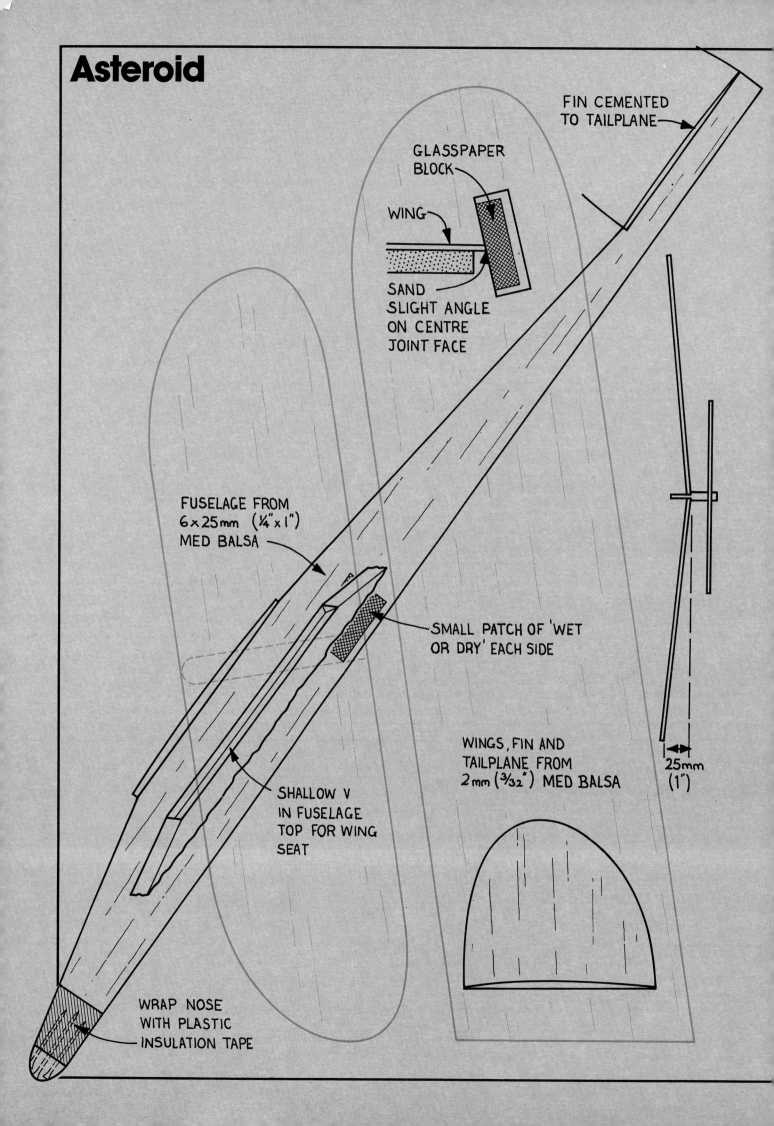

FIN CEMENTED
TO TAILPLANE

GLASSPAPER
BLOCK

WING

SAND
SLIGHT ANGLE
ON CENTRE
JOINT FACE

FUSELAGE FROM
6 × 25mm (¼" × 1")
MED BALSA

SMALL PATCH OF 'WET
OR DRY' EACH SIDE

WINGS, FIN AND
TAILPLANE FROM
2mm (³⁄₃₂") MED BALSA

25mm
(1")

SHALLOW V
IN FUSELAGE
TOP FOR WING
SEAT

WRAP NOSE
WITH PLASTIC
INSULATION TAPE

A simple chuck glider is an excellent introduction to aeromodelling and can provide experience in working with balsa as well as basic trimming technique. It's fun to fly, too.

Start by tracing the parts with a soft sharp pencil on to kitchen greaseproof paper. Turn the paper over, position on the wood, and draw over the lines from the back, which will transfer them lightly. Cut out carefully, using light cuts and a straight-edge for the straight lines.

Hold the wing panels on the edge of the building board and sand the wing with garnet or glasspaper on a wood block, to as close to the section drawn as you can manage. Repeat with the tailplane. Cement the joint faces of the wing halves, bring together, then separate and leave to dry. Recement and join, propping up to the dihedral angle shown.

Sand the fuselage, rounding the edges, then cement the tailplane in place. Add the fin; double cement all joints. Pare out a shallow V for the wing seat and double cement the wing in place. Make sure that the wing, tail, and rudder all sit true and square.

Use a small drill in the fingers to drill into the nose and push in strips of solder or headless nails till the model balances when held at the wingtips. Apply two coats of clear dope, sanding sealer, or banana oil and rub down with very fine paper. Polish model with wax polish.

Check glide into tall grass and add pins to nose to achieve smooth glide. Launch hard upward at 60° with model banked 45° to right. Adjust flight by breathing on the fin and holding a warp for a few seconds, and by modifying nose weight as necessary.

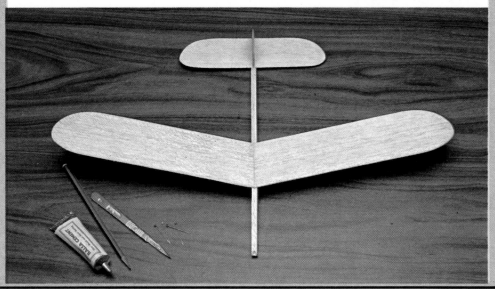

# Building a Simple Kit

Building and flying a simple beginners' free-flight kit gives a valuable grounding in the skills involved in using balsa and making accurate joints, as well as a feeling for the way an aircraft reacts to the air on which it depends for flight. This experience will be useful when you progress to high-performance control-line, radio-controlled or free-flight aircraft, and to the challenge and enjoyment of competition flying.

**Tools and Equipment**
With any flying aircraft, efficiency rather than appearance is the essential, and flat flying surfaces are the heart of the matter for model aircraft. To produce them a flat building board is needed, large enough for the biggest flat component of the aircraft and soft enough to push pins into. A piece of blockboard about 20mm ($\frac{3}{4}$in) thick and 300mm (12in) × 1000mm (40in) will do the job, but first check that it is flat, by laying a metal straightedge along the surface in several directions, ensuring that it touches along its whole length. For cutting on, a small flat piece of plywood or chipboard will save damaging the plan, which will be laid over the building board during construction.

While razor blades are the traditional tool of the model builder, the advent of stainless steel blades has made them almost useless for the purpose, since the edge bends and blunts very quickly when used on wood instead of hair. Carbon steel blades, if available, are well worth stocking up with, and can be identified by their greater thickness and a tendency to snap, rather than deform, when bent through a small radius. They can be carefully broken with pliers to give a pointed blade for delicate work.

While so-called 'modellers' knives' are advertised, by far the best cutting tool is a surgical scalpel; these take replaceable blades, which can either be discarded when blunt or else re-sharpened on a fine oilstone. Straight and curved blades are useful for different jobs; if a genuine scalpel handle is not available, several companies make Craft Tools that take similar blades and are a good substitute.

Cutting balsa is far easier to practise than to describe, but do not try just to push the blade straight down through the wood in one go. Use a stroking motion, holding the balsa firmly down on the board, and as near as is safe to the blade, which should be kept vertical to the wood. Be prepared to make several passes with the blade, especially when cutting sheet wood, and be aware of the wood grain, which will tend to divert the blade from the path you intend to take. Practise on some scrap wood first to get the feel of the material and the tool.

Balsa can vary from the very soft and light, about 65kg/m³ (4lb/ft³) to hard and comparatively heavy, 300 kg/m³ (19lb/ft³), and its grain type is also important, greatly affecting its stiffness and thus its suitability for various parts of an aircraft structure. Learn to recognize the characteristic speckled appearance of quarter grain or C-cut balsa, used for ribs and parts which must remain flat, compared with straight grained or A-cut wood, used for spars and components which need maximum strength in a lengthways direction. While a kit manufacturer will probably not select wood with as much care as a competition model flyer, try to assess the wood in your kit and use the stiffest strip wood for fuselage longerons and wing spars, rather than cutting it into short lengths for other components. Serious model flyers weigh each piece of balsa before buying it, for weight control is a vital part of any high-performance aircraft.

One of a modeller's most useful tools is home-made – a sanding block. Abrasive paper is vital for shaping and smoothing balsa, but is almost useless held as a loose sheet in the hand. Firstly, ask for garnet paper, or for wet-and-dry paper, rather than glasspaper, which cracks and sheds particles of glass all over the work as it rapidly wears smooth. Garnet paper is reddish-brown in colour and wet-and-dry (or silicon carbide waterproof paper) is grey; buy grades 320 and 120 in garnet, or 600 and 120 in silicon carbide. Next, cut some plywood or hardwood to about 150mm × 50mm × 10mm (6in × 2in × $\frac{1}{2}$in) and cut a piece of abrasive paper to cover the face and two long edges of this: stick the paper onto the block, using either rubber solution or double-sided Scotch tape, and ensure it is flat by rolling with a suitable cylindrical object. Curved sanding blocks can also be made, and are useful for reaching into concave parts.

A steel rule is useful for cutting along as well as measuring with, but any flat straight length of metal can be used as a cutting guide, although beware of nicking the edge if you use a soft aluminium alloy. A 300mm (12in) length will be

*Below left:* Quarter-grain balsa (bottom) compared with A-cut.

*Below:* Fuselage sides are lightly sanded; always sand away from where the component is being held.

adequate at first, but a metre or yard long straight-edge is helpful for cutting strip balsa and aligning long parts during assembly.

For sawing plywood or large sections of balsa a fretsaw is useful but not essential; a small 'junior' hacksaw taking a 150mm (6in) blade can serve in many cases, although parts will have to be rough-cut to shape with the saw before trimming and sanding to final outline. A razor saw, which is a thin, stiff-backed tenon saw, sold for model making, can be used for fairly light jobs where a straight cut across a large section is needed.

For shaping of balsa block a razor plane is handy and prevents the digging-in that occurs when a knife is used on soft wood; it can be adjusted to take a very fine cut, and uses a normal razor blade.

Pliers are used for bending light wire, up to about 16swg or 1.6mm (0.064in), and a pair of cutters incorporated will be satisfactory for most modelling jobs. Long-nosed pliers with flat faces tapering from about 3mm to 10mm ($\frac{1}{8}$in to $\frac{3}{8}$in) will be more versatile than larger ones, although parallel-action pliers of the Bernard type, with back cutters, can make light work of most cutting and bending jobs.

Some kind of drill, either hand or electric, will soon be necessary; a drill press is a useful accessory for the latter, to ensure that holes are drilled perpendicularly in the work. Initially it is possible to improvize when it comes to drilling holes in balsa or thin ply, since the materials are quite soft; a thin flexible file (i.e. soft-centred) can be a useful aid

*Below right:* Card or scrap balsa false formers with notched corners hold a fuselage square.

*Below:* Simple cutting jig when a number of equal-length spacers are needed.

for enlarging holes and slots.

For joining wire parts a soldering iron is essential; the type used for electronics assembly has too low a heat output to handle the larger masses of metal we will be dealing with. Look for something around 50 watts minimum; with this some solder will be needed, un-cored and of 40/60 tin/lead alloy. For joining steel wire a good acid flux like Baker's Fluid is needed, although acid-cored solders are also available, which some prefer; the resin-cored electrical solders have too high a tin content to give a strong joint. Cleanliness of the materials is important in soldering. Steel wire is always slightly greasy to prevent rusting in stock; fingertips are greasy too, so clean the metal thoroughly and wash it in a solvent like carbon tetrachloride to remove all contamination, for dirt, corrosion and grease prevent the molten solder from bonding on to the surface of the metal and forming a strong joint. The parts to be joined should first be tinned by applying flux, heating with the iron and then touching the solder, preferably with a drop of flux on the end of it, to the heated metal. The result should be a thin film of solder all over the surfaces to be joined; keep the iron in contact with the work for a few seconds to ensure that the solder has flowed where you want it to. When cool, assemble the parts, bind them with tinned copper fuse wire if possible, and then re-flux before re-heating and applying further solder to flow smoothly into the joint and form a fillet onto the surfaces of the metals. If the solder seems to be forming blobs on the metal, re-clean the work, re-flux, and let it get hotter before applying the solder again, and keep the iron in contact with the metal after the solder flows into the joint.

Pins are an indispensable item; while dress-making pins can be used, try to find steel ones rather than plated brass, which bend under pressure, have blunter points and cannot be kept on a magnet for convenience. Avoid the glass headed type of modelling pin, which can cause a nasty injury if the head breaks as they are being pushed into the building board. Large-headed pins can be made by rolling the head of a normal pin in epoxy glue to which balsa dust or talc has been added as a drip-retarding filler.

## Construction

The first thing to do on opening a kit is to read the instructions thoroughly and relate them to the plan; some instructions are written more clearly than others, but at least the person who wrote them has probably built the aircraft, so try to visualize each step as you go through them. The various views shown on a plan are used as a base over which to build the flat parts of the aircraft; wings and fuselage are usually built as sub-assemblies and later brought together, in the case of the wings, joined at the correct dihedral angle, while the two flat sides are joined with spacers to form a hollow fuselage. On some plans only one half of the wing is drawn, to save space; on these, either lay carbon paper face side against the back of the plan while the outline is traced on the printed side, or else rub the plan with a little cooking oil, which makes it transparent enough to see through. When building, double check everything before actually cutting any wood.

In building the St. Leonards *Performer* rubber-driven free-flight aircraft, the wing is started first. Like most beginners' models, this has a flat-bottomed airfoil section, which

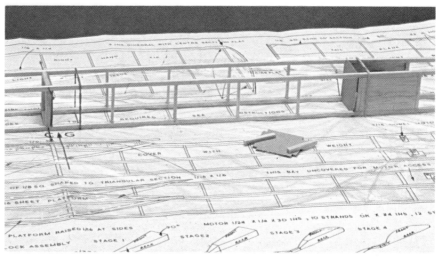

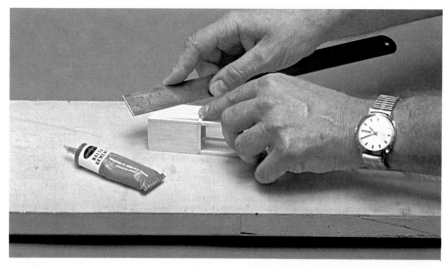

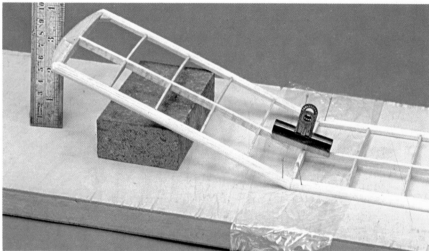

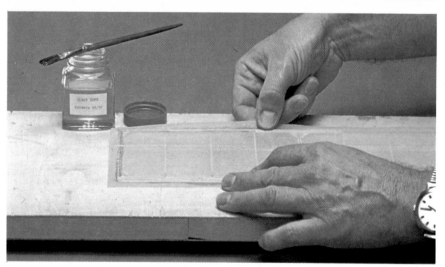

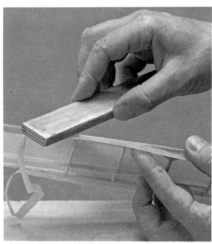

makes assembly simpler than an undercambered one. Most modern kits include die-cut ribs which theoretically just push free of the balsa sheet from which they are stamped; however, dies get blunted and some judicious work with the scalpel may be needed.

Lay the plan out smoothly on the building board, ironing it first if very wrinkled; cover it with a sheet of greaseproof paper or clear cooking film, which will both protect the plan and prevent surplus glue from sticking parts to it.

## Wing

After the ribs are separated from their sheet, it makes for a better final result to stack them together in a block, with a piece of scrap wood running through the spar slot to align them, while the upper and lower surfaces are lightly sanded with the block to remove any irregularities and ensure all are identical. Identify the leading and trailing edge wood and lightly sand the latter on both sides to remove any saw marks, which weaken the wood, as well as spoiling the finished appearance of the aircraft. Although not suggested in all instructions, it makes final shaping easier if some of the surplus wood is removed from the square section leading edge before assembly, so it is on the way to being rounded along one corner. Use the razor plane for this, being careful to work always away from where the wood is being steadied on the building board, to prevent the strip from buckling; follow this principle also when sanding wood. Mark the positions of the rib notches, if any, in the trailing edge and cut them, preferably with a small rectangular section file the same thickness as the ribs. If a razor blade is used make sure not to cut deeper into the wood than the notch depth; a bulldog clip can be used as a temporary stop to prevent doing so.

Pin the strips in position over the plan, pushing them against a straightedge to ensure they are really straight; use three ribs as a

*Top:* Wiping an inlaid sheet balsa panel into place with a metal rule.
*Second:* Use books or blocks to hold wingtips at correct height for dihedral; note centre panel pinned flat.
*Third:* Easing tissue in place and pressing on wet clear dope or paste.
*Bottom left:* Remove tissue surplus by sanding with fine paper when dry.
*Bottom right:* Use balsa strip for turn adjustment, or fit tab – both shown.

guide to check leading edge, trailing edge and spar spacing. Although the ribs are die-cut they may be of slightly different length, so check each piece by putting it in place dry – that is without glueing; if it needs forcing into place shave it down until it fits snugly. Discard any loose-fitting parts; bad fits can lead to warps and poor strength, so get used to building accurately, because it pays off in performance and reliability, whatever the type of aircraft.

## Fuselage

Select the hardest and straightest strips for the longerons; in the *Performer* these must be spliced to give the correct length. To do this lay strips side by side in pairs and carve and sand an absolutely flat chamfer on adjacent ends; try to make this at least four times wood thickness for maximum joint strength. Turn the strips so the chamfered ends line up and glue together, using a straightedge to keep the wood straight while the glue dries, and weights, tape and pins as necessary. Lay the strips over their marked positions, pinning them to the board in vertical pairs; make sure they *are* vertically aligned, or the two fuselage sides will not be identical. Use pins every 100mm (4in) or so, each side of the wood, or lined up with the positions where horizontal spacers will later be fitted, because the pin holes will help the glue to key the joints when the sides are later assembled.

With some models, if the longerons are sharply curved, it may help to pre-shape them before starting; to do this, hold them in the steam from a boiling kettle, and, being careful not to hold the fingers there too, bend the wood to the approximate curve needed. Remove the wood from the steam and hold it in shape for a few seconds while it cools; check against the plan and re-shape if necessary.

To cut the spacers to length, first trim square one end of a piece of the right sized balsa strip, and align this end accurately over the plan so it just butts against the longeron; use the blade to mark where it should be cut to length, being careful to sight down vertically over it, and to hold the blade upright. Do not try to cut right through the wood, but transfer it, probably with the blade still embedded in it, to the cutting board to finish the cut on a firm surface. If identical spacers must be cut, make a simple jig.

Glue the first pair of spacers in position. Do not worry if glue oozes slightly from the joint, but remove it with a pointed piece of wood, for excess glue adds weight. Fit the remaining spacers and let the glue dry. If using a PVA glue leave it overnight to dry before removing the pair of sides from the board. Balsa cement, while less satisfactory structurally, and hard to remove from fingers and clothes, dries much faster; this can make some assembly jobs harder, as the cement may be partly dry before the parts are accurately aligned. Whichever glue is used, the fuselage sides will probably be stuck to each other when the pins are removed; they can be carefully cut apart with a razor blade.

To fit the inlaid pieces of balsa sheet reinforcement to the nose and motor peg areas, sand one edge of the sheet dead straight and offer it up to one of the spacers against which it will be finally cemented; mark a parallel line along the edge of the other spacer and cut the sheet to this width. Observe the correct grain direction shown on the plan. Lay this strip of wood over the bay to be filled and cut the third edge to line up with the inside face of a longeron; finally ease the piece into place and cut the final edge. Glue it into place, using the flat edge of a ruler to 'wipe' the inlay flush with the surrounding fuselage structure.

Carefully sand the fuselage sides to remove fuzz and blobs of glue. Make rectangular false formers from cardboard or scrap balsa to fit the inside of the fuselage at its widest points; cut square notches out of each corner to locate the formers exactly on the longerons. Use rubber bands to hold the fuselage sides onto the formers, and cement the horizontal spacers into place, starting with the ones adjacent to the formers, which are removed when the glue is dry. The rear of the fuselage can be held together with bands and pins while the rest of the spacers are installed, being sure to keep the fuselage both square and symmetrical, and using the top view on the plan as a guide.

A plywood former at the nose is useful, in order to reduce wear and to prevent the joint between the removable noseblock and the fuselage from becoming sloppy. Face these two surfaces with 0.8mm ($\frac{1}{32}$in) plywood; cut a former with a square hole in it to fit exactly the rear spigot on the noseblock, and glue it to the front of the fuselage. A similar one is fitted to the rear face of the noseblock.

## Propeller

The lower surfaces of the propeller blades should be carved first; in the case of most basic aircraft the blade airfoil is flat-bottomed, and the X-shape of the blank, seen from the front before carving, ensures that the pitch reduces progressively towards the tips. Use a knife, long-bladed if possible, only for the rough carving; use progressively finer garnet paper for final shaping. Mark and trim each blade to outline after the lower surface is finished, and then carve the top surface to airfoil section; be sure not to over-thin the blades near the roots.

If the noseblock of your aircraft is laminated from several pieces of sheet balsa, arrange them with alternate grain directions at right angles, like plywood. Cut the parts oversize, drill a hole in the centre of each to take the propeller shaft bearing or bush, and use slow-drying epoxy to glue the laminations and bearing together. If the epoxy is slightly warmed it will become less viscous and will soak into the wood grain and strengthen the noseblock. Make sure the bearing is thoroughly cleaned and slightly roughened before starting.

When the assembly is complete, position it in the front of the fuselage and rotate the propeller blades so they fold flat along the sides; add the woodscrew stop so that it will prevent rotation of the blades as the motor tension declines, with the shaft in the correct rotational position to achieve a perfect fold. Several coats of clear dope and tissue covering will add to the strength of the blades. Mark the noseblock and fuselage to ensure that the former is always replaced the same way up.

## Tissue covering

This is far easier than most beginners think. First, give the entire structure a couple of coats of thinned clear dope everywhere the tissue will touch, sanding very lightly between coats with fine garnet paper. Next, cut the tissue about 10mm ($\frac{1}{2}$in) oversize all round, using a separate piece for each fuselage side, each surface of the tailplane and fin, and for the top and bottom of each panel of the wing (i.e. eight pieces for the polyhedralled wing of the *Performer*). Use a fresh blade for cutting tissue, as even a slightly blunt edge will cause tears.

Brush clear dope round the leading edge, trailing edge and dihedral joint ribs of the undersurface of one

Tailplane bowed -permissible

Tailplane warped-must correct

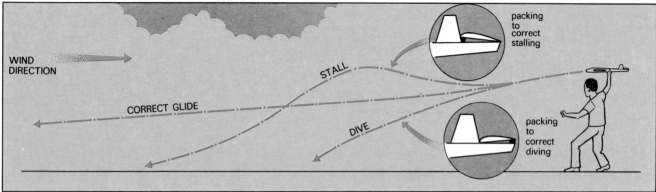

WIND DIRECTION

CORRECT GLIDE

STALL

DIVE

packing to correct stalling

packing to correct diving

wing panel and quickly lay the tissue on it; press the covering firmly onto a doped rib at one end of the panel, and gently ease it down onto the rest of the wet dope, all the time pulling the tissue gently spanwise and outwards, away from the first rib, herring-bone fashion. Do not try to get the covering drum-tight, but just reasonably wrinkle-free. If the dope dries before the job is finished, run some more dope on top of the tissue in the areas still to be stuck; tissue is porous and the dope will quickly penetrate and bond to the wood beneath. Do not be afraid to get dope on the fingers while smoothing the covering down; if a compound curve is to be covered, wet the tissue first, which lets it drape smoothly, as well as tightening it as the water evaporates. If the wing has undercamber, i.e. a concave undersurface, the tissue must be stuck to each rib, using tissue paste or wallpaper adhesive. Run a finger along each rib to press the tissue onto the paste; the dampness will show through the paper when the paste has penetrated. Overlap the tissue up onto the leading edge.

Once the adhesive is dry remove the excess tissue by rubbing gently round each component with fine garnet paper, which will cut the paper neatly. Finish the covering and spray lightly with water, using a scent spray; this will tighten the tissue. Further tightening will take place when you apply clear dope, thinned 50/50; keep the brush full, using it to flow the dope on, rather than trying to brush it in. Be careful with the first coat, as the tissue

is quite delicate until the dope stiffens it and fills the pores; with the lightweight Modelspan provided in most beginners' kits 3–4 coats of thinned dope will make the covering impervious to air. Avoid coloured dope which is far heavier than clear, due to the pigment, and does not tighten; it is best totally avoided for free-flight aircraft.

It is important to keep the flying surfaces free of unwanted warps. Pin each flat panel to the building board while the dope dries thoroughly, if possible overnight; allow the lower surface to become touch dry before pinning down, to prevent sticking. A small amount of washout (trailing edge twisted upwards towards the wingtips) is helpful, as this delays tip stalling, but avoid asymmetrical warps; to remove them hold the wing in steam from a kettle or in front of an electric fire (not gas, due to the fire risk), while twisting the warped panel in the opposite direction. Hold the twist and remove from the heat, allowing the wing to cool. Lay the panel on a flat surface and check that no corner is raised. Re-steam if needed. Re-check from time to time during the life of the aircraft, as sun and moisture induce warps.

To save space the building board with drying components still pinned to it can be stored vertically, making sure that the work will not be accidentally brushed against or damaged. Still on the subject of domestic harmony, plan your work so that sanding jobs can be done out of doors, or at least in an area where fine balsa dust can be kept

under control; doping, too, produces fumes which some people dislike, so ensure ventilation is good.

**Alignment and completion**
Before taking the aircraft out of doors make sure a clear name and address label is attached to it, with a request to the finder to contact you, and an offer to refund expenses. Correct alignment of wing and tailplane is vital if the model is to fly well; use a steel rule or even a length of string to measure between the same rib position at each wing and tail tip, and the end of the fuselage, to ensure that the distances are equal and the wing and tail are therefore square to the fuselage when seen from above. It is equally important to see that the flying surfaces *stay* correctly aligned during flying; D-section locating keys stuck on the leading and trailing edges, and butting up to the fuselage sides will prevent skewing, but will allow the wing to ride up against the tension of the hold-down rubber bands if it receives a sharp blow in a heavy landing.

The *Performer* uses a dethermalizer to prevent fly-aways in rising air currents; be sure that a snuffer tube of aluminium foil is used to retain and extinguish the slow-burning fuse that allows the tailplane to pop up to bring the aircraft safely down.

Install the rubber motor, using cycle valve rubber or plastic tubing on the wire hook of the propeller shaft to avoid cutting the rubber. See Chapter 6 for details of rubber

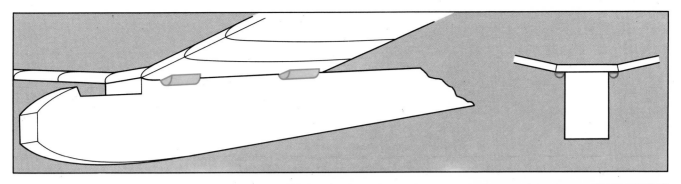

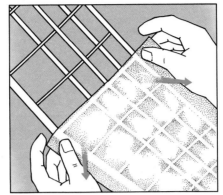

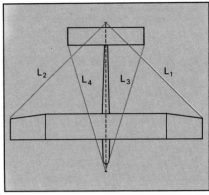

*Opposite, top:* Checking for warps on a flat surface. Some warps are acceptable, but it is safer to avoid them as far as possible.
*Opposite, bottom:* Trimming for a smooth glide is vital—do it over long grass to reduce the risk of damage, and wait for an almost calm day.
*Above:* Fitting little keys will ensure that surfaces are always correctly aligned but will knock off when necessary.
*Right:* Secure one end of each tissue panel, then ease diagonally along the panel to produce a smooth wrinkle-free surface.
*Far right:* Alignment checks are simple and take only a minute or two, but may save a crash. L1 = L2 and L3 = L4.

treatment and lubrication. Add a few turns to tension the motor and prevent bunching, and then check the centre of gravity (CG) by balancing the aircraft on a fingertip held under each wing root. Add modelling clay to the nose or tail until the CG is in the position shown.

## Flying

Attach the wing and tailplane with light rubber bands; for most small or medium sized rubber models bands about 1.5mm ($\frac{1}{16}$in) wide and 75mm (3in) long stretched to about three times their normal length will be adequate for holding the flying surfaces firmly in place.

Choose a calm day for first flights; windspeed should be 2m/sec (5mph) or less because a light aircraft like this is easily upset by gusts. Often the calmest time of day is about an hour before sunset. Adjust the glide first; try to find some long grass to cushion heavy landings, and start by launching gently into wind and slightly nose down, aiming at a point about 20m (60ft) away. Try not to throw the aircraft, but bear in mind that it glides at a little more than walking speed. If it stalls, add 0.8mm ($\frac{1}{32}$in) ply packing to raise the leading edge of the tailplane, cementing it in place to prevent loss. The aircraft may be stalling because of excess airspeed, so try a slower hand launch to see if the stall persists, before making the adjustment.

Repeat until the glide is stall-free.

If the result of these hand launches is a dive, add the packing to raise the trailing edge of the tailplane, until the aircraft just stalls; then remove the final piece, which should give the flattest glide. The aircraft should turn to the right, both on the glide and during the power run; the glide turn should be just detectable from a hand launch, the diameter being about 30m (100ft) for an aircraft like the *Performer*. The reason for the circling flight path is to keep the aircraft in sight for longer and to ensure that it stays in rising thermal air currents instead of flying straight across and out of them. Adjust the glide circle either by bending the trim tab (usually of aluminium foil) in the desired direction, or by adding a strip of 2.5 mm ($\frac{1}{8}$in) square balsa to the trailing edge of the fin on the side to which the model should turn. Try a short length at first and increase it until the turn is correct. This acts as a drag strip and is more reliable than a flexible trim tab, which can be accidentally bent.

Wind about 150 turns on the motor; see Chapter 6 for details of the technique. Set the dethermalizer fuse to about one minute. Hold the hub of the propeller with one hand and the fuselage under the wing with the other, releasing the propeller fractionally before gently launching the model forward into the air and slightly to the right of the wind. It should climb and turn to the right until the propeller folds. If it stalls under power or

does not show a definite turn to the right, add downthrust or sidethrust by cementing strips of thin ply to the top or one side of the rear face of the nose-block to angle the thrustline in the required direction.

Gradually increase the number of turns on the rubber, preferably after having found the number at which the motor goes tight and breaks, with a spare motor outside the fuselage, or from tables. The aircraft will climb steeper and fly faster at the beginning of the power run and as the motor is wound more, because the power delivered by the rubber decreases as the turns run out.

## Repairs

Most damage to model aircraft can be repaired fairly simply. Try to save all fragments; cut away the tissue from the damaged area and re-assemble on the building board, lightly cementing the broken wood together and pinning while the glue sets to re-form the original structure. Then cut replacement strips of wood with long chamfered ends; lay these over the damaged wood, which is cut away and replaced with the new. Alternatively, tapered doublers can be glued alongside breaks, or gussets added as reinforcements. The tapers are important in order to spread the stresses back into the sound wood; try to stagger the joints so they are not in a straight line across the component. Tissue damage can be repaired by doping round-edged patches over the perforations, or torn areas cut out and recovered.

# Free Flight
## Competition Power Models
## Rubber and Glider Classes
## Indoor Flyers

In breezy conditions gliders such as this A2 are safer if 'parked' upside-down with the dethermaliser in the operative position. Glass fibre fishing rod sections or archery arrows are often used for 'pod and boom' fuselages on high performance gliders. The magnificent flying site is a service aerodrome little used by full-size machines at week-ends.

Exciting and exhilarating, power models combine the thrill of aerial drag racing, during the powered vertical phase, with the graceful gliding of silent thermal soaring.

The attraction of tinkering with miniature engines, the fascination of simple clockwork activated gadgets and the over-riding constraint of power to weight ratio and model efficiency, in an effort to defy gravity, are all key ingredients of its inherent appeal. The real chal-lenge to the model flyer is how to control the very fast initial climb and achieve the transition into glide.

### Early lessons
One modeller's first venture into power model flying involved fitting a small motor to an old glider, with the nose shortened to compensate for the additional weight. Even the very first flight was a great success, indeed almost too successful for the

model was nearly lost. Using the integral fuel tank fitted to the engine resulted in an excessively long motor run. The flight pattern, too, was erratic. As the motor warmed up in mid-flight the model flew faster, performing an impressive series of loops, but by then the model was so high it no longer mattered.

## First principles

The inherent appeal of power model flying plus some of the problems to be encountered are illustrated by this anecdote. Firstly, the need to limit the duration of the motor run, second to control the increased flying speed. Gliders, or indeed power models after the motor has cut, are adjusted to fly in a gentle state of equilibrium, lift balancing gravity giving a slow floating glide. Upset that equilibrium with increased speed and all manner of aerobatics result as various elements take increasingly dominant roles in the flight performance. It is the balance of these two phases, the high speed launch and the slow glide, that offers the key and the enjoyment of power flying.

## Design considerations

How then are these problems overcome? In simple terms there are two solutions: by the geometry of model design itself or by the use of controls operated by simple clockwork timers. Slower power-assisted gliders or cabin-style sports models tend to give less difficulty because their power speed is little more than their gliding speed; a little engine downthrust is usually all that is required. But it is only natural that all modellers are tempted to push forward the limits of performance. It is these high performance types of model which will be considered, although naturally the aeronautical principles discussed hold true, in degrees, for all power models.

The ideally trimmed model will have a maximum rate of climb for a short period to gain altitude, followed by a long floating glide to achieve the maximum duration. Many factors affect the flight of a power model during power and glide phases. The ratio of wing area to tail area: the larger the wing the more it lifts at increased speed, producing loops, the larger the tail the more it lifts, balancing the wing's lift to retain equilibrium. The wing incidence: the more wing incidence or up elevator effect required to compensate for a for-

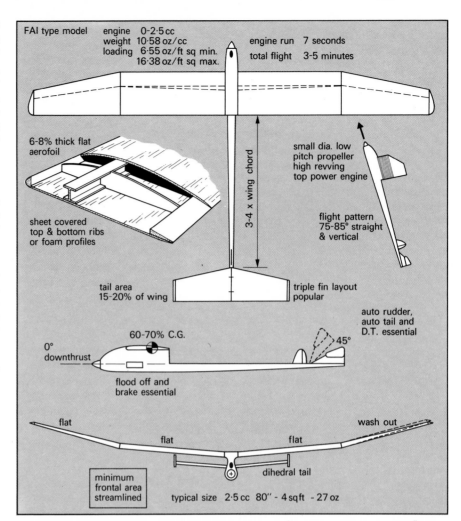

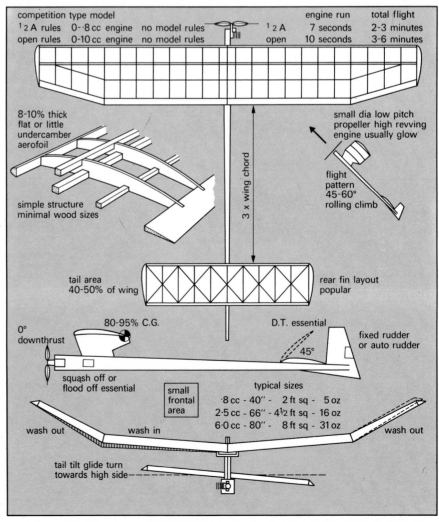

ward centre of gravity (CG) balance point, of a nose-heavy model, again the more the unwanted looping tendency there is; reduce the incidence and move the CG back to correct the glide, and this tendency is controlled. Wing sections also play their part, excessively under-cambered glider sections being most unsuitable at speed compared with the flatter sections preferred for power.

Rudder offset for glide turn can produce unwanted wing-overs at speed, diving the model sideways towards a potential crash. Tilting the tail relative to the wings produces the desired turn for the glide without the other unwanted effects during the power phase. Even the rotation of the propeller, normally clockwise (as seen from behind), results in a counter-clockwise twisting reaction known as torque which can roll the model upside down to the left. This rolling torque effect can be lessened by using a lower pitch higher revving propeller, or counteracted by turning the model slightly to its right, using rudder offset or small amounts of engine sidethrust. The danger of overdoing this turn, and ending up in an unwanted spiral dive to the right, is overcome by the use of increased wing incidence on the inboard right-hand wing known as 'wash in'. Wash in and torque on their own would result in a steady barrel roll to the left, so they need counteracting by the opposite turning effects achieved by rudder or sidethrust.

The secret of power flying is being aware that these forces exist and knowing the effect each has on the flight pattern. The simple balancing of equal and opposite forces is determined by a few trial flights.

## Clockwork gadgets

The use of an engine makes potential flight time almost limitless. The real challenge, however, is to obtain maximum flight time from minimum length of engine run, the permitted engine run being normally 7 to 10sec. Commercially available clockwork timers provide the answer for accurate control of engine run. A soft fuel supply pipe to the engine, such as cycle valve

*Above:* Checking and adjusting the engine. This model has sheet balsa-covered flying surfaces for truth and efficiency.
*Right:* Launching a ½A model. The pole in the background carries a bubble machine, releasing streams of soap bubbles which help to detect thermals.

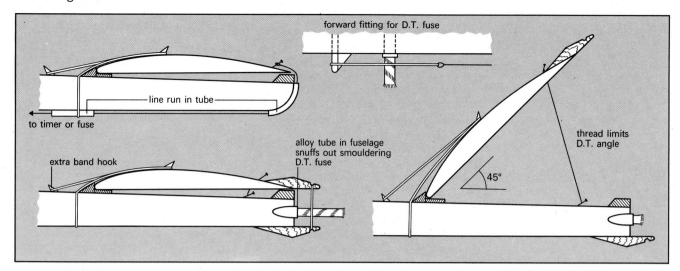

tubing, is squashed shut by a moving arm, called a 'squash off', which immediately starves the engine. Another option is to 'flood off' the engine, by releasing more fuel from the tank under pressure from the engine crankcase or a balloon type tank. An extra pipe runs from the tank feed, directly to the engine air intake, trapped closed by a wire arm during the run. When released by the timer the engine is extinguished with a squirt of fuel.

The aim is now a smooth transition between a fast nose-up climbing attitude into a slower level glide. The use of tail tilt has an increasing turning effect as the model slows and can produce good transitions on a simple model. The rudder ceases to balance opposite sidethrust as the motor stops, but the best answer is to use the clockwork engine timer as an automatic pilot, controlling other functions. A simple auto rudder, held straight for the climb, can be released to provide turn for the glide as the timer cuts the motor.

In competition classes, where rules dictate the total wing area be limited, modellers naturally want to use that precious area primarily on the wings, thereby achieving a better glide. The resultant proportionately smaller tail can cause instability, and the method of overcoming this is to use an auto tail, again operated by the timer after the motor cuts and producing a change of tailplane incidence from that ideal for a straight climb to the best for a stable glide.

The use of wing flaps or folding wings is the ultimate development. Either system radically alters the geometry of the model, into power and glide configurations, to attempt optimum efficiency for both phases. Flappers use a large spanwise hinged flap, which is raised to

*Top:* Dethermaliser details, essential to all high performance free-flight models.
*Above:* Operation of engine cut-out, variable incidence tail, rudder trim and D/T can all be carried out by one clockwork timer.
*Left:* Pan-mounted engines are common in top international models.
*Below:* The claw which controls tail angle is withdrawn, a rubber band tips the tail, and a restraining line stops it at the correct angle.
*Opposite:* Rudder and tail angle control methods.

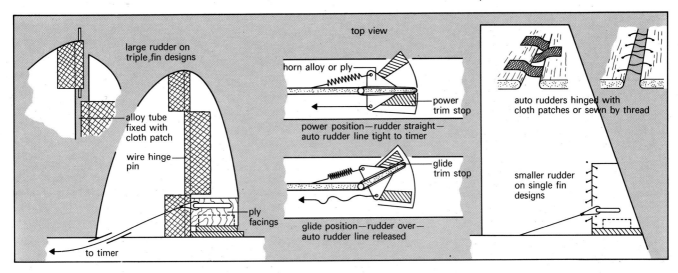

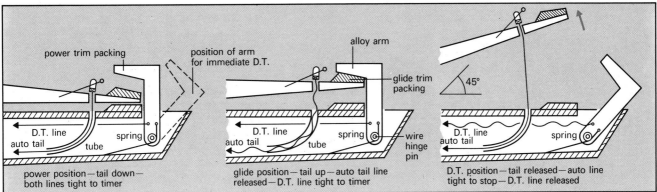

produce a flat bottomed aerofoil section for the fast climb, and lowered to give an under-cambered section for the slower glide. Folders hinge the outer half of the wing, tucking up under the inner half to produce a power model of half the span with a symmetrical section for the climb, re-opening out to full wing area for the glide. Such experimentation illustrates the variations open to the power modeller, although these are extreme examples so far only used by a handful of modellers throughout the world.

The final gadget, and the most universal, is the pop-up tail DT. The air in which models are flown, although invisible, is never still. We are aware of wind direction, but it also rises and falls in thermals and downdraughts, all the more prevalent on hot sunny days. In order to prevent models being carried away upwards by thermals, or to limit flights in a small field, a DT device is used. The tail, traditionally fixed in place by rubber bands, is released to pop up and be restrained at a higher angle, usually about 45°. In this position the model becomes super-stalled and settles gently back to earth safely, wings still level. Once again the operation can be actuated by a clockwork timer, but to save weight, most modellers use a small length of DT

fuse. This looks like thick string, and smoulders slowly, like a cigarette, until activating the DT by burning through an elastic band to release the tail.

## Structures

In general, the lighter the model the better the flight, depending, of course, upon the design of the model and its total wing area. The common criterion is wing loading: the lower the model weight per unit area, the better its chances of long flights.

The power model suffers in that for the largest portion of its flight, the glide, it is carrying an unwanted dead weight, namely the engine, tank and timer. The solution is obviously to build the model as light as possible, but if it were just that simple, then perhaps it would be less fun. For every piece of structure discarded the weight goes down, but the strength also decreases. No problem during the glide, but during the power phase strength and rigidity are needed to overcome the increased forces. What is required is that each part does its job to the utmost and is not just along for the ride. Balsa itself is very variable material, so choose the grade carefully, only the lightest, stiffest wood for spars and structural members, and soft light wood for ribs and sheet covering.

Hard and heavy balsa has other uses, but not for power models. Strips of spruce, cut from thin sheets, can be used sparingly to reinforce wing spars, especially for those all-important few inches at the centre, where a break might eventually occur. Lightweight structures may often be strong enough to withstand flight loads, but may not be rigid enough to stand flight speeds. Such structures will flex and flutter as the model accelerates. Tissue and dope adds greatly to rigidity, especially when correctly water shrunk first, or double covered. Extra diagonal ribs and bracing are used to produce a rigid geodetic structure. Covering with thin lightweight sheet balsa acts as a surface-active structure on larger faster models. Further developments include covering over tissue or sheet with ultra light glass cloth ($22gm/m^2$ or $0.6oz/yd^2$), using two part epoxy or polyurethane finishes, which, using the monocoque principle, improves the structure. Models that may look solid actually consist of thin balsa sheet over structural frames of ribs and spars or cores of lightweight expanded polystyrene. Fuselages, too, consist of hollow balsa boxes or tubes rolled to shape round simple formers such as billiard cues. Whatever the materials, the objects are lightness, strength and rigidity.

## Model flying

Model planes, even if built exactly to a well-known design or from a manufacturer's kit, will not fly automatically. In fact the chances are that they will not fly very well, if at all, without some simple adjustments made during the initial test flights, known as trimming the model.

Having chosen a design and constructed the model, how then does the model flyer go about trimming it for flight? The first stage is to resist the temptation to rush out and fly almost before the dope has dried. Then check out the model completely at home to ensure wing warps, balance and mechanical systems are in order. More models crash through lack of pre-flight checks and malfunctions of this kind than for any other reason.

## Pre-flight checks

Follow the check procedure outlined in Chapter 5. For high performance power models tailplanes and left inner wing panels should be dead flat. Right inner wing panels should have some wash in (1–2mm per 100mm chord or $\frac{1}{16}$–$\frac{1}{8}$in per 4in chord and both wing tips some wash out (2–4mm per 100mm chord or $\frac{3}{32}$–$\frac{3}{16}$in per 4in chord). If the wings differ from these desired warps by very much, they will need correcting.

Strap the wings and tail on the model using thin rubber bands, well stretched so that components cannot be lifted away from their mounts once in position. The forces acting during flight can be quite strong. Check and key components as previously described.

Run the timer and check that the mechanisms, if using any, always work and never jam. Ensure that, if using auto rudder or auto tail, they always move positively and are not liable to be moved by the force of air pressure. Now run the motor up several times, holding the model's nose vertically upwards, to check that the motor will be able to suck fuel up from the tank during the climb. Finally, check that the timer and all gadgets work with the engine running, to see that vibration or propeller thrust do not result in any malfunction. Time the engine run for various timer settings until fully familiar with the correct settings.

## Test flying

Calm weather really is essential for first flights; evenings are usually ideal, although once trimmed,

Extra height can legally be gained by a javelin-like launch enabling the model to reach climbing speed swiftly. Care is needed to avoid fuel surge interrupting the engine run.

models can be flown in literally any wind speed. A few hand launches at gliding speed are traditional to test for a smooth glide, adjusting with tail packing, rudder or tail tilt.

Now comes the critical moment, that first power flight. There really is no substitute for simply letting go and seeing what happens. No one can tell exactly how a new model will fly, that's why it is so exciting. The most important factor however, is to *watch what happens*. Observations from the first flight, followed by corrective adjustments, will help make the second more successful, and so on. Plan the desired flight pattern by deciding the length of engine run, 1 to 5sec is all that is required to start with. The safest possible way is to link the pop-up DT tail, even if only temporarily, so it operates the instant the timer cuts the motor. Models with auto tails will already have this facility, but others with no gadgets will need a temporary release wire fitting. With this method a very short run of 1 to 2sec, will lift the model 15 to 30m (50–100ft) into the air, to DT immediately and safely return to earth. This is just long enough to watch critically the direction of flight and allow any minor corrections before they develop into unwanted and dangerous loops, dives or spirals. Models without this inbuilt safety valve would simply stall and dive back to earth on such a short engine run, so they need slightly longer runs of 3 to 5sec, to allow them enough altitude to make a safe transition into glide. Go ahead, face into the wind, try it and watch what happens. Do make sure the engine run is genuinely short, a lot can happen to a power model in a few brief seconds.

Once that all-important first flight is over, and adjustments made, a second flight with the same length of engine run will show if unwanted tendencies have been corrected successfully. Patience is the key factor to start with. Once the model is performing as expected, gradual increase of engine run with further flight adjustments can be made, finally concentrating on adjustments to glide trim.

Ultimately, the flyer will have a perfectly trimmed model that he can confidently start up, launch and experience the thrill as it rockets skywards faster and faster until as a small speck overhead, suddenly quiet, it flips over into the glide for another long flight. That's the challenge of power models.

# Rubber and Glider classes

Historically, the first model aircraft were of the glider and rubber-powered varieties. Since then aeromodelling has progressed from being the province of the experimenter to that of the hobbyist and, more recently, almost to that of the sportsman. Inevitably the types of model fashionably popular have changed as well. The silent forms of free-flight model have been overtaken in the public eye by other classes, but nevertheless have a great deal to offer in their own right, and are well worth a long hard look.

**Rubber-powered models**

In their simplest form these are well known, most laymen being familiar with children's ready-to-fly all-balsa stick models, sold plastic-wrapped in many toy shops. These simple models can teach the basis of 'trimming' (the experimental adjusting of the model to make it fly properly), and indeed can fly remarkably well in expert hands. The principle of using twisted loops of rubber to turn a propeller is used on all rubber-powered models.

Commercial constructional kits are usually the beginner's first encounter with 'proper' aeromodelling. Those who attempt a duration design, as distinct from a scale model, can still run into real difficulties with building and/or flying.

Most of these kits feature built-up 'stick-and-tissue' construction which can be fiddling and time-consuming for the beginner. The design is usually a compromise between 'looks' (meaning a cabin and wheels) and function. Moreover, many designs are old, and intended for superseded contest rules. Even if satisfactorily completed, attempts at flying the model can be handicapped by inadequate knowledge of trimming, although the best designs *can* fly very well.

Nowadays, there is little 'sport' (or fly-for-fun) rubber model activity in the clubs. Consequently there is a tremendous gap between the models just described and the other extreme of modern contest designs intended for out and out duration flying. Such models use the energy stored in a tightly-wound rubber motor to climb as high as practical, while still preserving a reasonable length of motor run. When the turns have unwound, the model descends as slowly as possible in an unpowered

glide. Nowadays contest models are invariably hand-launched (so wheels and the like are superfluous) and are fitted with folding propellers. When the turns wound onto the rubber motor are expended the propeller stops and its hinged blades fold back alongside the fuselage. This decreases the drag (or air resistance) and improves the model's glide noticeably, hence prolonging the flight.

A tip-up-tail dethermalizer (DT), operated by either a burning fuse or a clockwork timer, is invariably fitted to curtail flights when required, either for ease of test flying or to prevent the model flying away. Contest rubber models fall into two main divisions:

1. *Open or unrestricted* ('unlimited' in America) designs.

This is the purest form of outdoor free-flight as there are no artificial limitations to the model design or its mode of flying. The usual approach of lightweight airframes and plenty of rubber gives too much performance for the facilities commonly available. Flights of four to seven minutes (without thermal assistance) will take the models beyond the bounds of most flying sites in any weather windier than a light breeze.

Competitions usually require three flights to a three minute maximum (max), almost a formality in good weather, and are settled by 'flying off' in an additional all-out effort. The Americans favour a progressively higher max for their fly-offs.

Open rubber is a test of structural design as much as aerodynamic considerations. Sophistication has to be worth its weight penalty, and it can be better and easier 'to simplify and add more lightness'. Various practical aspects such as strength, ease of building, visibility, etc. tend to restrain the models from becoming too extreme.

2. *Specification designs to the internationally agreed 'Wakefield' and 'Coupe d' Hiver' rules.*

Both sets of regulations (detailed in appendix) severely limit the amount of rubber, while simultaneously demanding high airframe weights. The World Championship Wakefield class also has tight limits on the wing-plus-tail areas. Contests usually have more flights (seven or five) than open events, but can still need fly-offs to resolve 'all-max' ties.

Although given heavy emphasis in the aeromodelling press, Wakefield and Coupe d'Hiver are not really suitable classes for the beginner; even a relatively competent modeller can find it far from easy to obtain high performance under such restrictive rules. Development has produced refined aerodynamics, much involved metalwork (often at true model engineering level), and assorted gadgets to alter the model's trim in flight. There still remains the necessity to wind the rubber motor right to its limit.

Experts can get over three minutes from a Wakefield in 'still' or 'dead' air, and around two minutes from its smaller brother. Contests, however, are rarely flown in such conditions, and to be successful the flier must avoid sinking air, and hence endeavour to launch his model into thermal lift. This situation has led to concentration on the detection and utilization of rising air-currents, as even the world's best Wakefield will not 'max' in a downdraught.

The universal motive power is strip rubber, commonly $6 \times 1$mm ($\frac{1}{4} \times \frac{1}{24}$in) in section, obtainable from specialist suppliers and many model shops. A suitable length of rubber is arranged in a number of loops to give the power required. Proprietary designs normally specify the number of strands appropriate to the particular model. The novice should note that a loop is *two* strands.

As it is hardly practical to 'finger-wind' such motors by turning the propeller by hand, some mechanical aid is required. Various adaptations of hand-drills are the usual approach. The tension of the rubber is such that merely fitting a hook directly into the drill-chuck is extremely risky.

Rubber should be washed to remove grit, and allowed to dry before being lubricated with either *medicinal* castor oil or a glycerine and soft-soap mixture. Motors will not take their predicted ultimate turns without some form of 'breaking-in'. This involves preliminary winding or stretching, and is often combined with test flying.

Stretching the rubber while winding is standard procedure intended to increase allowable turns

Ivan Taylor launches a Wakefield model. This class of rubber model originated over 50 years ago but has now become very sophisticated.

and assist the motor to unwind evenly. The latter aspect is particularly important on open models where the rubber motor is usually longer than the fuselage. The excess length is accommodated either by mechanically retaining some turns on the almost unwound motor, or by a 'pre-tensioning' process that effectively plaits the rubber round itself.

Regrettably, rubber quality is variable, and can affect model performance quite dramatically. While most modellers have to be content with what they get, 'Vintage Pirelli' can be quite an advantage. Even the best rubber breaks if overwound, and the worst can fall apart unpredictably. Clearly this can be a disaster for a fragile model. The use of a metal or hard plastic 'winding tube' to protect the fuselage is a more than sensible precaution.

Starting off on the right tack really demands a small, simple and strong model with a 'zippy' climb followed by a *poor* glide. This combination will provide real flying in a smallish space, and teach the beginner how to handle, adjust and fly his model.

If specific advice is required as a follow-up to kit building, then certain P-30 designs can be suggested as an up-to-the minute approach. They fit American ideas for a 'small-field event' using small models 76cm (30in) with a commercial plastic propeller and a limited amount of rubber.

Plans for P-30 models are available from several sources, one very popular one being 'Teacher's Pet', featured in *Aeromodeller* magazine. Even rough and heavy versions have proved capable of around 1¼min flights, ideal for local playing fields. Building from a plan and set of instructions may not be quite as convenient as the pre-packaged approach, but it can be much more educational.

Assuming there is the urge for 'bigger and better', the next in a logical sequence would be a 'Delinquent' (from the same source) partly because it involves carving a balsa propeller.

By now the modeller (no longer a beginner) will be able to cope with assembling built-up frameworks on a flat board, joining sides to form a box fuselage, covering with tissue, and a host of other techniques. He should appreciate trimming and the effects of CG (centre of gravity) position, thrustline offset, rudder, wing warp, tail tilt and the like. Hopefully he will have learnt to fly

a model – and to keep it by use of the DT! A contest model could now be a realistic project.

## Gliders
The unpowered free-flight model is often more involved than appears at first sight.

Paradoxically the deceptively simple all-balsa 'chuck' glider (outdoor hand-launch glider to be formal) presents the most difficult problem of all. The idea is to throw the glider as high as possible, after which it should glide down slowly and reluctantly. The usual trim to give a slow stable glide is unsuited for the high speed imparted by a hard throw. A series of tight loops might thrill a youngster with a rudimentary 'toy' glider, but is hardly the aim of the more knowledgeable modeller.

To resolve the conflict between climb and glide requirements, a 'zero-zero' trim of identical wing and tail incidences is accepted practice. Launch techniques are then similar to those described elsewhere. This approach is far from safe, but it is the only way to obtain durations of, say, 40 seconds or more without thermal assistance.

Another form of hand-launch gliding is slope-soaring. The model is launched off a hill, hopefully to ride the upcurrents produced by deflection of the wind by the hillside. For success the model has to remain flying into wind – a most uncertain procedure. A flight that turns out of wind usually goes *over* the hill, which can make for exhausting retrieval. Magnet steering is practical enough and far

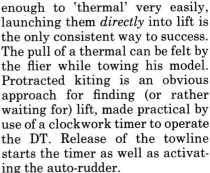

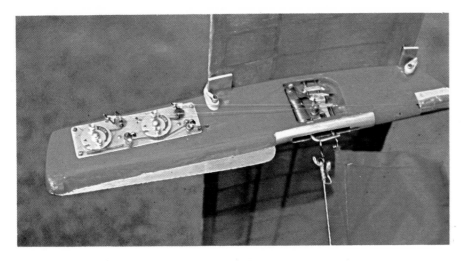

more predictable, but it must be conceded that the real answer is to use radio control for this form of flight.

The easiest method of obtaining long flights is to use a line to tow the glider to altitude, and then release the line from the model so it is free to glide down, or ride thermal upcurrents. The similarity to kite-flying is obvious, even solo launching is possible, although less reliable than making use of an assistant.

Release of the glider is achieved by a simple ring and hook system. The line ends in a ring which fits onto a rearward facing hook on the model. With tension on the line, the ring remains in position, but when the line goes slack, the ring

*Left:* Complex 'egg-box' construction of an A2 glider by Soave of Italy.
*Above:* A circle tow system and, for safety, a double D/T timer on an A2.
*Below:* Folding propellers from Wakefield models with (centre) a P30 plastic prop assembly.

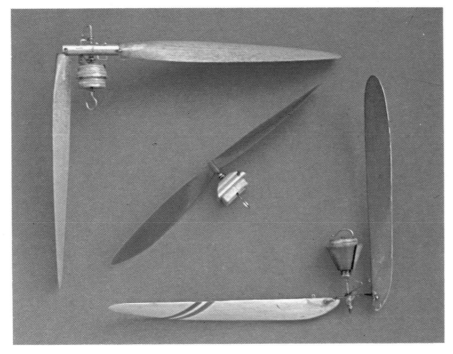

moves backwards and falls free, usually assisted by the drag of some form of pennant.

One peculiarity of the towline glider is its need for circling flight, to stay within reasonable bounds as well as to remain within thermal lift. Merely offsetting the rudder would give turn on tow as well as on glide, making height difficult to attain. Hence standard practice is to use an 'auto-rudder', a spring-loaded tab being held straight until freed by some device actuated by release of the towline.

Since lengthening the towline will increase the height attained by the glider, and hence its duration, contest rules restrict the length of line to 50m (164ft). This is insufficient for even the best models to fly long enough for a 'maximum' score without thermal assistance.

Remembering that air is rarely 'still' in the up and down sense, it is not surprising that glider contests have become a game of avoiding sink and catching lift. Although most of the models descend slowly

enough to 'thermal' very easily, launching them *directly* into lift is the only consistent way to success. The pull of a thermal can be felt by the flier while towing his model. Protracted kiting is an obvious approach for finding (or rather waiting for) lift, made practical by use of a clockwork timer to operate the DT. Release of the towline starts the timer as well as activating the auto-rudder.

Towing in calm weather requires the flier to run, and he can run out of space (or breath) before finding lift. The recently developed solution is to 'circle tow'. The line is *locked* onto the model to prevent premature release. The glider is towed up to height, then allowed to glide in one or more circles part way down (with the line still attached) before being towed up again. This process can be repeated, continuously testing the air until it 'feels' (literally, via line tension) good enough for a deliberate release. There are various approaches to the mechanics necessary to do all this, some very complex, and *none* recommended to anyone not fully competent at ordinary straight towing.

While many glider contests are 'open', or unrestricted, nevertheless the vast majority of the entrants fly models designed to the International A/2 rules (see appendix). This popularity is due to the A/2 being a good practical all-round contest model, of about 2m (6-7ft) wing span, and strong enough to wear well. While large or light designs can be advantageous under some conditions, the margin is insufficient to justify such models to most fliers. They would rather concentrate on A/2s, and fly them in both open and specialist events. Such contests require from three to seven flights, with a three-minute maximum and the usual fly-off procedure.

There is another popular specification, for A/1 gliders. These are small, heavy, and usually flown to two-minute maxs (see appendix).

Modern British glider design has settled down to a remarkably stereotyped and rule-of-thumb layout. High aspect ratio (over12:1) wings of constant chord (width), small light tailplanes (well under 20% of the wing), a pod-and-boom fuselage, and a mid-chord CG are virtually universal. Practical considerations require strong wings to withstand towing loads in wind, while the use of glass-fibre tubes has rendered fuselages virtually

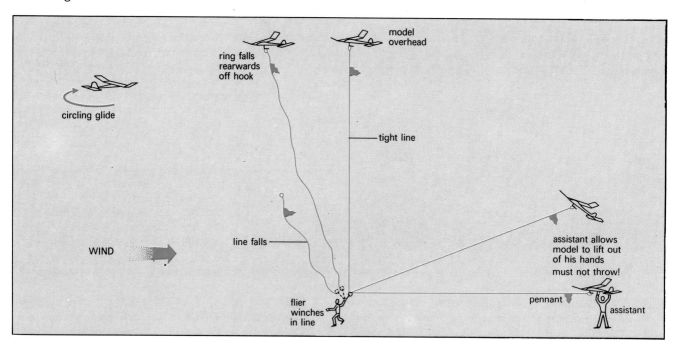

Top diagram labels:

circling glide

ring falls rearwards off hook

model overhead

tight line

WIND

line falls

assistant allows model to lift out of his hands must not throw!

pennant

flier winches in line

assistant

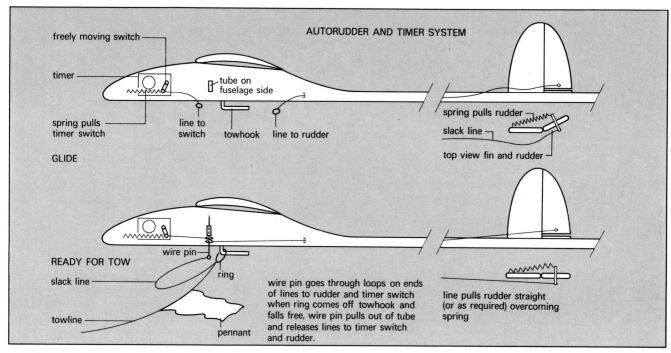

AUTORUDDER AND TIMER SYSTEM

freely moving switch

timer

tube on fuselage side

spring pulls timer switch

line to switch

towhook

line to rudder

spring pulls rudder

slack line

top view fin and rudder

GLIDE

READY FOR TOW

wire pin

ring

slack line

towline

pennant

wire pin goes through loops on ends of lines to rudder and timer switch when ring comes off towhook and falls free, wire pin pulls out of tube and releases lines to timer switch and rudder.

line pulls rudder straight (or as required) overcoming spring

unbreakable in normal use.

The newcomer would do well to avoid the very small models offered as towline-glider kits, as they are difficult to handle on tow. Models around A/1 size, say over 1m (about 40–50in) span, are far more practical. Suitable designs are available as plans and there are some kits. If in doubt, opt for simple straightforward designs rather than advanced contest winners. Construction is usually similar to, but more substantial than, that of rubber models.

Regular use of a DT is essential to avoid losing the glider in a thermal. Burning fuse is adequate as a timing device while learning to fly, but a clockwork timer is far more convenient (even though liable to disastrous stoppages if allowed to become dirty).

Trimming is easier than for rubber models as there are less variables. Unwanted warps should be removed, and sufficient nose-weight added to bring the CG to the designer's recommended position. Field adjustments are then limited to packing the tail to trim the glide, and altering the rudder settings to suit both tow and glide requirements.

The towline itself is important. Nylon monofilament fishing line is ideal and readily available, if a little difficult to knot. It needs to be kept on a spool, with some sort of geared winch being required to wind in the line after use.

One final word of advice. Put your name, address and phone number on any free-flight model. Otherwise, if it flies away, it is gone forever!

*Below:* Youthful P30 builder Allan Warman holds model and tube while father winds.
*Right:* Enormous 'open' rubber-powered model by John Carter.

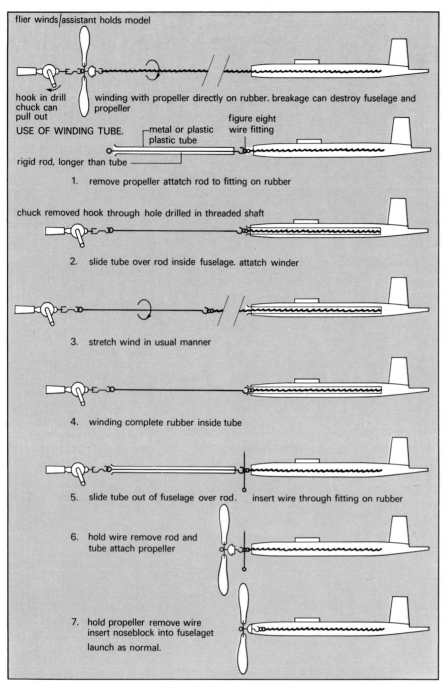

flier winds/assistant holds model

hook in drill chuck can pull out

winding with propeller directly on rubber. breakage can destroy fuselage and propeller

USE OF WINDING TUBE.

metal or plastic plastic tube

figure eight wire fitting

rigid rod, longer than tube

1. remove propeller attatch rod to fitting on rubber

chuck removed hook through hole drilled in threaded shaft

2. slide tube over rod inside fuselage. attach winder

3. stretch wind in usual manner

4. winding complete rubber inside tube

5. slide tube out of fuselage over rod.   insert wire through fitting on rubber

6. hold wire remove rod and tube attach propeller

7. hold propeller remove wire insert noseblock into fuselaget launch as normal.

## Characteristics of rubber driven models, world championship formula, 'Wakefield' (Class F1B):

Total surface area, 17 to 19sq.dm (263.5–294.5sq.in).

Minimum weight of model less motor(s), 190g (6.70oz).

Maximum loading, 50g per sq.dm (16.38oz per sq.ft) of surface area.

Maximum weight of motor or motors lubricated, 40g (1.41oz).

## Coupe D'Hiver rubber class (Class F1G):

Model specifications:

Minimum total weight of airframe (less rubber), 70g (2.46oz).

Maximum loading: 50g per sq.dm (16.38oz per sq.ft) of surface area.

Maximum weight of rubber motor (lubricated): 10g (0.352oz).

Minimum area of maximum fuselage cross section measured in the vertical plane with the model in a normal horizontal flight position: 0.20sq.dm (3.1sq.in).

## Characteristics of gliders, world championship formula, A/2 (Class F1A):

Total surface area, 32 to 34sq.dm (496–527sq.in).

Minimum total weight, 410g (14.46oz).

Maximum loading, 50g per sq.dm (16.38oz per sq.ft) of surface area.

The maximum length of the launching cable shall be 164ft (50m) when momentarily subjected to a tensile load of 4.4lb (2kg), and no cable in excess of this length shall be allowed on the cable holder. In order that the commencement of a glider flight can be correctly judged, a small pennant of minimum area 39sq.in (2.5sq.dm) must be fixed close to the free end of the cable.

## A/1 glider class:

Model specifications:

Maximum total horizontal surface area: 18sq.dm (279sq.in).

Minimum total weight: 220g (7.76oz).

Maximum loading: 50g per sq.dm (16.38oz per sq.ft) of surface area.

The maximum length of the launching cable shall be 50m (164ft) when momentarily subjected to a tensile load of 1kg (2.2lb) and no cable in excess of this length shall be allowed on the cable holder. In order that the commencement of a flight can be correctly judged, a small pennant of minimum area 2.5sq.dm (39sq.in) must be fixed close to the free end of the cable. The cable may be of any material.

# Indoor Flyers

**Rubber powered indoor models**
The aim of indoor microfilm models is purely to achieve the maximum possible flight duration. The duration record, set in an airship hangar in the United States, is almost 51min, a very long flight for a rubber-powered model. The International contest class has restrictions of 650mm span (25.6in) and one gram *minimum* airframe weight, but flights of 35min are quite common. Even apparently simple models can make long flights. The 'Easy-B' class is for models of simple construction with tissue covering. Fuselage and propeller blades must be of solid balsa and no curved outlines are allowed. In expert hands these models can fly for up to 20min and even the beginner can get flights of 5min from his first model.

There are various other classes of model flown, including so-called 'cabin models' (which must conform to minimum cross-section requirements and have a cockpit and undercarriage), helicopters, tailless models and even ornithopters.

With all these models, a prerequisite for long flights is a low wing loading. This usually means that the aircraft must be made as light as possible for its size, consistent with maintaining sufficient strength and stiffness for it to be handled and flown; it must be as efficient as possible aerodynamically and structurally, and great care must be taken to match the rubber 'motor' to the airframe.

**The power source**
The power to fly the model comes from the energy stored in the twisted rubber strip 'motor'. High flight times require many turns on the rubber run off very slowly. This means thin rubber and a big propeller, which will give a slow rotation speed, yet still provide enough thrust to keep the model airborne. Best performance is achieved when the model is under power for the whole flight, landing as the last turns of the rubber are used. The high initial power of the tightly wound rubber makes the model climb at first then, as the torque or twisting effect reduces, the model levels off – ideally just under the roof – and begins a slow cruising descent, using all the stored energy by the time it lands. If the rubber is too thick or too short the propeller will turn too fast and the model will run out of energy before it lands. If the rubber is too thin or too long, the model will land with energy still stored in the motor, and that energy will have been wasted. The adjustment and matching of the rubber to the airframe and propeller is essential for best performance.

Rubber, being a natural material, is very variable in quality and expert flyers will test as many types and batches as they can to find that with the best energy storage characteristics for its weight. The rubber motor used on a model can weigh more than the airframe: an International class model would be up to 60% rubber in a 2.5g total (0.088oz).

**The airframe structure**
Indoor model structures are built mainly of balsa, which varies in density between about 60 and 250 kg/m$^3$, (4–16lb/ft$^3$), so wood selection has a major effect on final structure weight. For a given weight, low density strip has a larger cross-section than high density and consequently has greater stiffness. Wood properties can even vary in different parts of the same sheet, so some selection is always necessary. The beauty of indoor flying is that we use so little wood, we can afford to be selective, and only the lightest balsa is chosen.

Structures used in indoor flying are often braced with wire to achieve maximum stiffness at low weight. The bracing causes drag, and to minimize this while retaining sufficient strength, a high tensile material is used. This is most often nichrome wire (Nickel-Chrome Steel) and is used in diameters from 0.015 to 0.03mm (0.0005–0.0015in).

Other metal parts in a typical model are the propeller shaft and rubber anchorages, which are made of 0.35–0.4mm diameter steel wire (0.014–0.016in). The propeller shaft bearing may be fabricated from

steel wire or aluminium alloy sheet. The metal parts of a microfilm model can account for about 10% of the airframe weight.

## Construction methods

The flying surfaces are built up from balsa outline spars and ribs and covered in tissue paper or microfilm. This construction is also used for the propeller on most models, although simple designs and some of the heavier types have sheet balsa propeller blades.

Wood sizes used in these built up surfaces vary from 0.5 to 2mm (0.02–0.08in), usually in rectangular sections with the greatest depth in the direction of the maximum load.

Fuselages are of solid balsa on simple models, but built up tubular units give a better strength to weight ratio for lighter models. The fuselage of a typical International Class contest model is in two sections. The forward part, which must withstand the torque and tension of the rubber motor, is a 6mm diameter tube (0.25in) which is rolled from 0.36mm (0.014in) sheet balsa. It has external wire bracing to help resist the bending effect of the rubber which hangs beneath it. The rear part of the fuselage, supporting tailplane and fin, is a tapered tube, going from 6mm to 1.6mm diameter (0.25–0.06 in). The wall thickness is 0.2mm (0.008in). Some classes of indoor model have built up fuselages similar to outdoor types but of lighter construction.

Any curved balsa outline spars or tubes required for a model are formed by soaking the wood with water and then binding it to a former while it dries. This process can be speeded by the application of gentle heat – even by baking in a very low oven. Curved strips for ribs are made by profiling the edge of a sheet of wood by cutting round a template, sliding the template down the required rib depth and repeating the cut.

Very thin strip balsa is easily damaged so it must be handled with care. Conventional tweezers will crush the wood but a lightweight pair of home-made balsa tweezers can be used.

The narrow balsa strip required for indoor models can be cut from thin sheet using a sharp pointed blade and a straight edge or a small custom-made wood stripper. The thinnest sheet balsa normally stocked by model shops is 0.8mm (0.03 or $\frac{1}{32}$in) but thinner sizes can be obtained by sanding this down.

Most flyers prefer to purchase wood from specialist suppliers who can saw wood down to 0.2mm (0.008in) and less. A thick bladed, high rotation speed saw is used but the difficulty of the operation and high wastage make the wood expensive by comparison with normal sheets. Costs are still low overall, however, because the last thing we want in a light model is a great deal of wood.

## Adhesives

The adhesive used for airframe construction is thinned balsa cement or a similar special glue, made for

*Left:* Climbing gently but steadily is a fuselage model – the 'bump' on the fuselage gives the required cross-section.

*Right:* Film colour is a guide to thickness.

*Below:* Transparency of the film is obvious; 100 parts nitrate dope, 30 amyl acetate, 30 methyl isobutyl ketone, 25 acetone, plus a touch of cellulose acetate butyrate is one formula!

indoor models. The glue is applied with a hypodermic syringe which has had its needle ground off square and blunt – not just for safety, you get smaller glue drops that way. Paper coverings are stuck to balsa with thinned tissue paste or white glue applied with a small brush. These adhesives will not melt the cement used to build the airframe. Microfilm is stuck to the framework with saliva or beer, both of which are said to contain enzymes which bond the film to the wood. Thin plastic covering materials used on some indoor models are stuck to the balsa with thinned rubber solution or contact cement.

## Covering materials

Indoor models are usually covered in tissue paper or microfilm. The tissue is normally condenser tissue, a very lightweight non-porous paper. It ranges in weight from 3.5 to 7g/m$^2$ (0.008–0.016oz/100in$^2$). Normal lightweight tissue for outdoor models is heavier at 10 to 15g/m$^2$ (0.023–0.034oz/100in$^2$).

Microfilm is the lightest covering material used, weighing as little as 1g/m$^2$ (0.002oz/100in$^2$). The most striking feature of the film is its beautiful iridescent colours which, apart from looking nice, enable the film thickness to be judged. The colours are due to interference effects, which means that the film thickness must be of the same order as the wavelength of visible light, about 0.0005mm (0.00002in). Silver/Gold is the lightest, and thicknesses range through Blue/Yellow, which most flyers prefer, to Red/Green, which is considered 'heavy', but is still much lighter than paper.

Some models, notably those powered by $CO_2$ motors, are covered in thin plastic film called mylar. This ranges from 0.0025 to 0.006mm in thickness (0.0001–0.00024in) and weighs 2 to 5g/m$^2$ (0.0046–0.011oz/100in$^2$).

## Covering techniques

Small structures are best covered by placing the framework onto the covering material, having first applied the adhesive. Tissue and mylar can be trimmed with a very sharp blade but microfilm is cut by melting it with a hot wire or a brush moistened with solvent. Large structures, which can distort if the method mentioned above is used, are covered by laying the covering over the framework, which is lying on a flat surface. Microfilm is kept on its lifting frame until the covered surface is finally cut free.

## Making microfilm

The film is prepared by pouring a cellulose solution onto the surface of clean water at room temperature. A shallow tank about five times the area of the required sheet is needed and may be made by draping a sheet of polythene over a wooden frame on a flat surface. Film thickness is controlled by thinning the solution or changing the amount poured onto the water. Film is poured by letting the solution run out of a 2.5 mm (0.1in) hole in a small container as it is drawn along close to the water surface. After 5 to 10min when the film has stopped shrinking and dried, it may be lifted from the water surface. This is done with a balsa frame with a border about 12 mm wide and 6mm thick (0.5 by 0.25in). The lifting frame is moistened with water and laid gently on top of the film. The excess film, outside the frame, is gathered by pushing the frame close to each edge of the tank in turn and folding the resulting narrow border of film over

*Below:* Tissue-covered Manhattan class model capable of 6 minute flights. Span is 500mm, weight 6g.

*Bottom:* Two indoor hand-launched gliders. The smaller is 315mm (12.4in) span and weighs 2g.

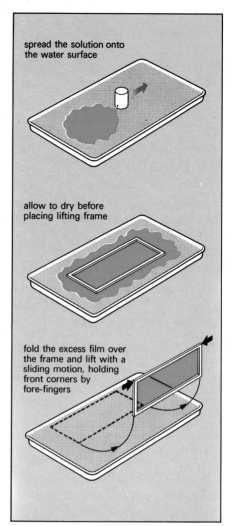

spread the solution onto the water surface

allow to dry before placing lifting frame

fold the excess film over the frame and lift with a sliding motion, holding front corners by fore-fingers

the edge of the frame. Lifting starts with the frame at the far side of the tank. Holding the frame lightly, with the forefingers at the front corners, it is drawn towards the body lifting it at the same time in one smooth action, finishing with the frame clear of the water and pivoted to a vertical position. When the excess water has drained off the film is hung in a safe well-ventilated place to cure before use.

When lifting microfilm some flyers use rubber solution to stick the film to the lifting frames. In this case, the 'excess' film outside the frame can be simply torn away. This method is more convenient but also more expensive.

### Hand launched gliders

The World Record for a hand launched glider flight indoors is 90 sec. This was made in an airship hangar in the United States, using a 560mm span (22in) solid balsa glider which weighed 22g (0.78oz). This type of duration is achieved by having a model which can be thrown very hard and uses the launch energy to climb to a good height, perhaps 35m (115ft), before beginning a slow glide back to the floor. As with other types of model, stiffness and strength are very important because the stress imposed at launch is very high. The model's size and weight must be matched to the available ceiling height and the thrower's strength. A heavier model will climb higher and a lighter model will glide better. In a low ceiling site the lightest model which can just be thrown to the roof is used, weighing perhaps 4 to 5g (0.14–0.18oz) for a 10m high site (33 ft) for example, with a span of about 450mm (18in).

### Flying sites

The best known indoor flying sites are the giant airship hangars which are 50m (164ft) or more high, but are only to be found at a few locations in the United States and one in England. Other large halls are available in most large cities, but perhaps the most curious site known is the salt mine at Slanic in the Transylvanian Alps, Rumania. This site is over 50m high (164ft) and more than 100m (328ft) underground!

A great deal of fun can be had flying indoor models in any size of site. Most schools and sports centres have a reasonable sized hall or gymnasium which could be used for indoor flying, allowing flights of several minutes duration.

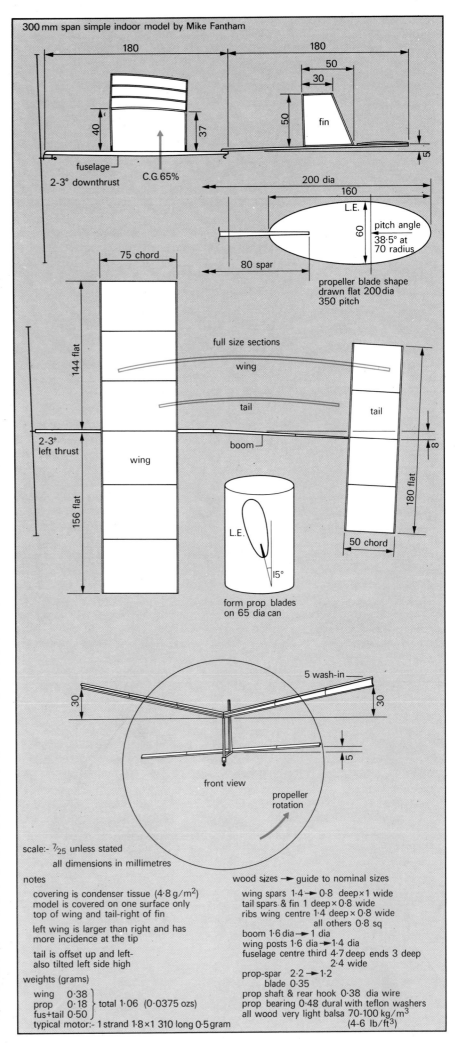

300 mm span simple indoor model by Mike Fantham

scale:- 7/25 unless stated
all dimensions in millimetres

notes

covering is condenser tissue (4·8 g/m²)
model is covered on one surface only
top of wing and tail-right of fin

left wing is larger than right and has more incidence at the tip

tail is offset up and left-
also tilted left side high

weights (grams)

wing    0·38
prop    0·18  } total 1·06 (0·0375 ozs)
fus+tail 0·50
typical motor:- 1 strand 1·8×1 310 long 0·5 gram

wood sizes → guide to nominal sizes

wing spars 1·4 → 0·8 deep×1 wide
tail spars & fin 1 deep × 0·8 wide
ribs wing centre 1·4 deep × 0·8 wide
              all others 0·8 sq
boom 1·6 dia → 1 dia
wing posts 1·6 dia → 1·4 dia
fuselage centre third 4·7 deep ends 3 deep
                           2·4 wide
prop-spar 2·2 → 1·2
    blade 0·35
prop shaft & rear hook 0·38 dia wire
prop bearing 0·48 dural with teflon washers
all wood very light balsa 70-100 kg/m³
                           (4-6 lb/ft³)

# Meteorite

This 36in towline glider introduces built-up structures and tissue covering in a straightforward model which will appeal to a novice.

Requirements are:

$2 \frac{1}{16} \times 3 \times 36$in medium balsa (fuselage sides, ribs etc.)

$2 \frac{1}{8} \times \frac{3}{8} \times 36$ medium balsa (fuselage frame).

$1 \frac{1}{4} \times \frac{1}{4} \times 36$ medium hard balsa (wing l.e.).

$1 \frac{3}{16} \times \frac{3}{16} \times 36$ medium hard balsa (tailplane l.e.).

$2 \frac{1}{8} \times \frac{1}{4} \times 36$ hard balsa (wing and tail spars).

$1 \frac{1}{8} \times \frac{1}{8} \times 36$ hard balsa (wing rear spar).

$1 \frac{1}{8} \times \frac{1}{2} \times 36$ medium balsa (wing t.e.).

$1 \frac{1}{8} \times \frac{3}{8} \times 36$ medium balsa (tail t.e.).

A scrap of soft $\frac{1}{8}$in sheet balsa, $\frac{1}{32}$in ply, $\frac{1}{8}$in dowel, 18swg wire, two sheets of tissue, cement, dope. (Possibly additional scrap $\frac{1}{16}$in sheet.)

Trace the fuselage side view on to kitchen grease-proof paper and pin to building board. Pin $\frac{1}{8} \times \frac{3}{8}$in strips top and bottom, cement in bottom reinforcement strip, then cut and cement spacers. Laminate nose from $\frac{1}{8}$in sheet. When dry, remove pins and sand top face. Apply cement and position $\frac{1}{16}$in sheet, weighting till dry. Remove from plan, trim round sheet, fit towhook, sand second face, and sheet cover. Trim and sand when dry. Add wing and tail platforms (accurately) and dowels.

Trace wing and tail — note that all wing panels use the same basic tracing. Trace wing rib on to thin ply and cut out accurately; use the ply as a template to cut out 22 ribs from the rest of the $\frac{1}{16}$in sheet. Repeat to cut 10 tail ribs. Pin ribs together over a piece of spar material and sand to ensure that they are all smooth and identical. Build wing centre panel, notching trailing edge and pinning down together with leading edge, then inserting ribs. Add mainspar. When dry lift and add rear spar.

Pin down one tip panel l.e. and t.e., then join centre panel to them, propping end to dihedral height. Build tip panel and add mainspar dihedral brace before lifting. Repeat for other tip. Alternatively build tip panels

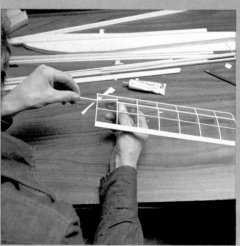

separately, trim spars, and join completed panels to centre, blocking each tip to dihedral height. Add centre sheeting, gussets at dihedral break and soft scrap to tip ribs. Sand all over, shaping leading edge and ensuring a smooth surface for covering.

The tailplane is a simpler version, without dihedral or a rear spar; the fin is cut from sheet and its bottom edge shaped to fit to the centre sheeting, though it needn't be cemented until after covering.

Dope tissue straight on to fuselage, one panel each side with sufficient overlap to cover the top and bottom edges. Cover wing with six panels of tissue, the three bottom panels first, and the tail-plane and fin with two each. (Read the notes about warps elsewhere!) Two coats of dope overall should be adequate; plus a *thin* coat of colour on fuselage.

Attach wing and tail with rubber bands and add lead in the ballast box till the model balances at the point shown. Follow the trimming procedure of hand launches, adding or removing weight to get a reasonable glide before moving on to gentle tow launches.

# Meteorite

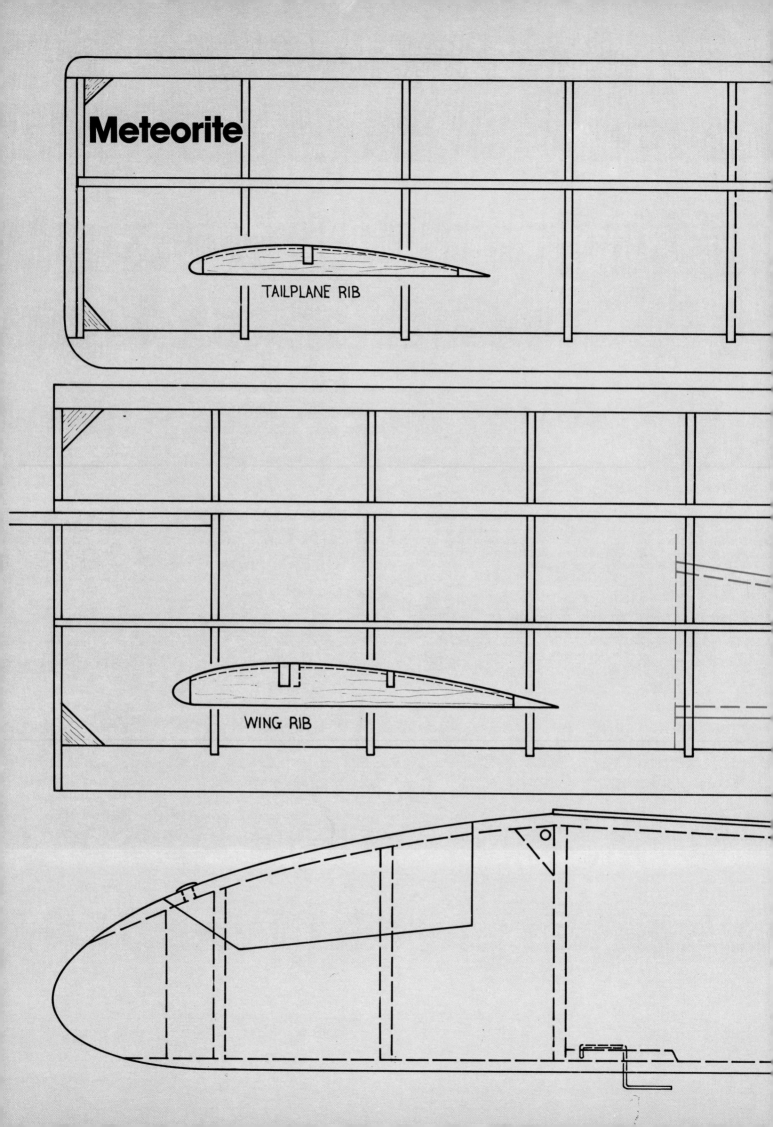

TAILPLANE RIB

WING RIB

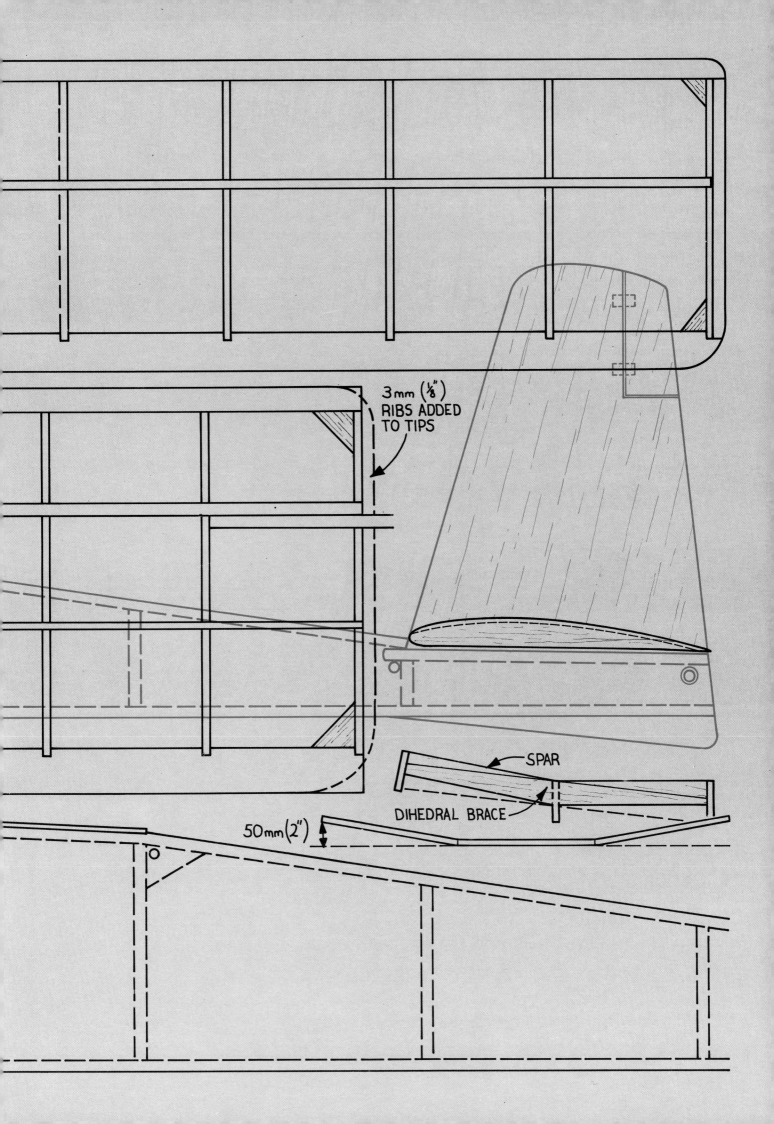

3mm (⅛″)
RIBS ADDED
TO TIPS

SPAR

DIHEDRAL BRACE

50mm(2″)

This Russian FAI stunt model, flown by
Alexander Listopad at the 1978
European Championships at Verviers,
Belgium, typifies the attractively
finished .40 powered modern stunt
model. This aeroplane was also an
entry at the 1977 World Championships
in Kiev.

# Control Line
## Basic Trainers
## Team Racing
## Speed and Combat

## What is Control-line flying?

Control-line flying, as discussed in Chapter 5, was developed by the American Jim Walker during World War 2 as a system of controlling a model aeroplane tethered to fly in a circular path. Early attempts were with free-flight models but these were unsuitable due to problems in maintaining line tension, principally caused by the wind as the model circulated. It was soon realized that dihedral was unnecessary to maintain stability in the rolling plane as the aircraft was automatically stabilized by the lines, and as the pilot had direct control over the elevators then the size of the tailplane could be reduced to more scale-like proportions. This immediately opened up wide possibilities to the scale aircraft enthusiast, who could now build and fly models which were previously impossible as free flight projects or even radio control at that stage. Even multi-engine installations were possible.

Another advantage of control-line flying is the relatively small area required, just a circle which is large enough for the length of the lines as a radius plus a safety margin. This is one reason why control-line flying is popular for displays in public parks for carnivals etc.; it can be done almost anywhere there is a reasonable surface.

## Principles of Control-line flight

The principles of control-line flight are outlined in Chapter 5, but it must be stressed that control over the model is only maintained while the lines are taut and several features must be incorporated in control-line models in order to help maintain the line tension, as it is termed. As it is conventional for the models to fly in an anti-clockwise direction, it is desirable to introduce a bias in the opposite direction trying to make the model fly away from the pilot in order to keep those lines tight.

1. The point of connection of the lines to the model, at the lead out guide, must be behind the centre of gravity of the model. The greater this distance then the more line tension.

2. There must be some weight added to the outboard wingtip: this counterbalances the weight of the lines and is very important, especially when the model is flying high, to make the model tend to roll outwards.

3. Engine and rudder offset,

where the engine thrust line and rudder are offset to the right, may be needed.

4. Centrifugal force, which is the product of the weight of the model and how fast it is flying, means that a light model flying slowly will have little tension and vice versa.

**What are the requirements of a training model to learn control line flying?**

Firstly and foremost it must be stable in that it does not require constant control movements in order to stay flying. Secondly, the controls must also be insensitive so that overcontrolling by the pilot does not result in violent reactions by the model. Thirdly, the model must be ruggedly constructed to withstand the inevitable crashes which occur as the pilot learns the skills required. Finally the model must maintain good line tension in reasonable wind conditions.

*Top left:* Japan's Hara fills the tank on his O.S.40 powered World Championship entry.
*Below left:* British semi-scale D.H. Chipmunk starting up.
*Below right:* Take-off by an Italian model starts the scoring manoeuvres. Another F.A.I. Class F2B machine.

The most popular type of model for learning to fly control line is the all-sheet profile trainer, so named because it is entirely made of solid sheet balsa with no built-up construction such as wing ribs etc. This makes it quick to build and also very tough. The fuselage is also solid sheet on its edge, but its side view or profile is representative of an aircraft.

Such a model would be about 500mm (20in) wingspan and be powered by an engine of 0.8–1.5cc (0.049–0.9cu.in) capacity, either diesel or glowplug. There are kits of this type of model available from most major manufacturers, or a plan for a suitable model is included in this book. Larger models are generally more stable and easier to fly than smaller ones.

Having built a training model, what equipment do you need to go flying? First of all the pilot needs a control handle to hold. These are available made of metal or plastic in many varieties, but the important features are that it should be comfortable to hold and light, and it should feature an adjustment to compensate for unequal line lengths, as the handle should be in a comfortable upright position with the elevators at neutral. Some

handles even make the vertical distance between the two lines adjustable. This is very good for beginners, because control is less sensitive when the lines are closely spaced, and vice versa. As the flier becomes more proficient then he can open up the spacing to give greater control response.

Line connectors are the next item in the chain to connect the handle to the control lines, and these must be strong enough to withstand the maximum line tension likely to occur. Also they must not have any sharp protrusions likely to snag. Proprietary connectors are available from model shops, of course, but there are similar items in any angling store which may be cheaper. Split rings are excellent in use, although a bit fiddly to connect. Do not in any circumstances tie the control lines to the handle unless they are the Terylene cord type, because knots will strain the lines and reduce their strength.

Control lines are the most important single item in the control system. For the simple lightweight trainer model it is possible to use waxed linen thread or light fishing twine. They are certainly cheap and easy to look after but suffer from the disadvantage that they are

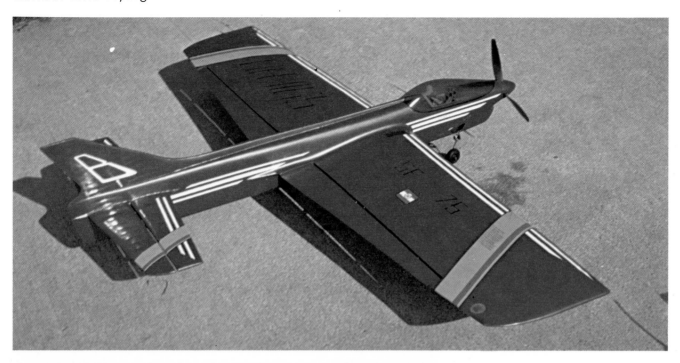

slightly stretchy, which imparts a 'spongy' feel to the controls when flying. They are suitable for use with models powered by engines up to 1cc capacity and can be up to 10m (33ft) long.

The most-used type of line is a three-strand, high tensile steel, braided wire known as 'Light Laystrate'. It is approximately 0.3mm (0.013in) diameter and is bought on small cardboard reels in lengths of 21m (70ft) or 30m (100ft). It is supplied in a tinned state to give protection from rust, which greatly aids soldering loops at the ends, but it is easily kinked, so the lines must be looked after very carefully, and always stored on a reel when not in use. They are suitable for any

*Opposite, top:* Aaltio of Finland used car paint on his HP40 model.
*Opposite, centre:* Three-blade prop, three-wheel undercarriage and three fins distinguish this Dutch model.
*Opposite, bottom:* Slightly unusual are the detachable wing and tailplane on Tindal's highly developed Chipmunk.
*Above:* Sbragia of Italy about to start his Facit model with Super Tigre 46; note silencer.

model up to 1500g (50oz) in weight. For heavier models or very fast models which therefore have a higher line tension a heavyweight grade at 0.45mm (0.018in) diameter is also available.

Fast becoming popular with competition fliers is a seven stranded American stainless steel line known as 'Pylon Brand' which has the big advantage of being almost impossible to kink and is very flexible and soft to the touch. A set of these lines is much more durable than the high

tensile lines, though rather more expensive. They are available with the ends made up with brass eyelets, which saves a tedious chore, and in a wide range of diameters for different weights of model from 0.2 mm (0.008in) diameter up to 0.5mm (0.021in) diameter.

For specialist applications such as speed and team racing where the absolute minimum line drag is required to maximize speed, then

single strand wire is used, as its smooth surface reduces wind resistance. However, it requires very careful use as it is very prone to kinking and damage. Large diameter storage reels are required.

All lines require loops or eyelets at each end for any connection to handle and model, but for safety's sake this must be done correctly. Follow the methods shown in the sketches. Recommended lines are:

| Type of model | Line length and diameter |
|---|---|
| Elementary trainer 500mm wingspan, up to 1cc engine | 8–10m Terylene thread, or very light steel line, 0.2–0.3mm (0.008–0.012in) diameter, 12m (40ft) length. |
| Sport combat models 1m wingspan, engine 1.5–2.5cc | 15m (50ft) 3-strand light Laystrate. |
| Competition aerobatic models 1500mm wingspan engines 4–7cc | 17–21m (56–69ft) light Laystrate 0.3mm (0.013in) or 7-strand stainless steel 0.4mm (0.015in). |

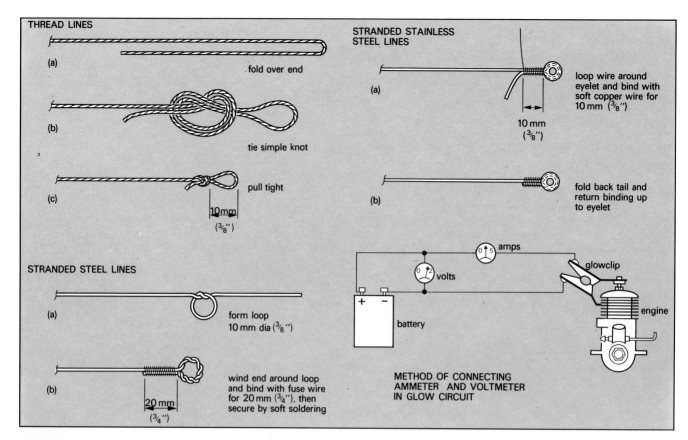

THREAD LINES

(a) fold over end

(b) tie simple knot

(c) pull tight
10 mm ($^3/_8$")

STRANDED STEEL LINES

(a) form loop
10 mm dia ($^3/_8$")

(b) wind end around loop
and bind with fuse wire
for 20 mm ($^3/_4$"), then
secure by soft soldering
20 mm ($^3/_4$")

STRANDED STAINLESS
STEEL LINES

(a) loop wire around
eyelet and bind with
soft copper wire for
10 mm ($^3/_8$")
10 mm ($^3/_8$")

(b) fold back tail and
return binding up
to eyelet

amps

volts

+ −

battery

glowclip

engine

METHOD OF CONNECTING
AMMETER AND VOLTMETER
IN GLOW CIRCUIT

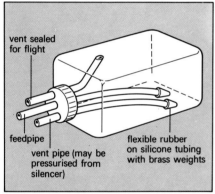

vent sealed
for flight

feedpipe

vent pipe (may be
pressurised from
silencer)

flexible rubber
on silicone tubing
with brass weights

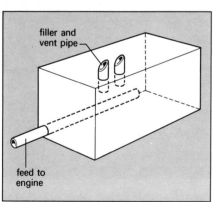

filler and
vent pipe

feed to
engine

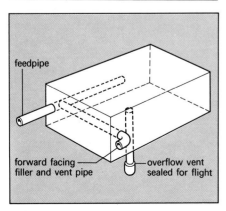

feedpipe

forward facing
filler and vent pipe

overflow vent
sealed for flight

## Fuel tanks

Fuel tanks can cause much trouble to modellers and are viewed with suspicion by those who feel there is a secret art to fuel systems in model aircraft. This is not true at all: all one has to do is to remember and take account of the forces which act on the fuel, that is gravity – which always acts vertically downwards, centrifugal force – which acts horizontally away from the pilot, and inertia, which only acts when the model changes speed or direction.

Traditionally fuel tanks are made of thin tin plate, fitted with copper or brass pipework soldered in place. Nowadays, although metal tanks are still in the majority, there is a growing tendency to use transparent plastic bottle tanks, fitted with flexible internal plumbing. They have the advantages that you can see exactly what is going on in the tank, and they are not prone to leakages due to split seams or bad soldering as the metal ones are.

A fuel tank for an aerobatic model must be capable of delivering fuel to the engine when the model is in any attitude, upright or inverted, climbing or diving.

Do not forget when deciding on the size of tank for your model that glowplug engines have about twice the fuel consumption of a diesel of the same size. On large glow powered models fitted with internal tanks, for instance, it can be quite a problem to find the space required for,

say, a half pint fuel tank (300cc).

Glow fuel is very much cheaper bulk-bought and is usually sold in plastic containers of 5 litres (1gal), although small tins are available which are much more convenient to use, as they are usually fitted with a spout to fill the tank direct. Most fliers make or buy a 'squeeze bottle' for filling their tanks, merely a small plastic bottle fitted with a spout. This enables a convenient quantity of fuel to be carried about and can be squeezed to pressurize the fuel into the tank.

## Batteries and glowplugs

If your model is fitted with a glow-plug engine then you need a battery of the correct voltage and a suitable connecting clip in order to start it. American and most small engines are usually fitted with a 1$^1/_2$ volt glowplug and therefore it is important to use a dry cell battery in order not to 'blow' the filament. Use as large a battery as is convenient

*Opposite:* The British team at the 1978 World Championship rallying round to start John Newnham's Merco 35 powered Nobler. Note model is started inverted, and timekeeper in background is checking elapsed time.

| Ammeter reading | Interpretation |
| --- | --- |
| 1. No reading. | Circuit incomplete, blown plug or loose connections somewhere. |
| 2. Full scale deflection. | Short circuit – clip shorting on engine, bad insulation on leads. |
| 3. Higher than normal reading. | Engine 'flooded' with fuel, cold plug element draws more current. |
| 4. Low reading. | Battery going flat, meter may read correctly initially but needle moves slowly down. |
| 5. Normal reading. | Learn by experience for each type of plug, usually 2–3 amps. |

in order to have a good working life. It can be very frustrating to have to stop flying due to a flat battery preventing the engine from starting. Wet lead/acid cells, or accumulators as they are sometimes called, are 2 volts per cell and have the advantage of being rechargeable. They have a longer working life than dry cells and the voltage falls off slowly as they become discharged with use, so giving adequate warning that a recharge is necessary. More expensive to buy initially, they are cheaper and far more satisfactory in the long run.

*Opposite, top:* Highly developed semi-scale Mustang by Al Rabe, USA, uses wet-moulded balsa fuselage and Super Tigre 60 engine. Runner-up in 1978 World Championships.

*Opposite, bottom:* Current World Champion as this book is prepared is Bobby Hunt, USA, a pioneer of hollow foam wings on stunt models. Unusual engine choice is Schneurle-OS40 FRS in his Genesis design.

The competition-minded enthusiast will have the battery mounted in his flying box complete with an ammeter and voltmeter in the circuit to give him information about the battery and glowplug conditions.

The voltmeter is used mainly as a confirmation check on the state of the battery.

## How to fly Control-Line

The model is complete, you have all the equipment and the moment has come to go out and fly for the first time. You need three things:

1. A person to help you hold and launch the model who is an experienced control line flier if possible. He will recognize and help to correct the mistakes.
2. A suitable flying site, which must be reasonably level and smooth if take-offs from the ground are expected, and preferably grass, as it is more forgiving than tarmac in the event of a crash. Check that model flying is allowed at the place that you intend to fly, as in some public parks etc. it is forbidden. Finally and most important of all, keep well away from any overhead electric power cables, since if the model contacts *or even approaches* high voltage lines then you may be electrocuted. It has happened.
3. A reasonably calm day is important for these first flights. A blustery wind can make the model lose line tension and crash.

Before attempting to fly, start and run the engine in the model for a tankful of fuel to check that everything is OK with the engine mounting and fuel system. Connect the lines and handle, making sure that up or a backward movement of the handle gives up elevator control. For safety's sake do a pull test on

the lines; with the helper holding the model securely pull on the handle approximately 5kg (12lb). This tests the strength of the whole system, handle, connectors, lines, leadout wires and bellcrank.

Now you are ready to fly. Position the model in the downwind side of the circle the model will fly in and check that there are no obstructions in the flight path; get onlookers to stand well back. Start the engine and walk to the handle, hold it the correct way up and signal your helper to release or launch the model. Hold your control arm fairly stiff in a straight line and raise or lower the whole arm when controlling the aircraft. This has a desensitizing effect, and enables the model to fly at the altitude that your arm is pointing at. To fly high raise the arm, to fly low lower it. Try to maintain a flying height of about 3m (10ft) initially. Be gentle in control movements and concentrate on looking at the model and not at the scenery passing behind it, which will alleviate any tendency to dizziness. When the engine stops lower the arm very slowly as the model descends on its glide down to the ground. Just before the landing is made apply some up elevator control to round out the glide and slow the model for a gentle touchdown.

## Aerobatic Control-Line flying

Once a pilot is competent at straight and level flying with a trainer it is time to become a little more adventurous and try an aerobatic or 'stunt' model. Such models are generally larger than trainers and much more lightly constructed in order to reduce the wing loading for stunts. The engine is larger to give the power necessary and the control systems are much more sensitive to ensure manoeuvrability. The wings are also very thick, which helps to produce more lift, although the wing section is symmetrical so that the model will perform equally well when flying inverted. On advanced stunt models the wings are fitted with flaps on the trailing edge rather like ailerons on a fullsize aircraft. These are connected to the control system to move in opposition to the elevators. When the elevators go up then the flaps move down in order to change the symmetrical section into a cambered section with a greater lift. This enables the model to perform sharper turns without mushing or stalling. Special fuel tanks are required to ensure a constant supply to the engine whilst the

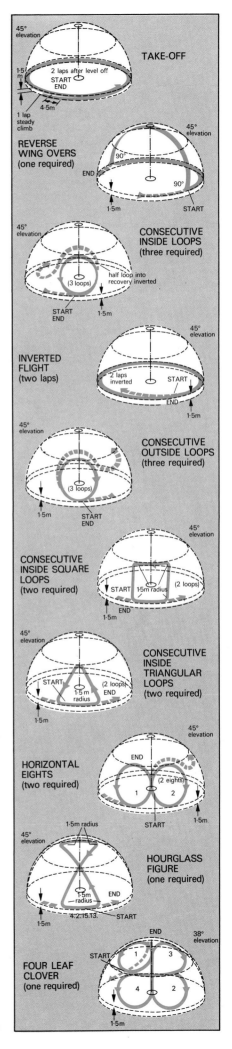

# STUNT MODEL

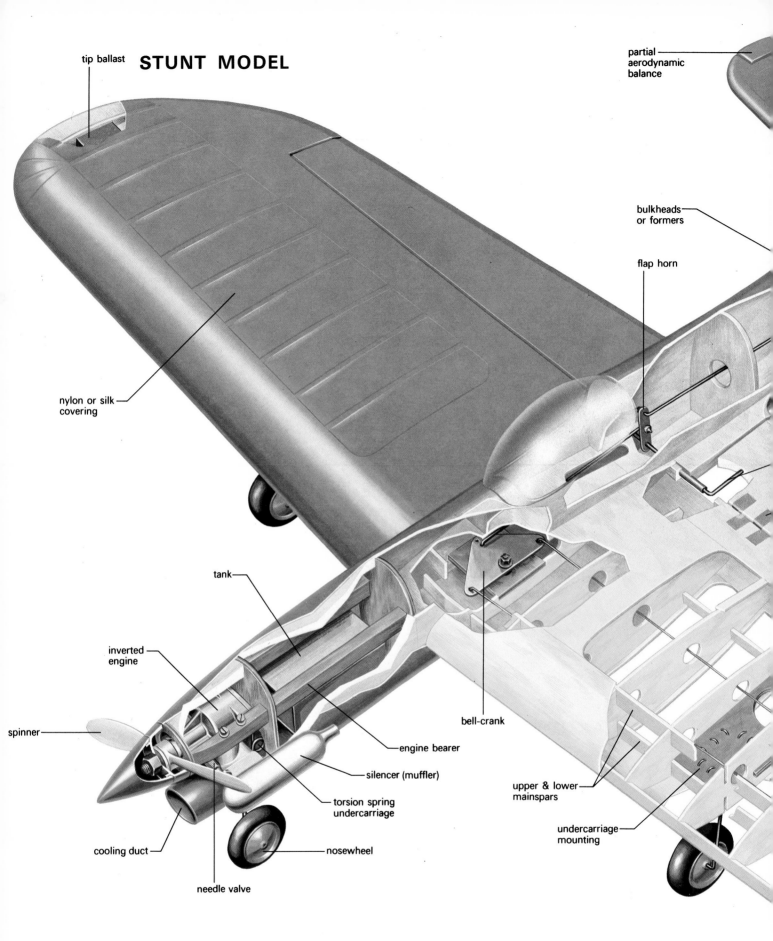

tip ballast

partial aerodynamic balance

bulkheads or formers

flap horn

nylon or silk covering

tank

inverted engine

spinner

bell-crank

engine bearer

silencer (muffler)

torsion spring undercarriage

upper & lower mainspars

cooling duct

nosewheel

undercarriage mounting

needle valve

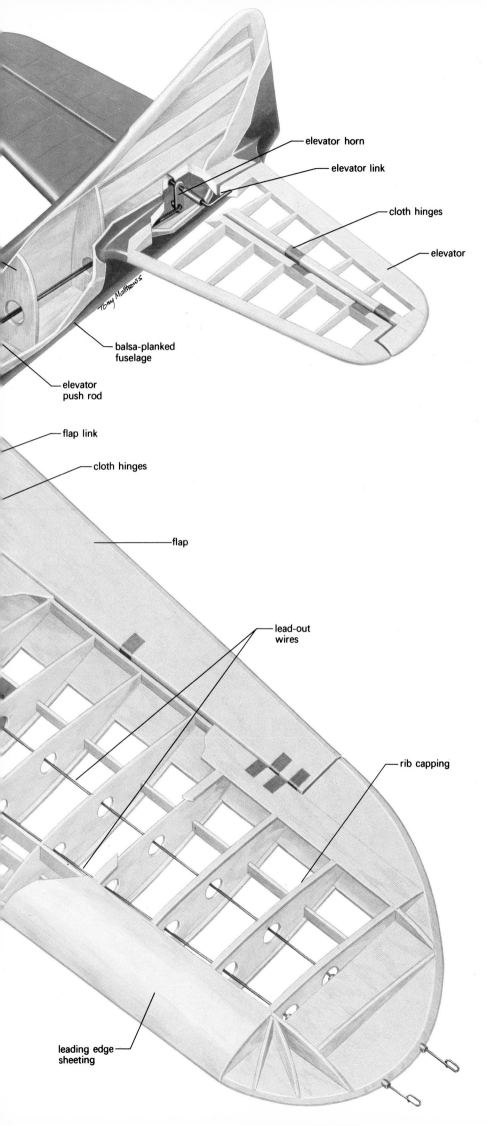

elevator horn

elevator link

cloth hinges

elevator

Tony Matthews

balsa-planked
fuselage

elevator
push rod

flap link

cloth hinges

flap

lead-out
wires

rib capping

leading edge
sheeting

model is climbing, diving, or flying inverted.

Once a pilot can master simple manoeuvres such as loops, eights and inverted flight, he (or she) is ready to enter competitions as a novice. In aerobatic competitions the pilot performs a set schedule of manoeuvres in front of a judge who marks each one out of a score of ten. This score is then multiplied by a 'K' factor which varies as to the difficulty of the stunt .Competitions usually have two or three rounds.

In international aerobatic competitions the models must conform to the regulations of the FAI – the Federation Aeronautique Internationale – class F2B, which say: The model shall have a maximum weight of 5kg (12lb) maximum surface area (wing and tail) of $150cm^2$ and a maximum engine size of $10cm^3$ (0.61cu.in). The line length shall be between 15 and 21.5m (49–70ft) and shall be pull tested to ten times the model weight.

The stunt schedule itself consists of fifteen manoeuvres, starting naturally enough with the take-off, followed by one of the most difficult stunts, the reverse wing-over. This is followed by the relatively simple inside loops, inverted flight, outside loops, and then the square inside and outside loops. The triangles are next, followed by a succession of figure of eight type stunts, the horizontal, square horizontal and vertical. A variation of the vertical eight is next, termed the hourglass, which has straight sides. The schedule finishes with overhead eights, the four-leaf clover and landing. There is a time limit of seven minutes for the whole period from the moment the pilot signals he is ready until the model stops rolling when it lands. An overrun will disallow the landing points. The pilot must raise a hand to signal the start of each manoeuvre and fly at least two level laps between each stunt to allow the judges to consider and write down their score.

Competition stunt flying appeals to individualists, as it is not a team event such as combat or team racing, and also, as the specifications have few restrictions, there is wide scope for variation in model design and approach to the whole event. The models can vary, the classical style of stunter and semi-scale jobs at one extreme to super sleek jet-style types at the other.

Whether or not you wish to enter competitions, the challenge of stunt flying is a most rewarding and satisfying form of control-line flying.

# Team Racing

The essence of any race is for two or more people to compete together to see, in direct comparison, who can cover a set distance in the least time, or possibly who can travel the greatest distance in a set time. This simple principle applies in most sports, and it should be no surprise to discover that control-line aeromodelling (held by its devotees to be the most versatile part of a versatile sport) has its racing aspects. To many, racing is the most exciting form of control-line aircraft competition.

For a race to be an exciting contest, the participants should be well matched in potential and the whole race should be well controlled, which means that rules are essential. With a considerable number of variables, many different sets of rules exist with, rather obviously, engine size limitation being the principal differentiating factor. So around the world control-line racing is seen in many forms and below are indicated just a few of these:

| Class | Engine Size |
|---|---|
| Mouse Race | 0.8cc (0.049cu.in) |
| ½A Team Race | 1.5cc (0.09cu.in) |
| FAI Team Race | 2.5cc (0.15cu.in) |
| Goodyear | 2.5 or 3.5cc (0.15 or 0.21cu.in) |
| B Team Race | 5.0cc (0.29cu.in) |
| Rat Race | 6.5cc (0.40cu.in) |

Airspeeds vary from as low as 110km/hr (70mph) in Mouse Race to as high as 240km/hr (150mph) in Rat Race.

Goodyear and FAI Team Race classes are probably the most popular in numerical terms around the world; these two classes show the greatest divergence in approach with respect to the governing rules, and yet both produce extremely close and exciting racing.

## Goodyear

Goodyear models are profile models of full-size racing aircraft and must have the engine un-cowled. The rules (as applied in the UK) may be summarized as follows:

Motors – 3.5cc maximum.

Models – Profiles to $\frac{1}{8}$ scale ($\pm 5\%$ error in any dimension allowed, except the tail, which may be increased in area to 25% of the wing area) of PRPA 'Formula 1' midget racing aircraft. Models must have profile fuselage and scale-like finish.

Lines – 15.92m from centre-line of model to centre-line of control-handle.

Races – Heats: 100 laps including two pit-stops.

Finals: 200 laps including five pit-stops.

There are additionally a number of rules covering matters such as race conduct, principally aimed at achieving safety and fairness; the aspiring competitor is recommended to study the rule book thoroughly.

This makes an apparently simple class, for the models are about as basic as can be, and many plans including all of the necessary mechanical and constructional detail are available. (The best sources are probably from England, the *Aeromodeller* magazine, and from America, *Model Aviation* magazine.) The catch, if it may be so described, is contained in the rule requirement for compulsory pit-stops. The rules state only that there must be the required number of pit-stops, and no requirement is stated concerning when these pit-stops need to be made, or whether re-fuelling must occur. Particularly, there is no limitation stated as to what fuel can be used or how much of it can be carried. It will be fairly obvious that, since fuel consumption is unimportant, success in Goodyear is all about engine-power – the more, the better. So for Goodyear, the most powerful engines available, used in their maximum power set-up, are essential, and this means racing glow motors using high nitromethane content fuels. In the UK with a 3.5cc motor size limitation, it is currently the American K & B 3.5 and the Italian OPS 21 motors that dominate, and a typical fuel formula is:

| | |
|---|---|
| Nitromethane | 40% |
| Methyl Alcohol (Methanol) | 40% |
| Castor Oil | 20% |

In America, where the engine size limitation is 2.5cc, the dominant motor is the Italian Rossi 15 FI and fuel with a nitromethane content in excess of 50% is common. Airspeeds of over 190km/hr (120mph) can be achieved and the pilot's job can be difficult with lap times of under 2sec and line pulls approaching 14kg (30lb).

What was intended to be a simple class for rather basic models has thus turned out to be just as challenging as any other. Goodyear

today still features cheap, easily built models, but the cost in fuel and 'blown' glowplugs is considerable.

## FAI team race

Perhaps the form of control-line racing that requires the most inventiveness and presents the greatest challenge is FAI Team Race – the challenge because it is the only World Championship class of control-line racing, and the inventiveness because it is the most rule-bound. The basis of the rules is summarized as follows:

Motors – 2.5cc maximum.

Models – wing and tail area, 12dm² minimum in total.

Fuselage at pilot location, 50mm wide × 100mm high minimum with a minimum cross-sectional area of 39sq.cm.

Pilot's head must have forward vision and must have minimum dimensions of 14mm wide × 14mm deep × 20mm high.

Motors must be fully enclosed with only controls allowed to protrude.

Fuel capacity – 7cc maximum.

Lines – 15.92m from centre-line of model to centre-line of control-handle.

Races – Heat, 100 laps.

Final, 200 laps.

A considerable number of rules exist as to the conduct of the contestants and the conduct of the races; this is one event where full knowledge of the rules is an absolute essential. There are at least 18 different 'offences' that may lead to a team being (a) warned with respect to their conduct (three warnings means disqualification from a race) (b) disqualified instantly from a race, or (c) disqualified from the whole contest.

The key feature of FAI Team Race is that the permitted fuel load is insufficient to complete the race without at least one re-fuelling pit-stop. There thus has to be a balance achieved between brute horsepower and fuel consumption; it is one of the very few events where engine efficiency really matters. Many people all over the world have become addicted to the search for this balance.

Two pilots flying together must clear each other. Handles held high and close mean minimum distance covered by model, important in a 5 minute race.

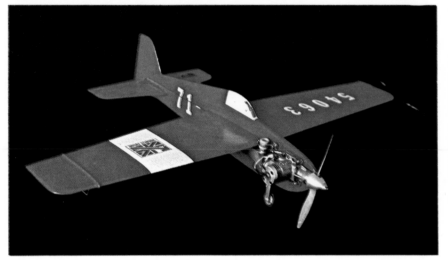

## Racing

All races are in essence the same: two or three teams flying in one circle race together from a cold start over the set distance or time, performing pit-stops as necessary, with the winner judged by the stopwatch or lap-counter. Typical set distances are as follows:

*Top left:* Catching a team racer at high speed takes skill and judgement.
*Top right:* Refuelling and restarting is helped by fuel line taped to finger and battery contacts on thumb and finger.
*Lower left:* A typical Goodyear class racer.
*Lower right:* the 'works' of a top-class team racer – compare with drawing opposite.

| Event | Line length | No. of laps | Distance |
|---|---|---|---|
| ½A Team Race | 14.00m | 100 (heats) | 8.8km |
| | | 200 (finals) | 17.6km |
| FAI Team Race | 15.92m | 100 (heats) | 10km |
| Goodyear | | 200 (finals) | 20km |
| B-Team Race | 17.69m | 90 (heats) | 10km |
| | | 180 (finals) | 20km |

At best, in all of these events, heat times are around 4min and final times in the vicinity of 8min. For FAI Team Race a heat time of 4min means an average speed of 150km/hr, (over 93mph), including the start, and all the pit-stops. Taking this example just a little further, it is possible to analyse such a performance as below:

Initial start at 4sec lost       4
Two pit-stops at 8sec lost each
100 laps at 2.2sec per lap    220
Total time in seconds      240

Even though over 90% of this time is spent in the air (and therefore sheer airspeed is all-important), the time spent on the ground during a race can be crucial to the result. The time allowed above for a pit-stop of just 8sec includes deceleration, landing, reception by the mechanic, re-fuelling, re-starting, launch by the mechanic and finally acceleration back to full racing airspeed. From model reception (the 'catch') to model launch during such a pit-stop, the time elapsed is

about 2sec, so it could be said that in a 4min heat the pilot is at work for 234sec and the mechanic for just 6sec, hardly an equitable division of work! Yet both jobs are highly exacting, and the result is the teamwork that sets control-line racing apart from most other forms of aeromodelling. In his 234sec, the pilot can make many minor mistakes without serious prejudice to the result, but the mechanic's 6sec have to be perfect – one mistake and it could be 16 or even 60sec!

## The anatomy of a team racer

For its size, it could be argued that a modern FAI Team Race model is one of the most complex forms of competition model in aeromodelling. However, as with all contest-aimed models, three basic principles apply:

KICK (Keep It Clean, Klaus). Aerodynamic cleanliness is important and this means gentle changes in cross-sections and smooth surfaces with the minimum of holes and/or protrusions, especially when it is remembered that the air displaced by the propeller is rotating rapidly and that this rotating air-stream flows over the fuselage.

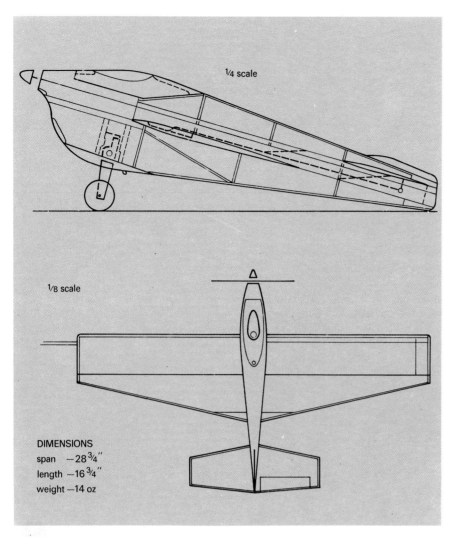

1/4 scale

1/8 scale

DIMENSIONS
span —28¾"
length —16¾"
weight —14 oz

The basics of one of Dave Clarkson's highly successful team racers are shown in this drawing.

the mechanics are standing ready to flick their motionless models into life. The whistle sounds and an instant later the models are airborne.

*Flight* Mechanics and officials stand around the edge of the circle watching while the pilots try to fly as quickly as possible within the constraints of the rules (no physical assistance, normal flight to be at 2 to 3m (6–10ft) altitude, no interference with other pilots). To fly quickly means that the model must progress along the shortest path possible, so it must fly at the maximum height permitted and have the control handle as close to the centre of the circle as permitted. Also the model must be subjected to the minimum of drag-creating circumstances – control handle as high as the rules permit and the minimum of disturbances to the intended absolutely level flight path.

*Pit-stops* The mechanic is in control here despite the fact that it is the pilot who has his hands on the flight controls. One lap away from the mechanic, the pilot operates the motor fuel supply shut-off by use of the mostly redundant full-down elevator mode on the model. With the minimum of time-loss, the pilot guides the model to the ground and into his mechanic's hand. Now one lap means about 100m in straight distance, and the air-speed at the start of that lap can be 170km/h, (105mph), so the only way for the model to be stationary at the end of that lap is for the mechanic to catch and stop the model. Another reason for light models is that they have less inertia and therefore slow quicker, resulting in reduced mechanic hand stress. Now in the mechanic's hand, the model is re-fuelled (in Team Races, by using a pressurized re-fuelling system strapped to the mechanic's arm) and the motor re-started; the team-race jargon 'a flick like an elephant' helps here – try to imagine what that means and then try to do it. Practice will ensure that you can, eventually! The sound of his motor going again secures the total attention of the pilot and, on release by the mechanic, a smooth low take-off puts the model back into the traffic for more 'boredom'.

'Practice makes perfect' is the key. In control-line racing perfection is very hard to achieve, but it can ultimately be reached; its pursuit is addictive . . .

KISS (Keep It Simple, Sam). Simplicity is vital, for what is not there cannot weigh and cannot fail; low weight and reliability are both vital in team race models. This principle applies not only to the woodwork (i.e. the airframe) but also to the motor/tank package, where a great aid to lightness and reliability is the elimination of systems by making what systems you have do everything, as typified by the so-called 'Multi-function Valve' where tank filling, in-flight fuel feeding and motor shut-off functions are all performed by one item.

'Light Is Right'. Every ounce removed from the model weight can mean an extra couple of seconds subtracted from the potential race times. It is no coincidence that the top three finishers at the 1978 World Championships had very light models, viz

1st Metkemeijer/
   Metkemeijer
   (Holland)     384g (13½oz)
2nd Geschwendtner/
   Mau (Denmark) 361g (12½oz)
3rd Heaton/Ross
   (England)    418g (14¾oz)

How these low all-up weights are achieved is not by 'magic' – there are no secrets. Select the lightest wood, use the minimum of glue by accurate joint fitting, and do not over-engineer anything. In other words, KICK, KISS and 'Light Is Right'.

## People matter

Control-line racing by definition is a competitive activity – there is no way for a race to happen without people competing together under the restriction of rules policed by other people. People to check that the models involved accord with the rule requirements, people to ensure that the arena for the spectacle is marked out exactly in accordance with the rule requirements, people to enforce the conduct necessary for a fair result, and, of course, the people on the centre-stage – the competitors.

It has been said that war comprises long periods of boredom interrupted by short periods of intense stress. Viewed in this light, control-line racing is war.

A race features:

*The Start* Immediately before the whistle, all pilots are crouched with control-handles grounded and

# Speed and Combat

Speed is a fascinating subject; take any object you can think of powered by any form of engine and someone, somewhere, will try to make it go faster. That applies to anything from jet-propelled motorcycles to pedal cars where a child is the 'engine'. Not surprisingly, then, control-line speed flying has been in existence for many years. Different capacities of engine result in different classes, and rules cover line lengths and diameters, and sometimes the fuel used. For example, the International class (FAI) calls for a maximum engine capacity of 2.5cc (0.15cu.in), a pair of control lines with a minimum diameter of 0.4mm (0.015in) 15.92m (52ft 3in) long measured from centre line of handle to the centre line of model, and a fuel consisting of 80% methanol, 20% castor oil; timing is over ten laps, exactly one kilometre.

Most countries have other classes to cover engine capacities from 0.8cc (0.049cu.in) to 10cc (0.61cu.in), flown on either one or two line control systems using lines of stated minimum diameter, or lines capable of withstanding the pull of (for example) 20 times the weight of the model, with no fuel restrictions.

Model design is not governed by the rules, but the requirements of a fast model are quite clear. Naturally, the engine must be the best available, or if you have the expertise and knowledge it must have the *potential* for being the best. Commercially available engines are mass produced to a greater or lesser degree, and frequently skilled workmanship can improve the engine in details where the manufacturer simply cannot afford to spend the time himself.

To achieve its full potential the engine must be mounted on a solid base and the most common method is to bolt it to a cast magnesium or aluminium 'pan' forming the entire lower half of the fuselage, rounded and tapered to provide a smooth aerodynamic shape. Alternatively,

a half pan may be used, forming just the front half of the lower fuselage. The pans are hollowed out extensively to save weight, carry the engine and fuel tank, and are bolted to the remaining structure.

Drag is the biggest enemy of the speed flier, so models are made to reduce it to the minimum. Traditionally mounted upright, the engine's cylinder head is normally faired-in by a tightly fitting cowl, while the wings are of high aspect ratio and have just sufficient area to enable the model to fly in a stable, level attitude.

The control lines themselves create a tremendous amount of drag and to overcome this a system of providing control from just one line has been designed, known as mono-line. In essence, the scheme works by twisting the control line itself, using the Archimedean spiral principle. The pilot holds a special handle in his right hand which has a spirally wound piece of stiff wire, some 600mm (24in) long projecting from it, to which the control wire is attached. In his left hand is a bobbin which, when moved along the spiral, causes it to rotate and twist the control wire, thus moving a torsion bar in the model which operates the elevator via a push rod. Unfortunately control is less precise and a thicker wire is necessary for both safety and adequate control.

An alternative to reduce drag in two-line systems is to fit line groupers holding one control line *behind* the other using tiny plastic airfoil mouldings or pieces of very fine tube and adhesive tape 'flags' every 150mm (6in) or so along the lines; wind pressure keeps the 'flags' all pointing the same way. Speed increases of 10% are easily obtained in this manner, but they are banned from international competition and also from certain domestic classes.

Again, to save drag, fixed undercarriages are not used, the models taking off from three-wheeled 'dollies', which remain on the ground when the model reaches sufficient speed to take off.

Recently, asymmetric layouts have become popular, with all (or nearly all) the wing area being concentrated inboard of the fuselage. An outer wing panel has to fly faster than the inboard wing as it has further to travel due to the

A speed flier places his handle in the pylon, which guarantees a constant-radius circle.

circular flight path, so it creates more drag, while by using a high aspect ratio inboard wing only, more of the control lines are faired-in, so once again drag is reduced. The result may be odd looking aircraft, but they certainly are fast; the 1978 World Champion FAI class model (2.5cc) recorded 255.5km/h.

Apart from modifying the engine and reducing drag, there are other ways of going faster. If fuel is unrestricted, there is plenty of scope for experiment. Nitromethane is the most common additive for increasing power, but other chemicals too are used. Castor oil does not blend so well with high percentages of nitromethane, so modern synthetic two-stroke oils are often utilized.

However, the biggest source of increased power concerns the exhaust system employed, often called a 'tuned pipe', consisting of two cones joined back to back, tuned to suit the engine, and operating on the principle of using the exhaust pulses to extract or scavenge the engine's exhaust port of the previously burnt charge. Properly set up, and matched perfectly to the engine, such an exhaust system can increase power by up to 50%. Unfortunately, it restricts the engine power to a very narrow rpm band, for example, with a 2.5cc engine, perhaps between 26,000 and 28,000 rpm. The problem is then how to get the model airborne and flying level in order to bring the engine rpm up to the power band; the best solution is a centrifugal switch with the engine set 'lean' on the ground, near the desirable rpm range. Then as the model gains speed, so more fuel is fed to the engine, keeping it in its power band. It's tricky to set up correctly, but the system works – ask the top ten fliers in the World Championships.

To make sure that the models fly *exactly* the right distance without 'assistance' from the pilot, the timed portion of competition flights are made with the pilot's handle held in a pylon, a U-shaped bracket revolving in the top of a metal pole. During a competition the pilot leads the model with the control lines during take off from the dolly, then pulls on the lines to bring the model up to speed. When satisfied that the engine has reached maximum rpm, he places his control handle in the pylon. The timekeepers allow him one more lap, then start the watches. When he has completed the required number of laps (usually ten) they stop the

watches and signal that the flight is over. The pilot then lifts his handle from the pylon and flies continually until the fuel runs out, landing the model at a fast glide on a wire skid secured to the metal pan.

## Combat

Combat is a very descriptive title for this form of competition flying. Spend a few minutes watching a combat 'bout' and you quickly appreciate why this branch of aeromodelling has such a vast following, particularly among younger enthusiasts. It has all the essential ingredients for a truly exciting competition; high speed manoeuvring (frequently very close to the ground), the need for lightning reflexes by the pilots, the necessity for first-class teamwork between pilot and pit-crew, and the inevitable crop of broken models as a reminder of poor technique!

Two models are flown together within the same flight circle. Each is fitted with a crepe paper streamer and the pilots, standing next to one another, have to try and manoeuvre their fast flying aircraft so that they can cut their opponent's streamer with the propeller. As points are awarded for cutting the streamers, and lost for time spent on the ground, each pilot must concentrate on keeping his model airborne, avoiding tangling control lines and bringing his model into a good attacking position, without having his own streamer cut.

Countries have differing regulations concerning engine sizes, line lengths and scoring, but most support the *Federation Aeronautique International* (FAI) rules which call for engines of 2.5cc (0.15cu.in) maximum capacity and control lines 15.92m (52ft 3in) long and that is the class of model described here.

Model design is unrestricted, but practical experience over the years has resulted in most top designs being very similar. For success, they have to be very fast and very manoeuvrable. The first requirement is achieved by using a powerful engine, and until the mid 1970s, the diesel engine reigned supreme in the FAI class due to its ease of operation, reliability and reasonable power. Today, racing type glow engines are the most popular choice, frequently operated on high nitromethane content fuel. A top quality glow motor can produce some 200% more horsepower than most diesels.

Unfortunately, glow engines are more difficult to handle because they have to run on pressurized fuel tank systems, either of the baby pacifier/surgical tubing variety or using crankcase pressure fed into a sealed metal tank. A pressure system is essential for steady supply of the vast amount of fuel that these high revving engines (24,000 rpm is not unusual) require. The models approach 160km/h (100mph) and can turn so sharply that the G-force is quite remarkable; normal suction feed fuel systems simply would not work. The practical disadvantage of a pressure feed system is that the engine is much more sensitive to needle valve settings, and that if (when!) the model crashes, the fuel is still being pumped into the engine under pressure, making it hard to re-start.

Most diesel engines operate happily on suction feed as they feature smaller bore intakes (which makes for good fuel draw) and usually operate at a mere 14,000 rpm. High performance diesels can be competitive, but then they, too, require pressure fuel systems.

To produce a really acrobatic model there is one essential ingredient: lightness. Or, to be more exact, a light wing loading. To save weight, every non-essential part is dispensed with. Conventional fuselages are unnecessary, they simply serve to carry the engine and tailplane, so mount the engine on simple hardwood bearers glued to the wing and save some weight! The tailplane can likewise be removed and the elevator hinged directly to the wing to save weight. Fins are not required either, so leave them off. After all, if it's not there then it cannot weigh anything or get broken. That is how the universally adopted flying wing of today evolved.

High mortality rate requires quick and cheap replacement. Complicated structures are out – what is the point of spending weeks making a model when its future competition life might well be measured in minutes, or even seconds?

Practical experience has shown that approximately 27.5dm² (425sq. in) of wing area is near the ideal; this, combined with a ready to fly weight of 425gm (15oz) gives a very favourable wing loading, without providing too much drag for a high performance glow engine to pull it through the air at 145km/h (90mph). A 15% thick wing section provides a good aerodynamic performance without loss of airspeed, while a wing leading edge to elevator hinge line measurement of around 330mm (13in) has proved best for a tight turning radius. Mounting the engine as close to the leading edge as possible means that a centre of gravity of approximately 10% chord can be achieved without resorting to adding tail ballast.

During the 1960s the models tended to be built quite strongly – 25mm (1in) square leading edge, 3mm ($\frac{1}{8}$in) balsa ribs and a 6mm ($\frac{1}{4}$in) sheet trailing edge, all nylon covered. There were no spars, the models being of quite low aspect ratio, and there was frequently spruce reinforcement for the leading and trailing edges. Typical weight for a 19.4dm² (350sq.in) model (near the ideal for a 2.5cc diesel) was 450gm (16oz). Gradually models became weaker as the experts strove to make them lighter and nylon covering gave way to iron-on plastic film. Then around 1975 the all-polystyrene model began to emerge. Produced from solid sheets of expanded polystyrene foam with the aid of hotwire cutters, the models now in use are extremely light and just sufficiently strong to withstand aerodynamic loads.

Typical construction consists of a wing cut from this super light material, often with internal portions hollowed out to reduce weight further. Spruce spars are frequently let into the top surface and the whole covered with brightly coloured gift wrap paper pasted on. The engine bearer assembly is then glued on to a central balsa rib, the tailplane fixed directly to the trailing edge and a model is quickly born. A competition modeller who has made his own assembly jigs can mass-produce models very quickly and cheaply. Six models in a weekend is not unusual!

To reach success in combat flying, a fast engine, a stock of good models and a great deal of flying ability matched to super-quick reflexes are not enough. The pilot must have a well-rehearsed pit crew of two mechanics.

Their task is to get the model in the air initially and to keep it off the ground for the duration of the match. The usual technique is for the pilot to have two models fully prepared (the maximum number of models per bout allowed under FAI rules). Each mechanic will be fully conversant with handling the models and their engines and while one model is airborne, the reserve

will be kept fully fuelled and the motor running, just in case. If (when!) the model being flown crashes, their duty is to retrieve it and decide whether to concentrate on re-starting the engine and getting that model back into the air again, or whether to transfer the streamer to the reserve model, running a new set of lines and control handle to the pilot, and then to continue battle again. Much will depend on the state of the crashed model. It may be broken or it may be fine. But has the engine been flooded with fuel from the pacifier tank? Has the glow plug burned out?

While the reserve model is airborne, all these points must be checked out by the pit crew and temporary repairs made to the model. Control lines too should be checked for damage. If all is well, the tank is refilled and the engine started just in case. All the while, of course, they must be aware of how 'their' pilot is faring and keeping an eye open for another contact with the ground. With penalty points being incurred for every second that a model is on the ground, they must work fast, and as a team. Misunderstood orders from the pilot cannot be tolerated if success is to be gained.

Yes, combat flying is fast, furious, and above all, fun.

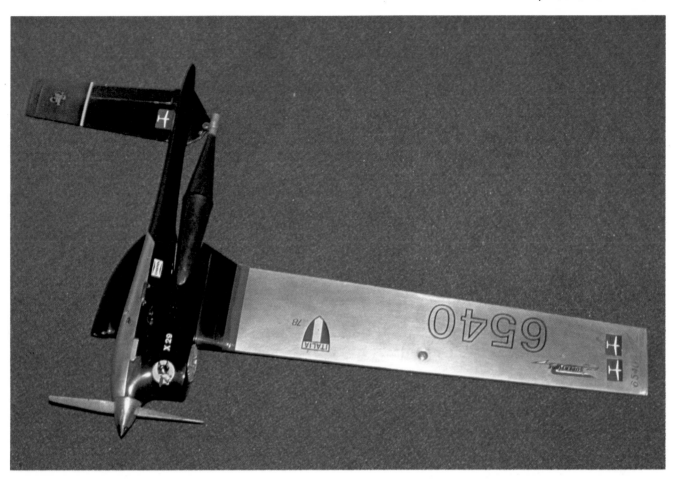

*Opposite:* Italian speed champion for 1978 was Renzo Grandesso whose model is shown above. Asymmetric layout has aerodynamic advantages in this form of flying. A similar model is Peter Halman's top class English machine, shown without propeller *below.* Note 'processing' label from a recent competition, validating entry.

# Pulsar

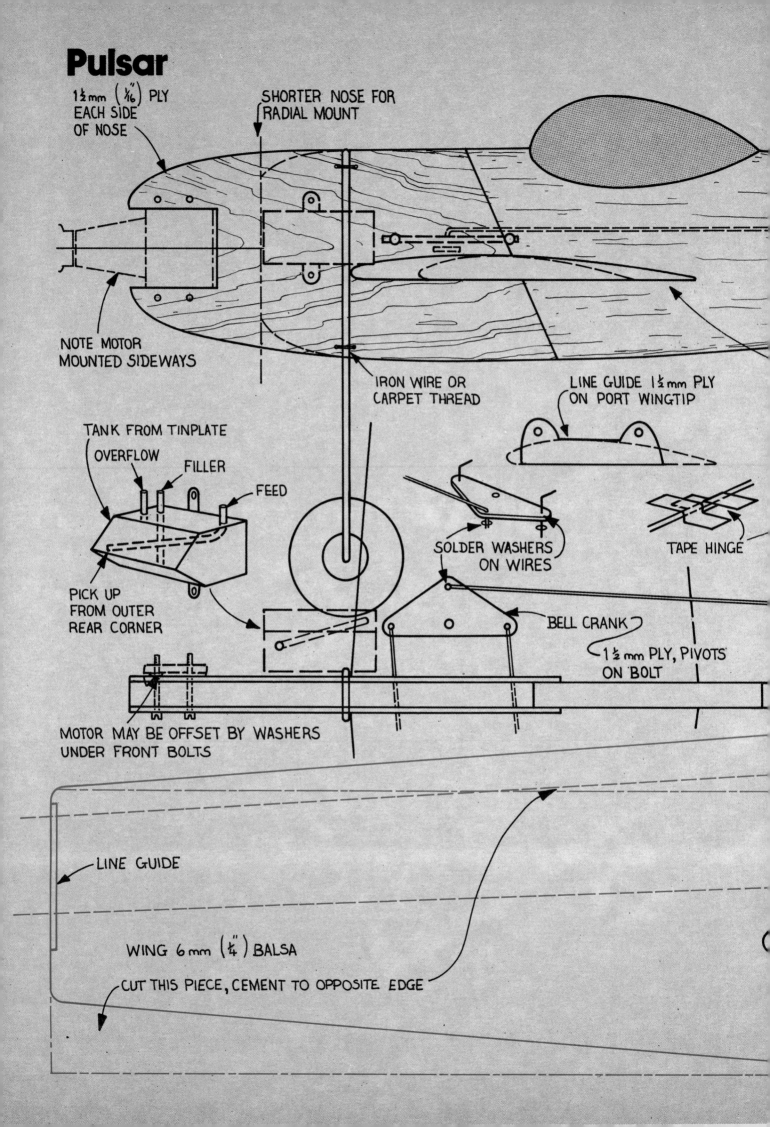

1½mm (1/16") PLY EACH SIDE OF NOSE

SHORTER NOSE FOR RADIAL MOUNT

NOTE MOTOR MOUNTED SIDEWAYS

IRON WIRE OR CARPET THREAD

LINE GUIDE 1½mm PLY ON PORT WINGTIP

TANK FROM TINPLATE

OVERFLOW

FILLER

FEED

PICK UP FROM OUTER REAR CORNER

SOLDER WASHERS ON WIRES

TAPE HINGE

BELL CRANK

1½mm PLY, PIVOTS ON BOLT

MOTOR MAY BE OFFSET BY WASHERS UNDER FRONT BOLTS

LINE GUIDE

WING 6mm (¼") BALSA

CUT THIS PIECE, CEMENT TO OPPOSITE EDGE

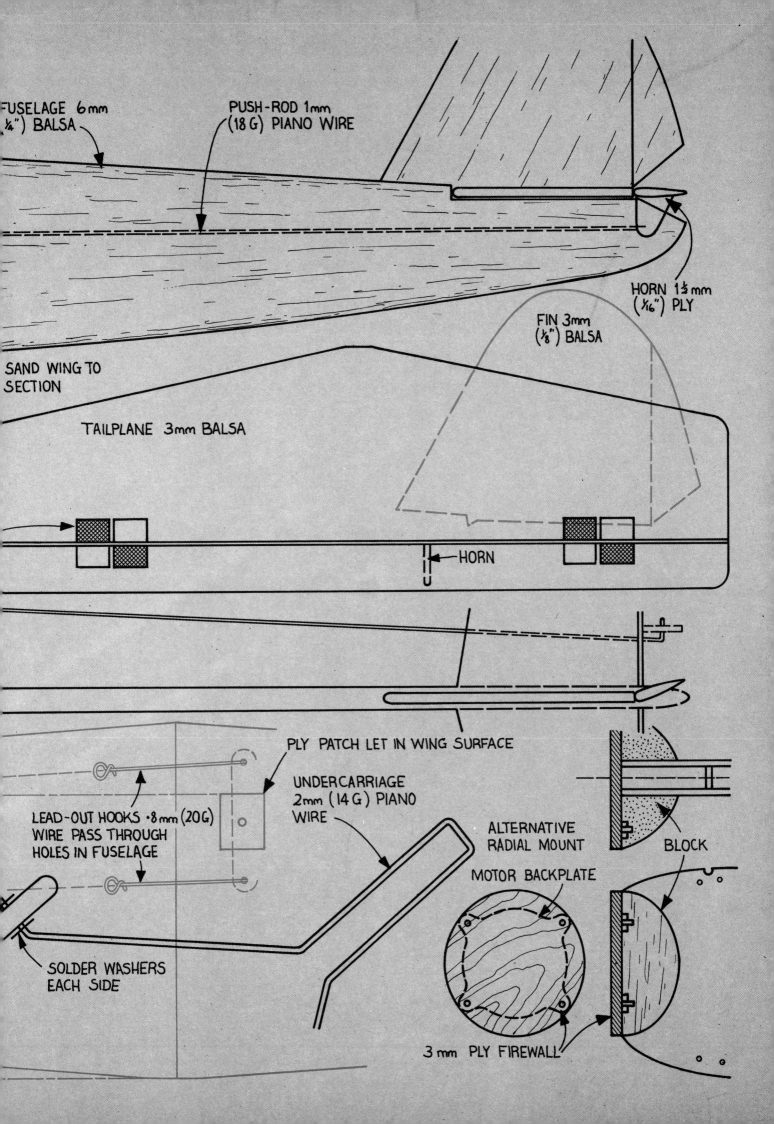

FUSELAGE 6mm
(¼") BALSA

PUSH-ROD 1mm
(18 G) PIANO WIRE

HORN 1½ mm
(¹⁄₁₆") PLY

FIN 3mm
(⅛") BALSA

SAND WING TO
SECTION

TAILPLANE 3mm BALSA

← HORN

PLY PATCH LET IN WING SURFACE

UNDERCARRIAGE
2mm (14 G) PIANO
WIRE

ALTERNATIVE
RADIAL MOUNT

MOTOR BACKPLATE

BLOCK

LEAD-OUT HOOKS ·8mm (20 G)
WIRE PASS THROUGH
HOLES IN FUSELAGE

SOLDER WASHERS
EACH SIDE

3 mm PLY FIREWALL

# Pulsar

Control-line flying can be fun. This little trainer is strong, simple and inexpensive to make, and capable of many hours of flying. If you crash it, it is easy to repair. Any diesel or glow engine of up to 1cc (.06cu.in) can be used, and alternative mountings are shown on the plan.

First trace out all the parts, 6mm ($\frac{1}{4}$in) balsa for the wing and fuselage and 3mm ($\frac{1}{8}$in) for the tail surfaces. Two 1.5mm ($\frac{1}{16}$in) ply panels are needed for the nose, and it is necessary to decide at the start which mounting will be required, depending on the engine to be used. Double cement the ply panels each side of the fuselage and leave to dry under pressure. Sand the wing to the section shown, and round off the tailplane, elevator, and rudder edges.

Cement the tailplane and fin to the fuselage and when dry, add the rudder, offset as shown, and hinge the elevator to the tailplane with four short lengths of tape. Try to avoid cementing the centres of the tapes, so that they remain flexible. Cut the elevator horn and fit it securely in place.

Slide the wing through the fuselage slot, filing the slot out as necessary, and cement firmly in place. Make sure that wing and tailplane are parallel and that the fin is upright. Add the wingtip leadout guides, make the bellcrank and mount and assemble securely. Pass the leadout wires through the fuselage, make the pushrod, and hook the three wires through the bellcrank. Soldered washers are the best means of retaining the wires while still allowing free movement.

Bend the undercarriage, slide over the fuselage and sew in place with strong thread before running a fillet of cement along the wire. Drill the motor mounting holes, or make up the radial mount from a ply disc epoxied to the fuselage and reinforced with balsa block, which can be laminated from 6mm. ($\frac{1}{4}$in) offcuts.

The tank should now be soldered, or a suitable commercial one bought, and mounted on the fuselage side as shown. Make sure that it does not foul the bellcrank. Remove tank and engine and apply several coats of sanding sealer. It is best to cover the whole model with tissue attached with dope or sealer. Rub down well and colour dope to taste. If a glow motor is used, apply a coat of fuel-proofer.

Replace engine and tank and connect up, add wheels (if not fitted previously) and propeller. Check that the balance point is on or in front of the front leadout line. Make up the control lines as described elsewhere, and you are ready to fly.

The manufacturer of your engine will have specified a suitable propeller; control-line props are usually slightly smaller in diameter and of coarser pitch than those used for free-flight, the extra pitch being needed because the smaller model flies faster. Reducing the diameter allows the engine to turn at the same speed despite the increased braking effect of the coarser pitch.

Line length for this model will be about 5–7m (say 15–22ft) depending on how powerful an engine is used and how windy the flying site may be. More wind requires shorter lines or you may have difficulty in maintaining line tension. Lay the lines out across wind so that the model takes off (or is launched) downwind; this means that the wind is blowing the model away from you in the first half-lap, while it is accelerating. Hints on flying appear in Chapters 5 and 7. Good luck!

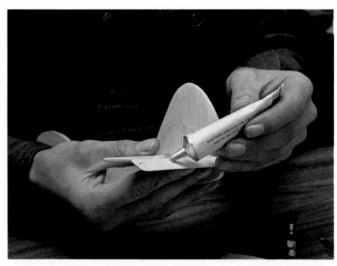

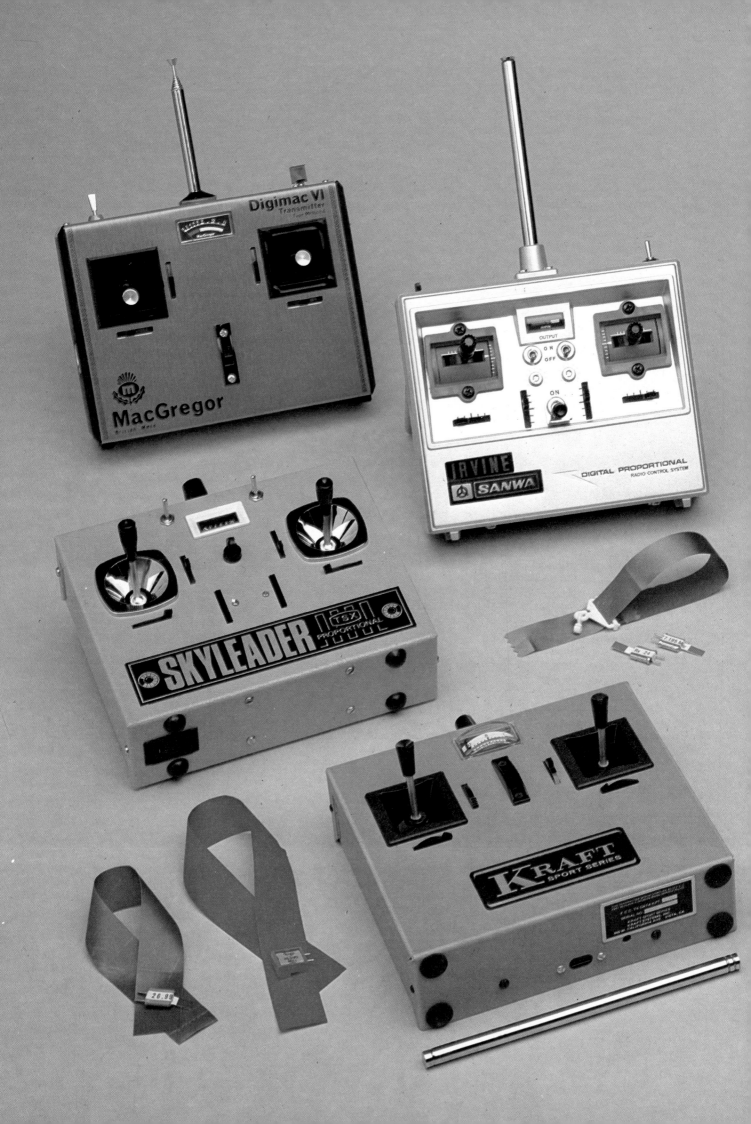

# Radio Control Equipment

Probably the most frequently used aircraft radio is the four-function set, usually used to control rudder, elevators, ailerons, and engine. Examples of such sets, from Britain, Japan and the USA, are illustrated; the basic form is common, but there are detail differences in circuitry and mechanics and, to some extent, in size and weight. The standard of performance and reliability of modern equipment is remarkably high.

Methods of exercising control over model aircraft have taxed the wits and ingenuity of modellers since the first successful flying models. The fact that aircraft move in three dimensions not only provides an extra fascination and challenge but also adds to the risk of operating the model at all. After all, the comparative fragility of a model aeroplane cannot withstand repeated heavy crashes and some degree of control over its flight path is essential. Careful trimming of free-flight models, use of pendulum operated controls and tethered flying systems are all means of controlling the flight path.

All the systems mentioned have disadvantages, and with the exception of control-line (C/L) flight, still contain elements of unpredictability and risk. Modern radio control, however, provides the modeller with the possibility of seeing his model aeroplane perform free of lines and virtually free of risk.

Most types of aircraft can be successfully modelled and controlled by radio control (R/C). Accurate scale models, aerobatic types, racing types, gliders and simple free-lance 'sports' models are all possibilities. Race, soar, perform aerobatics or just take off,

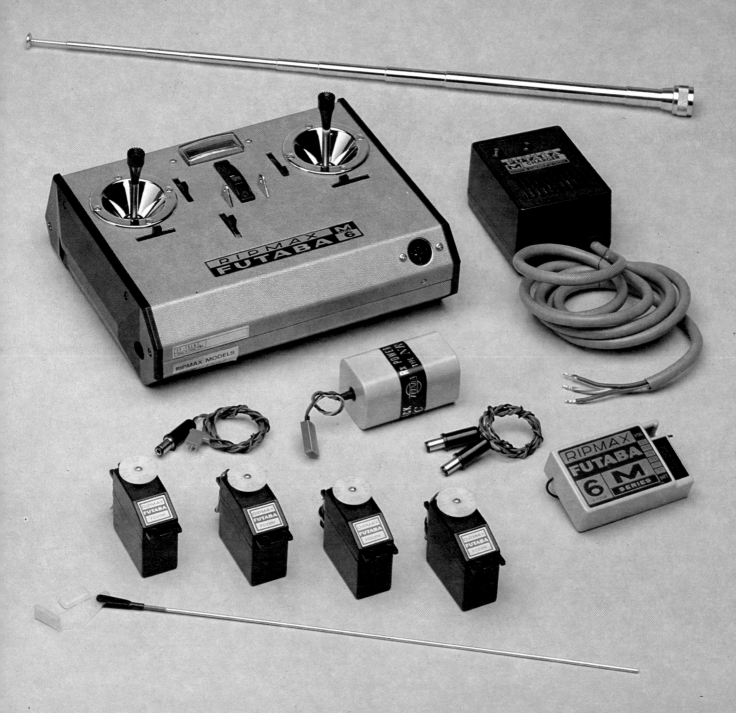

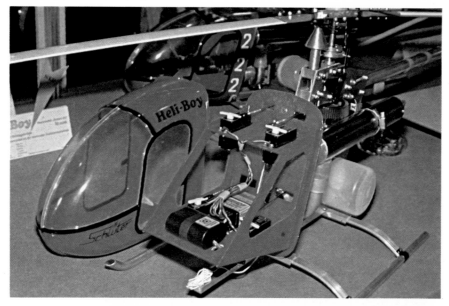

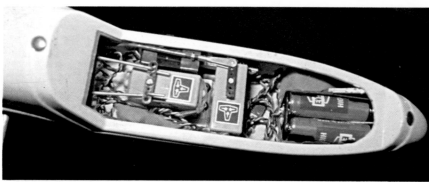

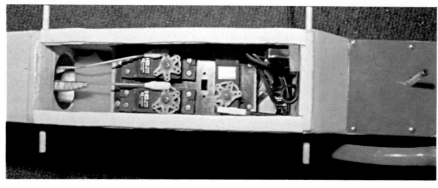

*Top:* Radio installation in a helicopter. *Centre:* A straightforward glider set-up, reached through a removable canopy. *Bottom:* Three functions in a beginner-type power model, where the wing must be removed for access.

fly around and land – the choice is yours.

Modern R/C equipment can quite reasonably be described as totally reliable, that is, as reliable as the other electronic equipment that forms a familiar part of the domestic scene. It is not necessary to possess any knowledge of electronics to install or operate it; manufacturers have all taken advantage of the electronic marvels of the computer age to produce control equipment that anyone can use. Plug in, switch on and operate is all the expertise needed.

Free from the necessity to understand the electronics, the would-be

R/C modeller can devote all his energies to building and finishing his model, secure in the knowledge that his efforts are unlikely to be wasted in an early disastrous crash.

**How it works**
An explanation of the principles of R/C for practical purposes need not go into detail of the more technical aspects. Several basic assumptions must be made, not least that the reader is aware that a Transmitter (Tx) is a device for broadcasting Radio Frequency (RF) energy, and a Receiver (Rx) is a device for detecting the presence of these energy waves. Explanations of how both the Tx and Rx perform these functions are beyond the scope of this introduction.

Before any form of R/C can take place an RF link must be established between the would-be con-

troller and his model. Once established, the RF link can be used to carry information from Tx to Rx. Currently the commonest method of carrying this information is to vary (modulate) the volume or amplitude of the RF link (or carrier, as it is sometimes called). This system of imposing information is called Amplitude Modulation (AM). An alternative system is one in which the rate of oscillation or frequency of the carrier is modulated. This system is known as Frequency Modulation (FM). Whichever system is used, the Tx contains electronic circuitry which controls the modulation. Consider a modern R/C transmitter, a simple box which is bristling with apparently mysterious knobs, switches, sockets and meters. To help understand what is actually happening, imagine that you have it in your hands and are about to switch it on for the first time.

Find the on/off switch and move it to the 'on' position. Most sets have a meter which should now indicate that the Tx is operating. The aerial fitting to the Tx is now radiating RF energy. If you have a portable radio, switch this on and move your Tx aerial close to the aerial of the portable. A buzzing noise should be heard over the portable's loudspeaker which is the signal your model control Rx will detect when in operation. (A good quality portable radio will only pick up the transmission of a model control Tx from a very short distance, usually only centimetres and rarely more than 1m.) Move the control sticks and a slight variation in the pitch of the buzzing may be heard over the loudspeaker. What is happening is that the Tx is transmitting a series of pulses. For a two-function system there will be 'frames' of two information pulses followed by a reset or synchronization pulse. For a three-function system there are three information pulses plus a reset pulse, and so on. These frames of pulses are repeated at a rate of around 20 times per second. When detected by a portable radio the pulses are amplified to a buzz like a front-door buzzer. The variation in pitch noticeable when the control sticks are moved is caused by the length of the individual information pulses being changed slightly. It is this variation in the length of the pulses which contains the information that the control system acts upon to operate the aircraft's control surfaces.

Continuing with the example of

the two-function system and moving one step forward, assume that the control stick which moves in the vertical plane, that is from the bottom of the Tx towards the top, controls the elevators in the aircraft, and assume that the second control stick, that which moves from left to right, controls the rudder. The information pulses are always sent in the same order (elevator, rudder, reset, elevator, rudder, reset and so on) and a movement of the elevator control stick towards the top of the case will, say, lengthen the elevator pulse and vice versa. A movement of the rudder control stick to the left or right will shorten or lengthen the rudder pulse, but, irrespective of the position of either control stick the reset pulse always remains the same length.

**The receiver**
So the Tx is radiating modulated RF energy in a high speed pulsed code which can be heard over a portable radio. What happens when the Rx is switched on?

The signal must first be detected via the long flexible aerial which emerges from one end of the Rx case. This aerial should not be coiled up or shortened, as either action will de-tune the Rx and seriously affect the range at which it is capable of detecting the signal from the Tx. The Rx detects the signal and filters out all the unwanted interference. Simple examples of the type of interference rejected are the noises caused in an ordinary radio by inadequately suppressed electrical appliances or car engines. The remaining signal, which should be as pure as the strident buzz heard over the portable loudspeaker, is now amplified and fed to the part of the Rx package known as the decoder. The decoder has to sort out the information pulses and distribute them to the appropriate control-actuating devices.

The decoder is designed to recognize the long reset pulse first. Then, when it has recognized its first reset pulse after being switched on, it sends the next pulse to the elevator actuating device, a servo; the next pulse goes to the rudder servo, then comes reset. Elevator, rudder, reset etc. Almost on the instant that the Rx is switched on, the decoder falls into step with the pulse train that is being transmitted. Moving the control sticks on the Tx does not affect the Rx or decoder, the varying length pulses are simply distributed in their ordained sequence to the servos.

Returning to the Tx for one moment and in particular to the elevator control stick, recollect that a movement of the control stick towards the top of the Tx case lengthens the pulse – a small movement of the stick, a small increase in length, a big movement of the stick, a big increase in pulse length. The pulse length is *proportional* to the position, or amount of deflection, of the control stick. Ultimately the control surface moves proportionately to the control stick movement. The servo is the electronic and electro-mechanical device which converts the carefully transmitted, detected and decoded pulse into actual driving force in the model.

Inside the servo case there are an amplifier, gearbox and electric drive motor. The amplifier contains circuitry for driving the electric motor in either direction, plus circuits for detecting whether or not the servo output arm is in the position demanded by the system operator using the Tx. Assuming that the whole system is in a neutral position what happens if the elevator control stick is moved? As already explained a lengthened (or shortened) pulse is transmitted, detected and decoded, finally arriving at the servo. Circuitry within the servo deduces that the lengthened pulse it has just received does not match up with what is necessary to maintain equilibrium, i.e. servo output control arm stationary in the required position. It therefore decides which way to drive the electric motor in the servo, which in turn drives a device called a 'feed-back potentiometer' as well as the output control arm. The feed-back potentiometer alters current levels within the amplifier until there is no error detectable between the position demanded by the lengthened control pulse and the output control arm position relayed to the amplifier by the potentiometer, which 'feeds back' information on the output arm position to the amplifier.

Whichever way the pulse length changes, the servo amplifier drives the servo motor until a state of equilibrium is achieved; however small an amount the pulse length changes, the servo moves a corresponding amount. Of course there are differences in accuracy, speed of response and driving power from one manufacturer's system to another, but all well-established systems on the world markets provide adequate performance for the average modeller and can be purchased with confidence.

Most manufacturers are able to offer a range of systems to cater for the varying demands of different modellers with regard to servo power (pull), accuracy (resolution) and speed (time of transit from extremes of movement). The actual Tx radio frequency section and the Rx and decoder do not affect these aspects: it is the quality of the control stick electronics and the servo mechanics and amplifiers which govern them.

**More than one?**
Most modellers will at some stage wish to indulge in their chosen hobby in the company of other fellow enthusiasts. It is often puzzling for the layman to appreciate how it is possible to operate several R/C models simultaneously without any apparent interaction. This is due to 'frequency' which was mentioned in the explanation of R/C principles. The frequency of the radio wave is the rate at which it oscillates. For model control purposes there are numerous frequency bands or slices of the total frequency spectrums available. Most common, world-wide, is 27mHz (27,000,000 cycles per second) but this is losing popularity as Citizens' Band (CB) voice communication radio (also on 27mHz) becomes more widespread. Other bands in use are 29, 35, 40, 53, 72, 433 and 459mHz. These frequency numbers do not indicate specific 'spot' frequencies, but bands or slices of available frequency. For example, in the UK the 27mHz 'band' covers 26.960 to 27.280mHz. All of these bands are subdivided by unwritten international agreement into sections or 'spots' carefully spaced out so that transmitters can operate simultaneously on all 'spots' without causing interference to operators using adjacent frequency spots.

To control the frequency on which a transmitter radiates a 'crystal' is used. This crystal is a thin slice of quartz, ground to extremely close tolerances, which will vibrate at precisely the required frequency and thus control the RF output frequency of the Tx. A matched quartz crystal is also fitted to the Rx, thus only signals of precisely the right frequency are passed through the initial section of the Rx to be amplified and fed to the decoder.

## Colour coding

All of the 27mHz spot frequencies have been allocated colour codes, and users are expected to attach a flag or pennant to their aerials to indicate with which spot frequency crystals their Tx is equipped. Most modern R/C systems are capable of accepting 'plug-in' or changeable crystals and can thus be operated on any one of the waveband spots.

A few words of caution to users of plug-in crystal systems are appropriate. Crystals are very delicate items and should be carefully stored in a tin or box. It is not a bad idea to keep the spare pairs of crystals wrapped up in their frequency pennant. This serves the dual purpose of protecting the crystals if they rattle about inside the box, and is a reminder to change the frequency pennant when changing the crystals over. The modern trend for identifying crystals is not to colour code them or stamp the frequency on the case, but to attach a strip of fabric or paper with a channel number printed on. Either can become detached, because with most R/C systems the only way to pull out the crystal is by tugging on this strip. A very good course is to paint with a suitably coloured enamel the spot identification colour (or colours in the case of split frequencies) plus the letter T or R to identify Tx and Rx crystals respectively. Although the R/C system will work with the crystals reversed, the Tx will, in most cases, then be operating on an *illegal* frequency.

It is not advisable to use crystals of doubtful origin: use only the crystals marketed by the manufacturer of the equipment, as these crystals will be selected to suit the requirements of the particular system. There are many different types of crystal of any nominal frequency and while all may apparently work, only the correct specification crystals will allow the set to perform at its best in terms of range and interference rejection.

Finally, avoid continuous changing of crystals; repeated pointless changing accelerates the wear of both Tx and Rx crystal sockets. Every time the crystal is changed there is a possibility of introducing dirt and corrosive perspiration into the socket and on to the crystal pins. A faulty crystal socket or poor contact between socket and pins can cause a malfunction that will crash a valuable model. The moral is: wait for five minutes until the frequency you wish to use is free.

## Range

As already intimated, the operational range of R/C equipment is quite extensive. Most modern R/C systems have a ground to air range in excess of 1000m ($\frac{3}{4}$ mile). Output power of the Txs is limited by the licensing authorities and is comparatively modest. The range of the system is not, however, totally dependent on Tx output power, but is a combination of factors which include aerial efficiency, Rx sensitivity and Rx selectivity. In fact some of the best systems on the market have comparatively low output power and rely on a sensitive Rx, as it is often the case that boosting the output of the Tx can also boost the spurious signals (side band emission) that it produces, which could interfere with R/C systems operating on adjacent spot frequencies. R/C receivers are designed to be able to operate from very close to the Tx up to a distance of possibly 1000m ($\frac{3}{4}$ mile). The variation in signal strength of the low power signal will be considerable over this spread and the receiver has to incorporate an Automatic Gain (volume) Control (AGC) to enable it to operate with the very high power signal close to the Tx, yet still have the sensitivity to pick up the signal at maximum range. Although it is possible to make the Rx operate at much greater ranges, this would be of little or no practical advantage, because without making it more complicated the greater sensitivity would make the Rx more susceptible to interference and, even more significant, it is not practically possible to control a model further away than it can be seen and 1000m ($\frac{3}{4}$ mile) is probably the maximum distance at which even the largest of models are visible. Much the same argument can be raised for vertical distances; human sight is the limiting factor.

## Power supply

Although the description of the principles of R/C systems began with the instruction 'switch on', more correctly this might have been either 'charge up batteries' or 'fit appropriate dry cell batteries'. Most systems are designed to fit *either* rechargeable batteries or dry batteries (torch-type batteries of the non-rechargeable type). Some are convertible from dry batteries to rechargeable, although it is less likely for R/C systems with more than two functions to be available as dry battery systems.

Both Tx and Rx have stated nominal operating voltages, commonly 9v and $4\frac{1}{2}$v, respectively. Most modern electronic components used in both Tx and Rx are capable of operating on any voltages in a range of 3 to 18v, so the fact that the voltage of the supply is not exactly the nominal voltage is not very important. What is important, however, is the current required, that is, how much electricity in milliamps the Tx and Rx consume. A typical four-function Tx will consume up to 150ma ($\frac{150}{1000}$ of an amp or 0.15a) while a Rx battery could be required to provide anything from three or four milliamps, with all servos at rest, to over one amp with all servos pulling hard. Obviously the Tx is working full out all the time, so the current consumption remains a constant; the only variation would be between aerial extended and aerial collapsed conditions.

It is possible for even a four-function Tx to operate on dry batteries where the current demand is constant and not too high, but the dry battery falls down where high currents are required, even for short periods, as can be the case with a four or more function system. The demand for high current results in the dry battery 'polarizing' and it is unable to supply any current, or at best a very much reduced amount, until it has recovered. The resulting voltage drop has adverse effects on the performance of the Rx, which loses range and is unable to reject interference. This situation can be avoided quite simply by only using rechargeable batteries for Rx and servos on systems employing more than two servos.

The rechargeable batteries already mentioned are invariably of the nickel-cadmium (nicad) type. Nicad cells are extremely robust, long-lasting cells capable of withstanding a great deal of abuse over a very extended period. Nominal voltage of a single nicad cell is 1.2v. There are two common styles of packaging, the button cell and the cylindrical cell. The former is similar in appearance to a chocolate peppermint cream while the latter, as the name implies, is cylindrical. Both types of cell are available in a range of sizes (or capacities) ranging from tiny button cells only 12mm ($\frac{1}{2}$in) in diameter to huge, doughnut-sized high-amperage monsters. The most common sizes for R/C applications are 225 milliampere/hours (ma/h) and 500ma/h. The capacity in milliampere/hours refers to the amount of current in amperes that can be drawn from the cell on a continuous basis for a stated number of hours. In general terms the 225ma/h size is suitable for airborne packs (Rx and servos) and Txs for two-function systems, while the larger 500ma/h cells will supply sufficient current for the requirements of the four-function and up systems. Unlike the dry cell, the nicad is capable of supplying very high levels of current for short periods, and for airborne pack application, where a servo motor could be stalled by overloading, thus drawing very high currents, the nicad will not 'dry up', but continue to supply power. It should be pointed out, however, that the long term result of overloading of nicad cells will be to shorten their life.

## Charging

Most modern R/C systems employ either eight cells (9.6v) or ten cells (12v) for the Tx and four cells (4.8v)

*Right:* A helicopter starting stand and tool box embodying accumulators for glowplug and electric starter.
*Below:* The complete radio modeller's outfit. Starter, transmitter, and other items fit in tool box/model stand for portability.

for the Rx. Either button cells or cylindrical cells are used, depending on the manufacturer. Chargers are supplied with rechargeable battery equipped sets and are usually of a very simple nature. An indication of charge is normally by a warning light, although some makes of equipment indicate that charging is taking place via the Tx mounted meter. As the charger is essentially very simple, it is important that the correct output from it is connected to the correct battery pack. It is also very important that correct polarity, i.e. positive to positive (red to red) and negative to negative (black to black), is observed. Connection of the charges with the polarity reversed will destroy the nicad batteries. The instruction manuals for most equipment contain a section on charging, but a few pointers and amplifications may be helpful.

A full charge with charger charging a 500ma/h pack with a 50ma current will take 16h. Subsequent charges will take a somewhat shorter time. The following simple

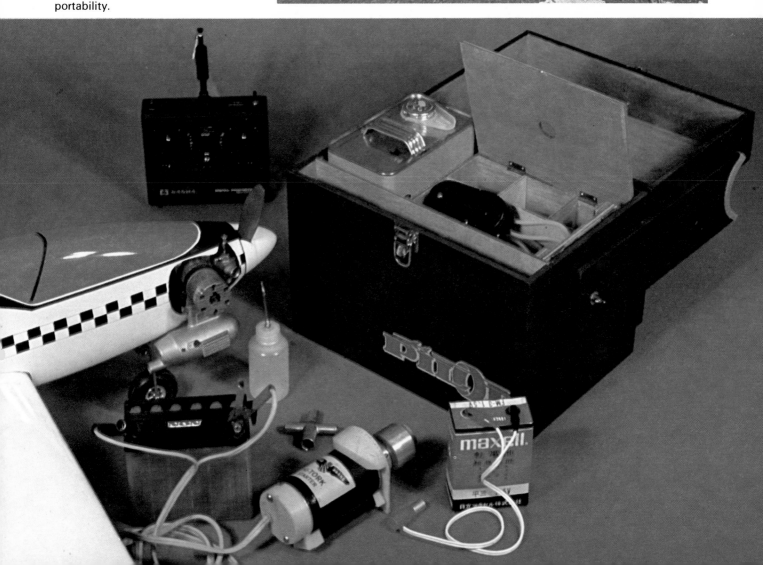

formula will help to calculate the amount of charge time required after all varying times of usage other than the aforementioned full charge:

Charge time

$= 2 \times$ number of hours of use $+\frac{1}{2}$h for each day that equipment has stood idle.

It is obviously not advisable to undercharge batteries, as failure in flight would be disastrous, but it is equally inadvisable to overcharge them. Most chargers are not capable of continuously supplying current into a fully charged battery and it is therefore difficult to overcharge, but continued pumping in of even a low level of current can cause the cells to overheat and eventually a breakdown of the cells' internals may occur. A simple rule is: do not overcharge the batteries.

Equally damaging to nicad batteries is over-discharging. This can be caused by leaving equipment switched on overnight. The requirement of voltages greater than 1.2v entails joining cells together (eight cells for 9.6v, four cells for 4.8v), and despite most careful manufacturing tolerances it is virtually impossible to produce even two cells of identical capacity. This slight variation in capacity means that if the cells are over-discharged, some cells in the pack may well be discharged to a zero voltage condition while others still retain a charge, with the result that the cells still retaining charge feed the zero charge cells with current, but in reverse polarity. Consequently some cells in the pack may be irreparably damaged by over-discharging the full pack. In most cases, however, this effect is only slight and a full charge of 16h will return the pack to full operating efficiency.

If there is any reason to suspect that pack of cells has been damaged by over-discharging, replacement of the pack will be necessary unless test equipment is available to identify the damaged cells within the pack.

Many sets of R/C equipment on the market at present are fitted with a new type of nicad battery, the sintered plate vented cell. This type of cell contains a vent, unlike the earlier sealed cell, which allows any gases developed during charging to escape. Unvented cells can be irreparably damaged by pressure build-up if overcharged. A bonus provided by the fitting of a vent is that the cell may be charged very

rapidly as compared with the unvented types. Not that they should be charged at a rate that causes them to gas, however; the vent is merely a safety device to prevent violent explosion which could result from overcharging. The secret of the cells' ability to withstand higher charge rates is not in the venting arrangement but in their construction. One very obvious advantage of this type of cell is that the batteries can be charged rapidly between morning and afternoon flight sessions, thus enabling the modeller to pack in more hours of flying during the day. A number of fast chargers are available on the market, both for mains electricity operation and for 12v operation. Twelve volt chargers are particularly interesting as they enable the modeller to charge Tx and Rx batteries on the flying site from a car battery. Some chargers incorporate a plug to fit the cigar lighter socket in many modern cars.

Different manufacturers claim different operating times for their equipment, varying between three and four hours. Modern equipment design using integrated circuits has cut down the current consumption of the detector and decoder stages of the airborne system, but the servos continue to demand the same level of current. The stiffer the linkage from servo to control surface and the more the servos are actually used to drive the control surfaces, the more current will be consumed. It follows that a two-function system installed in a glider with free-moving control connections which spends a high proportion of its flying time without the servos driving will be capable of staying airborne for far longer than a powered model fitted with many servos, all of which are operating continuously under high load conditions. A safe maximum for most airborne battery packs of 500ma/h capacity would be in the order of three and a half hours for a glider and up to three hours for a powered model with four servos. Tx battery life is far more predictable, as the current drain is constant. Usually about four hours is claimed, but the facility of a meter or battery condition indicator is a great help in monitoring the state of the battery in the Tx. It is advisable to monitor the battery condition indicator carefully until total familiarity with the system is achieved, so that the meter can be correctly interpreted. Possibly a

three-hour test on the Tx could be made to see to what point the meter needle falls; it is very easy to accumulate three hours of air time in one flying session without realizing, and a look at the Tx meter before each flight is a good habit.

Some manufacturers now offer users the option of 1000ma/h (1a/h) battery packs for their Txs, and those whose models spend very long periods in the air, particularly slope soaring enthusiasts, would do well to investigate the possibility of fitting these larger batteries.

It has been proved that nicad batteries have a peculiar property known as the 'memory effect'. Quite simply, if the cell is continually charged then only partly discharged, as would be the case if only one hour's flying was done between charges, then the apparent usable capacity of the battery is reduced. This means that after a prolonged period of partial discharge the battery is only capable of producing current for the one hour to which it has been accustomed. If this memory effect is allowed to develop, it can result in failure of the batteries the first time that the system is used for over one hour.

In normal service it is almost inevitable that the Tx or Rx, or both, will be left switched on and the battery fully discharged occasionally. The full 'discharge in error' is usually enough to break the memory effect, but should there be any reason to suspect that the cells are susceptible to developing a 'memory', steps should be taken to break the pattern. It is possible to buy expensive nicad 'cyclers' to perform the job, but they are of doubtful value to the individual, although useful as a model club property to be loaned to members as required. It would be cheaper to buy new sets of batteries than a cycler in some instances. A simpler method is to discharge the batteries with a car light bulb. A 12v 2 to 3w bulb suits the average Tx battery pack and a 6v 1w bulb the Rx batteries. A voltmeter is necessary to check the voltage of the battery so that the fully discharged point can be identified. Nicad cells are fully discharged at 1.1v. Therefore an eight-cell (9.6v) Tx battery will be fully discharged at 8.8v and a 4.8v Rx battery at 4.4v. When the fully discharged state is reached,

Radio frequencies permitted vary in different parts of the world. The chart opposite shows current allocations for major modelling countries.

| band | frequency | colour code | flag(s) |
|------|-----------|-------------|---------|
| 25 MHz UK USA Europe S. Africa Rhodesia Canada New Zealand | 26.975 | black | ■ |
| | 26.995 | brown | ■ |
| | 27.020 | brown/red | ■ ■ |
| | 27.045 | red | ■ |
| | 27.070 | red/orange | ■ ■ |
| | 27.095 | orange | ■ |
| | 27.120 | orange/yellow | ■ ■ |
| | 27.145 | yellow | ■ |
| | 27.170 | yellow/green | ■ ■ |
| | 27.195 | green | ■ |
| | 27.220 | green/blue | ■ ■ |
| | 27.245 | blue | ■ |
| | 27.270 | blue/grey | ■ ■ |

| band | frequency | colour code | flag(s) |
|------|-----------|-------------|---------|
| 35 MHz Europe New Zealand | 34.40 | yellow check/black | ▦ ■ |
| | 34.70 | yellow check/brown | ▦ ■ |
| | 35.00 | yellow check/red | ▦ ■ |
| | 35.30 | yellow check/orange | ▦ ■ |
| | 35.60 | yellow check/yellow | ▦ ■ |

| band | frequency | colour code | flag(s) |
|------|-----------|-------------|---------|
| 40 MHz Europe | 40.665 | green check/black | ▦ ■ |
| | 40.675 | green check/brown | ▦ ■ |
| | 40.685 | green check/red | ▦ ■ |
| | 40.695 | green check/orange | ▦ ■ |

| band | frequency | colour code | flag(s) |
|------|-----------|-------------|---------|
| 53 MHz Europe USA | 53.100 | brown/black | ■ ■ |
| | 53.200 | red/black | ■ ■ |
| | 53.300 | orange/black | ■ ■ |
| | 53.400 | yellow/black | ■ ■ |
| | 53.500 | green/black | ■ ■ |

| band | frequency | colour code | flag(s) |
|------|-----------|-------------|---------|
| 72 MHz Europe USA | 72.080 | brown/white | ■ □ |
| | 72.160 | blue/white | ■ □ |
| | 72.240 | red/white | ■ □ |
| | 72.320 | violet/white | ■ □ |
| | 72.400 | orange/white | ■ □ |
| | 72.640 | green/white | ■ □ |
| | 72.960 | yellow/white | ■ □ |

| band | frequency | colour code | flag(s) |
|------|-----------|-------------|---------|
| 29 MHz AM Australia | 29.745 | black | ● |
| | 29.785 | brown | 16 |
| | 29.825 | red | 20 |
| | 29.865 | orange | 24 |
| | 29.905 | green | 29 |
| | 29.945 | blue | 32 |
| | 29.985 | white | 36 |

127

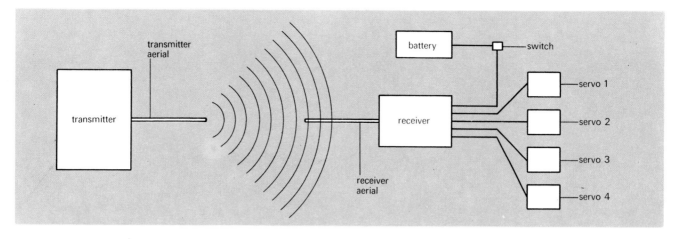

Diagrammatic illustration of the basic components of radio control equipment.

re-charge for a full 16h. This discharge/charge cycle should be repeated two or three times to break the memory. Commercially-produced cyclers carry out the operation described automatically and continuously for as many complete cycles as the operator desires.

Given that the user does not maltreat nicad batteries by over-discharging and charging they are capable of providing many years of trouble- and maintenance-free service.

**Dry cells**

If the system is designed for dry cell operation there will be no provision for recharging. When the battery voltage falls the dry batteries have to be replaced. As there are several types of dry battery available in each size, it is important to purchase the correct type of replacement. At the very least the batteries should be of the High Power (HP) series i.e. HP7 (pencell is AA size, HP7 is High Power AA size cell). Ideally alkaline cells should be used, as these have a much higher capacity than the conventional acid type dry batteries, but they are considerably more expensive.

It is desirable to check the on-load voltage of dry cell packs before flight, for while they last considerably longer than fully charged nicad cells (in a typical two-function system) they cannot be charged before use, thus guaranteeing their ability to perform satisfactorily. An on-load voltage check means checking the battery pack voltage while it is connected on the load i.e. Rx and servos, with Rx switched on. If the on-load voltage falls much below 1.5v per cell the batteries should be discarded.

It will soon become apparent to the experienced user when dry batteries are starting to flag. Servos will start to slow noticeably and the Tx meter or battery warning light will start to go down in level or brightness. Unlike nicad batteries, which almost appear to switch off when the 1.1v per cell level is reached, dry batteries will continue to supply current at a reduced level for some time before ceasing altogether. It should be emphasized, though, that in the interests of safety the batteries should be changed every other flying session. Batteries should ideally only be bought from a shop that appears to have a good turnover of stock to ensure that those purchased are as fresh as possible.

Before many sets of dry batteries have been bought the false economy of dry battery powered equipment will be appreciated and it is strongly recommended that rechargeable nicad batteries are purchased and fitted to the equipment as soon as possible.

**Controls**

R/C model aircraft are usually controlled in a similar way to their full-size counterparts in 'pitch', 'roll' and 'yaw'. Pitch control is via the elevator, a movable control surface attached to the tailplane (stabilizer) which makes the aircraft climb and dive. Roll control is effected by ailerons, one on each wing, coupled together so that when one rises the other drops, causing the wing with the down-going aileron to lift more. On most model aircraft the result of extended application of aileron control is a roll or axial rotation of the model. Rudder operation has a similar effect when applied to a simple model without ailerons but with a fair amount of dihedral, but on models with only minimal dihedral the rudder controls yaw, that is the fore and aft (directional) attitude of the aircraft, and it is quite possible for the aircraft to

continue straight ahead, albeit in a crabwise fashion, without turning when rudder control is applied. Many simple R/C trainer type models and gliders use only rudder and elevator control.

In addition to the basic aerodynamic controls, a powered model usually employs an engine throttle control. Other working features can be retracting undercarriage, flaps, brakes, carburettor mixture strength, bomb, torpedo and/or parachute dropping, simulated gun noises etc. Gliders are essentially simpler aircraft and after the full complement of aerodynamic controls, rudder, elevator, ailerons and flaps, normal additions would be spoilers and towlaunch line release.

All the primary controls are 'trimmable' by means of a small auxiliary lever set to one side of the control stick which provides an adjustable neutral offset to the servo. If, for example, when a new model is first flown it shows a tendency to turn to the right continuously, then by moving the trim control to the left this tendency is cancelled without moving the main control stick to an unnatural non-central neutral point. The same correction can be applied to all the controls, including fine tuning of the engine tick-over with the throttle control stick 'trim'.

**Installation**

Commercial R/C systems usually comprise Tx, Rx, servos and batteries plus an assortment of different sized output arms for the servos and the necessary screws for installing the airborne items into the airframe. The hardware necessary to connect the servos to the control surfaces or other features needing actuation on the model are the responsibility of the model builder, or in the case of a kit built model, the kit manufacturer.

Most R/C manufacturers include instructions on installation of their equipment, but they are usually brief. Some kit manufacturers are equally cursory in their instructions, tending to leave the details to the ingenuity of the builder.

There are several basic axioms that should be borne in mind when installing an R/C system: (a) Keep control runs short, direct and rigid. (b) Make sure all hinges are free from friction and slop. (c) Insulate all parts of the R/C system from vibration. (d) Prevent dirt and oil from reaching the R/C system. (e) Do not overload servos.

Control runs are usually considered right at the beginning of the design of the model. Most powered 'sport' models are designed around the engine, fuel tank and R/C system, so that all linkages are simple. Most gliders are also very simple, as the majority have only two servos. Scale models, however, are usually much more difficult.

Connection from servo to control surface can be made by: (1) push/pull rod, usually balsa or spruce with wire fittings at either end and never less than 6mm ($\frac{1}{4}$in) square; (2) flexible cable inside a tube; the flexible inner can be either 'Bowden' cable or plastic and it is essential to anchor the outer tube

securely both at the ends and at intermediate points; (3) closed loop cable, where a double control 'horn' is fitted to the surface and two cables are used, both in tension, connected to a double arm on the servo. A parallelogram action results. Each system works in a satisfactory way, but for freedom from friction and positive control the push/pull rod system is the best.

Various plastic moulded parts are available for fixing push-rods to servos and control horns, for providing adjustment and for improving appearance by fairing-in exits etc. Most good quality kits include the necessary items, and most plans illustrate the recommended methods of connection.

There are three methods in common use for hingeing control surfaces: (1) plastic film hinges; (2) moulded hinges; (3) sewn hinges. Plastic film hinges are usually of mylar or polypropylene film, resistant to fatigue fracturing and simply pinned and glued in slits in the control surface and wing, tailplane etc. Moulded hinges, similar to those on doors, are freer moving (but more expensive) and are installed in the same way.

Sewn hinges are gradually going

out of favour as mylar film can provide a similar cost advantage to thread used for sewn hinges, with the bonus of being completely rotproof.

Whichever form of hinges are used it is essential that they do not bind, which may load the servo or prevent the surface from moving to its full extent. Also the gap between main surface and control surface should be kept to a minimum to allow the surface to operate at maximum efficiency.

Vibration insulation of the servos is usually provided for by the manufacturer with rubber grommets in the mounting lugs of the servo. It is most important to follow instructions relating to the fixing of the servos. Servos should be screwed down to hardwood or plywood beams securely built into the model. A loose servo or servo rail will in all probability result in a lost model. A minimum of 6mm ($\frac{1}{4}$in) square hardwood or 3mm ($\frac{1}{8}$in) plywood is required.

Protection for the Rx is usually in the form of foam rubber packing.

The transmitter and receiver of a typical set giving four basic functions and two further optional auxiliary controls.

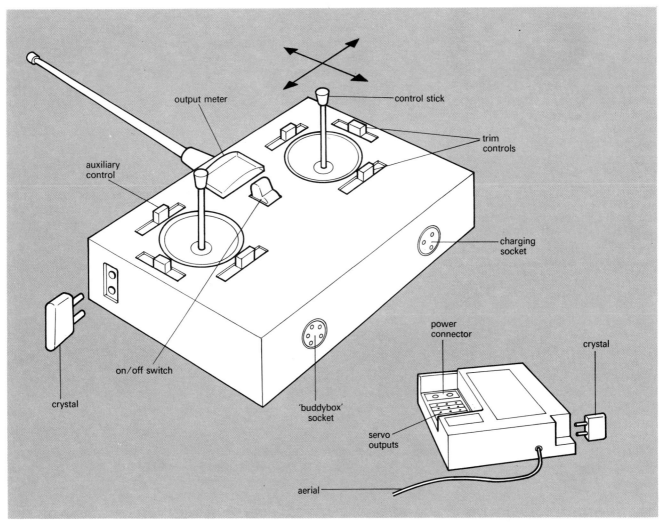

This insulates the Rx from engine vibration and also acts as a shock absorber in the event of crashes or heavy landings. A properly packed Rx can survive undamaged a crash which totally destroys the aircraft. Avoid foam plastics and rigid foams; rigid foams give no protection against vibration, and synthetic foams give little protection against shock, as they compress to virtually nothing.

The Rx battery pack should be protected in a similar way and placed so that it cannot shoot forward and crush the Rx in the event of a crash. Position the on/off switch on the fuselage side away from the engine exhaust so that the switch will not be damaged by oil.

A very important point frequently neglected is the correct routing and installation of the Rx aerial. The very fact that the Rx aerial is a simple length of flexible wire can lead to the R/C user not treating it with the respect that it deserves. Remember that it should never be shortened. It forms an integral part of the tuned detector circuit of the Rx and shortening it can seriously affect the sensitivity and range of the Rx. It should be carefully routed away from the servo and battery wiring harness, as it may pick up interference from these sources. Aim to get the majority of the aerial outside the fuselage, routed through a grommet to prevent chafe after first tying it round a piece of dowel or a button. This will prevent the aerial being tugged out of the Rx if it becomes snagged during transport of the model or is in a crash. The most common point of attachment for the aerial is the tip of the fin; a glass-headed pin can be pushed in to form an anchor point and a small elastic band tied to the end of the aerial to keep it taut. Try to avoid getting sharp kinks in the aerial or the stranded core may become fractured, effectively shortening the tuned length.

When the entire system has been installed a full check should be made, preferably with the assembled model supported to allow operation of all items such as retractable gear, steerable tail or nose wheel etc. Stand behind the model, switch on the Tx, then the Rx, and methodically check. Tx elevator stick back, elevator trailing edge should rise. Rudder stick right, rudder trailing edge right. Aileron control stick right, right hand aileron should rise, left hand depress. Operation of the throttle stick is normally forward for open, back for closed. Check all controls at the extremes of their travel, including full trim. If there are any foul-ups or any servo stalls before reaching the limit of its travel, correct now. Finally, before any attempt is made to fly the model replace dry batteries, or charge the nicads, as a surprising amount of current will have been consumed during installation and checking.

**Before flying**

In the excitement following the purchase of a set of R/C equipment it is all too easy to forget several essentials, an operating licence, adequate third party insurance protection and somewhere suitable to operate the model. Most national government departments grant a licence for model control purposes without formality and at a very modest cost; failure to obtain one could result in confiscation of the equipment plus a heavy fine. Insurance is a common-sense precaution that most modelling clubs insist on, and one which no responsible modeller would be without. The third item, the flying site, does not at first seem worthy of consideration; after all there are many commons, fields, and public open spaces around. Unfortunately very few of them are available or even desirable for first attempts at R/C flight. Many are ruled out by local bye-laws, or are too close to noise-sensitive areas of population; almost all are frequented by other leisure-pursuing members of the public. People could be described as a hazard to model aeroplanes but more correctly the reverse is true, particularly powered models. Few onlookers realize the space required, the lack of manoeuvrability (that is, ability to take violent evasive action) or the potential hazard of a fast flying model weighing several pounds, and thus fail to make the necessary allowances when they inevitably wish to take a closer look at the action.

The local hobby shop can usually help with information about the nearest model club, who will doubtless be able to recommend flying sites and even provide willing instructors. Beware of striking out into what appears to be virgin territory for those first flights, for that noise which sounded like a chain-saw may be the local R/C boat or car club just over the fence. Switch on your Tx and their models are out of control, launch your model and it goes out of control.

Beware of other R/C modellers and check out any new site very carefully before switching on your equipment. If you are a dedicated loner, purchase a monitor to check the airwaves with before attempting to fly.

When you do finally arrive at your chosen site complete with all modelling equipment, fully licensed and insured, there is a certain etiquette to be observed. Most sites operate a simple form of frequency control which is intended to prevent models being inadvertently 'shot down' by unauthorized transmission. Usually a board is set up with a series of numbered or colour coded clothes pegs. If such a system is in operation *never* switch on your Tx without the appropriate peg clipped to the aerial. Providing everyone abides by the system there can only be one person using each frequency at any one time. Sometimes a reverse system is used, in which each site user provides his own peg which he clips to the appropriate place on the board when it is vacant; with this system only switch on when your peg is on the board. (Flying is covered in detail in Chapter 9.)

**After flying**

When the model is safely back in the model room there remain the very important checks that help ensure a long and trouble-free life for the model and R/C equipment. Careful checking before the model is put away prevents essential points being forgotten when the model is next taken out. A thorough clean up of the whole model, including the engine, silencer etc. is first on the list, as the oil residue from the fuel soon becomes very sticky and hard to remove. Use a detergent and a stiff brush to clean the engine and wipe down the remainder with a soft cloth moistened with detergent. Make any minor repairs to covering that may have been damaged before oil has a chance to attack the structure of the model.

Adjust all control linkages so that the control surfaces are in their correct positions with Tx trims at neutral. It may have become apparent during flight trials that an adjustment to the engine thrustline is needed, if so, make the necessary adjustment now and remember to re-adjust the throttle linkage of the engine after doing so. If a flying session is contemplated the following day charge the nicads or check the on-load voltage of the

*Top:* Three basic types of hinge for control surfaces. The simple film and the backflap type are usually fitted in slits, the other in drilled holes.
*Centre:* The last short length of push-rod is often external, as on this glider. Exit bushes should be friction-free.
*Bottom:* Rear end of a scale Fokker D8. Note the sewn thread hinges and the engagement of the push-rod clevises in the control horns.

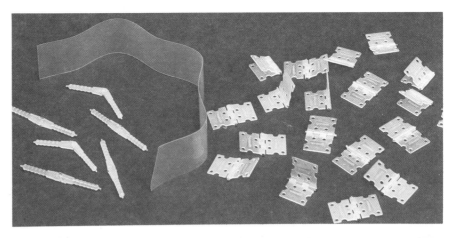

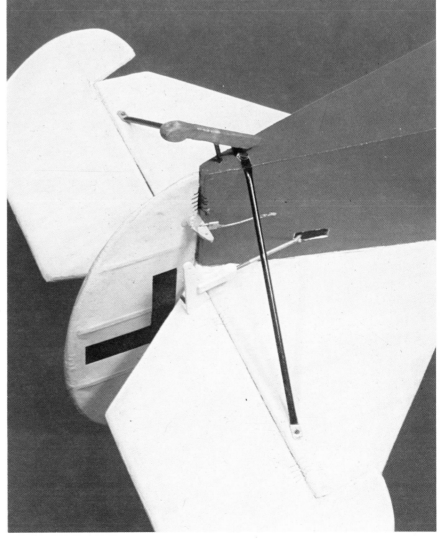

dry batteries. Check all plugs and sockets, including the plug-in crystal in the Rx, to make quite certain that they have not vibrated loose during the flying session. When all these checks are complete it can be assumed that all will be well for further flying.

## R/C maintenance

From time to time it will be necessary to check over the R/C system completely for signs of possible trouble. Likely trouble spots are all those points where plugs and sockets are employed or spring contacts carry current, that is battery boxes and switches. Use aerosols of switch cleaning fluid (from electronics specialist shops) to clean plugs and sockets periodically and also the contacts in the on/off switch and battery box. Examine all plugs and sockets carefully for signs of wear, particularly the aileron connection, which is the most frequently unplugged. If there is any cause to suspect damage to electrical leads into plugs have these repaired immediately by the equipment service agent. Check that the Rx aerial has not become chafed; if it has, have it replaced. Make sure that all servo mounting screws are tight and inspect servo arms; they can become cracked after a heavy landing, and the push-rod holes can become worn and oversize.

Last but not least clean the Tx. Avoid strong solvents, as some may attack the case surface. A strong detergent solution used on a *damp* soft cloth should be sufficient to remove all dirt. Do not forget to clean the aerial, pulled out to its furthest extent; check that it is screwed firmly into its socket. Clean charging sockets and 'buddy box' sockets with switch cleaner. Do not lubricate the stick mechanisms, since oil will attract dust and eventually the mechanism will become stiffer than it ever would without lubrication. Providing that the equipment is kept clean and not treated roughly these simple maintenance procedures should keep it in good operational order for years.

# Radio-controlled Models
## Gliders
## Power and Sport
## Helicopters

One of the greatest growth areas in model flying in the last three or four years has been in radio-controlled glider flying, or, as it is frequently termed, radio-controlled soaring. Soaring is the maintenance or gain of height relative to the ground of a gliding model, which might be a rubber or power model when the motor has stopped, but is more usually a glider or sailplane. At one time a glider was expected to lose height throughout its flight, whereas a sailplane was a more sophisticated and efficient machine capable of soaring, but in recent years the distinction between the two types has become blurred and the two words are synonymous.

There are two basic forms of R/C gliding, in slope lift or in thermals, with slope soaring the more popular, since flying is possible more regularly in slope lift. Flying 'on the flat', as thermal soaring is sometimes called, relies on reasonable thermal activity and although there are very few occasions on which there are no thermals at all, there are a good many days when a model can be launched without contacting usable lift. On a hill site, on the other hand, there is almost always a breeze, and provided a slope facing approximately into wind can be used, flying is possible, especially as models can often be changed to suit the conditions prevailing.

How the two types of lift are generated is touched on in Chapter 14; the methods of using them are considerably different, and there are some differences in the types of model used.

Cliff-top soaring at a popular Californian site, Torrey Pines, with a popular American R/C glider, a 'Hobie Hawk'. On-shore breezes make such flying possible on most warm days, and a flat cliff-top often means less violent turbulence behind the flier. On the other hand, loss of lift can mean a landing on the beach and a long climb to retrieve it!

## Launching

Hand-launching directly out from the slope, into wind, is almost universal on hill sites, and only very rarely is any other form of launch necessary. In hand-launching it is essential that the nose is kept well down to build up flying speed quickly, and the model should of course be well clear of obstructions such as bushes and trees, not only for the risk of physically striking them but because of the turbulent air surrounding them. The model should be steered straight out from the slope, probably 100m or so, into smooth air before turning to fly along the slope. Exactly how far out it is necessary (or at the other extreme, safe) to fly will depend on wind strength, angle of slope, and surface characteristics; a smooth grass hill will obviously create less turbulence than a rocky, irregular slope.

Thermal soarers are launched in several ways, but basically either by towline or catapult. Hand towing, where the towline is held at the winch end by the tower and the model launched, or released, by an assistant, makes the most of the towline length, since no line is wound in until the model is free. In a breeze, the tower can stand still and the assistant let the model lift from his hand; the tower may even have to walk or run towards the model to reduce the speed of ascent and the strain on the wings. In a light breeze he will walk or trot into wind, at least to start the model climbing, and in flat calm he would have to run. If the model has a high wing loading and thus a fast flying speed, he may not be able to move fast enough to tow it up, but winding in on the winch may produce the required speed. Once the model has climbed 15 to 20m (50–60ft) through the wind gradient it will often find enough breeze to carry on, and the line can be paid out slowly to achieve maximum height.

The usual winch is a converted small portable grindstone with a ply drum replacing the stone and the gear body clamped on to a handle, but purpose-made hand-winches can be obtained. A gear ratio of not less than 7:1, up to 25:1, is usual. The line is frequently 20kg (40–50lb) breaking strain nylon monofilament fishing line (which tangles fairly easily) with a maximum length, under most rules, of 150m (492ft). A small wire ring on the free end engages the glider's

towhook, and 60 to 90cm (2–3ft) from the ring a silk pennant about 20cm (8in) or so square is firmly attached. This pennant drags the ring off the hook when line tension is slackened, provides a visible indication of release to the timekeeper, and slows the descent of the line, enabling much of it to be winched in before it lands.

Power winches are beginning to be used, avoiding a lot of running, the drum being attached to a gear train on an electric motor powered by a car battery and having controllable speed. One disadvantage is that line is wound in and cannot easily be paid out. Where unlimited line length is allowed this is no real problem, but if a competition limits line length, valuable potential height is lost. The model, too, has to be carefully controlled on the line by radio, whereas in a running tow the tower can veer and slow at will, thus keeping a straight, constant-speed controlled climb.

Variations with towlines employ pulley systems to reduce the speed at which the tower has to move. If he carries a pulley with an anchored ground end to the line, the model, released above the

anchor point, will travel at the required speed when the tower is moving half as fast, and he can gradually work the pulley back towards the anchor to gain extra height. If the line runs from an anchor to the tower's pulley and thence to a second pulley beyond the anchor, the ring end can then return to the tower who can launch his own model. In calm conditions, the second pulley can be held by an assistant who runs in the opposite direction to the tower to create enough initial speed; once the model has settled in the climb, the operators can move towards each other to gain extra height.

For the second basic launch method, called 'bungee' or 'hi-start' launching, about one quarter of the launch line is 8mm latex surgical tubing or bungee rubber cord. Latex tube gives a better launch in that its recovery rate is slower than that of bungee, giving a steady pull, but it is necessary to keep it clean and stored out of light. Bungee is a nylon or cotton-covered multi-strand elastic rope available in various sizes, 6 or 9mm being usual for this purpose. The line is laid out downwind of the anchor point, the model hooked on and drawn back

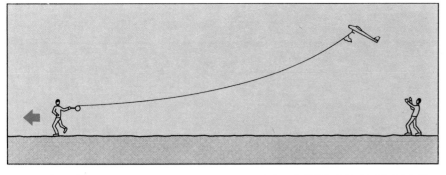

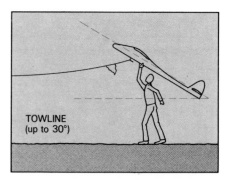

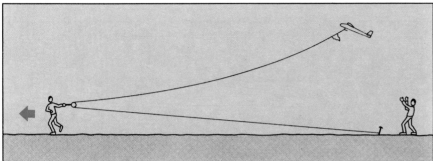

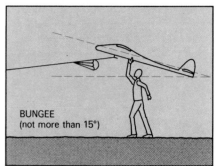

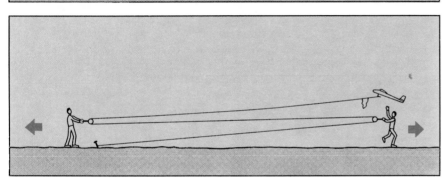

TOWLINE
(up to 30°)

BUNGEE
(not more than 15°)

SLOPE
(nose well down)

*Opposite, top:* Spoiler panel retracted flush with wing on large thermal soarer.
*Opposite, bottom:* Power-assisted or motor glider, limited to 2cc engine for competition work.
*Above:* Methods of towline launching.
*Above, right:* Launch attitudes for various methods.
*Right:* Correct hook position. DL is datum line, the line from which all angles are measured.

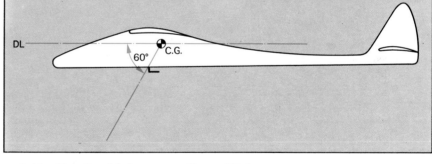

DL — C.G. 60°

to stretch the line. How much stretch depends on wind strength and model weight, but it will not often be as much as two times the length of the stretchable part of the line.

In anything but a light breeze the ring may be reluctant to leave the hook, because the line will remain tensioned from the kiting effect of the model. Using a parachute instead of a pennant provides a greater force to pull the ring off, but modellers who use the system regularly may incorporate a radio release mechanism for the hook, as on full-size gliders. Without such a release, the model may have to be flown free of the line by down-elevator to relieve tension on the line.

The hook position is quite critical

and ideally should be on a line drawn through the CG at 60° to the horizontal datum line. Small adjustments to the CG position during trimming should not make a significant difference, but with an unknown design it may be that an adjustable hook is desirable. A simple way is to make the hook longer than necessary and blank it off progressively to restrict how far forward the ring will slide, making it permanent and clipping off excess wire when the best position is found. Alternatively, a ply keel extending slightly beneath the fuselage can be drilled to receive a wire hook sprung into two holes and thus adjustable by drilling further holes. Epoxy will secure the hook when the best position is found.

## Flying

Most slopes good for soaring attract a number of fliers, most of whom are willing to advise a newcomer. Radio discipline is essential and most regularly-used sites have a peg-board or similar system. A wind of 16 to 25km/h (10–15mph) is ideal for new models and/or inexperienced pilots. Study the area and, if other people are flying, where they are launching and landing. As will be clear from Chapter 14, landing needs to be on top of the hill but the model must not fly too far back from the edge or it will be in heavy turbulence or down-draught.

Launch the model down the slope and fly it out into smooth lift before turning to fly parallel with the slope. Keep the flying speed fairly high, especially when turning, and do not fly too far along initially. Always turn outward away from the slope – the lift area is likely to extend out at least the same distance as the height of the hill – but bring the model back to continue a pattern parallel with the slope and just far enough out to avoid turbulence. If the model loses height in the turn it will regain it as soon as it heads back into the area of strongest lift, which is the band close to the slope but just clear of turbulence. Because of the sideways drift the model will appear to be crabbing when maintaining a course parallel to the slope, and if it is turned downwind its groundspeed may well take you by surprise.

To land, start with enough height, turn towards the slope and either maintain a gentle turn or fly only a very short downwind leg, then turn to fly parallel with the slope, 50m or so behind you. Allow the model to lose height to perhaps 10m, then turn into wind and land on, or close to, your pre-selected spot. If the last turn is made too high, the model may scrape over the edge, but in this case it will fly out into lift again and give a second chance. If, however, it is allowed to drift too far back from the edge, it may well be dumped on the ground by the downdraught, with the possibility of damage. Depending on the site, there may be a car park or spectators to be avoided.

Launching by towline for thermal soaring is usually more of a team effort, the pilot entrusting the actual towing to an assistant, though he himself may participate by holding and releasing the model. This may entail moving a few steps along with the tower until there is sufficient line tension and speed for the model to be virtually towed out of his hand. With a small or light model, one hand for the model and one for the transmitter is enough, but for large models a second assistant is desirable, even if only to hand the flier the transmitter quickly.

On tow the pilot can assist by holding on a little up elevator and may even be able to correct tendencies to veer by use of rudder. As with any teamwork, a little practice is necessary to achieve top results every time.

For single-handed flying the double pulley system can be used, but a bungee launch is much better provided the model is released only slightly nose-up and with its wings

level. Roll and yaw control are not too effective in the initial part of the climb, though pitch control is always present.

## Models

An obvious difference between slope and thermal soarers is that the latter tend to be larger and lighter than the former, on average. Wing loading (that is, weight related to lifting surface area) for a thermal soarer may well be in the range 2 to 2.5kg/m$^2$ ($6\frac{1}{2}$–$8\frac{1}{2}$oz/sq.ft), while few slope soarers are less than 3kg/m$^2$ (10oz/sq.ft) and many are much more, up to twice this figure in fact. This is partly because slope models are flown in winds and, if the wind is right, have an inexhaustible supply of lift, while thermal soarers have to be towed up and need to make the most of what lift can be found; a larger model is more efficient but too high a flying speed may make staying in lift a little difficult. A high wing loading means higher airspeed, in general, which in turn means higher groundspeed. The ability to make headway into wind, called 'penetration', is important in strong winds, especially on the slope.

The other reason is the type of competition which has evolved. On the slope, aerobatic models are entirely feasible, as are pylon racers and cross-country machines. Actual duration is fairly meaningless when a model can stay up till the wind dies or the batteries run out. Thermal models can measure skill in achieving minimum flight times (i.e. duration) and can com-

pete in speed and distance events, usually round a quadrilateral course. Both types of flying combine different events into multi-task competitions, and in both there is a growing swing to scale or stand-off scale sailplanes.

Model sizes vary from under 2m (6ft) for an aerobatic slope machine to 7m (23ft) scale-type models. Other than maximum sizes and weights allowed for any model by various governments there are no restrictions on slope soarers in average competitions, but for flying from the flat there are one or two categories, one of the most popular being the '100' class, limited to 100in (2.5m) span.

In some scale classes a division is made between vintage gliders, perhaps pre-1950, 'standard' and open categories. A standard machine is a model of one of the full-size 15m class gliders; scales in normal use are $\frac{1}{5}$ or $\frac{1}{6}$, and a 15m glider at $\frac{1}{6}$ size is 2.5m, or back to a 100in model. These models are becoming very popular for slope soaring; at present there is simply Class 2, which demands reasonable adherence to scale but does not require details such as a fully-fitted cockpit. No doubt in due course a Class 1 category will come into being. There is again a difference between models built for slope or flat soaring in that

*Below:* Slope lift in diagrammatic form.
*Opposite, top:* Even quite a gentle slope will provide enough lift in the right wind conditions.
*Opposite, bottom:* A high aspect ratio glider. Span is unlimited but area must not exceed 150sq dm and weight 5kg.

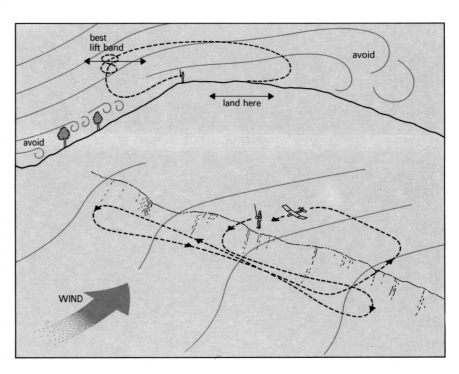

the former fly better with bi-convex section wings, but thermal soarers are likely to produce higher performance if built lighter and with flat-bottomed or undercambered wings.

Some multi-task models are fitted with storage for water ballast, or are designed to carry solid ballast, to increase flying speed while maintaining much the same rate of sink. For a cross-country or speed event, where the model can quickly find lift in an emergency, this may have advantages, as it may when flying in strong winds. In multi-task events, however, often three separate tasks are set in one flight, the first being aerobatics, where the additional ballast is likely to prove a disadvantage.

Many gliding events, slope or flat, incorporate points for landing on or close to a marked spot, and some incorporate with this a precise flight time. Air brakes or spoilers are helpful for accurate landings but for fun competitions are a complication that a newcomer may care to omit.

As a first model, something with reasonable inherent stability is desirable, and a guide is the amount of dihedral compared with other gliders. Reasonable dihedral, or polyhedral, suggests the likelihood of other stability factors being generous. Rudder and elevator control are all that is needed – most experts advise against ailerons for a first model. A built-up structure may take longer, but is cheaper and straightforward and, most importantly, is easier to repair. Something between 2 and 2.5m (80–100in) span is usual for a trainer for either slope or flat.

## Construction

A lot of R/C gliders use glass fibre (grp) fuselages, a few moulded ABS, but the majority use built-up wings. Veneer-covered foam wings are available in kits, or as separately-purchased wing kits, but a surprising percentage of models are built-up throughout.

Construction follows conventional style, except that the length of components is usually greater

*Above:* A simple boxy model equipped with a power pod. The engine is a means of gaining height in place of a towline.

are sometimes seen.

Ailerons are used on all aerobatic models and most top contest gliders, but it is illuminating to note that only one quarter of the scores of currently available kits are designed for more than rudder and elevator. To travel really fast round a quadrilateral speed (pylon) course requires vertical turns at the corners, for which ailerons are essential, and without them a full aerobatic task could not be performed.

A closely faired hinge line is required to maintain efficiency, since the aileron will of necessity be long and narrow on a high aspect ratio wing, and such a wing is less willing to roll, so the aileron needs to occupy a fair area. This reluctance to roll fast is why most top aerobatic gliders are under 2m span and usually have rather lower aspect-ratios. Some advanced models provide, by means of a second servo, a flap effect by drooping both ailerons without affecting the differential aileron action. These are called 'flaperons' and have the effect of increasing lift (and drag) for flying at reduced speed. A development is to have the entire wing adjustable in camber while still retaining differential movement for aileron control. Precise building is necessary to benefit from any of these refinements.

## Radio

There is little unusual in radio installation except that linkages tend to be longer and therefore care must be taken to prevent bowing. Frequently 'snakes' are used – a stiff nylon tube sliding inside another; the outer tube can be anchored at regular intervals to the structure and thus cannot distort.

Mounting the battery pack in the extreme nose is usual, depending on its effect on the overall balance of the model. Most builders try to avoid extra ballast on the average model, moving the radio gear to balance out before permanently installing it. Wrapping the batteries and receiver in foam is customary, as is the use of adhesive pads for the servos. The aerial can be taken outside or, if the fuselage is long enough, carried inside, through a plastic reed from a sunblind or a series of drinking straws to prevent possible tangling with the control linkages.

Radio functions are usually rudder and elevator, and possibly ailerons. Other functions might be

than the average building board; veneered chipboard can provide a reasonable board up to about 2.5m long. Wing mounting depends on the degree of cleanliness required, and for a first model or a trainer the crash-resistant advantages of rubber-banding the wing in place, with the halves tongued or dowelled together, should be employed. Shoulder-wing gliders can use a fuselage tongue or dowels with boxes or tubes in the wing halves, and it is also possible to buy moulded wing-mounting strips which adequately locate the wings, using concealed rubber bands, passing through tubes, in the fuselage.

This type of fixing is not always recommended for large towline models, which take a considerable strain on the wings, but enables a a nice clean joint to be made on slope models and moderate size towliners. Because of the strain when towed, spar strength is higher than on most other types of model.

All-sheet tail surfaces are frequently employed, with the tailplane often fixed in place with nylon bolts, the idea being that these will shear if enough force is applied. The amount of force is, however, likely to damage the structure. Some experts use nylon bolts to secure the wing, with the philosophy that a bad landing with the model is going to damage it anyway. Fully floating (i.e. all-moving) tailplanes and even fins

spoilers, flaps and releasable tow-hook or water ballast release, the water being carried in a plastic bottle on the CG and dumped through a large diameter thin rubber tube normally kept folded closed by a servo.

**Other launch methods**
On quite a number of gliders it is possible to attach a small power pod with an engine of 1 to 1½cc (0.06–0.09cu.in) which will climb the model to a good height in a minute or so, when it reverts to being a soarer. The drag of the pod and small propeller has some effect on the glide, but long flights are common and it is a simple means of getting the glider up, especially for single-handed fliers. The pod is usually mounted above the wing

centre-section and if over the CG, does not affect the towing or slope-soaring capabilities with the pod removed. A limit of 2cc (0.12cu.in) is placed on engines for competition flying, with a run of 45 seconds.

Aero towing is quite feasible, using a docile and very controllable power model and 15m or so of nylon monofilament line. The line is attached above and slightly aft of the tug's CG and to the extreme nose of the glider. Flaps on the tug and airbrakes on the glider help to balance flying speeds and keep the towline straight, but the line should be releasable from either model in an emergency. This is rather getting away from the basic advantages of gliding – simplicity, virtually nil running costs and no noise – but is an enjoyable diversion.

*Above:* Preparing for a towline launch with the flier making a last-minute check on controls. Note the pennant on the line just ahead of the model and the nose-up attitude in which the assistant is holding the model. Towing must be dead into wind, checked just before launch by observing the curve of the towline, which should hang vertically between model and tower.

# Power and Sport

It is often suggested that a glider is the best sort of model on which to learn to fly R/C, and this is true so far as self-tuition is concerned. Many model gliders will almost fly themselves and, as long as they are kept straight into wind, will land themselves in a way that few power models would. Unfortunately, learning to fly the glider qualifies the beginner to do no more than that. It is still likely to take time and practice to adapt to a power model, particularly the tricky landing phase.

For this reason, it is considered better for the prospective R/C flier to start with a conventional engine-powered model and learn to fly with the help of an experienced instructor via one of the various 'dual control' systems, where the transmitters of the student and instructor are joined by a special link and the instructor is provided with a switch which enables him to 'hand over' to the student or take control himself at will and instantly by releasing the 'over to you' button. This is particularly important during the phase of instruction where the pupil is learning to land. From about 15m (50ft) until the model is on the ground, split-second reversion to instructor control is often the only factor in deciding whether the model lands intact or is reduced to a pile of expensive litter.

## Choosing a model

A bewildering array of models claimed to be suitable for beginners is now available, and, since the novice will not yet appreciate the finer points of model design, he would probably be well advised to get his prospective instructor to decide for him.

A few years ago it would have been considered imperative to start with one of the established, docile 'trainer' types, but many beginners now start with a more advanced type of model, sometimes even a low-wing scale design. Provided that an experienced instructor and dual control are available, this approach has the merit of making a better pilot of the novice, though it will usually take longer before he 'goes solo' than if he had elected to use the 'stable trainer' course. The best advice is to find the instructor first, then be guided by him as to the choice of model.

For the beginner unable to find a willing and qualified instructor, a primary trainer is absolutely essential, or, better still, one of the excellent 'powered gliders' available in kit form. The 'do-it-yourself' trainee would also be wise to study the various magazines and books on the subject; although this has its pitfalls, there is much to be learned and the study of the working drawings usually appearing in magazines can be particularly useful.

## Construction

Confusion for the beginner is likely to arise on the question of the most suitable type of construction for his first model. In the early days of R/C flying there was very little choice – a strip balsa framework covered with paper, silk or nylon. The first variation on this theme was the 'foam wing' described in Chapter 12; tail surfaces are another obvious use of the foam/veneer formula. In recent years they have even been used for quite major fuselage components such as curved rear top decks, engine fairings and so on. More commonly, however, plastic materials are used to mould the entire fuselage; sheet plastic 'ABS' is perhaps the most common. Vacuum forming is used to produce two thin plastic half shells which the modeller is left to join and complete with the necessary internal fittings and stiffeners. These fuselages work quite well in spite of their flexible, 'squeezable' nature, but sometimes, especially with more powerful engines, they tend to develop cracks at stress points, which recur even after repeated repair.

Best of all, perhaps, is the glass fibre fuselage, usually presented to the kit purchaser as a complete shell with just the internal fittings to be added. These fuselages are very resilient and usually have a fine finish but are expensive and usually, for a given strength, rather heavier than the corresponding fuselage of conventional balsa construction.

Properly designed, the old-fashioned balsa skeleton type of construction is by no means outmoded, for some applications, at any rate. Because of the low inertia of the light individual members of the structure, crash damage is often limited to the actual point of impact and the paper or fabric covered structure is easy to piece together again. Modern sheet/block/plastic structures, on the other hand, have relatively high inertia and often parts of the airframe quite remote from the 'scene of the accident' are badly damaged. Foam wings damaged by crumpling or crushing can be repaired only by cutting out and replacing all the damaged material, followed by the tricky process of splicing into place a new section of veneer covering. If the damage affects more than about one tenth of the total structure, replacement is more economical than repair.

There is plenty of room for both old and new construction techniques; the achievement of a satisfactory end product, that is, a flyable model aeroplane, is mainly dependent on the knowledge, skill and patience of the builder.

## Before flying

Assuming that the beginner has produced an appropriate model, installed a suitable engine, fuel system and R/C outfit and found an experienced pilot to teach him to fly it, it might be thought that nothing remains but to go out to the flying site and get on with it. There is, however, just one final, important formality which should be completed at least a day or two before the proposed first flight. This is an all-embracing check of the aeroplane and its control system. The whole airframe should be checked for integrity and compliance with design. All units, screws and other fixtures should be locked against vibration and the fuel proofing of the outer finish carefully checked. If fuel gets into any of the woodwork, this can be considered a disaster of the first magnitude. The engine installation and fuel system should receive a careful going-over. Engines of the almost universal single cylinder two-stroke type cannot be completely balanced, so some level of vibration is bound to be present and anything that *can* shake loose, sooner or later *will* shake loose, perhaps with serious results.

Fuel tanks are usually of the plastic bottle type, described in Chapter 13, in which three pipes run through the cap. This kind of system is nearly fool-proof as long as the flexible pipes are secured to

*Opposite:* Radio-controlled pylon racers require experience and quick reflexes—among four models at perhaps 240kph (150mph) on a tight course is no place for a beginner!

the rigid ones by a tight turn or two of copper wire and the tank cap seals properly. The flexible pipes should be renewed from time to time, especially the one inside the tank, while the vent pipes inside the tank should point vertically upwards to end at the highest part of the tank; these sometimes 'creep' out of position which makes it impossible to fill the tank completely. Obviously, the tank should be made accessible so that it can be got at with the minimum of dismantling, in order to make these periodic examinations.

The radio equipment should be installed in accordance with the maker's instructions, paying particular attention to antenna location. The most common error made by beginners is failing to get full and free movement of all the controls. Check, particularly, that the throttle servo is not stalled at the full throttle position, a position normally occupied for most of the flight, as this can easily result in complete loss of control after a few minutes, due to the abnormally high battery consumption, especially if the flight controls are also a bit stiff and causing their servos to take more current than normal.

The flying surfaces should be carefully checked for alignment and compliance with the designed rigging. An experienced modeller can do this by eye, sighting the model from some distance directly astern, but the less experienced should chock up the model in the level flight position on a bench and verify the rigging by measurement. At the same time the centre of gravity should be checked. If this is incorrect, small adjustments can be made by re-locating the radio battery or in more extreme cases, adding ballast. In this connection it should be noted that, due to the balance point being about a quarter of the model's total length back from the nose, a tail heavy condition of 28g (1oz) will need 85g (3oz) of ballast in the nose to correct it, so it is well to keep in mind during the entire construction of the model that the tail end must at all costs not be overweight.

This final check-out phase should always be a leisurely, contemplative operation. Nearly always,

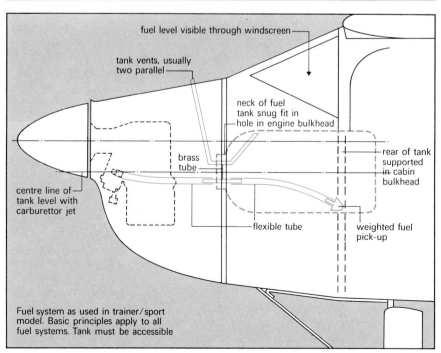

fuel level visible through windscreen

tank vents, usually two parallel

neck of fuel tank snug fit in hole in engine bulkhead

brass tube

rear of tank supported in cabin bulkhead

centre line of tank level with carburettor jet

flexible tube

weighted fuel pick-up

Fuel system as used in trainer/sport model. Basic principles apply to all fuel systems. Tank must be accessible

the modeller will find that by simply looking at and thinking about the new model, a number of important snags will be eliminated that might have gone unnoticed in a check-out conducted at a brisker pace. One thing is quite certain. It is impossible to give a new model a sufficiently thorough inspection at the flying field, with its distractions and lack of facilities, and any R/C model aeroplane, even of the simplest type, costs far too much in time and effort to risk flying it without the most strenuous probing to eliminate all possible snags. It should be noted that, when the model is in flight, almost any malfunction or structural failure will lead to immediate disaster.

## First flights

And so, finally, the great day arrives when the model is taken to the flying site for its first flight. In the early days, there would probably have been a long wait for suitable weather, but, providing that an experienced pilot does the test flights, the weather is not now a very important factor. If the instructor helped with the previous check-out, he will be able to proceed more or less at once, but if not, he will do a careful test of the controls and probably range-check the radio; a typical set is considered to be 'within limits' if the radio functions perfectly at 50 paces with the transmitter antenna fully retracted. The instructor will want to check the flying surfaces for any mis-alignment that might have gone unnoticed, as well as the location of the all-important balance point. The engine will be run-up to check that it will hold full power and idle slowly and reliably. Most instructors have got fairly blasé about first flights, and if all has gone well so far, take off will be marked with little more than a nod of the head by way of ceremonial – an epic occasion for the beginner but an everyday experience for the instructor. For this reason, he is unlikely to have overlooked any serious snag.

The first and essential part of any training flight is the 'pre-flight briefing'. Little will be achieved unless the pupil knows exactly what he is supposed to be doing, why he is supposed to be doing it, and, most important, given a few minutes to think about it. Flight training is one of those activities where going too quickly can waste a lot of time!

The first exercise will consist of

the instructor taking the model off, bringing it round in a climbing circuit and first giving the student control just after the model has gone overhead, into wind, the object of this phase being simply to fly the model straight ahead, into wind at a steady height. This is perhaps the most difficult and discouraging part of learning to fly. Most people who have not flown R/C tend to think, 'You push the stick to the left and it goes left, to the right and it goes right, what could be simpler?' Anyone who has 'had a go', however, knows that there is a lot more to it than that. The first shock is to find that with both sticks central, the model does not necessarily fly straight and level, much less does it recover to straight and level flight simply because the sticks have been released! Another difficulty is that of deciding just how much the individual sticks should be displaced and for how long, to achieve a required

change of attitude. This is complicated further because the effect of the controls varies with airspeed, and, as soon as the model starts to turn, the nose starts to drop. This in turn causes the airspeed to increase which further causes the rudder effectiveness to increase. So that what frequently starts as a gentle turn quickly develops into a screaming downward spiral with no help from the pilot at all!

So when the prospective pilot has learned to fly more or less straight at a more or less constant height, while the model is *going away from him* (the significance of the underlining will be apparent in a minute) he is then introduced to turns.

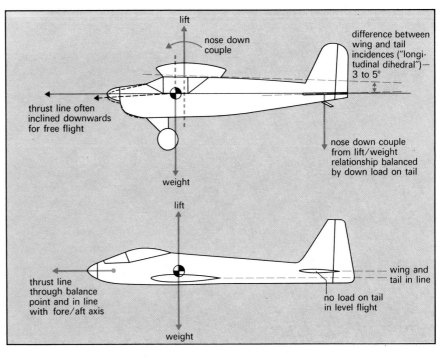

lift
nose down couple
difference between wing and tail incidences ("longitudinal dihedral")— 3 to 5°
thrust line often inclined downwards for free flight
weight
nose down couple from lift/weight relationship balanced by down load on tail

lift
thrust line through balance point and in line with fore/aft axis
wing and tail in line
no load on tail in level flight
weight

Contrary to possible expectation, these do not consist of applying rudder until the desired heading is achieved, then bringing it back to central. What really happens is that rudder (it is assumed that the trainer will not have ailerons, if it does, simply read 'aileron' for every reference to 'rudder') is applied in the appropriate direction. This causes the model to both yaw and roll in that direction, but while the rudder is held on, it *continues* to build up the roll and yaw, so that as soon as the model's wings are banked over at, say 30° (usual for training turns) the rudder has to be centralized or even moved a little in the opposite direction, to prevent the turn steepening. At the same time, the nose will have markedly dropped so that some up elevator will have to be applied to maintain height and airspeed. To *stop* the turn, the correcting control movements have to be applied a little before the desired heading is reached (because of the time taken for the controls to take effect, plus the inertia of the model). This consists of applying rudder in the direction opposite to the turn, neutralizing as the wings level, releasing the up elevator, or, if as is likely, the speed *has* been allowed to build up during the turn, apply a little down elevator to prevent the consequent 'zoom'.

The final obstacle to be overcome before going on to take-offs and landings is to learn to operate the rudder 'back to front' when the model is coming towards the pilot. Obviously, when the model is going away, left is left and right is right. But when it is coming back, a turn to the model's left becomes a turn to the *pilot's right*. All a bit tricky to work out in the split seconds available, so it pays to do the thinking before the flight rather than during it. Even after getting the hang of it for some time, most novice pilots will suffer the odd lapse of concentration and try to recover from a right turn by applying the right rudder.

All this will take some time – quite a few flying sessions, perhaps, and can be quite discouraging in the early stages as the novice makes the same old mistakes time after time and begins to wonder if there is a streak of insanity in his family! However, it really does get easier, and by the time the instructor deems it appropriate to start circuit training, the pupil will be reasonably confident that he can direct the model into a specified piece of

sky and even keep it more or less the right way up in the process. From all this, it will be appreciated that, even with a docile training aeroplane, an experienced instructor and dual control, learning to fly R/C models is not easy. It is certainly not impossible to teach yourself, but the difficult bit comes right at the beginning, so you cannot 'work your way up' to the tricky bits.

*Below:* This Sopwith 1½ Strutter makes a docile flying model, though not too easy on takeoff and landing. The name comes from the wing strut arrangement.

**"CROSSWIND LEG"**

3 reduce power to fly level before turning downwind

height about 100 m

model has to crab to maintain track at 90° to runway centre line

practise circuits both ways

wind

2 gentle turn crosswind

climbing on full power

100 m

"DOWNWIND LEG"

1 after take-off, maintain track on extended centre line to about 100 m upwind

6 aim to be at 30 m height about 70 m from runway threshold. Vary power as necessary, keep speed constant

if wind is not lined-up with runway, model will have to "crab" to fly along centre line

4 reduce power to start descent

if too low increase power and bend base leg toward runway

"FINAL"

5 vary power as necessary to give required rate of descent

if much too high, bend base leg downwind

"BASE LEG"

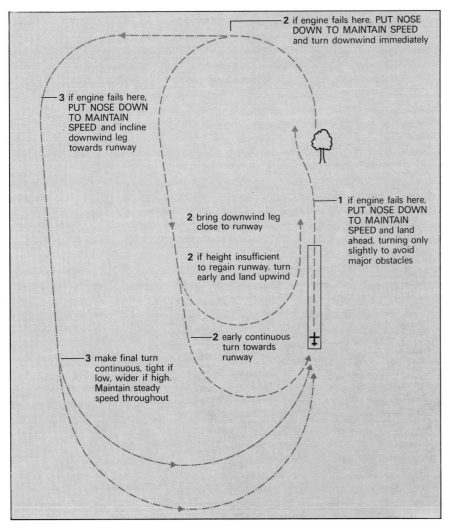

2 if engine fails here, PUT NOSE DOWN TO MAINTAIN SPEED and turn downwind immediately

3 if engine fails here, PUT NOSE DOWN TO MAINTAIN SPEED and incline downwind leg towards runway

2 bring downwind leg close to runway

2 if height insufficient to regain runway, turn early and land upwind

1 if engine fails here, PUT NOSE DOWN TO MAINTAIN SPEED and land ahead, turning only slightly to avoid major obstacles

3 make final turn continuous, tight if low, wider if high. Maintain steady speed throughout

2 early continuous turn towards runway

With trainers of the type specified, take-offs are relatively easy and most instructors will encourage the pupil to have a go as soon as he has shown that he can keep the model straight without dramatic losses of height. With the usual tricycle undercarriage model it is a matter of applying full power, keeping the model straight into wind and holding some up elevator until the model leaves the ground, then adjusting the elevator to give a steady climb. The circuit will be best understood by reference to the diagrams. Although apparently straightforward, such terms as 'adjust base leg as necessary to arrive at final position one hundred feet high and fifty yards downwind' do involve shrewd judgement of speed, height and distance. As in full-size flying you cannot do a good landing unless you first do a good approach. This again takes time. First exercises will consist of dummy approaches when the model will 'overshoot' back into the climb after getting down to, say, twenty feet, but thereafter, any approach that looks good will be continued right down to the ground.

With the usual tricycle undercart, the landing, although involv-ing quite a bit of quick judgement, is relatively simple. The model is held straight in a steady glide down to about six feet, then up elevator is progressively applied, a little at first, more as the decreasing airspeed reduces the effectiveness of the elevator. Just before touch down, the stick will have to be fairly well back to ensure that the main wheels touch down before the nose wheel. If the nose wheel hits first, a pretty horrific bounce usually follows, and if this happens it is safer to open the throttle fully and climb away for another try. A somewhat illogical error many novices are guilty of is to open up the throttle less than fully when they have decided to abandon a landing. Staggering around on part-power at very low altitude is the very last thing you want, so, whenever you decide to 'go round again' always apply full power, smoothly, of course, but fairly quickly.

Some instructors regard this as the end of the matter, but the more imaginative ones include one final stage before the pupil is allowed to fly on his own. This consists of dealing with emergency situations. Loss of power soon after take-off is perhaps the most common one. The

remedy seems obvious, simply put down the nose to maintain airspeed and land straight ahead. But even this is complicated, in that, having taken off – say fifty yards – climbed to fifty feet – then glided down, the model is quite a long way from the pilot and so judgement of the landing is quite difficult. If there are obstructions or irregularities in the lie of the ground the pilot may not be able even to *see* the model at the point of touch-down.

Engine failures later in the circuit entail doing something of a normal circuit but much abbreviated, and the important thing here is to decide what to do and then do it quickly. The widespread practice of getting the model some way-downwind of the landing area, quite low, then 'dragging it in' with quite a lot of power is another possible cause of serious trouble if the engine stops unexpectedly. If there is smooth ground downwind of the landing area, all well and good. If not, unnecessary damage will be done to the model which will hold up the training. The best technique is to turn 'final' at such a height that the throttle will be more or less closed from that point down to the runway. If the engine then stops at some point during this phase, although the glide will steepen slightly with no engine – 'dead stick' or 'fan stop' are the slang terms – unless you are cutting it pretty fine, you will still get into the landing area.

By this stage, the budding R/C pilot will have already flown several times entirely unassisted with the instructor merely standing-by in case of difficulty, but there are one or two final points that the conscientious instructor will want to cover. Most important and usually demonstrated rather than practised, is to acquaint the pupil with what happens when a heavily loaded, possibly under-powered model leaves the ground when it is travelling too slowly. This often takes the form of a sharp climb to about ten feet followed suddenly by an uncontrollable roll to either side. This is caused by the model stalling as soon as it gets out of the 'ground cushion' familiar to hovercraft enthusiasts, and the roll is caused by the fact that the engine, running at full power and generating a lot of torque reaction, suddenly overpowers the controlling force as the wing stalls. This will be demonstrated at a safe height, of course, and with a more advanced type of model.

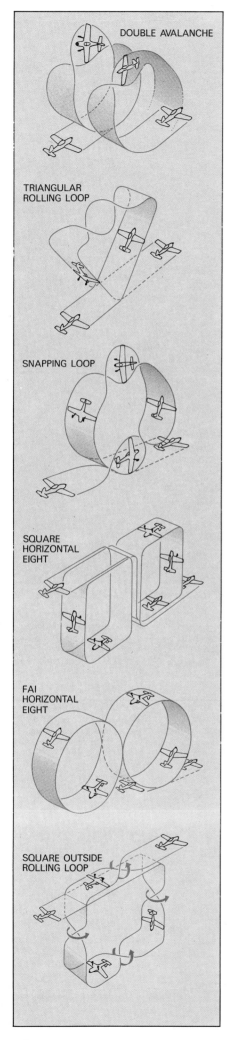

DOUBLE AVALANCHE

TRIANGULAR ROLLING LOOP

SNAPPING LOOP

SQUARE HORIZONTAL EIGHT

FAI HORIZONTAL EIGHT

SQUARE OUTSIDE ROLLING LOOP

The same model will be used to demonstrate what happens if full power is applied suddenly when the model is flying on the point of the stall – probably an uncontrollable 'flick' or 'snap' roll in which the falling wing is *stalled* while the other is still flying. A spin is exactly the same thing in a different plane. In these circumstances, the model cannot be brought under control until the offending wing is un-stalled, either by an opposing yaw from the rudder or by increasing speed or both.

The novice will by now be getting quite competent, and will be able to operate on his own and at this stage will be looking around for his 'follow on' model. If he has started with a simple trainer, it is a good idea to have the construction of his second model actually under way while his initial training is still going on. That way he is ready to make the transition to the 'intermediate' type as soon as his flying skill reaches the required level.

Since flying scale models seems to be the ultimate aim of most R/C modellers, an ideal choice for the second model is one of the semi-scale 'stand-off scale' or 'S.O.S.' models of which there are a number on the market. The 'stand-off' bit refers to the fact that they are not intended to be subject to close scrutiny and that, in contests, the judges do not approach closer than 5m (5½yds) when marking them for their 'static' scores. The choice of types is very wide. A 'Great War' type, such as the Sopwith '1½ Strutter' illustrated, is as easy to fly as most trainers and takes the same type of engine. It is mildly aerobatic, capable of loops, half rolls, rolls off the top, stall turns, and so on, but not very good on rolling manoeuvres. With its high centre of gravity and narrow undercarriage take-offs and landings have to be executed with care to avoid tipping over. Cross-wind landings are not its strong point.

Perhaps more modellers are attracted by the World War 2 fighter types, however, and there are plenty of these to choose from, Spitfires being, of course, the most popular, closely followed by Mustangs and Me 109s. The Mustang with its long nose and wide track undercart is perhaps the easiest for the not-too-experienced modeller and again, need not be any more difficult to fly than the average non-

Advanced aerobatics demanded of fliers at the annual Championship of Champions at Las Vegas.

scale intermediate model. Landings and take-offs, however, again need rather more accuracy than the novice will have been used to, particularly if he has trained on tricycle undercarriage types.

It might be apposite to point out that, from the take-off and landing point of view, the properly designed tricycle (main wheels well apart and 'at rest' attitude slightly nose down) is superior to the 'old fashioned' tail-wheel type undercarriage in every respect. To start with it is directionally stable whereas the tail-wheel type is not – sometimes to a distressing extent! Secondly, provided that the main wheels land before the nose-wheel touches, the nose will always pitch down on touch-down, so that the aeroplane 'stays down' with no tendency to bounce. The tail-wheel type is just the opposite in that if the mains and the tail-wheel do not touch down together – pretty difficult to do with most models – the nose pitches *up* and the model starts flying again, so the favourite is the 'wheel landing' in which the model is 'held-on' in the usual way, but not got down into the full 'three-point' tail down attitude. The moment the wheels touch, the back pressure on the stick is released and, if timed just right, this counteracts the natural 'pitch up' and the model stays down. Anyone who has tried it will realize that nice timing is involved.

For the modeller with interests other than scale, the delta is an exhilarating alternative. These models because of the elimination of parasitic appendages such as fuselage, tailplane, etc., have very low drag and can be fast even on quite modest engines. A model of the type illustrated, for instance, can be expected to attain speeds of up to 100mph, have a sparkling aerobatic repertoire (but in most cases not including spins and other flick manoeuvres) and yet be capable of flying slower than the average trainer, and landing and taking-off in the same or even less space. This latter feature is because the ultra-low 'aspect ratio' wing – that is, one in which the span is short, relative to the chord – has the unusual property of being able to fly at angles of attack something like twice as high – around 25° – as a conventional wing. Furthermore, instead of the fairly sharp 'break' at the stall experienced by a normal wing, the delta comes up to the stall so gently that no clearly definable break is usually detectable, so that it is virtually impossible to stall the delta accidentally. Every good proposition has its price, however, and the delta's drawback is that its triangular plan form makes it appear as just a flat 'line' when it is coming towards or going directly away from the pilot. This makes orientation – the beginner's number one problem – more difficult than usual, as it is very easy to misinterpret what is visible and misjudge the model's attitude. The high speed and, usually, sensitive controls tend to aggravate this situation.

Something quite different is the *autogiro*. This looks like a helicopter but at first acquaintance seems to handle like an aeroplane. In fact it is in many respects quite unlike either. Unlike the helicopter, however, it is easy to fly, once its idiosyncracies are appreciated, and anyone who has graduated from an ordinary trainer should have no difficulty converting to the autogiro. In some respects it is even easier to fly, as like the delta (but for a very different reason) it is impossible to provoke a normal, sharp stall. Instead, if the autogiro is flown too slowly, the rotors slow down and sink follows, but this speeds up the rotors. So, as long as there is height to spare, it is difficult to get into trouble with this configuration. One thing that has to be guarded against, particularly at low altitude, is the normal aeroplane pilot reaction to a too-slow situation of putting the nose down. This actually slows down the rotors at first, and a very high rate of sink develops before the rotors have time to catch up. A 'party trick' with the autogiro, in fact, is to do this deliberately – at a safe height, of course – if the nose is slammed down really hard the rotors stop altogether, which can be guaranteed to quicken the pulse!

Having become pretty competent with a range of different types of models, most enthusiasts, now approaching the 'expert' class, will want to specialize in some particular branch of the hobby. Some might go in for aerobatics, a pastime that needs practising as others practise the piano. Others might decide on pylon racing, in which four models at a time race around a triangular course at speeds occasionally exceeding 150mph. This combines many skills, particularly as far as tuning engines and 'cleaning up' the airframe is concerned. But it seems that the vast majority want to graduate to pure scale.

However much the specialists argue that model aircraft are aircraft in their own right and need owe nothing to full-size practice, most modellers, throughout the history of aeromodelling, have longed to produce models that look and fly like 'the real thing'. Some splendid free-flight and control-line flying replicas have been made and, less often, flown, but both forms have limitations, and it was not until reliable R/C arrived on the scene (and until modellers developed the necessary skills to complement it) that realistic scale model flight became a reality. Models that are realistic in appear-

*Top:* Autogiros are fun machines, almost guaranteed to mystify onlookers, since the rotors freewheel.
*Above:* Deltas always seem far faster than conventional models but can be more sensitive.

ance have now become so relatively commonplace that contest judges place great emphasis on requiring that the flight performance – speed, manoeuvrability, landing and take-off performance – shall simulate that of the original, too. Models of this standard invariably represent a vast investment in building time and nearly always in money as well, so be pretty sure of yourself before trying to fly anything of this sort!

# Helicopters

Although experiments with rotary winged aircraft may be traced back to Leonardo da Vinci, successful flights were not achieved until the 1930s, and it was not until 1941 that the first practical, full-size helicopter was built by Igor Sikorski.

Model enthusiasts are notably quick to emulate full-size aviation achievements, but were not as successful with rotary wing aircraft, and it was not until 1968 that the first fully controllable R/C model helicopter appeared, built by by Dr Dieter Schlüter of West Germany.

Many modellers were convinced that the single rotor autogiro would be an easier subject to tackle than the helicopter and were conducting their experiments along these lines, but in fact the first really successful British R/C autogiro, a semi-scale model of the Wallace Autogiro, was first flown in 1978, ten years after the first appearance of the R/C helicopter. Designers and manufacturers the world over were quick to take advantage of Schlüter's success and, in the early 1970s, model helicopter kits were on sale in the model shops.

## Basic principles

In order to appreciate the reasons for the slow development of the model helicopter, at least a few of the problems which faced the pioneers must be considered. These problems were many and complex; for instance: in order to achieve flight with any heavier-than-air machine, the lift force generated by its aerofoils must overcome the aircraft's weight. In the case of a conventional aircraft this is achieved by its forward speed through the air which flows across its aerofoil-sectioned wing, causing a speeding-up of the air, and thereby a reduction in pressure, over its upper surface. At the same time, pressure increases across its under-surface (Figure 1–1b).

The helicopter generates lift by the movement of its main blades through the air as it rotor turns. The blades have to be moved at high speed and at a comparatively high angle of attack in order to produce sufficient lift to raise the model into the air. Weight is critical and experimenters who discovered that their chosen engine had insufficient power to produce the required

lift were faced with a vicious circle. Fitting a larger engine to increase the available power also meant an increase in the weight to be lifted. Bigger engines require more fuel – more weight! Increasing the angle of the rotor blades in the airflow produces more lift, up to a point, but this also increases the drag of the blade which now requires more power to move it at the required speed.

All problems were eventually overcome and the fully controllable R/C model helicopter had arrived. There were, however, no short cuts in its development: engines, drive gears, rotor blades, control methods, etc. all had to follow a similar design to full-size helicopters, and be built to the same exacting standards.

How difficult is the model helicopter to control in flight? Well, it has been described as similar to balancing a steel ball on a knife edge while riding a bicycle! But more on that later – first we shall examine the methods by which helicopters are controlled.

Imagine the helicopter at rest on the ground, rotors stationary. Air

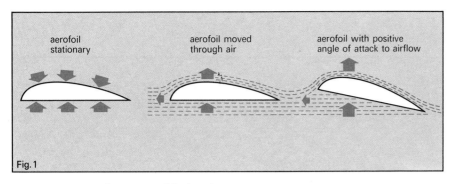

Fig. 1

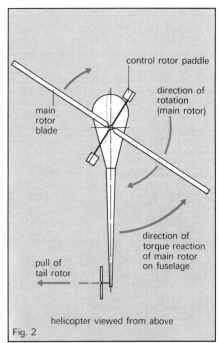

control rotor paddle

direction of rotation (main rotor)

main rotor blade

direction of torque reaction of main rotor on fuselage

pull of tail rotor

helicopter viewed from above

Fig. 2

pressure over the rotor blades is consistent with Figure 1. Now start the rotor turning and gradually increase its speed of rotation. Lift will, of course, increase as the speed of the airflow over the rotor blades increases and if the rotor speed is increased to a point where the lift generated is greater than the aircraft's weight, it will be lifted into the air. As the model becomes free of contact with the ground, the torque reaction of the lifting rotor will turn the fuselage of the model about the rotor's axis in the opposite direction to that in which the rotor blades are turning and it is to counteract this torque effect that the tail rotor is fitted, mounted vertically at the rear of the fuselage (Figure 2). The angle at which the tail rotor blades meet the airflow as they turn (angle of attack) is controllable by the pilot and he adjusts this angle to produce the exact sideways force required to counteract the torque of the lifting rotors.

The model is now in the air with the fuselage under control directionally, and, by use of the motor throttle control, the speed of rotation of the lifting rotor is adjusted to produce just sufficient lift to balance the weight of the helicopter, which is now hovering a few feet above the ground (Figure 3).

In order to achieve horizontal movement, an aerodynamic force in the direction required must be produced. Note that in Figure 3 the lift is acting at right angles, vertically upwards, to the rotor. If the rotor is now tilted as in Figure 3a, the lift (which will still act at right angles to the rotor blades) is also tilted, producing a force to move the helicopter in the direction of the tilt.

The plane of rotation of the rotor can be tilted either by tilting the rotor axis relative to the helicopter fuselage, or by varying the angle at which the individual blades of the rotor meet the airflow through certain sectors of the plane of rotation. The second method is the most common and, by this

*Opposite:* A Morley helicopter in flight. The main rotor is invisible but the flybar and tail rotor are clearly seen.

*This page:* The principles of helicopter flight must be understood before building or flying one. Lift and directional motion are straightforward, but precession is a phenomenon whose effects take a little grasping; the illustration overleaf may clarify it.

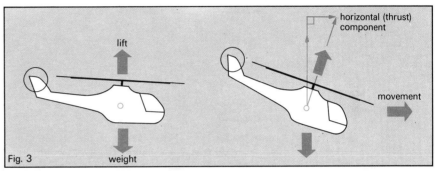

lift

weight

horizontal (thrust) component

movement

Fig. 3

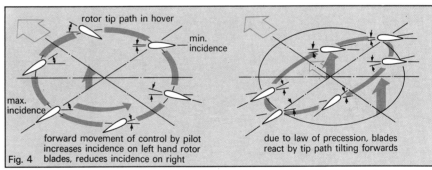

rotor tip path in hover

min. incidence

max. incidence

forward movement of control by pilot increases incidence on left hand rotor blades, reduces incidence on right

due to law of precession, blades react by tip path tilting forwards

Fig. 4

means, the angle of incidence of the rotor blades can be made to increase at one part of their rotation and decrease on the opposite side, producing the effect of tilting the rotor. This is known as cyclic pitch variation (Figure 4).

Note that in Figure 4 the maximum lift point of the blades is 90° before the point at which the maximum lifting force is needed to tilt the rotor forwards. The minimum incidence point is similarly 90° ahead of the required minimum force point. This is not an error: the Law of Gyroscopic Precession is used to effect control.

## Gyroscopic precession

One of the more complex problems which had to be overcome during the design of the helicopter was the

gyroscopic effect of the main rotor. Briefly, gyroscopic principles apply to any rotating mass such as a flywheel, propeller, etc., the main principle being 'rigidity in space', or the tendency of a spinning mass to resist any changes in its plane of rotation. 'Precession' is the reaction of any rotating mass, or gyroscope, to any force applied in an attempt to change its plane of rotation.

Figure 5 shows a disc at rest, balanced at its centre, which will react to an external force at the point at which that force is applied. Figure 5a shows the disc spinning; it has now become a gyroscope which, when subjected to an external force, will not react at the point of the applied force, but at 90° to that point – in the direction of

*Right:* The law of precession illustrated. Owners of toy gyroscopes will already be familiar with the effects.
*Below:* Cyclic pitch control of the fly-bar paddles by means of a swash plate is the most usual method of control.
*Below, right:* The operation of the fly-bar is to tilt the rotor head, producing horizontal movement of the whole machine.
*Bottom:* Scale appearance of model helicopters is helped by similar principles of control.

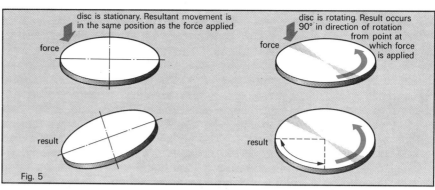

disc is stationary. Resultant movement is in the same position as the force applied

force

result

disc is rotating. Result occurs 90° in direction of rotation from point at which force is applied

force

result

Fig. 5

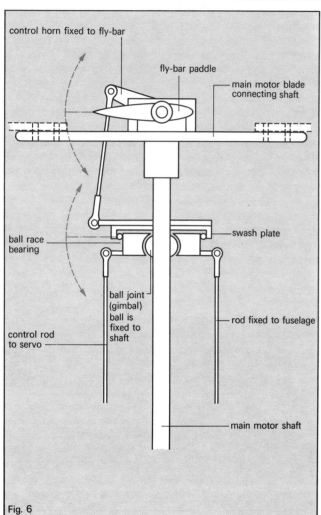

control horn fixed to fly-bar

fly-bar paddle

main motor blade connecting shaft

ball race bearing

control rod to servo

ball joint (gimbal) ball is fixed to shaft

swash plate

rod fixed to fuselage

main motor shaft

Fig. 6

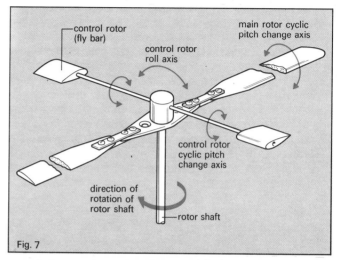

control rotor (fly bar)

control rotor roll axis

main rotor cyclic pitch change axis

control rotor cyclic pitch change axis

direction of rotation of rotor shaft

rotor shaft

Fig. 7

rotation of the disc. This is the Law of Gyroscopic Precession and, as the rotating rotor of the helicopter is a gyroscope, this law must be taken into account when a force is applied to tilt the rotor. Figure 4a shows the resultant forward tilt of the rotor caused by the gyroscopic precession of the forces (maximum and minimum lift) applied to the rotor in Figure 4.

Full control is now achieved: vertically by adjustment of engine power, horizontally by use of cyclic pitch, and fuselage pointing in whichever direction we wish by use of the tail rotor.

A further control feature, collective pitch (not used on all model helicopters as it is not really necessary in order to achieve controlled flight), allows the pilot to control the average angle of incidence of all the rotor blades simultaneously. Models which do have this control normally use it coupled to the throttle control, in that, as power is increased, blade angle is also increased and vice versa. It does have many advantages, but can be complicated and costly.

## Model practice

Model helicopters of various designs are now readily obtainable in kit form, or ready-built: these include purpose-designed training models with stark, open frame fuselages, semi-scale and true scale models. Practically all of these follow the same general layout of mechanical components.

The interests of R/C enthusiasts vary considerably. Some find equal interest in both the construction and flying of their models, others build but do not fly, while a high percentage of enthusiasts dislike all aspects of construction and purchase models ready-built. The latter course is quite acceptable even for the raw beginner, but only if the model is one of a conventional aircraft. The newcomer to the exacting hobby of R/C model helicopters *must* build his model, for it is essential that he fully understands the working of even the most minute component. Before each flying session, even after he has become fully competent as a pilot, he must check thoroughly every part of his model for security and correct operation. One loose bolt or out-of-balance rotor blade could result in a very expensive crash. The individual components can be taken in turn to go through an imaginary building sequence.

Fuselages vary, but they are all basically a platform for the mechanics and are straightforward as regards construction.

The motor will be air cooled and, if the fuselage used is one of the stark, open-frame type, will, apart from added cooling area of the cylinder finning, be indistinguishable from a standard model aircraft glow motor. It will rely on the downwash from the rotor blades and airflow around the fuselage for cooling. If the motor is totally enclosed within the fuselage, as on scale models, it will be fitted with its own cooling fan, normally connected to the motor drive shaft.

Model helicopters are fitted with a centrifugal clutch which disengages the drive to the rotors at low engine rpm. It is therefore necessary to fit a weighted flywheel to the crankshaft of the motor to achieve smooth, slow running. The flywheel is normally integral with the clutch, forming its inner cone, clutch shoes and centrifugal weights.

The model helicopter engine is normally started at a low throttle setting or 'idling' rpm. As engine speed increases, when the throttle is opened, the centrifugal weights of the clutch move outwards, engaging the clutch shoes with the outer body of the clutch, which is connected to the shaft which drives the reduction gears of the main rotor. The main rotor reduction gears are the answer to the pioneers' vicious circle power-to-weight problem.

The gear ratios are carefully calculated to permit the motor to produce its maximum torque while driving the rotors at the speed and angle of incidence which produce the maximum lift.

It is the normal practice, in order to keep the power section as compact as possible, for the reduction gearbox to include an angled drive to the main rotor shaft. The driving shaft of the tail rotor is normally an extension of a direct drive from the engine, and the tail rotor assembly includes its own reduction gearing.

The next component, one of the most important parts of the control system, is the Swash Plate. This is fitted on the main rotor shaft, below the rotor head. The swash plate is an infinitely variable stroke cam, and its function is to alter cyclically the angle of incidence of the control rotor blades (Figure 6).

Note that it is the 'angle of incidence of the *control* rotor blades', not main rotor blades. The helicopter rotor is subject to air irregularities: i.e. gusts of wind, ground effect, turbulence, etc., and if not fitted with a stabilizing device would be very difficult to control. A variety of such devices is used on full-size helicopters, but the most popular for use on models is based on the Hiller system. This is, in effect, a servo system. A bar, generally called the fly-bar, passes through the centre of the rotor head, set at 90° to the main rotor blades but in the same plane of rotation (Figure 7). Two small aerodynamic 'paddles' are fixed to the ends of the fly-bar, set at zero degrees incidence to the airflow. Turning, or twisting, the fly-bar will cause one paddle's angle of incidence to be increased and the

other's to be decreased. As the rotor turns at flying speed, the paddle having positive incidence will lift; the other, on the opposite end of the fly-bar, having negative incidence, will descend. The effect of this is to tilt the rotor head, increasing the angle of incidence of one rotor blade and decreasing the angle of the other.

By fitting paddles of carefully calculated size to the fly-bar, a damping force is obtained and the extra mass of the fly-bar improves the gyroscopic stability of the rotor. A further advantage of this sytem is that the force required to control the fly-bar is much less than would be required if the control system were connected direct to the main rotor.

The remainder of the components to be fitted makes up the rotor head assembly. There are basically three main types of rotor head which concern the modeller. 'Teetering', 'Articulated' and 'Rigid'. The 'Rigid' type is considered by the majority of enthusiasts to be the most suitable for all models; it is also the simplest to construct. As the name implies, it is fixed rigidly to the rotor shaft. The main lifting blades are interconnected by a shaft which passes through the rotor head; they can move as a single unit in the 'twisting' plane.

The fly-bar, which also has movemen in the 'twisting' plane, connects to the main blade shaft. It will now be apparent that the fly-bar is able to move around two axes: its own, and that of the main blade shaft, as, moving up or down, it changes the incidence of the main rotor blades. It is essential that the main rotor blades and the fly-bar are in perfect balance; if they are not, the vibration caused as the rotor turns can lead to structural failure.

## Radio installation

Most model helicopters require a four-function control system: two functions connected to the swash plate for cyclic pitch control, one to the tail rotor control and one to the engine throttle. The throttle control also serves the collective pitch control if fitted.

Positioning of the R/C system – receiver, servos and battery pack – within the helicopter fuselage varies with model type. The position is normally chosen with two

A scale Bell Jet Ranger. Flying a helicopter is totally different from any other type of model and by no means easy.

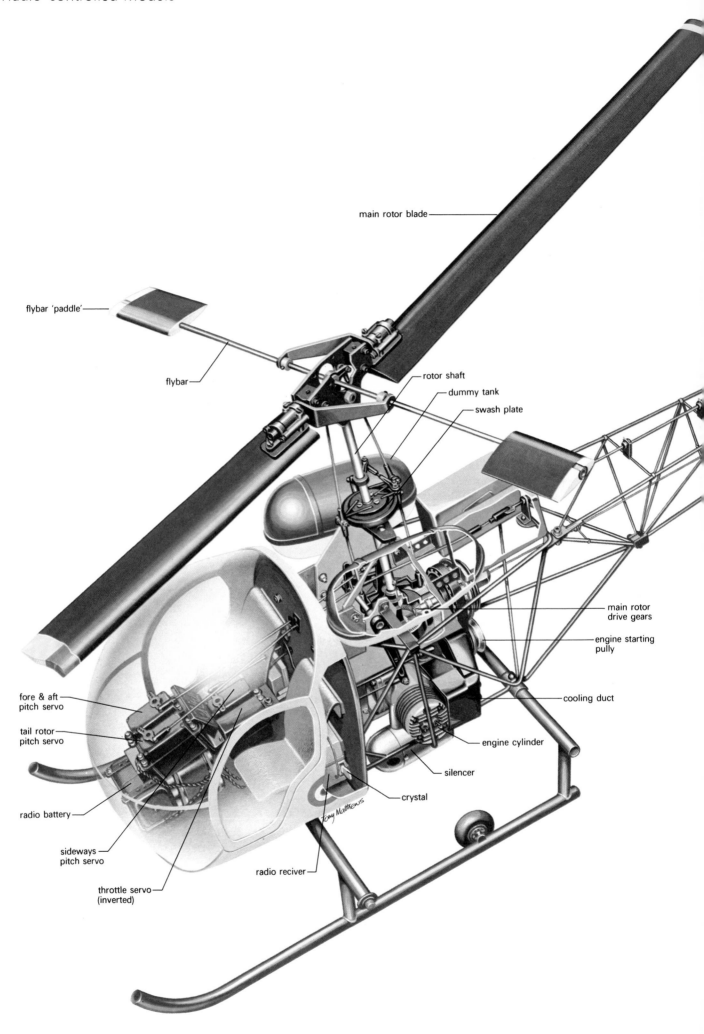

main rotor blade

flybar 'paddle'

flybar

rotor shaft

dummy tank

swash plate

main rotor
drive gears

engine starting
pully

cooling duct

engine cylinder

silencer

fore & aft
pitch servo

tail rotor
pitch servo

crystal

radio battery

sideways
pitch servo

radio reciver

throttle servo
(inverted)

Tony Matthews

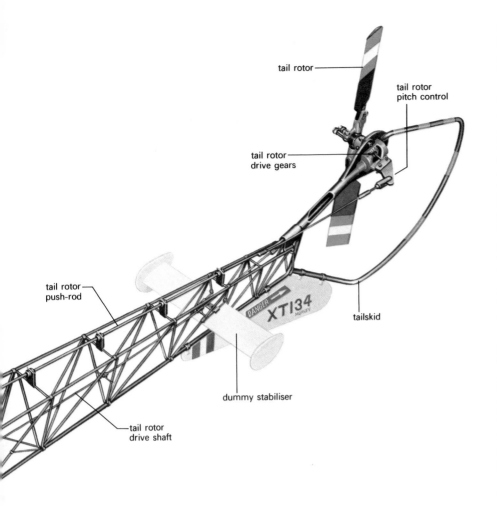

tail rotor

tail rotor
pitch control

tail rotor
drive gears

tail rotor
push-rod

tailskid

XT134

dummy stabiliser

tail rotor
drive shaft

noted. It is at this stage that the final rotor check for correct setting-up and balance is carried out – and the first lesson begins.

The power should be increased until the helicopter attempts to lift clear of the ground and the torque of the rotor starts to turn the fuselage. The trainee must now practise control of the tail rotor, with the object of keeping the fuselage pointed into the wind, at the same time continually adjusting the throttle control to maintain slight 'skidding' contact between ground and undercarriage. Having gained proficiency with the throttle and tail rotor controls, the trainee pilot is ready for 'hovering' practice and the right hand now comes into use with the cyclic control.

Starting again from the beginning, power should be increased until the undercarriage lifts clear of the ground, the tail rotor control being simultaneously adjusted to keep the fuselage pointed into the wind, and the trainee pilot should now practice 'hovering' the helicopter, or moving it gently away from himself.

It is unfortunate that these early training exercises have to be carried out in the worst possible conditions – just above the ground, where the model is subject to wind turbulence and ground effect of the rotor downwash. It will probably take hours of constant practice before the trainee can go further in the trainee programme; but once he has become proficient at hovering his model a few feet above the ground, the rest of it is comparatively easy – if flying a model helicopter can be said, at any time, to be easy! – and the trainee can now increase power and climb the model up and out of the ground effect.

It was often said of the model helicopter that once its controls had been mastered, it was boring to fly. In the early days of the model helicopter, there may have been truth in that statement, but not today. No longer is the helicopter pilot confined to take-offs, circuits and landings: now there are fully aerobatic models which satisfy even the most demanding pilot, and interest in the helicopter is fast increasing. They are now accepted in national competitions and world-wide associations have been formed. In the foreseeable future the radio control enthusiast will not have 'arrived' until he has completely conquered the controls of the model helicopter.

aims in mind: (1) to get the servos as close as possible to the control they operate; and (2) to place it where weight is most needed to adjust the model's centre of gravity to its best position.

When learning to fly, R/C enthusiasts would probably be unanimous in their agreement that the helicopter is the most difficult of all models to control and also the most difficult on which to instruct, as the early training exercises take place with the model so near the ground that it is practically impossible for the instructor to take over control from the pupil at a critical point to avoid mishap.

Most R/C model helicopter pilots teach themselves after carefully studying the detailed instructions which most manufacturers include with the helicopter kit. All of these follow practically the same system of teaching. The trainee pilot is advised to tackle one control at a time, starting with the tail rotor.

The R/C transmitter will normally have two control sticks; each of these will operate two control functions, all of which may be operated singly or simultaneously. It is usual to operate the tail rotor by lateral movement of the left control stick; vertical movement

of this stick operates the throttle control. The right-hand stick operates the cyclic pitch control; lateral movement controls the lateral movement of the rotor; vertical movement controls the pitching movement of the rotor. Helicopter controls are usually very sensitive, and very rarely during flight is either of the control sticks 'at rest'. Transmitter trays are now becoming very popular with helicopter pilots, supported by a neck strap and featuring wrist rests either side of the transmitter compartment. They provide a firm control platform, and cannot be recommended too strongly for the trainee.

**First Flights**

The model should be placed on flat ground, facing into the wind, with the motor idling just below the clutch engagement rpm; the pilot should stand about ten yards behind and to one side of the model. The throttle should be gradually opened; the rotors will commence to turn and the power should be increased until the rotors can be seen to be taking much of the model's weight. Next, the cyclic pitch control should be operated and the movement of the rotor

# Quasar

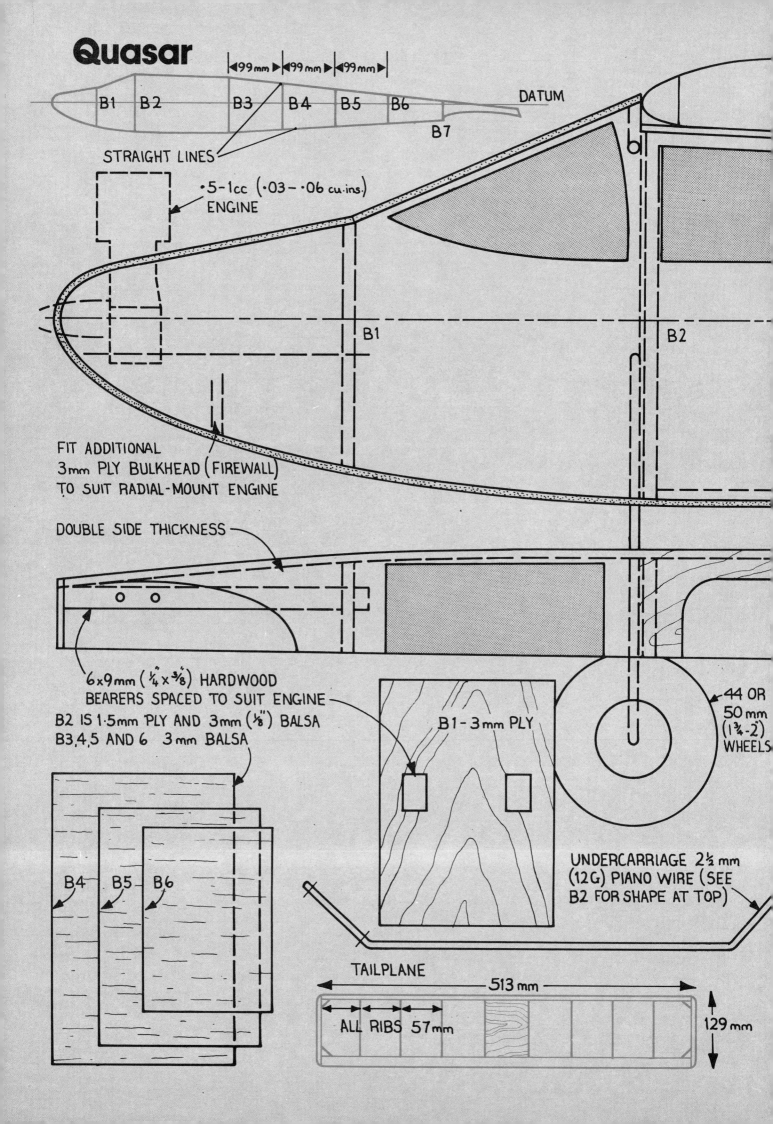

|←99 mm→|←99 mm→|←99 mm→|

B1  B2  B3  B4  B5  B6  B7

DATUM

STRAIGHT LINES

•5–1cc (•03 – •06 cu.ins.) ENGINE

FIT ADDITIONAL 3mm PLY BULKHEAD (FIREWALL) TO SUIT RADIAL-MOUNT ENGINE

DOUBLE SIDE THICKNESS

B1

B2

6×9mm (¼″ × ⅜″) HARDWOOD BEARERS SPACED TO SUIT ENGINE
B2 IS 1·5mm PLY AND 3mm (⅛″) BALSA
B3,4,5 AND 6  3mm BALSA

B1 – 3mm PLY

44 OR 50 mm (1¾ - 2″) WHEELS

B4  B5  B6

UNDERCARRIAGE 2½ mm (12G) PIANO WIRE (SEE B2 FOR SHAPE AT TOP)

TAILPLANE

|←————— 513 mm —————→|

ALL RIBS  57mm

129 mm

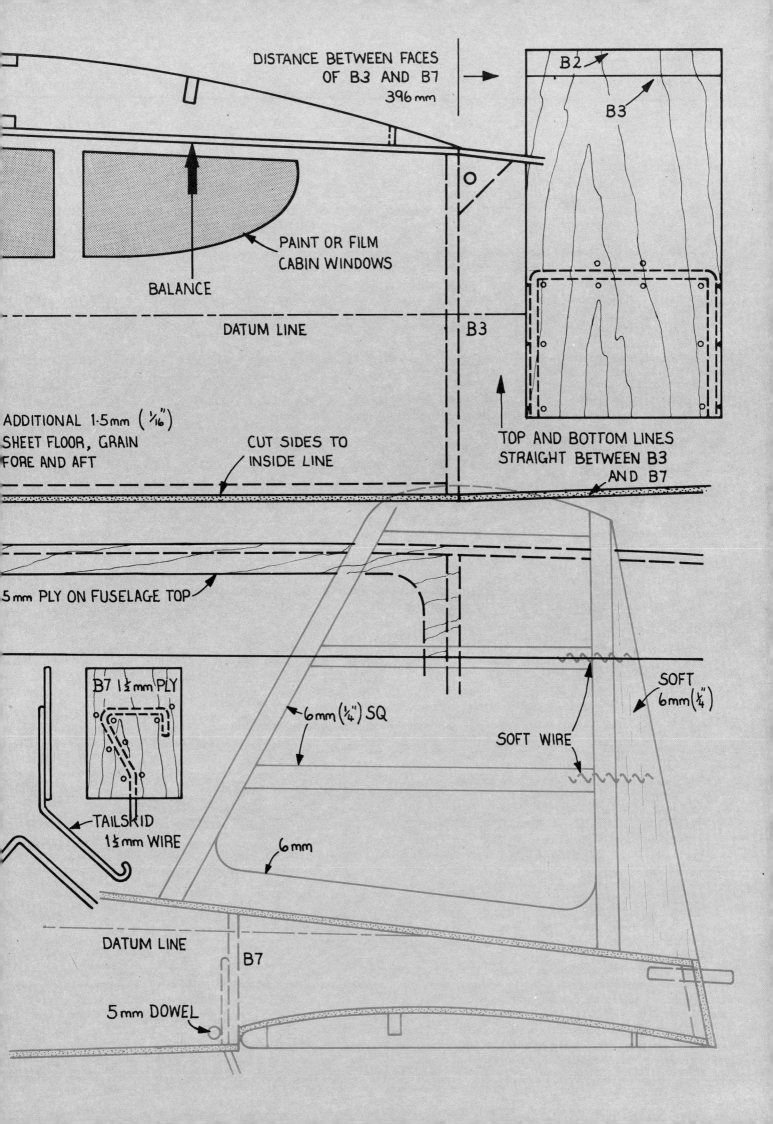

DISTANCE BETWEEN FACES
OF B3 AND B7
396 mm

B2

B3

PAINT OR FILM
CABIN WINDOWS

BALANCE

DATUM LINE

B3

TOP AND BOTTOM LINES
STRAIGHT BETWEEN B3
AND B7

ADDITIONAL 1·5mm (1/16")
SHEET FLOOR, GRAIN
FORE AND AFT

CUT SIDES TO
INSIDE LINE

5mm PLY ON FUSELAGE TOP

B7 1½mm PLY

6mm (1/4") SQ

SOFT
6mm (1/4")

SOFT WIRE

TAILSKID
1½mm WIRE

6mm

DATUM LINE

B7

5mm DOWEL

# Quasar

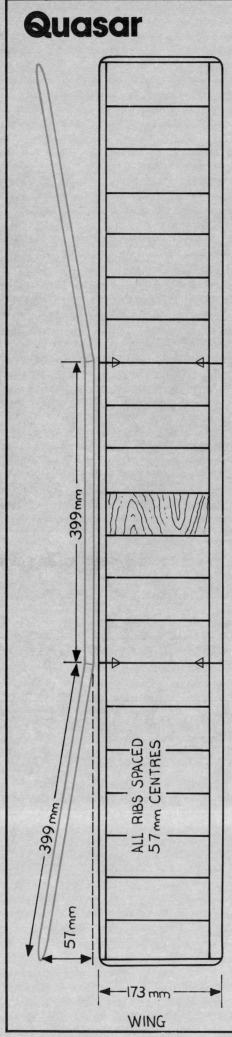

ALL RIBS SPACED 57 mm CENTRES

399 mm

399 mm

57 mm

57 mm

173 mm

WING

This model is designed as an excellent beginners' project which is straightforward to build and, despite its comparatively low power, has a pleasing performance. A biggish model with a small engine, it is easy to fly and forgiving over minor faults in construction; it has the further advantage that simple radio control – rudder only, or perhaps rudder and throttle – can be installed with only minor changes. For free-flight, it is recommended that a 1cc (.06cu.in) engine is the maximum, for radio, with throttle, 1.5cc (.09cu.in).

Basic materials are listed but depending on economy of cutting, it may be necessary to buy an extra sheet of $\frac{1}{16}$in (1.5mm) balsa. Unless specifically mentioned, 36in (915 mm) lengths are intended.

3 $\frac{1}{16} \times 4$ (1.5 × 100) medium balsa (fuselage sides, top, bottom, ribs)
1 $\frac{1}{8} \times 3$ (3 × 75) medium balsa (fuselage formers etc.)
2 $\frac{1}{2} \times \frac{1}{2}$ (12 × 12) medium balsa leading edge (or 1 48in length) (wing)
2 $\frac{1}{4} \times \frac{3}{4}$ (6 × 18) medium balsa trailing edge (wing and tail)
5 $\frac{1}{8} \times \frac{1}{4}$ (3 × 6) hard balsa (wing and tailplane spars)
1 $\frac{1}{4} \times \frac{1}{4}$ (6 × 6) medium/hard balsa (tail l.e., fin)
7 × 5in (180 × 130) $\frac{1}{16}$in (1½mm) ply (wing seat, formers)
18in (450mm) 12swg (2.5mm) piano wire (undercarriage)

Plus small piece of $\frac{1}{8}$in (3mm) ply, engine bearers ($\frac{1}{4} \times \frac{3}{8}$ or 6 × 9), $\frac{3}{16}$in (5mm) dowel, soft $\frac{1}{4}$in (6mm) balsa sheet scrap, 16swg (1½mm) wire for tailskid, tissue, dope, cement or PVA glue, pins, engine bolts, etc.

## Wing
The wing is basically the same as the towline glider except that it has a double mainspar and it will be necessary to draw out a simple full-size plan. Use a piece of uncreased paper – decorators' lining paper or even smooth brown paper will do – and draw a *straight* line about 1200mm (48in) long. Mark off accurately at 57mm intervals and draw a parallel line 172mm (6¾in) from the first. Use a set-square to extend the marks through.

Mark and cut the leading and trailing edges to length, remembering a slight bevel at the dihedral break, then mark the rib positions and notch 1.5mm ($\frac{1}{16}$in) wide and deep to receive the ribs. Trace the rib shape on to a piece of 1.5mm ply and cut out accurately, including spar notches, then use this as a template to cut the balsa ribs. Pin all

the ribs into a block and sand lightly to ensure that they are identical. Take two and with the template trim off 1.5mm from top and bottom edges; these will be the centre ribs and the trimming is to allow for balsa sheeting. Note that the spars will project above the rib surfaces and the sheeting will be between spar positions to give a flush surface. Two soft 6mm ($\frac{1}{4}$in) ribs will also be needed for the tips, without spar notches.

Pin the lower mainspar of one panel in place, positioned by a rib at each end. The leading edge can be lightly slotted to accept the ribs; it is also necessary to block it fractionally up off the building board, using slips of card or scrap balsa. Build the panel and leave to dry, then block it to the correct dihedral while the next panel is built. As the three panels are of equal length (except for the extra tip blocks) the dihedral dimension can be used at the free end of any panel. Add gussets and dihedral braces (which should be ply or very hard balsa) plus centre bay sheeting and soft tip blocks. If square timber was used for the leading edge, this should now be carved and sanded to shape, using a little template. Check for warps and that all glue joints are sound, then sand lightly all over ready for covering.

## Tailplane
This is exactly the same as the towline glider tailplane, but a plan must be drawn as for the wing. Use the material left from the wing for the spar and trailing edge – there will be just enough. The centre two ribs are reduced to receive balsa sheeting top and bottom, and there are again soft block tips.

## Fuselage
It is possible to draw out a fuselage side directly on to a sheet of balsa 100mm (4in) wide, but safer to draw it out on paper first. Draw a straight datum line, then trace the full-size 'front end' shown, carefully aligning to the datum. Measure off the distance shown between the formers at the wing trailing edge and tailplane leading edge, then trace the tail end, again accurately positioning on the datum line. Complete the outline with straight lines top and bottom, and mark in the former positions with lines at right-angles to the datum.

Trace or pin-prick the shape on to the first sheet of balsa, cut and check against plan and use to cut a second identical side. Note that the outline of the sides is 1.5mm ($\frac{1}{16}$in) smaller all round than the full outline, to allow for top and bottom sheeting. An option now exists; some builders will make a stronger and more symmetrical fuselage if 3mm ($\frac{1}{8}$in) square balsa strip is glued along all straight edges, on the inside face. This would mean nicking a suitable square out of the corners of the formers. The strip forms a fillet between side and top and bottom skins, giving more area for glue and helping smooth curves, but it is not absolutely necessary. Beginners would find it helpful, however.

Cut all formers; B1, B2, and B7 require further work before assembly. In the case of B1, check the mounting dimensions of the engine to be used and adjust the bearer spacing accordingly. If a radial mount is to be used, B1 could be 3mm balsa and an additional ply firewall mounted ahead of it. The distance will depend on the engine length, but as the ply will be only a simple rectangle it is easy to determine its height and width. Probably 25–30mm (1–1$\frac{1}{4}$in) ahead of B1 would be near for a motor fitted with a tank. Reinforce the inside of the area between the firewall and B1 with 3mm balsa to ensure a strong mounting.

B2 is a lamination of 1.5mm ply and 3mm balsa but could, if preferred, be a single piece of 3mm ply. The undercarriage must be secured to it before assembly, so bending this is the next job. It has been designed flat (i.e. bends all in one plane) to make it as simple as possible, since heavy piano wire can be difficult to shape. A small vice is desirable rather than trying to use hand pliers. Measure and bend the square top first to make a long square U, then bend out the legs to the angle shown. Carefully measure and bend the axle angles, check the wheel hub thickness, mark and cut off. Filing a deep nick all round and then snapping is usually the best way to cut this tough wire.

Lay the unit on to B2 and pencil round. File nicks in the edge of the former and drill 1.5mm holes as shown, then sew the wire in place with carpet thread, making the crosses from one hole to the next on the back of the former. Rub cement into the thread.

The tailskid is bent from thinner wire and sewn to B7 in a similar way. Ensure that it is vertical and roll the end to prevent a sharp tissue-tearing projection.

Now lay one fuselage side flush with the edge of the work-bench to clear the undercarriage, and glue in place B2 and B3. Cut a rectangle of 1.5mm balsa exactly fitting between them, and the exact internal width of the fuselage, and glue in place, flush with the bottom edges. Add the second side, on top, check, with a set-square, that the tail-ends are aligned, and leave to dry. The ply wing seat can be cut while waiting, ready to glue in place when the initial assembly can be lifted.

Draw the tail ends together and insert B7. Check most carefully that the sides bend equally, i.e. that the fuselage is symmetrical. This can be done by eye and by drawing two parallel lines 58mm (2$\frac{1}{4}$in) apart and aligning the fuselage between them. Insert the intermediate formers, checking constantly that no distortion occurs. Fit the internal gussets, drill through, and glue in the dowels for wing and tail retaining bands, which should project about 15mm ($\frac{5}{8}$in). Now sheet from B3 back (on top) and B2 back (beneath) with 1.5mm balsa, with the grain running *across* the fuselage, i.e. with short lengths cut to the required width from across the balsa sheet.

Slip a rubber band round the nose end and insert B1. Line the sides forward of this with 1.5mm balsa, grain vertical. Glue the bearers in place, checking that they are parallel and at 90° to B1. Cut pieces of 6mm ($\frac{1}{4}$in) sheet to fill the spaces between the bearers and the sides. Though not a 'computer-calculated crumple zone', this assembly is intended to give way in a bad head-on crash, limiting damage and hence repair work. Place the engine in position and mark the bolt positions, then drill these and insert the bolts from beneath with a touch of epoxy round the heads.

The sheeting can now be completed round the nose, its shape in the engine area being suited to the engine. Moderately hard sheet, applied in narrow strips round the sharp curves and sanded smooth, is desirable.

For a radial-mount engine, much the same procedure is adopted, but if it has an integral tank, the run of the fuel feed line must be borne in mind. It would be possible (though not so attractive) to cut the fuselage sides off at the firewall, leaving the engine exposed.

There remains the fin, which is built flat, sanded to shape, and simply glued centrally to the top of the fuselage; again, damage would be limited if the model flipped over on landing. The rudder can be hinged with tape for radio (with a horn fitted to one side near its base) or for FF secured by soft iron (florists') wire or thin aluminium.

If radio is intended, line the fuselage forward of B3 with an extra thickness of 1.5mm soft balsa, grain vertical, before assembly, and cut clearance through all formers for a rudder push-rod to emerge through the fuselage top just ahead of B7. A small klunk tank can be installed between B2 and B1, with access through a hatch forming the front windscreen. The battery pack should be stowed against the bottom of B2 and a shelf fitted to mount the receiver and servo. Radio weight should be not more than 200gm (7oz).

Inspect the whole structure carefully and sand all over ready for covering. Heavyweight tissue is intended; the original was all white and water-shrunk with a cold-water dye added to the water and applied with a big, soft brush. It was then clear doped (three slightly thinned coats) and the simple decor applied with contact film. The whole model was subsequently given a very thin coat of polyurethane varnish, almost watery in consistency, to seal the decor and make sure it was fuel-proof. Two coats were applied in and around the engine bay.

Soldering on the wheels is the last job, apart from bolting in the engine. Sponge rubber balloon wheels are intended, and their weight and size are taken into account in the design, so do not be tempted to use small and very light substitutes. Solder a washer on each axle, near the bend, slip on the wheels, and solder another washer to retain them, allowing only a small amount of play.

The final finished weight in flying trim of the original was just 14oz (392g) and no ballast or incidence change was necessary for a smooth glide. If hard balsa is used for the fuselage, it could turn out slightly tail-heavy; with a long nose, a small amount of clay pressed into the front of the engine bay, or a small amount of solder secured to an engine bearer, will have quite a marked effect on the C.G. position.

A very small amount of right rudder is likely to be needed, depending on whether any flying surface is warped. Keep motor runs very short, and run the engine rich to the point of erratic running for initial flights. When trimmed, motor runs still need to be short, as the model is a real wafter. Your name and address in a prominent place are definitely desirable!

# Electric Flight

Electric flight has developed from the realm of the experimenter to an accepted everyday aspect of model flying in the space of less than ten years. Some of the credit for progress in motors and batteries must go to electric model boats and cars, but aircraft pioneers in the USA, Japan, Germany, and Britain have played a large part in making it practical and popular. Flying close to houses, as in these photographs, with any other type of power model could soon lead to complaints.

**Introduction and History**

Electric flight first came to the attention of the public in 1946, at a national model exhibition in Dorland Hall, London, where models were flown attached by twin wires to a central pylon. In the absence of suitable commercially-available motors, the idea was not widely taken up until the late 1960s, when it was found that the small, powerful motors developed for electric slot-car racing were excellent for flying models RTP ('round the pole'). Soon supplies of quite sophisticated equipment came on the scene, and electric RTP is now practicable for anyone having nothing more than a kitchen table for a workbench; it will be dealt with more fully at the end of this chapter.

The problems of electric powered free-flight (FF) and radio control (R/C) provided even more headaches to the prospective experimenter in that, unlike RTP, batteries need to be carried in the model.

In 1957 the late Colonel H. J. Taplin (UK) installed a fairly large 24v permanent magnet (PM) motor and a quantity of silver zinc cells in

a large, heavy radio model, the ED *Radio Queen*. It should be remembered that this was the pre-transistor era and radio equipment was large and heavy, demanding necessarily a big model. It flew, providing other experimenters with an incentive by proving it could be done.

Three years later a small free flight model designed by the late Fred Militky was flown and developed into a commercial kit, the Graupner *Silentius*, in Western Germany. A very efficient and expensive small PM motor and gearbox (15:1 ratio) drove a large fold-

*Above:* A neat field-box carrying transmitter and test and charging equipment. Fast re-charge cells allow many flights during a session at the flying field.
*Below:* The airborne equipment tidily and firmly stowed. There is still a weight problem with electric power, but aerobatic models are entirely feasible.

ing airscrew assembled into a very light model which could fly with a dry battery, miniature lead acid cells (from cigarette lighters), salt cells, or button type nickel cadmiums. The model's efficiency was such that a slow-burning fuse-operated switch was required to stop the motor and curtail the flight.

Almost simultaneously with *Silentius* the Sanwa *Electra*, a small FF Japanese model, was introduced. It was a total contrast to *Silentius*, very inexpensive, requiring only a few minutes to assemble from expanded polystyrene mouldings (itself an innovation at the time), and used an ungeared PM motor and a 'one shot' salt cell, activated by a quick squirt from a syringe of water. The motor would run for about one minute with the model climbing in that time a hundred feet or so. The occasional superior battery coupled with good air would tax the athletic ability (and eyesight!) of the very best.

A decade was to pass before the next milestone was achieved, when Robert and Roland Boucher (USA) demonstrated the first modern-generation radio electric model, a semi-scale Sportavia RF4. This was a reasonably light model using an ungeared PM motor (which originated from a toy automobile) and cylinder type nickel cadmium cells (nicads) that could be recharged in 15min ready to fly again. This was followed by much improved production versions of the motor in two sizes, known as the Astro 10 and 25, together with battery packs and a charger panel.

Fred Militky introduced a twin motored RC model, the *Silencer*, followed by a commercial and improved version, the Graupner *Hi*

*Fly.* At about this time the Mattel *Superstar*, an almost ready to fly FF model of low toy-like performance, became available. These three models all used geared motors. Since that time (1971) a variety of motors, both geared and ungeared, kits, plans, batteries and accessories have become readily available. The cylinder type nicad is the almost universal choice, with methods of charging similar to those introduced by the Boucher brothers.

## Airborne equipment – Motors, Batteries, Switches and Accessories

Newcomers to electric flight normally purchase a commercially available motor and matching battery pack for their first experience of this branch of flying, and may need guidance on how to get the best out of them in respect of motor control, installation, choice of airframe, flight operation and charging. To use the various electrical circuits shown here a knowledge of circuitry is required, to obtain tailor-made installations for individual applications, as the circuits are drawn to demonstrate the essential detail only and omit such items as charging sockets and isolator switches.

As already stated, the PM type motor and cylinder type nicad battery have been universally adopted for practical and economical electric flight. It is unnecessary to explain how the motor and battery work, but desirable to state briefly why the choice falls on certain motors and nicad cells. Expressed in the simplest terms, a motor must be capable of producing high power regardless of whether it is geared or not, and equipped with an airscrew capable of providing the maximum thrust with the lowest power consumption. The nicad cell (1.2v per cell) must be able to provide all the power required by the motor to produce its maximum thrust for a sufficient flight time to make the whole exercise worthwhile. As can be imagined, all this is matter of compromise. Furthermore, the nicad cell must be capable of accepting rapid discharge and recharge many times over. The cell will get hot while it is being used (as will the motor) and adequate provision for cooling must be made. Two schools of thought on cooling are, first, to remove the battery for recharging, or, second, to have a permanent or semi-permanent installation with perhaps better pro-

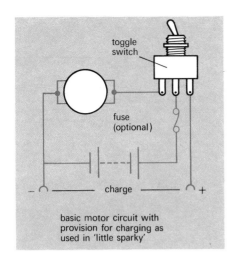

toggle
switch

fuse
(optional)

— charge +

basic motor circuit with
provision for charging as
used in 'little sparky'

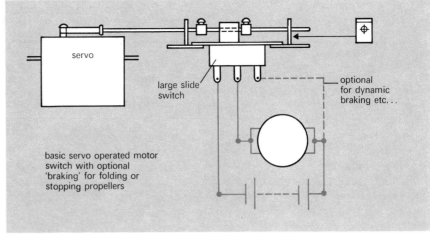

servo

large slide
switch

optional
for dynamic
braking etc...

basic servo operated motor
switch with optional
'braking' for folding or
stopping propellers

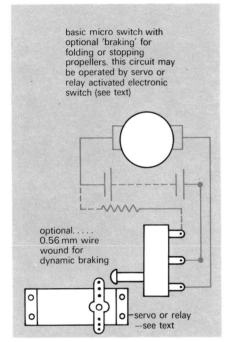

basic micro switch with
optional 'braking' for
folding or stopping
propellers. this circuit may
be operated by servo or
relay activated electronic
switch (see text)

optional.....
0.56 mm wire
wound for
dynamic braking

servo or relay
—see text

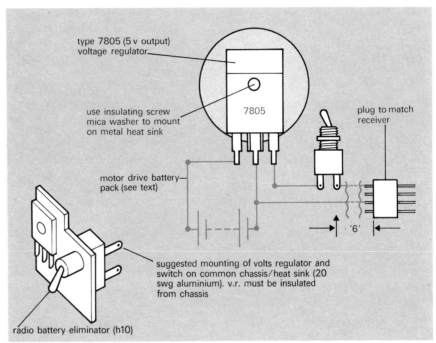

type 7805 (5 v output)
voltage regulator

use insulating screw
mica washer to mount
on metal heat sink

7805

plug to match
receiver

motor drive battery
pack (see text)

'6'

suggested mounting of volts regulator and
switch on common chassis/heat sink (20
swg aluminium). v.r. must be insulated
from chassis

radio battery eliminator (h10)

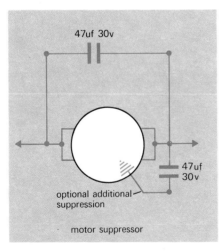

47uf 30v

47uf
30v

optional additional
suppression

motor suppressor

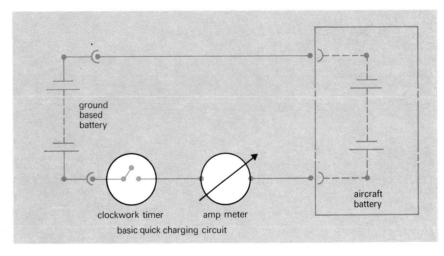

ground
based
battery

aircraft
battery

clockwork timer          amp meter

basic quick charging circuit

vision for cooling.

The smallest motor size commonly available is based on Mabuchi
(Japanese) RE26 components and
is 24.7mm (almost 1in) diameter and
31mm (1.2in) long. It is available as
the Astro 01 and the Mabuchi A1,
and is normally powered by a two
cell battery (2.4v) of 100ma/hr (milli-
ampere/hour) capacity, and used
exclusively for free flight.

The second motor size is based on

*Top left:* The basic motor circuit is
simple but as drawn includes the
facility of direct charging without
disconnection of any wiring, simply by
moving the switch to the 'off' position.
*Top right:* Using adjustable collets on a
rod to operate a conventional slide
switch. When a PM motor is switched
off but still rotating, it generates
current, and if its circuit is closed, the
short-circuiting of this current creates a
braking effect.

*Centre left:* This circuit introduces a
resistance to increase braking effect,
for rapid stopping of the propeller,
particularly when a folding propeller
is used.
*Centre right:* Weight can be saved by
eliminating the radio battery and
drawing the current needed for
receiver and servo operation, via a
voltage-regulator, from the main
motor battery pack.

161

Mabuchi RE36 components and measures 27.4mm (1.1in) × 37.2mm (1.5in). It is available as the Astro 02, normally powered by a four cell battery (4.8v), 225ma/h for free flight and 550ma/h for radio.

A third motor size is based on Mabuchi RS54 components, 35.3mm (1.4in) × 56.4mm (2.4in). It is available as the Astro 05 (Pup), Cyclone 15, Graupner 540, Hummingbird 15 and Robbe 76.11, in both geared and ungeared forms, is powered by a seven or eight cell battery of between 450ma/hr and 1.2amp/hr capacity and is exclusively used for R/C.

The largest motor size to be dealt with in detail is based on the same components, but in this instance the length is stretched to 63.4mm (2.5in) to accommodate a longer armature and magnets. It is available as the Astro 075, Graupner 550, Hummingbird 20 and Mabuchi CVR, powered by an eight or ten cell battery of similar capacity to the above, and again it is exclusively used for R/C.

Larger motors such as the Astro 10–15 and 25 and Bullet 30 are available, but are rather beyond the scope of this chapter, which is intended as an introduction to electric flight.

## Cells

The cylinder type nicad cell incorporates a safety feature in the form of a 'blow-off' valve that permits the cell to 'vent' (rather than explode) should the internal gas pressure build up, usually due to overheating or overcharging. *This feature is not incorporated in button type nicad cells and such cells must never be quick-charged under any circumstances.* The design of these valves varies with different suppliers – some have a plastic cap which distorts, allowing the gases to escape, while others have a small visible hole about 1mm diameter. This hole must not be soldered over or blocked in any way, nor should the plastic cap be in any way damaged. 'Venting', which may be heard, should be avoided as it effectively reduces the future capacity and life of the cell. Quick charging will be dealt with more fully later.

The requirements of free flight and radio operation vary in certain respects. In the former, generally a shorter motor run is required, and this should be precisely regulated by a fuse or timer-operated switch which would allow a fully-charged battery to be used, resulting in more available power. No commercial device is at present available, but small clockwork timers normally used to regulate glow or diesel engines (up to 30sec) or dethermalizers (up to 6min) can be adapted to operate a sub-miniature micro-switch installed in place of the more usual toggle switch.

A more commonly used method, preferred on the grounds of simplicity, is to charge the battery for a very limited period – as little as 30 sec – and rarely more than 2min for the longest hop. Before such a charge the motor must be switched on to drain the battery completely, to ensure that an excess charge is not introduced. If a switch is installed on the bottom of the fuselage, launching the model can be a one-handed operation, with one finger operating the switch at the point of launch to obtain the maximum advantage from the limited charge.

## Motor control

For R/C, except for the very smallest and lightest models, some form of motor control is desirable. A large slide switch can be operated by a servo by means of a push-pull rod, two adjustable blocks, such as wheel collets, being positioned so that the servo operates the switch and stops – *not stalls* – which would put the servo under load. In practice it is a good idea to 'park' the control stick on the transmitter in the mid-position after selecting motor 'ON' or 'OFF', as this removes any chance of the servo being stalled and the time lag to the next motor command is halved. The dynamic braking effect of the motor is used to stop the airscrew. In the case of folding airscrews it is essential to stop them, as they will never fold whilst turning, due to centrifugal and aerodynamic effects. When dynamic braking is applied to fixed airscrews, the additional drag of a stopped, as opposed to freewheeling, airscrew may make landing in a confined space easier, as the model will be flying more slowly. This arrangement provides the option (and it looks impressive!) of being able to stop the airscrew in flight, then allowing it to freewheel before re-applying power.

As an alternative to a slide switch, a micro-switch may be incorporated, with reduced mechanical complexity; micro-switches have built in over-riders to perform the function of the pushrod and adjustable blocks. Also the present generation of electronic ON/OFF switches have a slave relay that operates the micro-switch, thus providing an alternative to the servo. These electronic switches, which plug directly into the radio receiver, are approximately half the current price of servos, which makes them an economical proposition. The only drawback is that they are suitable only for the smaller available commercial motors (up to the stretched RS54-based types using up to ten-cell batteries). These switches are usually adaptable, by changing the location of a single wire, to reverse operation, helpful if the complete system is wired so that the motor switches 'ON' with the control stick in the 'OFF' position. It is recommended that the system is wired up temporarily to check out the complete function and arrange that when switched 'ON' (the control stick pushed forward) the relay is energized, thus providing a safety function; should the radio malfunction or the battery go flat the relay is de-energized, causing the motor to cut.

For progressive (i.e. proportional) motor speed control, normally used only with larger motors, a number of commercial electronic controllers are available, also plugging directly into the radio receiver. The wiring harness is usually built into the unit and varies in detail from one type to another. The disadvantage of such controllers is that they consume power from the system (depending on their efficiency), which obviously shows itself as loss of rpm at full speed – it may only be a couple of hundred rpm, but it lowers the performance of the model. This loss may be eliminated by by-passing the controller at maximum speed, electronically or mechanically. The use of mechanical speed controllers (rheostats) is not recommended on the grounds of weight, size, power loss etc.

Switches are very often a source of frustration to anyone looking at electric power for the first time. Realizing that motors draw perhaps 10–15amp or more, they go on to examine the size and weight of commercial switches designed to accept such loads. It should be remembered that most of these switches are intended for a life of many thousands of hours and many thousands of operations in locations where a few extra ounces (or pounds) matter little. It is possible to select quite small switches without much fear of failure. The smallest toggle switches found able to draw the highest loads are those supplied by Astro Flight and Radio Shack (Tandy in Western Europe) type 275.324 and 326. These are rated at 10amp (which in itself is exceptionally high for such small switches) but will happily accept twice this load.

### Fuses

The use of a protective fuse is a matter of choice, though for the beginner it is advisable. A miniature cartridge type is preferred (either 20mm or $\frac{5}{8}$in) clipped in a panel type receptacle mounted in the fuselage side for ease of access. The problem is that fuses of the desired high ratings are generally hard to come by in these small sizes. However, it is easy to substitute the correct size copper wire by drilling through the solder at each end of the cartridge and extracting the fuse wire before threading through the new and resoldering. A table of copper wire diameters for fuses is published in most electrical data handbooks, but as a guide 0.15mm (0.006in) rates 5amp, 0.25 mm (0.010in) 10amp, 0.30mm (0.012

*Right:* Folding propellers reduce drag.
*Below:* With small capacity cells, as suitable for power-assisted gliders, large dry batteries provide a convenient source for recharging.

in) 15amp and 0.38mm (0.015in) 20amp; for safety a test should be made and each cartridge marked with its new value. As an alternative to a cartridge fuse it should be possible to break the wiring at a convenient point and install two terminal screws about 12mm ($\frac{1}{2}$in) apart in the fuselage side. Run a *single* strand of the appropriate copper wire across these terminals and secure with nuts and washers. The recommended fuse rating should be included with the motor instructions.

Charging sockets should ideally be impossible to reverse, since re-

verse charging will almost certainly destroy the nicads if left on for any period. Standardization at this point would be helpful, particularly if two or more enthusiasts fly together. A phono socket (the plug being fitted to the charge cord) is recommended as a cheap universally available connector; the accepted wiring is that the centre terminal is always positive.

### Suppressors

Suppressors – to reduce the chance of radio interference – are also a matter of choice. If the supplier of your motor fits a suppressor, use it.

Modern R/C units should not be affected by a good motor with a proper installation. If your installation is affected ensure that the motor brushes and commutator are clean and properly aligned in order that no sparking is visible and ensure that all *radio* wiring is routed away from the motor switches and battery wiring; this particularly applies to the radio aerial.

## Wiring

Wiring should be carried out with the utmost care, trying to reduce the need for plugs and sockets as far as possible. Good soldering and adequate wire diameter of minimum length commensurate with reliable installation all help to reduce resistance and improve the performance of the installation.

## Geared Motors

Spur gears, epicyclic and belt drive are all available commercially with gear ratios of $2\frac{1}{2}$:1 down to 6:1, but what advantages does a geared motor have? It can turn a large and relatively efficient airscrew at what may not be very efficient speeds (too low) and the opposite may be said of ungeared motors. Add to this a loss of power by using gears! But to apply the matter in more practical terms, a large slow-flying lightly loaded model would benefit from a geared installation. For example, the vintage K.K. *Junior 60* powered by an ungeared RS54 or the stretched version of this motor, with a $180 \times 100$mm ($7 \times 4$in) airscrew, would not sustain itself in the air. However, an M.F.A. Olympus belt drive fitted to the motor, driving an enlarged airscrew ($280 \times 150$mm, $11 \times 6$in), provides ten minute flights without difficulty. A

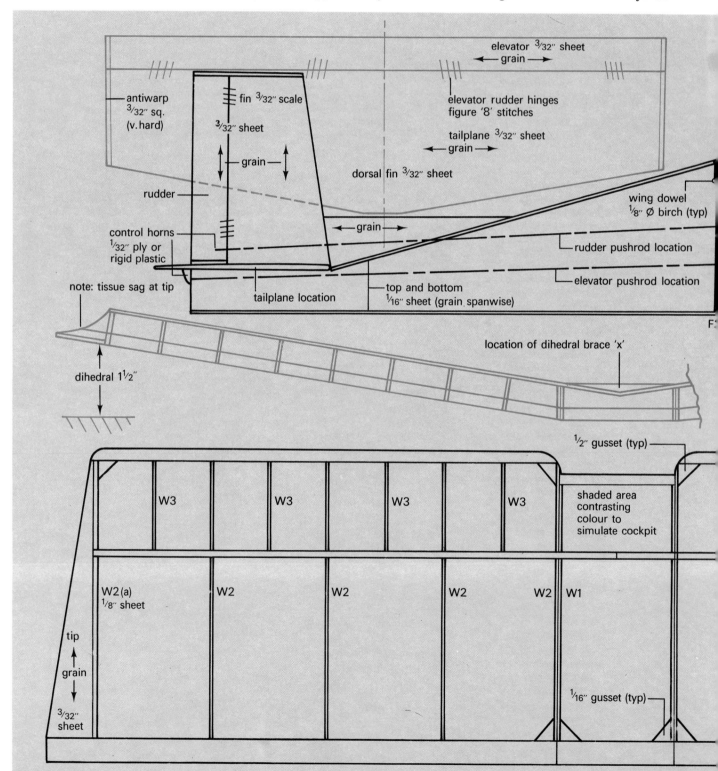

similar geared arrangement applied to an aerobatic style model, particularly if it was built as small as possible, would produce a very mediocre performance.

**Quick charging**

The simple charging panel developed by the Boucher brothers has proved to be a highly reliable means of rapidly charging batteries on the field, but understanding the theory and practice involved avoids pitfalls. Take as an example an eight-cell (nominally 10v) battery, commonly used with a RS54-based motor, when the model has landed with the battery discharged to the extent that it will no longer provide power to sustain flight.

The charge source is plugged into the battery (in this example it would be a nominal 12v lead acid accumulator, perhaps a car size battery or smaller) and the timer is started. Dependent on the amp/hour capacity of the cells to be charged, an initial reading on the ammeter of 4amp for a 500ma/hr or eight amps for a 1amp/hr battery should be expected. This will progressively reduce on the meter until after 15 minutes about ½amp or 1amp respectively should be registered. The battery is now fully charged and ready for flight. The rate of available charge will vary as to the capacity and state of charge of both the battery and the charge source.

How are these rates of charge arrived at? If a 1amp/hr battery is taken as an example and the meter reading is observed, it can be deduced that the average rate over 15 min is 4amp, which when divided by a quarter (15min being a quarter of 1hr) gives 1amp, the amp/hour capacity of the battery. For reliability and long battery life it is recommended never to exceed these charge rates – if necessary, to reduce the charge rate, some resistance should be introduced, best achieved by lengthening the charging cord. Conversely, if the charge rate cannot be achieved, perhaps when using a small capacity charge source battery or one which is partially discharged, reduce the length of charging cord. Certain makes of nicad cells have a higher internal resistance and in practice are not able to accept a high initial rate of charge, so a longer charge time (based on the above calculations) is required. As a rule, nicad cells manufactured in the USA are able to accept this high rate of charge, those of other origins may be suspect in that respect. It is recommended that the supplier's instructions as to charging are followed, when these are supplied.

To charge a four-cell battery a 6v charge source is required and to charge a two-cell battery a 4v (or slightly less) charge source is required. In the case of a ten-cell battery a 14–15v charge source is required, which can be achieved by adding either a 2v lead acid cell (as used to start glow motors) or two nicad cylinder cells of at least 6amp/hr capacity in series to a 12v accumulator. Remember that the ammeter reading always relates to the capacity and the degree of discharge of the battery.

The most common fault to occur in rapid charging is the breakdown of insulation between two or more adjacent cells. This effectively reduces the total voltage of the battery, by shorting out the affected cells. This results in a higher reading on the ammeter, and more heat in consequence is generated within the battery, possibly causing a further breakdown of insulation between more cells. *Shut down immediately and repair insulation before further use.*

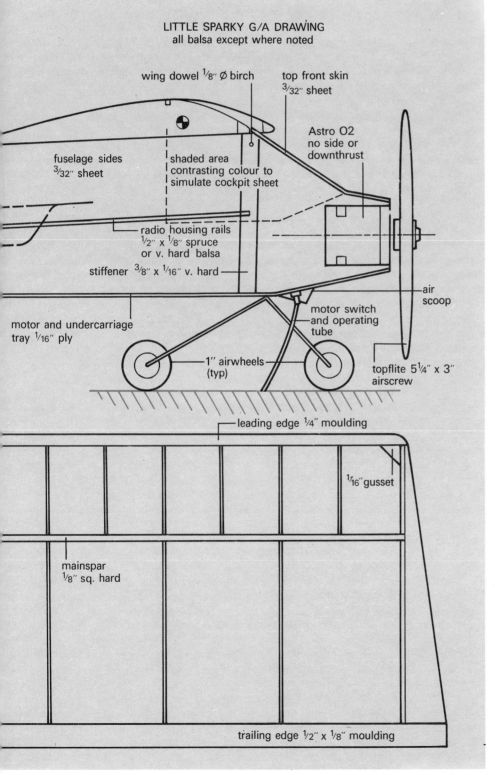

LITTLE SPARKY G/A DRAWING
all balsa except where noted

wing dowel ⅛″ Ø birch

top front skin ³/32″ sheet

Astro 02 no side or downthrust

fuselage sides ³/32″ sheet

shaded area contrasting colour to simulate cockpit sheet

radio housing rails ½″ x ⅛″ spruce or v. hard balsa

stiffener ⅜″ x ¹/16″ v. hard

air scoop

motor and undercarriage tray ¹/16″ ply

motor switch and operating tube

1″ airwheels (typ)

topflite 5¼″ x 3″ airscrew

leading edge ¼″ moulding

¹/16″ gusset

mainspar ⅛″ sq. hard

trailing edge ½″ x ⅛″ moulding

## Model designs

There are now many kits and plans available for electric flight and many more that can easily be adapted for both radio and free flight. Build a light, strong and rigid structure, ensuring that all equipment is accessible. When building from kits and plans originally designed for electric flight, follow closely the designers' recommendations for types of motor, battery and accessories to be used.

For the more experienced who may wish to adapt an existing kit, plan, or perhaps an existing model, or attempt an 'own design', the installation of equipment should be carefully planned, paying particular attention to cooling. Studying published designs will provide useful pointers.

## Building and flying

As a basic design and construction exercise *Little Sparky* is probably the smallest size electric R/C model capable of flying in all but the roughest (above 25mph winds) conditions, and even in those in the hands of a skilful pilot. It is cheap and quick to build and incorporates such features as a complete 'motor and undercarriage tray' and 'radio mounting frame' in to which the most complex parts of the model are assembled with complete accessibility and ability to be tested before installation in the model. The motor and battery used are the Astro 02

(radio control version). The radio comprises two of the sub-miniature servos each weighing no more than 21g ($\frac{3}{4}$oz) now being introduced by several manufacturers, a two channel radio receiver, stripped of its protective case then mounted on foam rubber, and four 100ma/hr cylinder nicads. The complete radio is mounted in a frame as shown in the full-size parts layout, the final shape and size of this frame being determined by the equipment used. The all-up weight of the 'radio mounting frame' complete should be about 100g, say 4oz. The radio battery (if using cylinder cells) may be rapid charged if required, but is capable of more than one hour's operation, which should be sufficient for most purposes. The flight duration is approximately five minutes with a full charge.

Construction: Start by making and assembling the motor and undercarriage tray. If the pilot is left-handed it would be as well to reverse the location of the motor ON/OFF switch and the airscoop. The lever of the switch (Astro or Tandy (Radio Shack) 274–324 or 326) should be arranged to push *forward* for 'ON'. A semi rigid plastic tube

'Little Sparky' is a tiny model, but if you can cope with the radio-mounting frame, the rest is straightforward. The design is based on a full-size home-built, 'Big Willie', built in Holland. Top picture shows the ink-tube 'off' lever clearly.

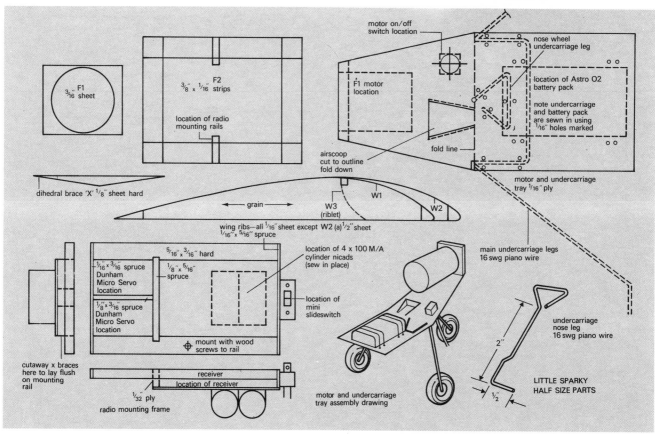

(an empty ink tube from a ball-point pen is ideal) long enough to extend about 12mm ($\frac{1}{2}$in) beneath the under-carriage is slipped on to the lever; when it strikes the ground it will move the switch to the 'OFF' position. Obtain or make a thin cardboard tube capable of accepting the motor and holding it firmly, cutting away at the back for cooling air exit, then assemble to F1, using an oversize piece of balsa for this purpose. When dry cut to final size and chamfer edges as on G/A (general arrangement) drawing. Assemble all parts to the tray and wire up. Fix the airscrew and give a short charge (no more than one minute). Check that the charging is correct. Switch 'ON' (avoiding the airscrew) whilst holding firmly then simulate the method of launch, ensure that the motor rotation is correct and that the motor switch is conveniently positioned. If you are not absolutely satisfied now is the time for changes, not when the tray is assembled to the model. When finally satisfied discharge the battery, remove the airscrew and motor operating tube, then tape over the motor cooling holes to prevent the introduction of foreign matter during remainder of construction.

Cut out the fuselage sides and assemble to radio mounting rails and stiffener. Assemble F2. When all dry, assemble fuselage sides to F2 and motor/undercarriage tray, then add the top *front* skin from nose to wing position only. When all dry, pull the rear fuselage together with a gap of 6mm ($\frac{1}{4}$in) to allow for elevator pushrod and cooling air exit. Then add tailplane, together with remainder of top and bottom sheeting. When all dry, sand to finish, adding fin and dorsal fin.

Cut all wing parts and assemble – note the location of dihedral brace 'X'. When all dry, sand to finish.

Cover model with lightweight tissue and dope using the minimum required to seal the tissue. While drying the wing should be held or pinned down to incorporate 6mm ($\frac{1}{4}$in) washout (negative incidence) at both wing tips. Ensure no warps are present in structure – steam out if required.

Sew on rudder and elevator with strong thread using 'figure eight' stitches and making sure they move freely. Make and fit control horns and wing mounting dowels.

Temporarily slide in radio mounting frame, with radio installed. Strap on wing, using rubber bands. Check the centre of gravity, moving the radio frame to obtain correct balance, and when finalized drill and attach with woodscrews. Make up rudder and elevator pushrods and assemble in the correct sense, adjusting the location to provide no more than 3mm ($\frac{1}{8}$in) left and right movement, together with 6mm ($\frac{1}{4}$in) up and down on the elevator. Remove tape from the motor, fit the airscrew and motor operating tube, charge the radio battery and finally check again for balance and warps.

**Flying**

Choose a very calm day. Charge the battery for no more than 20 seconds, switch on radio (check the operation) and launch smoothly into wind, switching on motor. Watch for a smooth straight descent, adjust controls if required, and repeat the procedure, increasing the charge time when satisfied to one, two, and four minutes before using a full charge. Small models are sensitive to any control changes. Whenever any work is carried out on the model or the radio is removed, always go through this trimming procedure. It is quick and easy and reduces the chances of damage enormously.

One final point, small models are difficult to judge at any distance – try to fly close to yourself when near to the ground but don't try any violent turns to do so. Select a good colour-contrasting tissue for covering and keep the weight as low as possible.

**Maintenance of equipment, improvements and repairs**

A limited amount of maintenance may be carried out on motors with a minimum of tools, but as motors are relatively cheap the cost of purchasing tools or commissioning professional repairs should be considered before embarking on extensive maintenance and repairs. To replace will often be cheaper than to repair.

Where recommended a very small amount of oil may be added to bearings, wiping off excess and ensuring that none reaches the armature and brush assemblies.

When motors are geared, turning the motors through 180 degrees before refitting can reduce the chance of localization of bearing wear. When this is done adjustment of gear mesh or belt tension should be carried out.

Bent motor shafts generally require professional attention. However, if you drill a hole in the side of a heavy workbench (or similar) exactly the same diameter as the shaft, insert the shaft, start the motor and apply a slight side load (the motor is best held in the hand for this operation) then remove from the drilled hole, all within a couple of seconds, you may straighten the shaft. Try again if necessary. This operation appears dangerous but is no more so than using a hand-held electric drill.

Sweated-on gears on some RS54-based motors require an extractor, something more substantial than those available from instrument makers but smaller than those used for motor cycles and automobiles. Sweated-on airscrew adaptors as fitted to Astro Flight motors are best removed by drilling through the front of the adaptor to the motor shaft, using a drill the same size as the motor shaft. Then, with the hexagonal part of the adaptor firmly gripped in a vice, the motor shaft is smartly tapped using a parallel pin punch and hammer. The adaptor is re-usable.

When the tabs that are an integral part of the case (bent over to secure the plastic end plate) break off, clean away the metal plating, make a tab from tinplate and solder in place, using acid flux and solder.

In the event of burning out armature windings, enamelled copper wire may be obtained from specialized suppliers. Ensure by measuring with a wire gauge or micrometer that the exact diameter is purchased. It is as well to practise re-winding on cheap toy motors first to ensure you have the technique and can get these motors to run reliably first. Where the wire attaches to the commutator it must first be scraped clean and preferably soldered.

Motor commutators, on which the brushes rub, are best trued up in a small lathe. With small motors, there is very little material and re-metalling is not feasible. Where possible a quick wipe with a very fine emery cloth glued to a stick and touching only high spots that are visible to the eye is all that is usually needed.

As far as possible avoid dismantling motors – 'inside' work is best avoided. It is generally best to install a new motor and hold the old and damaged motors for spares. Remember that every time you remove the armature from the motor you are effectively removing the magnet 'keeper' (the equivalent of the iron bar used to preserve the magnetic power of normal magnets). Keeping motors clean and checking the brushes for wear and tension is generally all that is required 'inside' – and try to do this with absolute minimum of dismantling. Always put the motor back together as quickly as possible, not forgetting the small fibre washers fitted at both ends!

No maintenance is possible on nicad cylinder cells, the care of which was mentioned earlier under 'quick charging'.

Do not try to dismantle switches; it is possible to check at least part of contacting areas in the case of slide switches to ensure that there are no sooty (i.e. burn) marks. On all switches ensure that connectors where they enter the body are not loose, the operating toggle or slide portion is not sloppy due to wear, overheating etc., and finally and most important ensure they make and break every time.

Charging Sockets – make sure they grip the charging plug, making good electrical contact without undue force needed to remove, and not so loose that they shake out if the model rocks a little in the breeze. Wiring – check everything, particularly for corrosion and chafing. Corrosion is most likely to occur between the cells.

Improving Motors – very little can be done here that doesn't come under the heading of maintenance. It may be worthwhile fitting a 1.5 mm ($\frac{1}{16}$in) soft iron clamp (mild steel is a slightly inferior alternative) but frankly the improvement is likely to be very slight and it would be only seriously worthwhile if you had a model which was tail-heavy and wished to increase the motor weight to compensate, with perhaps a marginal improvement in performance. An improvement in motor magnet power may be worthwhile if you have access to an old-time automobile magneto regenerator or suchlike.

Improving armature windings is always possible by increasing the copper wire diameter and reducing the number of windings. This may be worthwhile for a very specialized fast climbing duration model that doesn't already consume the major portion of its most efficient battery capacity in an allotted motor running time. In general those motors commercially available produce the best consumption-to-thrust compromise available. For the average enthusiast performance enhancement is more likely to be achieved by improvement and innovation in model design and construction, providing that you are using the best available motor and battery.

## Miscellaneous applications and future developments

This chapter so far has been an introduction to electric flight both for the practising and 'armchair' enthusiast, and has purposely avoided the larger motors available and more advanced applications. To at least scratch the surface of these:

Solar Power – an American Government-funded experiment into the use of solar power (sun-energized cells) was undertaken by Robert Boucher (Astro Flight). The present state of development of solar power and general aerodynamic efficiency together with the need to carry a bulky payload aloft produced a very large (more than 9m or 30ft wingspan) but remarkably practical model with solar panels mounted as an integral part of the top surface of the wing. This experiment was later duplicated by the late Fred Militky with a relatively small model of about 2m (80in) wingspan, the resulting performance of which was (without denigrating his achievement) quite modest, but this may well be a future practical application of electric flight. At present big solar panels on necessarily big models work best, but perhaps one day, when solar panels are made up in a form resembling adhesive tape 75–100mm (3–4in) wide, with the necessity only to couple up the two edges (i.e. positive and negative) via a switch to the motor, this will be quite feasible – and that day is not really that far away.

Multi Motor Models – at least five kits are currently available. This is an ideal application for electric power in that conventional engine reliability has always been a serious disadvantage to regular and reliable flying of multi models. Theoretically, motors wired for series operation give advantages in operation, but the majority available are for parallel operation. More batteries are required in the model, and it is as well to remember that battery weights do not increase pro-rata to capacity, i.e. two battery packs of 8 × 500ma/hr weigh more than one battery of 8 × 1amp/hr.

Battery Eliminator – to avoid the unnecessary payload of a radio battery when using a flight battery comprising nine or more cells it is well worth considering the use of a voltage control regulator (for example, a Type 7805) as a substitute. It works satisfactorily between 7 and 30v input to provide a regulated 5v output for the radio. The reason for suggesting that its use should be confined to nine cells or more is to provide an ample safety margin against low voltage or damaged cells. It must be mounted on a suitable heatsink using an insulated (nylon) bolt and a mica backing washer between the regulator and the heatsink. The radio switch is best attached to the heatsink, and the whole assembly may be fitted and removed as a single unit. This device is only suitable for use with 'three wire' type servos (i.e. servos that require no centre tapped battery to function).

*Below:* Solar-powered 9m (30ft) experimental model used two Astro 40 motors geared to one 760mm (30in) dia × 405mm (16in) pitch propeller. A model of this size needs a special Permit to fly, but this was a US Government-backed project.

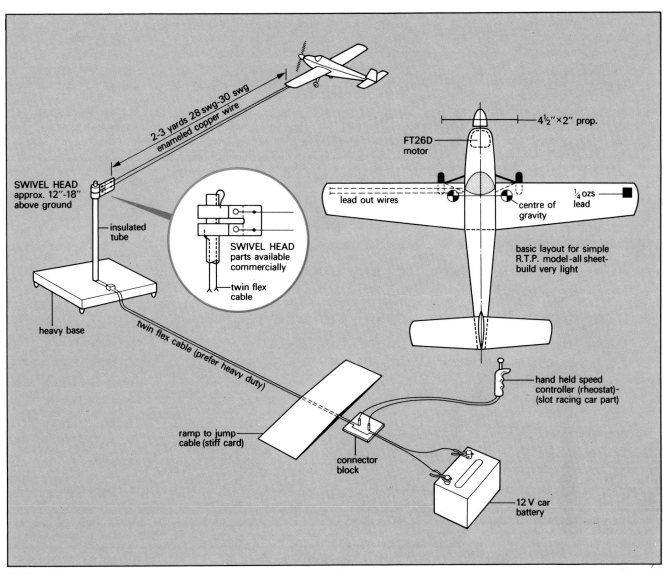

SWIVEL HEAD
approx. 12"-18"
above ground

2-3 yards 28 swg-30 swg enameled copper wire

insulated tube

SWIVEL HEAD
parts available
commercially

twin flex cable

heavy base

twin flex cable (prefer heavy duty)

ramp to jump cable (stiff card)

connector block

hand held speed controller (rheostat)-
(slot racing car part)

12 V car battery

4½"×2" prop.

FT26D motor

lead out wires

centre of gravity

¼ ozs lead

basic layout for simple
R.T.P. model -all sheet-
build very light

*Above:* Simple set up for flying a single model RTP. Kits for models are available.

## Round the pole flying

This was briefly mentioned in the opening paragraphs of this chapter. A simple arrangement using only one model flying on 2 to 3m wires would serve as an economical introduction to a rapidly growing interest that in its present advanced forms uses 10m or longer wires, flying two or three models simultaneously (some models are capable of loops and wingovers) and many multi-motor types of quite extraordinary complexity. The advanced ground equipment necessary to achieve all this requires large capacity transformer/rectifiers to convert mains alternating current to a manageable direct current of 12v at the motor; the longer wires are responsible for quite a large voltage drop and the choice of a transformer must reflect the planned length of wires and the capacity if two or more models are to fly. Sophisticated flying such as this really requires an adequately large indoor site and a number of enthusiasts to

share the work and cost.

A basic circuit requires a fairly high capacity 12v lead acid accumulator (car battery) joined to a swivel head by about 4m of twin flex cable (of mains carrying capacity) with a single break with two terminal ends on a connector block close to the accumulator, to plug in a rheostat. A hand-held speed controller as used on model slot-racing cars is almost universally accepted for this operation. A heavy wooden base with a well supported tube of electrically non-conductive material is needed; should the base prove to be unstable a few bricks to weigh it down would be needed. The swivel head assembly is mounted on the tube, and two thin enamel-insulated wires lead out to the model. All parts can be made fairly simply, but can if preferred be bought from specialist suppliers advertising in model magazines.

The model should be built as lightly as possible, and the centre of gravity should be well forward, at least for the initial flights. Leadout wire positions and weight in the outboard wing tip are similar to

control-line models. Quite a number of kits, plans and suitable motors are commercially available.

Before flying, the wheels should be checked so that the model will roll straight or tend to roll out of the circle. Set up the model and ground equipment, check that the rotation of the motor is correct and ensure a clear flight path is available to the model. Run up the motor until the model moves, and ensure that it holds the lines tight while increasing speed until the model is airborne. Ideally the model should cruise at a constant height at less than full throttle. More power will then make it climb, but watch carefully that line tension is maintained and avoid sudden changes of power. If the model will not take off, move the centre of gravity back a fraction. If it tends to zoom, add a little weight to the nose. Should the lines require more tension, apply a little rudder or more weight to the tip. Possibly a slight adjustment of the elevator is required. Obtaining the best performance from 'RTP' can be just as involved as any other branch of the sport.

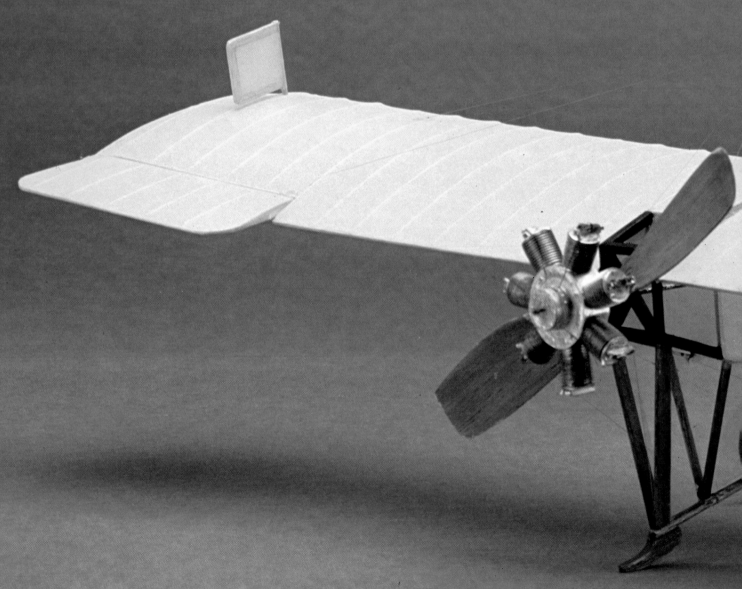

# Flying Scale Models
## Free Flight
## Control Line and Radio-controlled

*Left:* Early aircraft with their low flying speeds and simple boxy construction had much in common with models, and it is therefore no surprise to find that they make excellent subjects for flying scale models, especially with rubber power. Only the out-of-scale flying propellers on three of the four pictured make obvious the fact that they are models.

*Below:* Models have proved that many early experimental designs were practical. Note that the propeller on this pusher canard is ahead of the rotary engine and that it is left-handed. Machine is a Bleriot Canard by John Blagg.

Of all types of flying scale model the free-flight model was the first to evolve historically. Well before the advent of radio control and control-line systems, the simplified rubber-powered scale model had already enjoyed popular success during the decade leading up to World War 2, at a time when great pioneering flights and aviation achievements were headline news. A stimulated interest in aviation, particularly in the USA, brought forth a great profusion of small scale kits of varying quality from many different manufacturers, and the attractions of a model of a real aircraft that was meant to fly just like the real thing, but unaided, were enormous. Many modellers who

were later to be instrumental in the growth of every other branch of aeromodelling most probably made their initial entry to the hobby with this type of model.

Those attractions still exist today, but standards have improved to the extent that the best competition-type free-flight scale models would grace any museum, and the best models flown only for sport will leave very little to be desired in the way of performance.

Why continue to fly highly-detailed scale models free flight when very effective and arguably safer methods of control have been invented? There is no straight answer to this question, except that the achievement of first making a

Smooth launching is essential for any flying model. Notice the modeller's follow-through as he gets his Comper Swift away.

superb model and then getting it to fly really well specifically without these aids doubtless provides enough subtle satisfaction in itself to fulfil many modellers' ambitions. There is great charm in the deceptive simplicity of it all.

Choosing a suitable subject for free-flight scale is very much a question of personal preference, since practical models ranging from a Bleriot Monoplane to Concorde have been built and flown successfully. The most easily-manageable subjects are those with large tailplane areas, good dihedral or sweepback to the wings, and generally normal proportions, together with a simple undercarriage. It is probably true to say that single-engined biplanes, high-wing cabin monoplanes, and, less frequently, low-wing fighters are the most common types to be seen. Multi-engined models are something of a speciality usually only tackled by the experienced modeller.

In competition flying one is partly dependent for choice on the amount of documentation that can easily be gathered together to make up a folder of information used in proving the accuracy of the model for the benefit of the judges. Some full-size aircraft have been exceptionally well documented throughout their active careers, with many plans, sketches, photographs and details of colour schemes having been kept for posterity and published. Others, including many quite suitable for free-flight scale modelling, have been less well served. This makes the added challenge of research and discovery of relevant material all the more rewarding when success is achieved.

Many commercially available kits and plans are accurate and well-researched, but hardly any of these will provide one with a model to be compared with the very best original design from a scale specialist. A model built specifically for competition will have every detail of the full-size aircraft simulated as closely as possible in the appropriate materials, i.e. formed metal cowlings and fairings, hardwood struts and propellers, plywood panels, steel wires and turnbuckles, rubber tyres, etc., whereas a simpler model not intended for competition flying will have many of these parts made in balsa sheet and strip which is then painted to look like the real thing. Occasionally this is done with such skill that from a distance one is quite unable to distinguish between the two.

The basic framework of a free-flight scale model is usually built from the most traditional aero-modelling materials: balsa, spruce or obechi and spring steel wire. Covering materials used on outdoor models are also usually traditional: tissue, silk and nylon, and occasionally a combination of these will be used on the same model.

An excellent finishing technique that results in a very stable surface is to cover the open framework initially with tissue, and then to add a layer of best quality Jap silk to the surface, using dope as an adhesive. This can be used on all parts of the aircraft – wings, fuselage and tail surfaces – and it gives a skin that will not shrink or expand very much due to temperature and humidity changes. Any small accidental punctures or tears will not spread very easily because a laminated surface has effectively been created, and the weave of the silk will show through the final finish to resemble the fabric on the real aircraft. Admittedly the weave will be slightly over-scale on anything but a fairly large model, but it well maintains the attractive texture of a correct fabric surface. It is a commonly held misbelief that all scale models should have an extremely glossy, smooth finish, when this in reality is only to be found on relatively few meticulously maintained museum or private aircraft, or on specially-prepared racing types. Compared to these, most popular fabric-covered military and civil types have a relatively rough finish.

To go with the traditional covering materials, normal model aircraft dope usually constitutes the finishing medium, since it is capable of giving perhaps the lightest painted finish. Most enamels and two-part epoxy finishes are less resilient than dope when applied to a fabric surface, and can be measurably heavier unless very expertly applied. It is also much easier to repair a damaged surface if the types of paint have not been mixed since they can occasionally react very unpleasantly with each other. It may be possible on a suitable subject to accept a straightforward coloured tissue finish with all markings and trim simply being cut from the relevant coloured sheet and doped in place, but this is more suitable for a very lightweight model where flying performance is of greater importance than absolute realism.

Engine-powered models all need to be fuel-proofed to some degree, while the rubber-powered model obviously does not. With a diesel motor it is usually only necessary to fuel-proof the engine bay and its immediate surrounds. Diesel fuel does not violently attack cellulose dope, but it is still important to ensure that the pores of the covering are filled and sealed to prevent the fuel soaking into the structure. With a glow-plug motor it is essential separately to fuel-proof the entire model because the fuel will dissolve normal dope very quickly. Having to do this adds yet more weight to the model, and can add a further complication in that most fuel-proof lacquers are very glossy, and so a further coat of matt or semi-matt finish may be necessary to achieve the desired surface. Naturally this all creates additional weight which is almost always unwelcome. This is yet another point in favour of the diesel motor for use in this type of scale model.

The motors themselves are almost invariably not high-performance types. The scale builder is more interested in using a powerplant that can be easily controlled over a range of speed settings, and which will not require a great deal of fastidious maintenance and attention. For this reason most free-flight models are powered by 'sports' motors that are quite docile in operation. In Great Britain there is among scale fliers a distinct preference for diesel motors; perhaps the most celebrated are the Mills 0.75 and Mills 1.3, both of which are very easy to start and adjust when running, and because of their rear-facing air intakes are relatively easy to accommodate inside a typical scale upright or inverted engine cowling. These motors will each turn a relatively large propeller quite steadily at low speeds, which is ideal for simulating the type of scale performance that the modeller aims to achieve. The Mills and almost any other 0.75cc (0.046cu.in) diesel will power a scale type such as a high-wing cabin monoplane up to approximately 1100mm (43in) span, and a diesel of 1.5 to 2.5cc (0.09–0.15cu.in) will power a biplane of up to 1300mm (51in) wingspan; these two groups are representative of the sizes most popularly chosen.

It is a wise precaution to have a timer device fitted to the engine,

and simple clockwork fuel cut-offs can also be arranged to trigger a working feature on the model such as a bomb or torpedo release, or even a retractable undercarriage. In competition flying the engine run is usually limited to about 20s, and the working feature set to go off within the first ten seconds while the motor is still running. It is also possible to use the timer to operate a throttle if an R/C glow plug motor is used, so that if the motor is throttled down towards the end of the run the model will make a more realistic approach to a landing. The limitations on the use of timers are set only by the builder's imagination and a typical variation is in using a single timer to cut two engines simultaneously on a twin-engined aircraft.

A better way to fly a multi-engined model free flight is to use Motor units connected to a common power source, such as electric or $CO_2$ motors. The disadvantages of the electric system lie in the weight of the motors and rechargeable cells to be carried, thus demanding

*Top:* Biplanes offer low wing loading which can help scale modellers, but also suffer from extra drag. They have a romance which attracts modellers. *Above:* Squadron markings on warplanes and liveries of early airlines add to the interest of scale modelling.

a rather lightweight airframe to achieve a reasonable gross weight. Lighter and more efficient cells are constantly developed, and the ease with which one can match the speeds of electric motors offers great potential for the future. Any number of $CO_2$ motors may be connected to a suitably large common tank, and if each is very carefully adjusted they will all gradually lose power, slow down and stop running at the same time.

One rarely seen form of power is the ducted fan, a multi-bladed impeller fitted to a very high-revving engine running inside a closely-fitting tube or duct completely enclosed within the fuselage of a jet model. A very powerful motor is needed to give the equivalent performance of a normal model

In all scale contest flying the models are judged statically for fidelity to scale and quality of workmanship, and separately for realism in flight, the two scores then being added to give a final result. Models normally have to achieve a minimum flight time, generally in the region of 20 to 30s, to qualify properly. When possible, models are allowed to rog (rise off ground), or can be hand-launched on forfeit of all potential take-off points. The intended flight pattern of any free-flying model is of necessity something of a compromise, and with the exception of any timer-operated feature, the flier has no control at all over the model once he lets it go. Most models are trimmed to fly in circles, and only very rarely are deliberate attempts made at aerobatics or any other manoeuvre. Take-offs from a suitably smooth surface can occasionally be quite excellent and realistic, but landings only by very great luck ever resemble anything other than a rough and tumble arrival. There is very little that can be done about this, and in all forms of contest flying the actual touchdown itself is not marked, whereas the landing approach is. The model must be designed to withstand this type of treatment with impunity, and the most successful designs have strongly sprung under-carriages as well as detachable, 'knock-off' wings. The latter feature gives an added bonus in that it greatly facilitates storage and transport of the model. One of the best methods of attaching the wings is to slide them on to short wire or timber dowels built into the fusel-age or a rigid centre-section, and hold them in place using concealed hooks and small rubber bands. With a biplane it is possible to use the exposed rigging wires to do this. The method of retention should not be absolutely rigid, since it is intended to form a weak link in the system and give way completely in the event of something like a very violent cartwheel landing. Rigid, one-piece models fare very poorly when this happens.

The most typical sort of shock-absorbing undercarriage is based upon the principle of a wire torsion-bar loop. This is aligned laterally across the fuselage, and allows the main legs of the undercarriage to flex rearwards as the model touches down. On the normal type of under-carriage to be found on the average biplane, consisting of two front legs and two rear legs connected to

*Top:* The finishing work on this Albatros DV is the result of many painstaking hours.
*Above:* A convincing Westland Wallace. The builder has gone to some trouble to ensure authentic markings.

with exposed engine and propeller, and the air intakes and outlets frequently need to be enlarged over-scale to enable the desired amount of thrust to be achieved. Obviously many subjects well outside the normal range of free-flight scale models may be tackled if this form of power is used, but experimenta-tion is required for each individual aircraft.

The rubber-powered scale model was in existence long before suit-able small spark ignition, glow-plug, or diesel engines became generally available, but once these made an appearance, general inter-est in rubber power fell; the attrac-tions of a 'real' little motor in a scale model were, and still are, quite obvious. Rubber, however, still maintains its own particular attraction for a number of reasons: models can be much lighter because

there is no need for a fuel-resistant finish, there is no oily exhaust to soil the finish, and they are, like $CO_2$-powered models, beautifully quiet in operation and so may be flown in such places as public parks where engine-powered models are not usually allowed. In flying, there is none of the stalled transition from powered to gliding flight that occurs with the engine-powered model, since the thrust dies away gradually rather than suddenly, and being naturally lighter the model will land much more gently, therefore risking less damage to itself. It is at its best when flown in very calm weather, but this is also true of most free-flight models. The majority of rubber-powered scale models require a very much en-larged propeller to give their best performance, and on a typical bi-plane this may be anything up to one third of the wingspan. In con-test flying, when the model is being judged for static marks, a correct scale propeller may be substituted; this also applies to engine-powered models.

a rigid cross-axle, the rear legs are usually non-structural and simply slot into holes on the underside of the fuselage at their upper rear attachment points. When the front legs are pushed backwards, the rear legs slide even further into the fuselage, and then move back to their original position when the loading is released.

Used together on one model, these two features, or slight variations on them, will ensure that it will have a long and useful life.

Free-flight scale is not an area where radical changes occur with great frequency as, for example, in some classes of high performance model when a new motor is introduced on to the market or a major contest rule change is implemented. Two developments, however, have left a lasting mark in recent years. The first, in the early 1970s, was the advent of indoor scale flying, with models being flown in sports halls, gymnasia, aircraft hangars, and best of all, airship sheds, which are ideal sites due to their vast size. The second was the re-introduction of small $CO_2$ motors which had not been generally available in large numbers since the late 1940s and early 1950s, before very small glow-plug, diesel or spark ignition engines had been developed. The $CO_2$ motor runs on a charge of highly compressed carbon dioxide carried in a metal tank and is the smallest really practicable form of reciprocating engine. It will power models ranging approximately from 350mm (14in) to 650mm (26in) span.

To many people the choice of indoor scale flying is a means of overcoming in one simple step the greatest problem to outdoor flying, being dependent on good weather. Scale types are not naturally the most inherently stable kind of free-flight model, and to fly them in anything but calm conditions is to put a great deal of intricate and time-consuming work to unnecessary risk. Certain parts of the world, such as the west coast of America, are blessed with excellent weather throughout the year, but in contrast the weather in Britain may provide ideal conditions for outdoor scale flying perhaps six times in twelve months. This means that the contest flier may work very hard to prepare a model for a special event, such as the National Championships, only to find that the weather on the day is very poor, and he may be forced to risk his work in less than ideal circumstances. The indoor scale flier, however, can

carry on building his model until the night before a contest, confident in the knowledge that on the following day conditions will be perfect with absolutely no wind to worry about!

Being flown under such ideal conditions, indoor scale models reveal that certain well-known aids to stability found on outdoor models are no longer absolutely necessary for good flight performance. Enlarged tail surfaces and increased dihedral are two of the most common modifications made to improve outdoor stability, but their disadvantages are obviously that they are deviations from true scale and will cause a model to lose marks in a contest. The indoor model can happily be flown without the need for such modifications, and so it is actually possible to build a far more accurate replica despite the fact that such models rarely exceed 700mm (28in) wingspan.

Indoor scale flying makes necessary an entirely new approach to the design and building of models, since they benefit from being abso-

*Top:* Three-engined aircraft such as this Airspeed Ferry are rare, but go some way towards making flight safer. *Bottom:* Large spans with engine nacelles close in reduce the effects of one motor running out before the other.

lutely as light as possible in order to give good performance. The standard approach to outdoor flying of simply fitting a more powerful motor to an unexpectedly over-weight model simply cannot be adopted, and increasing the wing-loading of an indoor type only makes it perform less well. Such models require every piece of material used in construction to be very carefully considered and even weighed before being used. As an example, an expertly made biplane of 450mm (18in) span should weigh 28 to 45gm (1–1½oz). The uncovered framework of a very lightweight model will seem extraordinarily flimsy and flexible, but a great deal of the finished model's strength is derived from the covering itself, so that a miniature stressed-skin structure is created. The most commonly used covering material is super-fine Jap tissue which is quite similar to normal model tissue except that it is appreciably lighter, has a smoother surface which helps in achieving a good painted finish, and it has a better strength-to-weight ratio. When moistened before application to any framework it will readily conform to mildly compound curves without wrinkling, and will draw up tightly when it dries out. Colour schemes and markings are applied using extremely thin mixtures of dope and thinners and are invariably sprayed using an artist's airbrush, and very fine details, together with lettering, can be achieved using a draughtsman's drawing pen.

The great majority of indoor scale models are designed for rubber power. Although $CO_2$-powered models are quite capable of being flown successfully indoors, they require a comparatively much larger space in which to fly safely. They are usually heavier than a rubber model of approximately the same size due to the weight of the motor and its tank, and they tend to fly faster as a result of this. The $CO_2$ model is better suited to outdoor flying where the extra weight and power available will allow it to cope with unsettled wind conditions, and longer flights may be attempted with much less danger of the model damaging itself. The advantage of the $CO_2$ motor lies in the degree of control that one has over its speed and power output. It has a much wider range of usable speeds than an unthrottled diesel

or glow-plug motor, and it will run perfectly steadily at any chosen setting. This is very useful during the initial test flights of a new model since it is possible to slowly build up to the desired flying speed in small increments without putting the model to undue risk.

Almost coincidental with the emergence of interest in indoor scale flying came the birth of the 'Peanut' scale model, originating from the USA, also in the early 1970s. The precise origins of the name remain rather obscure, but the intention was to devise a very simple informal competition class of model that was in marked contrast to the more serious super-scale types. Initially all models were to be built to a wingspan of not larger than 330mm (13in), but an amendment to this rule introduced in mid-1978 allows a model to be built as an alternative to a 230mm (9in) limit on fuselage length, with none on the wings. Because these models are restrictively small, it is rather difficult to build them very lightly using the average quality of balsa wood found in most model shops. This meant that the only way to reduce wing loading effectively was to choose a subject on which the wing had a very broad chord, in the hope of achieving the greatest possible wing area within the 330mm (13in) span limitation. The more obvious way of gaining area, such as choosing a biplane, does not quite work because the additional wing and bracing wires of this type causes

more undesirable drag than can easily be overcome. The effect of this was that the choice of suitable prototypes began to narrow down to a mere handful of rather obscure homebuilt lightplanes which limited the appeal of the class. So, to increase the incentive to build other types and widen the choice of suitable subjects, the new 230mm (9in) fuselage alternative limit was devised so that models with quite high aspect ratio wings are now eligible.

The average weight of a good well-detailed 'Peanut' model lies between 10 to 20gm ($\frac{1}{3}$–$\frac{2}{3}$oz) approximately, but it is certainly possible to build much lighter than this by using the best indoor quality balsa wood and by paring down the weight of every structural member to the absolute minimum consistent with strength. A very accurate model that will fly superbly may weigh as little as three grammes when built using highly refined techniques and covered in condenser paper of the type used on indoor duration models. The heavier type of 'Peanut' model will fly for approximately one minute, whereas the very light-weight types may return times of three or four minutes.

The very great range of strength, stiffness and weight of balsa wood shows up quite markedly in the small sections of material generally used in indoor scale models, and such variations mean that this timber is not always the best one to use in certain applications. The

main fuselage longerons of a model are a case in point. Here, a grade of balsa wood that is stiff enough to resist the shrinking effect of the tissue covering as it pulls tight through doping will be quite heavy, and a lighter grade will distort badly under the same stresses. To overcome this it is possible to use some of the very small sections of basswood that are sold for use on model railways. This timber is much stiffer than balsa, yet the very small sections that can be used, such as 0.8mm sq ($\frac{1}{32}$in), weigh little more than balsa of four times the cross-sectional area, and the weight is more consistent. It is possible, using this material, to attempt structures that would be extremely difficult to equal in strength-to-weight ratio if made in balsa wood, and some of these advantages could be well used on much larger outdoor flying scale types. While indoor scale has opened up a whole new facet of scale flying for many people, the stimulation of ideas and building techniques that it has brought about can do little but benefit all other forms of free-flight scale modelling.

*Opposite:* High wing monoplanes such as this Fieseler Storche make perhaps the safest subjects for flying scale.
*Top:* An early racer, the Bristol Bullet, has adequate tail areas but the lack of dihedral can make it difficult to trim.
*Right:* Knock-off flying surfaces can prevent damage in awkward landings.
*Below:* Modern jet aircraft are not the easiest of subjects, but can use ducted fans driven by internal motors.

# Control Line and Radio-controlled

There are a number of factors which make the flying of scale models by the control-line (C/L) method an attractive alternative to free flight, perhaps the most important one being that, since the model is tethered, the design requirements for stable flight are far less restrictive and thus a wide range of subjects which would otherwise be difficult to tackle become practical propositions, although it must be accepted that the model's performance in flight may be less than realistic.

A particular advantage for scale models is that since the wing loading of a C/L model can be quite high, a strong structure such as balsa planking or sheeting can be used, and there is no weight limit to restrict the amount of scale detail which can be incorporated, including full cockpit interior, working navigation lights, metal cowlings, dummy engines etc. Furthermore, additional working features such as throttle control, operating flaps, bomb dropping and retractable undercarriage can be added. Such features can be operated by the use of an extra control wire or wires which can be pulled to operate certain functions directly, such as release of a bomb or throttle closing and opening or, alternatively, the extra wires can be pulled to operate switches in the model which then operate various electrically-powered functions such as a retractable undercarriage driven by suitably geared miniature electric motors powered by batteries carried in the model. Another method is to use insulated lines carrying an electric current to operate a relay in the model and thus trigger off the desired function. The control-line handle is fitted with the necessary triggers or switches to operate these extra features.

Multi-engine aircraft are especially good subjects for C/L models – the problem of asymmetric power, or failure of one of the engines, which could be troublesome or even disastrous to a free-flight model does not apply, and this opens up a further wide range of suitable prototypes. The choice of subject is therefore completely open and will depend to a large extent upon the modeller's whim – the C/L medium is especially suited to those aircraft which have marginal stability, such as low wing configurations with minimal dihedral typified by the Hawker Hurricane, Messerschmitt 109 and other World War 2 fighters. Also twin-engine types, perhaps with retractable undercarriage and operable flaps, exemplified by the Lockheed Lightning and the DH Mosquito, or there are the multi-engine civil airliners such as the Vickers Viscount. Aerobatic prototypes such as the Great Lakes Special or the Zlinn Akrobat are ideally suited.

It is equally possible to choose a simple high-wing monoplane such as the DH Puss Moth, a World War 1 SPAD biplane – eminently suitable with its lack of dihedral – a Caproni multi-engine triplane, or a four-engine Avro Lancaster complete with flaps, retractable undercarriage and bomb-dropping capability.

Choice may also be influenced by cost, and compared with a R/C model, the C/L counterpart is far less expensive. A suitable flying site may be an over-riding consideration – a C/L model only requires an area which can accommodate a 45m (150ft) diameter circle in order to fly, rather than a large field.

The model engine most suitable for C/L flying, except for a small simple model, is undoubtedly the glow-plug motor, for a number of reasons. Firstly, it is far less messy in operation than the diesel, which throws out rather a lot of oil and can spoil the appearance of a finely-finished model. Secondly, it is easier to fit a silencer which, when coupled to a suitable exhaust, will throw the comparatively small amount of exhaust sludge clear of the model. Thirdly, it will throttle efficiently, most important if engine speed control via a third line is fitted.

Plans for C/L models are available from most aeromodelling magazines and an upper and lower limit of engine size for any particular model is usually given. It is better to over-power rather than under-power the model, especially if throttle control is incorporated, since excess power can be reduced after take-off. The modeller may prefer to design his own scale model, and as detail design and constructional methods do not differ significantly from those used for R/C scale models this aspect will be dealt with in that section.

## Radio-control scale models

The control by radio of a perfect miniature flying replica of a full-size aeroplane is perhaps the ultimate achievement which aero-modelling can offer and the comprehensive range of controls available, coupled with the high degree of reliability provided by modern radio control equipment, makes it possible to tackle virtually any subject, from the early fabric and wire veterans, through the scouts and bombers of World War 1, the colourful aircraft of the inter-war years, both military and civil, including the early airliners, racers and record-breakers, down to the fighters and four-engine bombers of World War 2. Present-day light aircraft, aerobatic specials, home-builts and even jet airliners add to the wide range of prototypes from which to choose. Retractable undercarriages, operating flaps, crop-spraying, bomb-dropping and innumerable other working features are all easily incorporated in the modern R/C scale model.

## Choice of subject

The choice of a subject depends upon personal preference and practical considerations such as whether the model is intended for competition purposes or as a rugged weekend sports flyer, how much radio control equipment is to be installed, and what experience the modeller has in building and flying. The standard form of radio offers four functions (aileron, rudder, elevator and throttle) possibly with one or two extra controls for ancillary items such as retractable undercarriage and flaps, and with this type of equipment virtually any prototype can be tackled. This does not rule out the popular two-function outfit for scale use, though the choice of prototype is slightly restricted.

Aircraft types most suitable for two-function control include high-wing and parasol monoplanes, shoulder and midwing aeroplanes and many examples of biplane. The subject should possess a good degree of inherent stability, which is indicated by fairly large tail surfaces and reasonably generous dihedral, although the latter is not essential in high-wing or parasol types which have a fair amount of pendulum stability, that is to say, the low cg position tends to return the model to a level attitude.

*Above:* Fokker EV/DVIII C/L scale model, 48 in. span, OS40 engine. A past British Nationals winner by H. Venables.
*Right:* A 66in Handley Page 42 Hannibal by J. Shelley. Two 1.3cc and two 0.75cc diesels, radio-controlled.
*Bottom:* Another past national R/C champion, this 72in DH9 is twelve years old. Built by Dennis Thumpston.

Taking the parasol wing group first, this includes such attractive aircraft as the Sopwith Swallow, Fokker D8, Luton Minor and Westland Widgeon, while high-wing cabin monoplanes, which are eminently suitable subjects for the beginner, are exemplified by the DH Puss Moth, Piper Cub, Fieseler Storch, and the wide range of Austers and Cessnas. There is also an interesting selection of shoulder-wing types such as the Tipsy Nipper, Bristol Monoplane, Antoinette and Comper Swift, and the midwing Fokker Eindekker.

Most of the earlier biplanes are also suitable for rudder control, for example, the Sopwith Pup, Avro 504K, most of the De Havilland types, Albatross C1 and the Curtiss Jenny (but *not* the Fokker D7 or Sopwith Camel which do not have sufficient stability). Later biplanes, as typified by the DH Moths, may also be flown by this medium.

Low-wing types are not generally suitable for rudder control, since turns induced by rudder on these types tend to build up into spiral dives, but this category can still be flown successfully using the two-function system by substituting aileron control for rudder and choosing a simple fixed undercarriage type such as the Miles Magister, Fairchild PT 19 or Druine Turbulent.

Three-function radio brings in elevator control which improves take-off and makes flying easier in windy weather by enabling the pilot to push the nose down and make headway upwind. Also, a wider range of aerobatics becomes possible and landings are much more realistic due to the ability to flare out before touch-down and land the model at a slow groundspeed in a three-point attitude, which also minimizes the possibility of damage to a complicated scale undercarriage.

With four or more function radio, including of course trim control, the choice of subject is virtually unlimited. While many scale fliers prefer a fully-aerobatic fighter type with retractable undercarriage and operating flaps, such as the Spitfire, others use the full range of controls to build a four-engine bomber such as the Boeing B17 Fortress with opening bomb-bay doors and bomb-dropping capability, since multi-engine types are perfectly practical subjects – an engine failure in the air can be dealt with by applying opposite rudder trim to offset the effects of asymmetric power, or if this fails, the remaining motors can be throttled back and an emergency landing made.

At the same time, full radio control may equally be fitted into a model of a slow-flying, non-aerobatic type such as the Aeronca C3, for its is unnecessary to choose a fully-aerobatic or complex multi-

# CURTISS TOMAHAWK
## control-line model

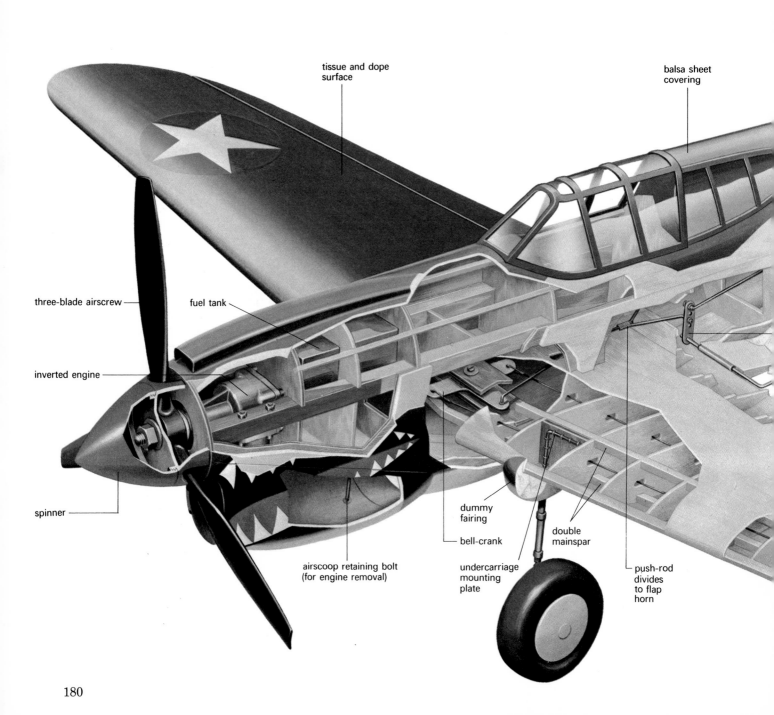

three-blade airscrew

inverted engine

spinner

fuel tank

tissue and dope surface

balsa sheet covering

airscoop retaining bolt (for engine removal)

dummy fairing

bell-crank

undercarriage mounting plate

double mainspar

push-rod divides to flap horn

engine prototype – the radio is merely the means by which any chosen model may be flown in a manner which simulates as nearly as possible its full-size counterpart.

Other interesting subjects exploiting the advantages provided by full R/C could include a sky-writing SE5 using a controllable smoke canister, a parachute-dropping Douglas Dakota, a crop-dusting Auster Agricola or Stearman, a rocket-firing Hawker Typhoon, or a dive-bombing Stuka or Douglas Dauntless.

Considerations of automatic stability are not especially critical when choosing a subject for radio control, since the model is controllable in all axes and will be flown in exactly the same way as the full-size. It will only be necessary to ensure that the correct wing and tail incidences are used, as will be mentioned later, and that the cg is in the correct position, usually between 20% and 30% of the mean chord.

**Plans, power and weight**
There are three ways in which to approach the building of the model, by purchasing a kit or a set of working drawings, or by scaling up one's own working drawings from accurate drawings of the full-size aeroplane. These last can be obtained from aeromodelling magazines, contemporary issues of aeronautical journals which can usually be found at the reference library in most large cities (where duplicating facilities are usually available), from one of the 'Profile' publications, or even from the actual aircraft manufacturers. Scale details not shown on the drawings may be obtained by close study of photographs, or from the actual aeroplane if it still exists.

The size of the model will depend to a certain extent on the type of radio equipment to be installed, and for a two- or three-function set, the optimum span is between 1 to 1.5m (40–60in), with a maximum weight of approximately 2kg (5lb). A model of this size would require an engine of 5 to 7.5cc (0.29–0.45cu. in), depending on whether the prototype was a slow or fast-flying aircraft. For a four or more function model, the span should be 1.5 to 2m (60–80in) with a maximum weight of 6kg (13lb) for the upper size. The engine power for this size of model should be 10cc (0.6cu.in). The larger models are certainly more impressive in flight and scale speeds tend to be more realistic, but once the span exceeds 2m (80in), weight becomes a problem, as does the question of adequate power.

It is advisable to tend slightly to over-power the model; an under-powered model can be difficult and even dangerous to fly. Another point to consider is the amount of drag or air-resistance. For example, a biplane with a large radial engine cowling, struts and bracing wires would require the same power as a streamlined fighter type of the same weight despite being a slower flying machine.

Regulations on maximum permissible weight and power for model aircraft vary in different countries, and the upper limits quoted here are those in use for international competition. The larger category of model mentioned above, weighing 6kg (13lb) could in fact take a motor of 13cc (0.80cu.in) if local regulations permitted. Models exceeding the national maximum levels for weight and power can, however, be flown if permission to fly is obtained from the governing body, and appropriate insurance cover obtained.

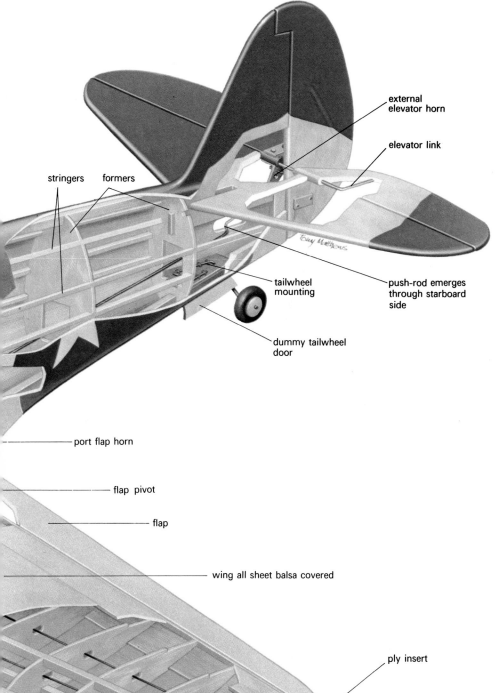

stringers
formers
external elevator horn
elevator link
tailwheel mounting
push-rod emerges through starboard side
dummy tailwheel door
port flap horn
flap pivot
flap
wing all sheet balsa covered
ply insert
ribs
adjustable lead-out guide
lead-out wires

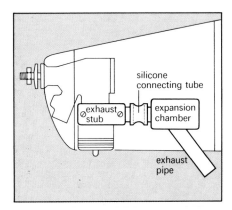

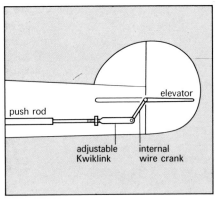

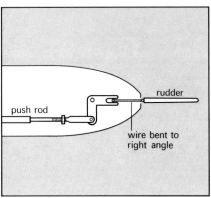

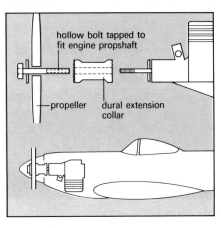

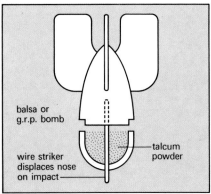

## Design and Construction

Having scaled up the drawing (as detailed elsewhere), the result is a basic outline of the aeroplane, which must now be filled in with the design detail required to build the model. The aim must be to construct the airframe in such a way that, when it is covered, it will present the same external appearance as that of the prototype.

Taking the fuselage first, a fabric-covered aircraft necessitates the faithful reproduction of the full-size construction – longerons of scale thickness (spruce giving the required strength) and the correct number of vertical spacers and stringers; every surface detail will show through nylon covering. Any ply-covered areas on the original must be sheeted on the model, using either balsa or 1mm ply. A ply-covered aircraft is easier to simulate, again using balsa or thin ply, but the perfectionist will place the fuselage formers in their correct scale positions so that any slight sag noticeable in the ply on the full-size aircraft will be reproduced.

The modern metal stressed-skin fuselage is best simulated by using a planked balsa covering over the basic formers, and after this has been sanded and tissue covered, and rivet detail applied, the effect is most realistic. It is possible to use thin aluminium sheet covering, and although this is not too difficult if there are no compound curves, any later damage is very hard to repair.

The siting of the radio gear should as far as possible leave the interior of the cockpit or cabin clear so that realistic interior detail can be fitted. The radio on/off switch and battery charging point must be accommodated in an easily accessible position, using, if possible, existing opening hatches on the full-size to hide these functional items on the model. The aerial should be hidden away along the inside of the fuselage well away from the servos, which might cause interference.

Wing construction should also simulate the appearance of the full-size, making sure that a fabric-covered type has the correct num-

*Top:* Enclosing a silencer in the cowling. Brass chamber is home-built.
*Second:* Internal elevator linkage, to avoid out-of-scale external rods.
*Third:* A similar hidden linkage arrangement for the rudder.
*Fourth:* An extension shaft allowing the engine to be out of sight.
*Bottom:* A bomb which gives a realistic 'smoke' puff on impact.

ber of wing ribs and riblets as well as any areas of sheet covering. It is important that the correct wing section should be retained, since deviation alters the characteristic appearance of the aircraft; in order to achieve adequate strength in a thin undercambered wing, spruce spars should be employed. Similarly, the correct dihedral angle and wing incidence should be used. This type of wing is associated chiefly with biplanes, and is best attached to a rigid cabane and centre section structure, with dural tongues, bent to the dihedral angle, protruding from the centre section and fuselage sides, locating in ply-wood boxes in the wing roots. The bracing wires should be functional in order to withstand flying loads.

Ply-covered or metal stressed-skin wings are dealt with in the way described for fuselages, and as this type of wing is usually featured on low-wing monoplanes, a one-piece structure may be used, fixed to the underside of the fuselage with nylon bolts. Some low-wing aircraft feature separate wing halves attached to wing stubs, and this can be duplicated on the model, the thickness of the wing at the root providing ample space for a good deep tongue and box. High-wing aircraft usually have two separate wing halves rather than a one-piece structure, requiring two anchorage points at each wing root and relying upon the wing-struts for strength.

The tail unit is made similarly to the wing, and is a permanent fixture to the fuselage. All control surfaces on the wings and tail should be of the correct scale size, and they should be hinged in the correct manner, using inset or shrouded hinges.

The engine cowling can sometimes be realistically represented in balsa, but it is usually preferable to make a glass fibre moulding for a radial cowl, or one of complex shape. Side panels may be made from tinplate, or thin aluminium sheet if a natural metal finish was a feature of the full-size aircraft's cowlings. The model engine should be mounted in such a way that the cylinder head does not protrude from the cowling, which may mean an inverted installation. Even this may not suffice if the prototype has a fairly pointed nose; an extension shaft can be fitted to move the cylinder head further back where increased depth will hide it. A silencer is necessary and this should be enclosed within the engine cowling, an added touch of realism being obtained by connecting the silencer outlet to the actual scale exhaust pipe.

## Finish, colour and markings

The final appearance of the model depends to a very large extent on the application of the covering material and the colouring, the success of this in turn depending on the finish of the basic airframe. With fabric-covered models it is essential that all wood which will come into contact with the nylon covering material should be sanded smooth, doped with clear dope and then sanded again, repeating until the grain is filled. Particular attention should be paid to the edges of the wing ribs and the wing trailing edges. The nylon covering should be applied damp, and after it has dried out, given three or four coats of *thinned* clear shrinking dope, rather than one or two thick coats, thus acquiring a more even distribution.

Models with a sheet-covered or planked construction must also be sanded smooth, doped and filled with two or three coats of thin sanding sealer, sanded down between each coat, before finally doping on a layer of lightweight model tissue.

Many aircraft have a semi-matt appearance, and this can be reproduced by using an eggshell polyurethane paint, using several *thin* coats brushed or sprayed on, which will give a fuel-proof finish. For a gloss finish, there is a wide range of colour dopes with fuel-proof properties in addition to clear fuel-proof varnishes.

Markings may be transfers (decals) or painted directly on to the model. Ink compasses, filled with thinned paint or dope, can be used to outline roundels which are then filled in by brush, and large letters can be painted using masking to get a clean edge. The correct size, style and positioning of lettering and markings will add appreciably to the realism of the model.

## Scale detail

There are innumerable small items of scale detail which will add immensely to the final appearance of the model, and the following items will help to give a convincing impression.

Flush rivets can be represented by using a short length of brass tube of appropriate diameter as a tool. By pressing and twisting the sharpened end at each rivet posi-

tion, a realistic rivet mark is created, but this should be done just before the final coat of paint is applied. Raised rivets can be made from shortened pins or by applying small dots of white glue from a hypodermic syringe.

Cockpit edging can be made from very thin skiver leather fixed with contact adhesive. Some cockpit edging was studded, in which case shortened brass pins can be inserted, but some was stitched, and this can be accurately reproduced with needle and thread.

External control cables may be difficult to connect to the servos,

*Right:* Fuselage detail of a 68in CA Wirraway by D. Vaughan. The model weighs 8.3kg (9½lb).
*Below:* A popular subject for R/C is the Spitfire. This one is a Mk 9E in an authentic colour scheme.
*Bottom:* Also a popular choice is the Vought Corsair, as this example in Pacific colours, built by J. Palmer.

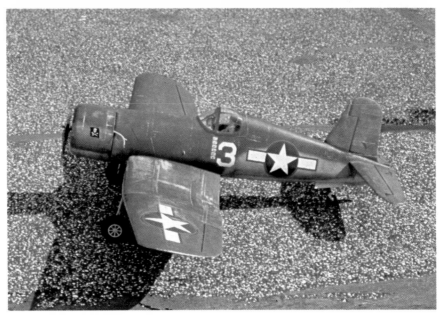

and to overcome this controls can be fitted with hidden internal linkages and dummy external cables. Dummy turnbuckles can be made by sliding a small length of thin brass tube, with a tiny nut at each end, over the bracing or control cable and gluing in position.

Machine guns can be purchased ready-made, but it is quite simple to make them using aluminium tube for the barrels and carved balsa block for the body of the gun. To get the right gunmetal colour, mix a little silver and a touch of blue with the black.

Wheels are also commercially available, but the hubs may need to be reworked to give a true scale appearance, and the tyres can also be given the correct tread by careful scoring. Retractable undercarriage units can be obtained ready-made, but the keen modeller may wish to build his own to give a truer scale effect.

Venturi tubes, such as those seen on the fuselage sides of the DH Tiger Moth, can be made by flaring out each end of a short piece of aluminium tube and fixing it with a small tinplate bracket. Piano hinges on small hatches can be simulated by filing score marks along a length of brass tube – the hatch can be made to open by inserting a piece of thin piano wire through the tube, bending the ends at right angles, and pushing them into the airframe.

Part or all of the engine will probably be visible on the full size aircraft and this should be represented on the model by making dummy cylinders which can either be turned from wood or built up from circular discs of different diameters to represent the fins, and appropriately painted. Spark plugs can be represented by sliding a tiny sleeve of white insulation stripped from bell wire over a piece of fine piano wire and sliding a tiny nut over the white sleeve. In the case of a rotary or radial engine, the cylinders are then grouped around a balsa crankcase.

The interior of the cockpit or cabin should not be overlooked, the instrument panel being perhaps the most important item. Instruments can be merely painted on the dashboard, but perfectionists have been known to photographically reduce the full-size dials to the correct scale size, add working pointers and fit glazing! Control column, rudder pedals and throttle levers are easily reproduced from scrap tube and balsa, and the seat for the pilot

does not present much difficulty, whether it be of the metal bucket variety or upholstered leather. Safety harnesses, maps and other items, such as tiny fire extinguishers, all add to the effect.

## Flying

Radio-control scale flying, whether for sport or in competition, consists of flying the model in a manner similar to that of its full-size counterpart. For example, when taxying out for take-off, an aircraft with a conventional undercarriage and limited visibility would zig-zag from side to side, and the model should do the same. The climb after take-off should be at scale rate, and when operating height has been reached the engine should be throttled back to give cruising speed as in full-size practice. Scale speed is most important, a common fault being to fly too fast, and overcontrolling should be avoided.

*Above:* Ducted fan model of scale appearance; true scale models of jets are not so far a practical proposition.
*Below:* American-entered Fairchild 24W Ranger at the 1978 World Scale Championships held in England.
*Opposite, top:* 1978 World Scale Champion was Mick Reeves of Britain with a fine Fournier RF4.
*Opposite, bottom:* A World Championship entry from France was this enormous model of the German Bucker Jungmeister.

Extra power would be used for aerobatics, but a non-aerobatic prototype such as the Druine Turbulent would be restricted to course-flying manoeuvres. A rectangular landing circuit should be flown prior to the approach, not only to enhance realism, but also to aid judgment of height and distance when coming in to land – not forgetting to lower the undercarriage on the downwind leg!

# Materials and Building Techniques

An advanced structure for a rubber-powered scale model, following closely the full-size airframe. Balsa has been the main model aircraft material for nearly 50 years, and though new materials have been introduced, remains first choice for the vast majority of enthusiasts.

## Materials

To the majority of aircraft modellers balsa wood is considered the prime building material. However, it was not always so, and may not be in the future; a myriad of new products, stemming mainly from the plastics industry, have entered modellers' workshops and many are equal to balsa, even if few surpass it.

Early flying models were built from bamboo, cane and wire with a covering of oiled silk. Slowly spruce and birch crept in until the early 1930s, when balsa arrived on the scene. The light weight and high strength obtainable from this wood, coupled with lighter covering materials such as Japanese tissue paper, enabled massive weight savings to be achieved, with corresponding increases in flying performances.

Found mainly in Ecuador, the balsa tree (*Ochroma lagopus*) grows very quickly, reaching a height of around 6m (20ft) in about a year and growing to around 20 to 30m (70–100ft) within the next 6 to 10 years. This is the correct time for the tree to be felled, for as it gets older the tree deteriorates and rots. Because the growth is so rapid, wet and dry spells have a marked effect on its density, leading to wide variation in the quality of the cut wood.

Botanically, balsa is a hardwood with an almost unique strength-to-weight ratio, on a par with oak.

For many years its harvesting was a sideline – it was cut wild to make rafts to float bananas down river (balsa means 'raft') – and only a small percentage of the balsa cut was suitable for models. Only in recent years has any attempt been made to cut wood especially for modelling.

Because of the wide variation in quality, modelling balsa is available in an equally wide range of densities from as low as 70 to 90kg/m³ (4–5lb/ft³) to as high as 280 to 350kg/m³ (16–20lb/ft³) although for modelling, densities of between 100 to 200kg/m³ (6–12lb/ft³) are most common. The choice of the correct grade of balsa for any given job is of paramount importance and the more expert modeller will shop carefully to choose the many different grades to be used in any one aircraft.

However, the story does not end here for not only is the density of the wood important but so is the 'cut', the way the grain runs in the finished sheet has a marked effect on the stiffness of the sheet and therefore on the way it can best be used in the aircraft's structure. In general terms balsa may be cut from the log in one of three ways,
(A) Tangentially to the log,
(B) Radially to the log,
(C) Diagonally, or quarter-sawn.

'A' cut has broad grain and is flexible; it is used for tubes, curved sheet covering, and the like. 'B' cut is very stiff and will bend only slightly before splitting or snapping. Its grain pattern is close and straight, and it is best suited to spars and similar rigid members. Most useful, but least easy to find, is 'C' cut or quarter-grain wood. Distinguished by gold or silvery speckles in the grain, it offers the best stiffness/strength for the lightest weight. It is ideal for wing ribs and fuselage formers, and at least one distributor has recently taken to stamping 'Rib Stock' across suitable sheets. The rest of the balsa log provides random cut timber, which may be stiff on one edge and flexible on the other; care is needed in selection so that pieces with the right characteristics are employed for the part of the structure in hand.

Although balsa is of adequate strength for most modelling, additional reinforcement is often needed in areas of high stress. Most common is the use of thin plywood (usually birch), spruce and beech. Spruce in small sizes is often used in place of balsa for wing spars on those aircraft subject to severe

flight loads. Beech is favoured for additional strength in areas where internal combustion engines are fitted and may be found in model shops under the description 'engine bearer'. Plywood for modelling comes in a range of sizes rarely seen in timber merchants, being too small for the DIY market. Common sizes range through 0.4mm ($\frac{1}{64}$in), 0.8mm ($\frac{1}{32}$in), 1.5mm($\frac{1}{16}$in) and 3mm ($\frac{1}{8}$in) although these are all approximate as quite large tolerances are allowed in manufacture.

Modern materials have crept somewhat slowly into the model aircraft world, some as a balsa 'substitute' and some as genuine alternatives. Many plastics can now be found, particularly in kit models, some of which exhibit useful properties and others being somewhat marginal. Glass fibre, or Glass Reinforced Plastic (GRP) to give it its proper name, finds a ready use for reinforcing tradi-

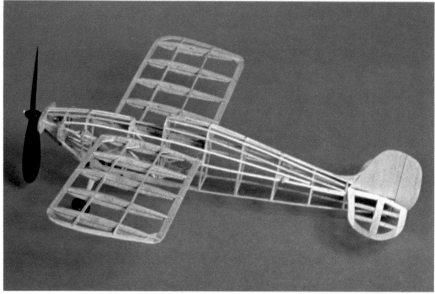

*Top:* Another close-to-scale structure, though this example incorporates solid sheet ribs and basic fuselage sides.
*Above:* A simplified structure achieving a scale outline with very light weight but adequate strength.
*Below:* The effect of cut on the grain formation of a balsa sheet.
*Opposite, top:* Extensive use of sheet and block balsa in a control-line model produces considerable strength at acceptable weight.
*Opposite, lower:* Light sheeting and planking combined with tissue or fabric covered areas creates the right strength/weight ratio for this model.

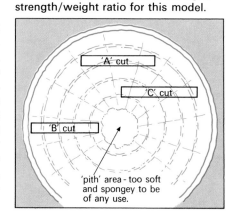

## Adhesives

Modern materials may have been slow to oust the traditional, but it is not so with adhesives, almost every year brings a startling new product. Balsa cement, for years the mainstay of model aircraft construction, is now challenged by water-based PVA glues (white carpentry glue). Balsa cement is a rapid drying cellulose-based adhesive, having a virtually transparent appearance when dry; high stress balsa joints require a double dose of cement, thereby largely negating the advantages of quick drying time. On large areas, it tends to dry before application is completed. Its shrinkage during drying is also a disadvantage, especially on small light models where distortion may well occur. White glues take longer to dry and penetrate further into the grain, giving a more satisfactory joint. They are water soluble and therefore are best not used on seaplanes and flying boats! They do, however, make removing surplus glue from fingers and clothes quite easy. One major snag is that PVA dries clear with a slightly rubbery feel, and on models which are planked or sheeted it is likely to 'pick up' on glasspaper, and in extreme cases may even pull out from the joint.

Aliphatic resins similar to PVA and also marketed as a woodworking glue, are usually creamy in colour and may be used like PVA. The prime difference is that they dry hard (if slightly yellow) and can be sanded to a smooth finish. Many other modern adhesives are used for specific reasons. For instance contact adhesives are widely used for large area fixing. Ply and balsa reinforcing doublers are often stuck to, say, the fuselage sides with such adhesives. These petroleum-based glues, more usually associated with fixing plastic laminates to kitchen work tops, are not fuel-proof and therefore their uses must be restricted to areas free from fuel. They must also be kept away from styrofoam as the glue (even the fumes) will dissolve the foam completely away. Latex-based contact adhesives are more often used for large foam areas, such as skinning the foam with balsa wood, veneers or thin ply.

Epoxy resin adhesives are especially good for high strength joints, particularly where metals are involved. These resins are incredibly strong and cure chemically rather than by evaporation. They consist of two parts which only

tional materials in areas of local high stress. More recently whole models, or major parts of models such as fuselages, have been made entirely of GRP. Glass and resin work needs a different approach and different tools from those used with balsa, and some of the techniques are not so easily mastered. Adhesives, too, differ.

Expanded polystyrene (styrofoam as it is sometimes known) is another recent innovation. Styrofoam can be as light if not lighter than balsa, depending on how it is moulded, but at comparable weight it has little strength. Suitable reinforcement to achieve this strength brings weight penalties, and finished sub-assemblies often weigh more than their balsa equivalents. However, other attributes, such as speed of construction and accuracy of outline and section, can often render the foam-built unit more attractive; to the R/C model flier, whose attitude is often that of 'no

time to build – all my spare time is spent flying', ready-moulded glass fuselages and ready-finished foam wings and tail offer a welcome time saving.

Another high strength plastic to make its mark on the model scene is nylon. Rarely used for whole models, nylon appears in a vast number of smaller assemblies such as engine mountings, propellers and precision small parts such as undercarriage retraction units and the like.

It perhaps should be emphasized that although many modern models are constructed entirely from plastic products, the weight penalty is usually such that those built from traditional balsa and ply will almost certainly have a superior performance. Consideration must also be given to repairs – few modellers get away with never breaking a model and in most cases the plastic materials prove more difficult to repair than wood.

start to 'cure' when brought into contact with each other. At normal temperatures, most epoxies require 24h to cure, although raising the temperature will accelerate this process. More recently, fast-setting epoxies (with curing times varying from 90sec to 20min) have made great inroads into modelling, allowing almost as much strength of joint in a much more convenient time scale.

Newer still is the expanding range of cyano-acrylate adhesives which have, quite literally, revolutionized construction. Most of these adhesives will work on the majority of modelling materials, producing a truly 'instant' joint in a matter of a few seconds. Like all 'wonder products', however, they have their snags. First they are not gap-filling, which in turn means that the modeller must produce excellently fitting joints to benefit from these glues. Secondly, and probably more important, is their ability to bond human flesh in seconds. While it really should not be necessary to advise the use of caution on *all* modern adhesives, cyano-acrylates *must* be used with great caution to avoid accidentally sticking one's fingers together, or to the model. (Methanol is one of the few solvents which is effective on cyano-acry-

lates and it is a good idea to have some handy in case the modeller becomes accidentally stuck.)

Care is needed in the selection of the right glue for any one job. Most common jobs may safely be tackled with white or yellow woodworking glue, but many specialist jobs require specialist adhesives. Glass fibre makes an excellent example, for while most glues *appear* to work, they will part company under quite modest stress (even strong glues like epoxies). Only glass/resin-based glues are of any use with this material, a point not always appreciated. However, the stores specializing in GRP products will be able to supply the necessary adhesives. Many of the surface fillers used to fill local nicks and dents prior to painting may also be obtained from such a specialist supplier.

## Structures

The use of traditional and/or modern structures depends as much on personal whim as it does on the type of model. Lighter weight models, free flight in particular, tend to be more dependent on traditional materials, while the less weight-conscious, such as C/L and R/C models, make greater use of newer materials.

Most used of all the traditional structures is the built-up frame-work made from a multitude of small balsa parts. It produces a very light but strong frame which can readily be reinforced at high stress points. Such structures may be made inherently weak, especially when light weight is imperative, and then the skin over the structure forms part of the strength.

Additional use of balsa sheet is quite common as both a reinforcing technique and as a means of simplifying construction; many novice models are of 'all sheet' construction which, while both simple and strong, must carry a weight penalty. Either way, the basic fuselage consists of a 'box', usually square or rectangular in section, perhaps with additions outside to enhance overall appearance or produce a better aerodynamic shape. Wings and tail are usually more straightforward, the aerodynamic attributes stemming from the basic construction of spars running from wingtip to wingtip supporting shaped 'ribs' fore and aft which, when covered, produce the 'lift' by which the aircraft flies.

The 'half-keel' technique is also common, particularly in scale modelling, and is formed by fitting half bulkheads to one side of a basic

covering adds much strength (and not a little weight) and provides a more rigid surface for carrying extra detail as, say, in a scale model.

Modern structural techniques make maximum use of 'stressed skin' design where the internal structure is minimal or non-load-bearing and reliance is placed on the outer skin being strong enough in its own right; examples are GRP moulded fuselages and veneer covered foam wings. Both these recent innovations have much to offer the modeller and lend themselves to ease of mass production, so it is quite common to find C/L and R/C model kits produced in this manner, featuring quite complex moulded fuselage shapes and aerodynamically clean wing panels. Much of the work is done by the kit manufacturer, offering the modeller rapid assembly and superlative surface finish.

The time and materials involved show no advantage for the home modeller producing a single model. GRP is a difficult material to work with at the weight levels required, and specific knowledge is needed to get the best from it. Constructing a fuselage requires a wooden master from which to work; accuracy is important, for once a female mould is formed any defect or deviation will be faithfully copied in the GRP replica. Most usually the female mould is made in two halves, also from GRP, using several layers of glass cloth to produce a high level of rigidity. The insides are polished to remove any small defects and then coated with a special wax polish (release agent) to which resin will not adhere. Layers of glass cloth and resin are then used to line the inside of the mould. If required, stiffening is provided internally by working in more glass cloth and resin and, where necessary, adding transverse bulkheads. When dry, the fuselage halves are carefully prised out of their moulds and joined together with yet more glass cloth and resin.

Veneered foam wings are also an easy item to mass-produce, and are not as daunting to the home constructor as working in GRP. Expanded polystyrene foam is a light and homogeneous plastic that can be worked with traditional modelling tools. It can also be melted at quite low temperatures, for example with the tip of a soldering iron. It

*Above:* A smart colour scheme need not be elaborate. Transfer or contact film, ruler and knife did this.
*Right:* Just a little colour smartens this combat model enormously.
*Bottom:* Tissue registration letters and stripes add negligible weight. Wing in foreground shows typical double spar construction, but with riblets and rib gussets.

keel of balsa strip. Longitudinal stringers cut from thin balsa strip are added and, when lifted from the construction table, half a fuselage results. The second side may either be built in a similar fashion and the two halves joined or, more usually, constructed directly on to the reverse of the first side. This technique is found in many kits for rubber-driven free-flight scale models, but may equally be applied to larger models, in particular C/L and R/C. The specific advantages of this structure are extreme rigidity and accuracy with light weight.

Heavier (and usually larger) models may use this basic structural approach but with the framework covered with thin sheet balsa, usually around 1.5 to 3mm ($\frac{1}{16}$–$\frac{1}{8}$in) thick, compound curves being dealt with by dampening the sheet or by cutting it into strips and 'planking' the outer surface as in boat construction. This all-wood outer

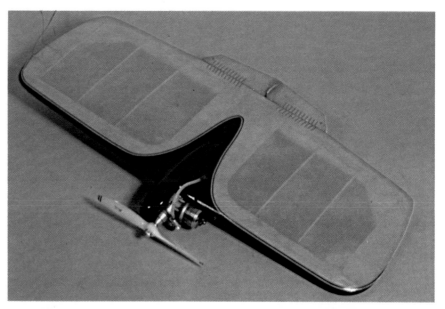

is, therefore, much easier to produce an accurate wing panel by cutting with a heated straight wire, cheese-board fashion. The wire most commonly used is nickel-chrome, and as such may be purchased for the purpose, although thin piano wire or even control-line flying wire may be used. Heat is obtained by connecting the wire to a 12v car battery or similar source (but *never* the mains!) until 'black' heat is achieved and the foam cuts cleanly. To keep the wire taut, it is usually fitted to a cane bow, archery fashion. Templates are made for the sections for root and tip of the wing and these are pinned to the ends of the foam block from which the wing is to be cut, and the hot wire run, spanwise, around the templates to produce the finished 'core'; practice soon builds proficiency. Pieces of 'hot wire' bent to specific shapes can be used to cut out awkward areas for fitting undercarriage blocks etc.

Polystyrene foam on its own is quite light, but yields little strength, therefore a skin must be fixed to it. Furniture type veneers are common in UK and Europe, but balsa sheet is also used. Some foam wings are even skinned with thick paper or thin cardboard. With practice, surface skinning becomes very simple, using latex glues. Other glues may melt foam, so try it on a scrap piece first. Lightweight glass cloth with epoxy resins has some advantages, but only epoxy glass resins are suitable, as polyester resins will dissolve the foam.

**Covering**
Like structures, covering is a 'horses-for-courses' subject, with traditional and modern approaches. Mention has already been made of the 'stressed skin' requirement and for lighter free-flight models this is still achieved using tissue and dope. Various grades of tissue are available, those referred to as 'Japanese tissue' being lightest and available in colours. Self-coloured tissue may remove the need for painted decoration, with subsequent weight saving. Special colours may be obtained by dyeing the tissue in conventional clothing dyes.

Tissue may be applied to the model framework with clear cellulose dope or with tissue pastes made for the job, and may be applied dry or damp. Dampening helps the tissue to follow compound curves in the structure without wrinkles, drying to a smooth, taut, surface

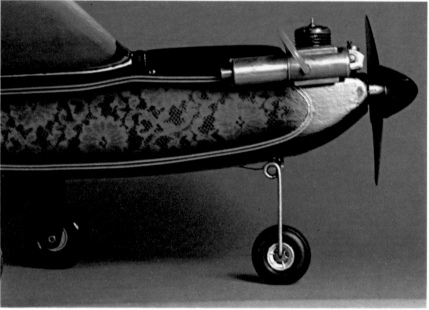

that requires only one or two thin coats of clear dope to provide the final tautening and fill the pores. Fragile structures achieve most of their strength from this method of covering but it must be approached with care. Light structures should always be carefully pinned down flat during shrinking to avoid warping.

A logical extension of this technique is to use stronger and heavier materials. Close woven nylon cloth may be used on larger models in exactly the same manner as tissue and exhibits tremendous strength for its weight. On models subjected to the punishment of, say, novice flying, it will amply repay the slightly higher cost. It may be purchased coloured, or can be dyed to save painting, time and weight. Silk is sometimes used, being somewhat lighter than nylon and almost as strong. As with tissue, the silk or nylon may be applied either wet or dry, with either clear dope or adhesives such as office paste. Clear dope will fill the weave of the material and pull it taut.

A more recent innovation which

Spray finishes offer scope for many effects. This model used lace masking and pinstripe adhesive tape to produce an unusual decor. A good basic surface must be prepared before any such special effects are applied, though this of course applies to any finish for a model.

has had a far-reaching effect on modelling was the introduction of polymer films as a covering medium. These plastic films offer a totally different covering method, providing a high gloss, super-taut finish in a matter of a few minutes, without the mess and smell associated with dopes. They come in a multitude of colours, including transparents and metallics. The tough plastic film is sensitive to heat and under its application will shrink by about one-third. The film is translucent and is coated on the rear with a coloured, heat sensitive adhesive which in turn is protected by a clear backing sheet.

The backing sheet is removed and the film is laid, adhesive side down, on to the surface of the model. A domestic iron set to 'low' may be used to tack the film to the edges of

Mottle camouflage such as used on the Me109 and other German aircraft can really only be applied convincingly by spray techniques. These pictures also show the effects of structure and panelling which can be achieved with suitable masks and a little practice.

the model. Having stuck the edges, apply heat from the iron, or from a hot air source, such as a hair dryer, and the film will shrink to adhere closely all over the surface. Careful working with the iron will allow the film to negotiate compound curves. Multi-colour schemes may be achieved by laying one coloured film on another, thin strips of film may be ironed on to achieve effects such as stripes, and decoration may be cut from contrasting colours and ironed on top.

These films are immensely strong, but by virtue of their strength gradient they add nothing to the surface strength of the structure and cannot be considered to act as a stressed skin. Structures must therefore be of sufficient strength in their own right, such as sheet-covered models or foam wings. Where open structure air-frames are to be used with plastic film covering, sufficient internal strength *must* be designed into the structure.

Plastic films are impervious to model aircraft fuels, but the adhesive is not, so seal carefully any exposed edges of these films where they come into contact with raw fuel or exhaust residue. This is particularly important in engine and fuel tank areas, for once the film has lifted, no amount of re-ironing will induce it to stick down again.

**Finishing**

Finishing models is largely a question of personal whim, functional requirements, technical skill and artistic flair.

Where weight saving is of paramount importance, tissue covering is usual, with paint kept to a minimum and used only for the purposes of good visibility. However, this is not to say that this type of model is lacking in visual appeal, for skilful application of coloured tissue can result in some quite eye-catching schemes.

Even simple application of the model's name or competition entry number can enhance appearance, not to mention trim lines, easily achieved with overlays of more than one colour of tissue simply doped in place. Lettering, often a source of difficulty to aero-modellers, can be traced from news-paper headlines or advertisements.

Where tissue covered surfaces must be painted, as for example, in free-flight scale models, care is needed in the application of the paint to avoid unnecessary weight build-up and in any prefinishing work attempted. Thin coats of clear dope or sanding sealer are commonly applied as a base for the final colour coat, and benefit from a light sanding down between coats. Obviously it requires a delicate touch, for it is all too easy to sand right through the tissue, parti-cularly at high spots such as wing ribs or fuselage stringers.

In the quest for weight saving, an airbrush or small spray gun becomes desirable, since one coat of brushed on colour can well weigh up to 10 times that of a sprayed coat. Extreme care is needed in applying masking or stencils – or, rather, in removing them from a tissue covered model.

Prefinish techniques are easier on larger models, where weight is, perhaps, not quite so critical. Balsa sheet covered or GRP and foam models have a stronger surface and therefore may take rubbing down with less likelihood of damage. Traditionally, balsa surfaces are sealed with coats of dope and/or sanding sealer and, more often than not, tissue covered as well to pro-vide a suitable surface upon which to spray. Each prefinish coat is thoroughly rubbed down, using progressively finer grades of garnet or wet and dry paper. Final pre-colour preparation will most likely be a primer similar to that used on cars, although it is well to check that the final finishing material does not specify some particular primer, again well rubbed down.

Polyester and epoxy finishing resins may be applied over balsa, but only epoxy can be used on bare foam; ultra light glass cloth may be incorporated during the application of these finishing resins, adding enormous strength to the surface of the airframe.

It must be apparent that, as in any high quality paint job, tremendous effort is used in the preparation and indeed in the final coats. The novice modeller's natural instinct for a good paint scheme should be subdued until the 'bent' model becomes a rarity rather than the commonplace. Ready coloured nylon will yield, as with tissue, a simple, eye-catching scheme that offers good airborne visibility with ease of repair following the inevitable 'prang'. The ease with which a chosen scheme can be repaired and its ability to be seen clearly when airborne are the important factors.

A very wide choice of spray guns, airbrushes, aerosols of propellant, compressors, gauges and so on tend to confuse a newcomer, but an obvious precaution is to choose equipment compatible with other items to make up a spraying system. All spray guns and airbrushes consume air, some more than others, and the compressor chosen must be capable of providing both the air-flow and pressure required by the gun in question. Similarly, differing guns offer differing areas of cover and differing degrees of finesse; the need is to select a gun or guns to fit closely the jobs envisaged for it. To spray a 2m (6ft) R/C biplane, for example, requires a totally different unit from that needed to spray a $\frac{1}{72}$nd scale plastic kit.

Similarly the wide range of available paints requires careful thought. For many years coloured cellulose (dope) was standard, and its use is still widespread. Fast drying and with a good surface finish, cellulose is compatible with most modelling materials except polystyrene foam. However, cellulose is not proof against model fuels, nor the hot exhaust waste, and this means a final coat of some clear, fuel-proof lacquer. Many of these lacquers 'yellow' with age, destroying the shades of the original colours, and in the past some were not really very fuel-proof. Modern synthetics go a long way to overcome these problems, with epoxides, acrylics and urethanes now readily available from specialist paint retailers. Some require specific primers, and this should be checked. Most of the better quality synthetics are of the two-pack variety mixed just before applying to the model, curing by chemical action (rather than evaporation as in cellulose) and forming an extremely tough, high gloss, third substance. Scrupulous cleaning of spray guns is essential *before* the chemicals set, for once hard it may prove impossible to dismantle the gun.

Spray painting offers the scale modeller the ability to copy the

full-size counterpart in every way. Feathered edges, mottling and shadow shading can all be copied with ease, while insignia, codes and serials may all be sprayed through masks and stencils. A visit to any graphic arts dealer will yield vast ranges of helpful self-adhesive films and tapes. The effective use of an airbrush will allow the creation of the 'well-worn look' so characteristic of military aircraft, while the use of, say, urethane gloss paints will enable a civil model to match its prototype, even down to the brand and type of paint, let alone the shade.

Many functional aircraft, whether for competition or fun, benefit from a slick coat of paint. Here one is not tied down to resembling the 'real thing' and artistic imagination may be given full rein. Within the realms of weight, many varied and vivid schemes can

*Opposite:* Bright and startling colour schemes on functional or non-scale aircraft can be extremely helpful to visibility, in flying radio models or timing free flight machines, and finding the latter after a chase.
*Above:* Most Air Forces can provide colourful scale subjects but the blue and yellow of the USAAF of the 1930s had a particular impact.

be sprayed: 'custom finishes', metallics, and 'candies' can be used to decorate the plainest model. Many of the custom paint techniques used on cars and vans lend themselves to adaptation for model use, and can produce truly devastating effects, if you like that sort of thing. Here again, choose the paints wisely, and if special primers and/or undercoats are needed, plan for them

during the prefinishing stage. If you are short on artistic talent, be reassured – many custom finishes can be obtained purely on technical ability to handle the spray equipment.

*Below:* Examples of commercial spray-guns and compressors. What you need, or whether you need one, is a matter of personal attitude and the type of model which attracts you.

All the parts can be seen in this demonstration engine, skilfully sectioned. Notice the two ball races carrying the crankshaft and the way that the crankweb and back cover reduce crankcase volume to, effectively, clearance for the connecting rod, which increases crankcase compression. The space between the cylinder casting and the liner provides transfer passages of considerable size. Engine is an Irvine 40 /6.6cc) sectioned for display by an Irvine engineer.

There are two main types of model aero engines – glow engines and diesels. Glow engines are by far the more numerous and popular, faster revving and generally more powerful size for size. They are suitable for powering all types of model aircraft and are produced in three general categories – 'standard' engines for general use; 'racing' engines for competition models; and 'R/C' engines for radio controlled aircraft. 'Standard' engines may also be used for radio controlled models fitted with a throttle control or R/C carburettor. This applies particularly to smaller engine sizes. Larger 'R/C' engines are generally specially designed to produce maximum power at more moderate revs than either 'standard' or 'racing' engines.

*Glow engines* have three particular disadvantages, although these are outweighed by the simplicity of operation and general flexibility of the type. First they need a special type of ignition plug, known as a glow plug, which can burn out and need replacement. They also need a battery connected to the plug for starting (and if the battery is 'flat' the engine will not start!), and special alcohol-base fuels which are a little more costly than diesel fuels and also attack paints and cellulose dope finishes. For this reason, model aircraft powered by glow engines must be finished in fuelproof dopes, or given a final coat of special fuel-proofer.

*Diesels* are 'self-contained' engines in that they need only a supply of suitable fuel to run. They are generally heavier and more robust than glow engines, so they are usu-ally longer lasting. They vibrate more and are less responsive to throttle control than glow engines, so are not generally recommended for powering radio controlled models. They cannot rev as fast as a 'racing' glow engine, so are less competitive in this respect. On the other hand they can be excellent power units for small and moderate size free flight 'sports' models and certain types of control-line models.

Diesels are produced in a much more restricted range of sizes than glow engines. Very small diesels (smaller than 0.5cc) are difficult (and costly) to produce and can prove tricky to start and adjust. At the other end of the scale, diesels larger than about 3.5cc generally prove disappointing in perform-ance. Thus diesel production is virtually limited to a size range from 0.5 to 3.5cc, with the 1cc and 1.5cc sizes being by far the most popular.

## Engine sizes – and how they are specified

Engine sizes are specified by displacement or the interior volume swept by the piston in making its stroke up and down the cylinder (swept volume). In the case of diesels, displacement is always quoted in cubic centimetres or cc (mainly because the model diesel originated in Continental Europe). In the case of glow engines, displacement is (nearly) always quoted in cubic inches or cu.in (because this type originated in the United States).

Manufacturers produce glow engines in a more or less standard range of sizes, originally representing logical steps in power output. These are: 0.049cu.in (also known as $\frac{1}{2}$-A); 0.09cu.in (also known as Class A); 0.19cu.in; 0.29cu.in; 0.35 cu.in; 0.49cu.in and 0.60cu.in. Quite often the 'cu.in' is dropped and just the figures quoted – 049, 09, 19, etc.

Some manufacturers produce additional sizes, e.g. smaller than 0.049cu.in for powering tiny models, and intermediate sizes to cater for a particular size or type of model, such as 0.40cu.in for R/C models. The need for 'intermediate' sizes is rather more commercial than realistic, however.

## Classification of porting

Nearly all present-day model aero engines are of similar layout, the main differences being in the method of inducting the fuel/air mixture into the crankcase and then transferring it to the top of the cylinder. Induction is controlled by a rotary valve, either a hole opening into a hollow section of the crankshaft, or a disc with a hole, driven by the crankshaft. In either case, when the hole in the crankshaft (or disc) comes opposite the end of the 'carburettor' tube the intake port is opened and then closed by subsequent rotation of the crankshaft. The circumferential length of this hole determines the intake timing.

When induction takes place in front of the cylinder (through the crankshaft), the layout is known as front rotary (readily distinguished by the 'carburettor', or strictly speaking, the intake tube) coming in front of the cylinder. With rear rotary engines the intake tube attaches directly to the back of the crankcase.

Transfer of fuel/air mixture drawn into the crankcase to the top of the cylinder is controlled by piston movement opening the top of a transfer port (or ports) formed in the side of the cylinder. This porting may be conventional, or specially arranged to give a 'boost' to the charge to fill the cylinder head in the most effective manner. The latter is a relatively new development with model aero engines and is known as Schnuerle porting. It is now a feature of many high performance glow engines.

### Classification of construction

A major constructional feature of model aero engines is whether the crankshaft is carried by a plain bearing or ball bearings. A plain bearing engine is simpler and cheaper to produce and so is commonly adopted for standard engines, both glow and diesel. Mounting the crankshaft on ball bearings (sometimes called a BB engine) reduces friction and enables the same size of engine to develop more revs and power. It is thus universally employed for 'racing' engines and preferred for R/C engines. Most large glow engines (i.e. above 0.35 cu.in) are of BB type, regardless of design purpose.

### Pistons

Piston design is another distinguishing feature. Diesels and small glow engines employ a plain piston. Larger glow motors normally

The components of a glowplug engine tend to be rather lighter than those of a diesel.

have a piston with a single ring; the latest development in this respect is a special type of ring fitted to the top of the cylinder, which expands and seals when the piston is travelling up the cylinder and 'relaxes' on the downward stroke to give less friction than a conventional piston ring. This is known as a Dykes ring and is a feature of many modern high performance glow engines.

The shape of the top of the piston can also vary. A simple flat shape is (normally) used on diesels. Glow engine pistons are usually fitted with a deflector or a contoured top to direct the incoming charge up-

wards and away from the exhaust opening (the actual working cycle of a two-stroke engine is described in detail later). Such shapes are more efficient, but are not practical on diesels because the top of the piston has to approach a contra-piston very closely. However, some diesels compromise by having a conical shaped piston top matching a conical depression in the contra-piston.

### Materials

The more or less standard form of construction for model aero engines is a light alloy crankcase/

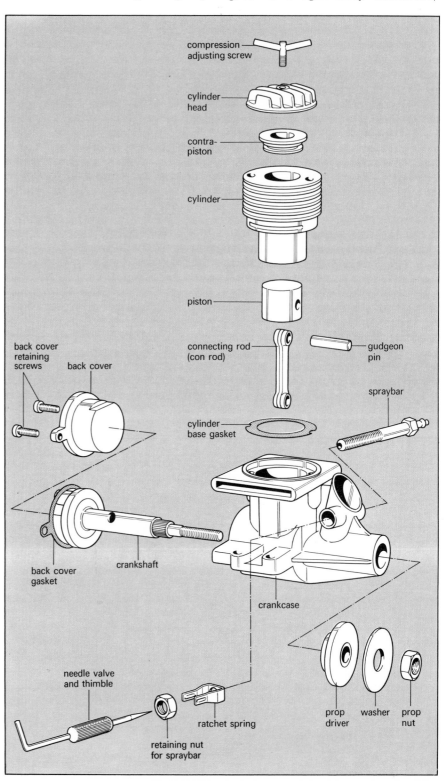

compression adjusting screw

cylinder head

contra-piston

cylinder

piston

connecting rod (con rod)

gudgeon pin

spraybar

back cover retaining screws

back cover

cylinder base gasket

back cover gasket

crankshaft

crankcase

needle valve and thimble

ratchet spring

retaining nut for spraybar

prop driver

washer

prop nut

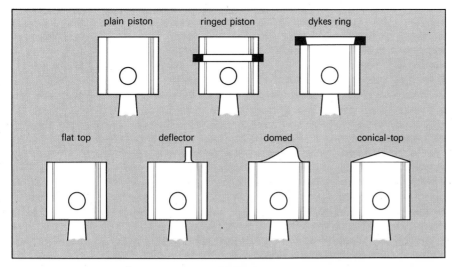

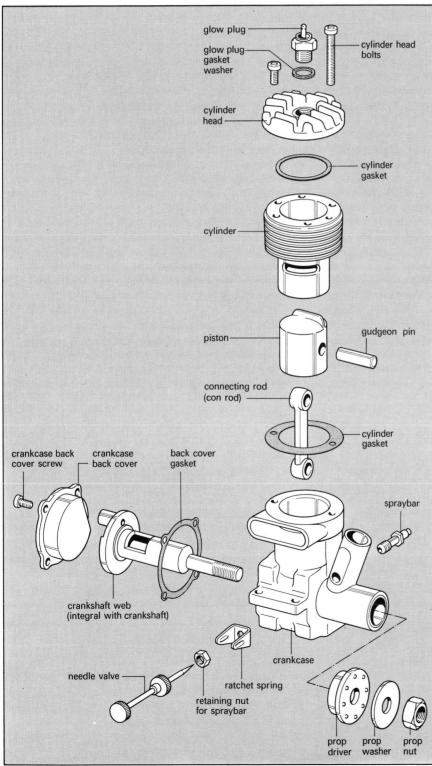

Various piston crowns, all designed to improve scavenging and hence overall performance.

cylinder casting(s) with a steel liner and light alloy head. The crankshaft is of steel and the connecting rod (usually) a light alloy forging.

Plain pistons are machined from cast iron, lapped to fit the cylinder liner. Ringed pistons are of aluminium.

There are exceptions. Small glow motors may have the complete cylinder machined from mild steel, including the fins. Larger glow motors may use an aluminium piston in a brass liner which is chrome plated. This is known as ABC construction. In this case the piston may be plain or ringed.

**Mounting**
Model engines are also distinguished by their method of mounting. The majority have lugs cast in with the crankcase, drilled to take bolts to secure the engine to a pair of wood beams or a commercial motor mount. This configuration is known as a beam mounted engine.

Other engines – notable small glow engines – may not have mounting lugs. Instead a metal fuel tank is attached to the back of the crankcase, so shaped and pre-drilled that the engine can be bolted directly to the front of the fuselage or firewall of a model. This is known as radial mounting.

Beam mounted engines can also be radially mounted by first bolting them to a suitable commercial motor mount which itself is designed for bolting to the firewall.

**Other engine types**
Glow engines and diesels are normally of two-stroke type (see later). This makes it possible to achieve high running speeds and power in a simple design with a minimum of moving parts, with minimum weight. In other words, two-stroke engines can achieve higher speeds and a better power-to-weight ratio than any other type.

Other types are, however, produced in relatively limited quantities. Glow engines, for example, can also work on the four-stroke principle, like an automobile engine. Inevitably they will not develop the same speed and power, for only one out of every two revolutions is a 'power' stroke, and they carry the penalty of extra complica-

Because of the contra-piston, diesels often appear slightly taller than other types of engine.

tion and weight in the valve gear required. They do have two favourable characteristics, however. They develop their maximum power at lower speeds (desirable on sports-type and scale R/C models) and are quieter running and therefore easier to silence. They are also more economical on fuel, but that is of lesser significance.

The Wankel rotary engine is another type which has been dupli-cated in model size, but is much more complicated in construction and thus very expensive to produce. Its power/weight ratio is vastly inferior to a two-stroke, in model engine sizes, but it does have the virtue of very smooth running. This can make it an attractive proposition for types of R/C models where a competitive performance is not required.

Similar comment applies to twin-and multi-cylinder model aero engines which are produced in very limited quantities. They have a specialist appeal – particularly for scale models – without being competitive in performance. They are also costly productions.

At the other end of the scale, the $CO_2$ engine offers a practical – and low cost – answer for a simple-to-operate sub-miniature power unit. Working on the two-stroke prin-

*Top left:* A four-stroke Kittiwake 10cc engine, designed in the 1930s, installed in a 2.5m (8ft) Vulcan model of similar vintage.

*Top right:* Only the carburettor reveals the presence of a model engine incorporated in the scale motor of this Stearman model.

*Above:* Two delightful small scale models, typical of the revival of interest in such machines brought about by the availability of $CO_2$ engines, well concealed in each of these examples.

ciple again but using compressed carbon dioxide ($CO_2$) for 'fuel' it really gives its best performance in diminutive sizes (less than 0.1cc) which would be quite impractical to construct as glow engines or diesels. It thus offers a practical form of engine power for flying models of 300 to 600m (12–24in) wingspan with an installed weight of 14g ($\frac{1}{2}$oz) or less.

Mention should also be made of

another form of power for flying model aircraft – the electric motor, discussed in detail in Chapter 10.

**The glow engine in detail**

Component parts of a typical glow engine are detailed in the cut-away illustration, which is readily identifiable as a front rotary, ball bearing, beam mounted engine. It is a two-stroke engine, meaning that a full working cycle is completed with

# A TYPICAL GLOW-PLUG ENGINE

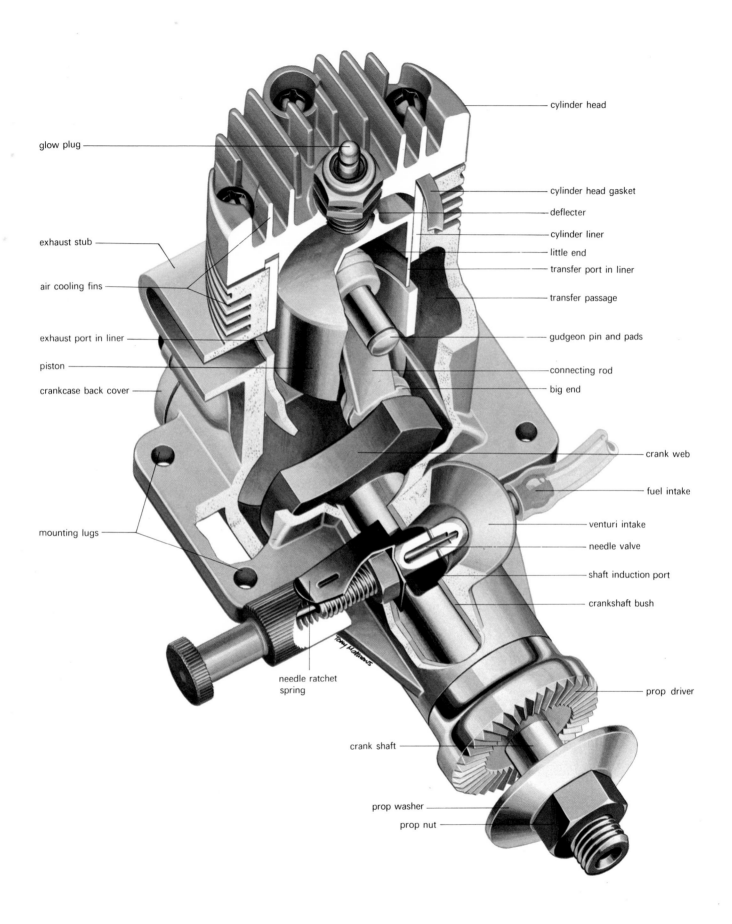

glow plug

cylinder head

exhaust stub

cylinder head gasket

deflecter

cylinder liner

little end

transfer port in liner

air cooling fins

transfer passage

exhaust port in liner

gudgeon pin and pads

piston

connecting rod

crankcase back cover

big end

crank web

fuel intake

venturi intake

needle valve

mounting lugs

shaft induction port

crankshaft bush

needle ratchet
spring

prop driver

crank shaft

prop washer

prop nut

each revolution of the crankshaft, or one upward and one downward movement (two 'strokes') of the piston.

The various stages involved in a complete working cycle are also illustrated. Several stages overlap. For example, when the piston is moving upwards, shutting off the transfer port and compressing fuel/air mixture in the top of the cylinder, more fuel/air mixture is being drawn into the crankcase because at this stage of operation the intake port starts to open. Similarly, on the downward stroke the piston first opens the exhaust port, allowing burnt gas to escape, then starts to compress the fresh charge sucked into the crankcase, and finally opens the transfer port to allow the fresh (compressed) charge to escape into the top of the cylinder.

A check on the appropriate diagram shows that the transfer port is open at the same time as the exhaust port. This means that the charge rushing into the top of the cylinder helps push out any remaining burnt charge – a process known as scavenging. The trick is to prevent too much of the fresh (incoming) charge from escaping through the exhaust port as well, before this port is closed off again by upward movement of the piston. That is the purpose of the deflector or special crown shape on a piston. The incoming charge is directed to flow in the form of a 'loop' around the top of the cylinder (called loop scavenging). Schnuerle porting is an even more effective method of scavenging.

Apart from the rotary intake valve, which is 'timed' by revolution of the crankshaft, the timing of exhaust and transfer is governed by the position of the piston (which of course is also related to crankshaft revolution) and the depth of the exhaust and transfer ports, respectively.

Most glow engines have non-symmetrical timing in that the intake port opens about 120–130 degrees of crankshaft revolution before the piston reaches it uppermost or top dead centre position (usually written TDC); and closes some 30 degrees or more after TDC. Exhaust timing is usually arranged for the exhaust to open about 135 degrees after TDC and close about 45 degrees after bottom dead centre (BDC). Transfer timing is similarly disposed equally about BDC, but with a more restricted opening than the exhaust; the exhaust port must open before the transfer port.

The non-symmetrical intake timing means that the engine will only run properly in one direction of rotation, normally anticlockwise, viewed from the front. It *may* run in the opposite direction – e.g. following a backfire on starting – but not as smoothly or as powerfully.

Certain engines will run equally well in either direction of rotation. These include reed valve engines where the opening and closing of the intake port is controlled by a flap of springy metal instead of a rotary port, or sideport engines where the intake tube connects directly to a port in the cylinder with opening and closing controlled by piston position. A number of smaller glow engines are of reed valve type, and it is readily possible to find them running 'backwards' rather than 'forwards' after starting. Side port engines are a much older design, used on earlier diesels and, before that, spark-ignition engines.

## Glow engine controls

A glow engine has only one control – the needle valve which adjusts the proportion of fuel sucked into the intake tube to mix with the inducted air. Adjustment is simply a matter of getting this 'mixture' right for smooth, two-stroke running. A rather 'richer' mixture setting is usually needed for starting, however – see later. R/C engines have a more elaborate carburettor in which both the quantity and fuel-to-air ratio can be varied to make the engine run at different speeds.

With a standard carburettor – that is, a simple spraybar with a needle valve – the speed at which the engine will run is governed by the size of propeller fitted, and there is only one needle valve setting which will produce the right mixture for running smoothly and powerfully. If the mixture setting is too 'rich' (i.e. too much fuel), the engine will run roughly with reduced power ('four-stroking'), or stop if excessively rich. If the mixture is too 'lean' (not enough fuel), the engine will be starved of fuel and stop.

## Glow engine fuels

Glow engine fuels are based on methanol and a lubricant, such as castor oil (not mineral oils which do not mix well with methanol) or a synthetic lubricant. This is known as a 'straight' fuel, usually with a ratio of 3:1 methanol:lubricant. To improve performance nitromethane may be added to a 'straight' fuel in proportions ranging from about 3% upwards. These are known as 'nitro' fuels and the greater the nitromethane content the more powerful or 'hotter' the fuel becomes.

The controlling factor is the design of the engine, or more specifically its compression ratio. Glow engines are normally designed to run on a specific fuel mixture – straight or low nitro (up to 5%) fuels for standard engines (and most R/C engines) but much higher nitromethane content (even up to 40%) for racing engines.

There is little point in trying to run a glow engine on other than its 'design' or recommended fuel, although a modest increase in nitromethane content may improve performance slightly. A 'hotter' fuel may need a change in compression ratio to produce satisfactory starting and running, and almost certainly a change in glow plug type. Also the hotter the fuel the more expensive it is.

Exceptions are racing engines and some of the smaller high revving glow engines. Both are normally designed to operate on fuels with a fairly high nitromethane content. Neither type can be expected to run well, or even start properly, on glow fuels with a much lower nitromethane content.

## Glow plugs

A glow plug is like a miniature spark plug with a coiled element of platinum or similar wire instead of 'points'. The plug works by catalytic action. When surrounded by alcohol vapour platinum glows at red heat. This heat, supplied by a glow plug element, is sufficient to ignite the (alcohol) fuel/air charge compressed in the top of the cylinder of a glow engine as the piston approaches TDC – provided the plug is of the right 'heat'.

This is really a case of matching the plug to the fuel used. Glow plugs are made in three heat ranges – hot, medium and cold. The difference is mainly in the arrangement of the element within the plug and the mass of the element. A medium plug is designed to match most standard fuels and standard engines – a general purpose type, in fact. In adverse conditions – e.g. very cold weather – the plug may not perform so well, particularly on engines with low compression ratio using straight fuel. In that case a hot plug, which realizes a higher element temperature, can give a better performance.

On the other hand, if the plug is

too 'hot', it can cause pre-ignition. This can happen particularly with engines having high compression ratios and/or being run on 'hot' fuels. The answer in this case is to use a cool plug.

Apart from giving smoother running and easier starting, the right type of plug will also have a longer life. A plug which is too 'hot', for example, will be subject to overheating and early failure of the element.

There are two other variations in glow plug design. The first is the threaded length or 'reach' of the plug. A long reach plug lowers the element farther into the fuel mixture (provided there is sufficient clearance at TDC to accept it without the top of the piston striking the bottom of the plug). This will give it slightly 'hotter' characteristics than a short reach plug with the same element design.

The other variant is the idlebar plug. This is the same as an ordinary glow plug with the addition of a bar fitted right across the bottom, partially shielding the element. The object is to prevent liquid fuel being thrown onto the element which would cool it down and prevent it igniting the charge when the engine is running on an over-rich mixture. In other words, it is designed expressly for use with throttled engines where closing the throttle

also richens the fuel mixture. For that reason it is often called an R/C plug. Like the other types it is made in different heat ranges and in long and short reach versions.

There are other individual designs of glow plugs, differing in element design. Some are general purpose types, and others special types (e.g. for high speed racing engines). Choice can be a little bewildering at times. However, most glow engine manufacturers recommend a specific type or types of plugs for their engines, or the model shop supplying the engine can supply that information. For general use glow plug selection is not particularly critical and if an engine runs well on a particular plug, there is no reason to change. However, for specialized competition work it may be necessary to experiment with a number of different plugs in order to obtain the best results, and a satisfactory plug life in service. Nothing is more frustrating than a glow plug which seems to give the best performance, but has a very short life. Glow plugs are relatively expensive items for what they are, so the 'best' plug is often the one that gives satisfactory starting and lasts longest!

### The model diesel
The main difference between a diesel and a glow engine is in the

cylinder construction. The cylinder is deeper to accommodate a shallow secondary piston, known as a contra-piston, above the TDC position of the main piston together with a length of screw with a tommy bar fitted through it, located in a tapped hole in the cylinder head. The contra-piston is made a fairly tight fit in the head so that it acts as a seal forming what is in effect the top of the 'working' cylinder. Its position in the cylinder can be lowered by screwing in the adjusting screw. To raise it the screw is backed off and the engine turned over. Natural engine compression as the piston approaches TDC will blow the contra-piston up the cylinder until it is stopped by the end of the screw.

The setting of the screw thus determines the clearance space between the bottom of the contra-piston and the top of the piston when the piston is at TDC, or the compression ratio. In other words, the screw is a compression adjustment control.

Otherwise the components of a diesel are essentially similar to those of a glow engine. The usual layout is front rotary with a plain bearing. Construction is generally more rugged to withstand the higher stresses of diesel operation, and cylinder height tends to be further exaggerated by adopting a longer

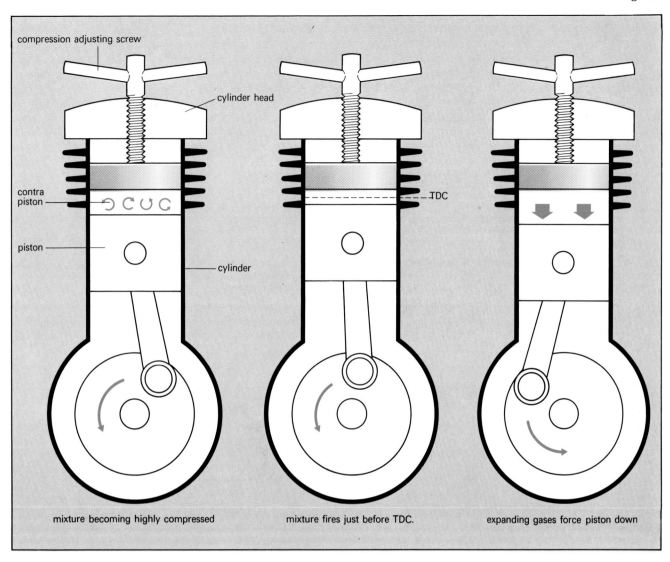

compression adjusting screw

cylinder head

contra piston

piston

cylinder

TDC

mixture becoming highly compressed

mixture fires just before TDC.

expanding gases force piston down

*Opposite, left:* A typical glow plug. This is a short reach type (governed by length of threaded portion). The centre pillar is one contact for the battery and the plug body, through the engine, the other.

*Opposite, right:* Rear induction is through a drum valve in the crankcase of this engine, but needle valve and throttle are similar to front rotary designs.

*Above:* The diesel, or compression ignition, principle.

stroke (total up-and-down travel of the piston) as a further aid to generating good compression. This means that diesels are bulkier and heavier than glow engine of similar displacement.

## The diesel working cycle
All model diesels work on the two-stroke principle. This is exactly the same as that described for glow engines except for the manner of 'firing' the mixture in the top of the cylinder. This is achieved automatically by the heat generated as the fuel/air charge is compressed in the small space between contra-piston and piston top as the latter approaches TDC.

The secret lies in getting the clearance space just right (i.e. the compression adjustment correct) for the fuel to self-ignite at just the right point in the working cycle – a little before the piston actually reaches its TDC position. If the clearance space is too large (i.e. not enough compression), not enough heat is generated to fire the mixture. If the clearance space is too small (too much compression), the mixture will fire too early, producing a backfire. Thus compression adjustment is quite critical.

## Diesel controls
In addition to the compression adjustment screw on top of the cylinder head diesels also have the same sort of fuel mixture control as glow engines – i.e. a spraybar and needle valve. This means that two controls have to be adjusted to get a diesel to run satisfactorily. If the mixture is too lean it will not self-ignite at any compression setting. If the mixture is too rich, again it will not fire properly and there will be a build-up of liquid fuel in the top of the cylinder which could fill the clearance space between piston and

contra-piston and produce a 'hydraulic lock'. Once 'locked' in this manner, any attempt to turn the engine over past TDC could cause damage to the engine. The same thing can occur without fuel being present if the compression adjustment is screwed in too far so that the clearance space disappears and the piston strikes the contra-piston approaching its TDC position. Either condition can be relieved by backing off the compression adjustment screw and flipping the engine over to 'blow' the contra-piston up to a 'clearance' position.

## Diesel fuels
Most diesel fuels are based on more or less equal mixtures of paraffin, ether and lubricating oil. A small amount (not more than 4%) of anti-knock additive such as amyl nitrite is also normally incorporated to improve starting characteristics and also produce smoother ignition.

Unlike glow engines, all diesels will run satisfactorily on a standard fuel of this type. Once a diesel has been fully run-in its performance can be improved by using a fuel with slightly reduced ether and lubricant content – e.g. a 60:20:20 mixture of paraffin:ether:lubricating oil. Actual gain in performance can be quite small, however, particularly if the port sizes are designed for running on a standard fuel. Thus there is little point in running a sports type diesel on anything but a standard fuel, when the extra proportion of lubricant can be beneficial in improved engine life.

### Diesel speed control

Like glow engines, the speed at which a diesel will run, when compression and needle valve are set for smooth two-stroking, is governed by the size of propeller fitted. This applies to all types of two-stroke engines fitted with a simple spraybar and needle valve 'carburettor'.

Diesels can be fitted with R/C type throttles, but their response to throttle control is not as good as that of glow engines. This is mainly because a change of throttle setting also really needs a readjustment of compression as well.

Another way in which diesels are less flexible than glow engines is that a change in engine speed which *can* occur in flight – for example, engine speed will increase in a dive – can result in the diesel becoming over-compressed (or under-compressed in a steep climb) so that it starts to run roughly, or even stops.

### Propellers

All engines develop maximum power at a certain speed, known as peak rpm (rpm = revs per minute). To get the best performance out of an engine, therefore, the propeller size used must be one which allows the engine to reach this speed. (Remember, propeller size determines engine speed.)

This problem does not have a simple answer. It is easy enough to use a rev counter to check the rpm an engine will develop when the model is held stationary, but not when the model is in flight. The difference is important. In flight, the propeller offers less load on the engine, so the engine will increase its speed. That means a propeller size chosen on the basis of measuring rpm when the model is stationary must be slightly 'oversize' – i.e. holding the revs down to below peak rpm – to allow for this speeding up in flight.

This difference between 'static' and 'flight' rpm varies widely with different types of models. It is not

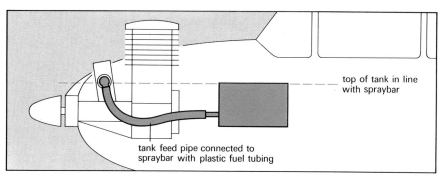

top of tank in line with spraybar

tank feed pipe connected to spraybar with plastic fuel tubing

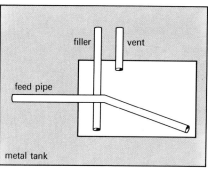

filler    vent

feed pipe

metal tank

*Above:* A spraybar works by the air sucked in drawing off a spray of fuel through an aperture controlled by a tapered needle valve. A throttle controls the amount of air inducted.
*Left and below:* Types of fuel tank for various applications.
*Opposite:* Side mounting of engines is often more convenient, especially with scale-type models. This one is on a radial mount casting, with a plastic bottle-type tank behind the firewall.

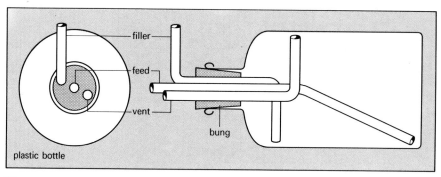

filler

feed

vent

bung

plastic bottle

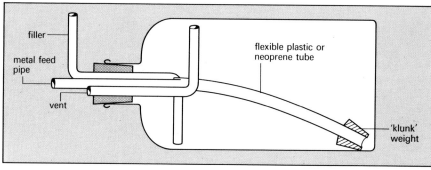

filler

metal feed pipe

vent

flexible plastic or neoprene tube

'klunk' weight

particularly significant in the case of sports models where a generously oversize propeller can be used (which can have the advantage of making the engine easier to start). Although the engine may never develop peak rpm in flight, it should still have enough power to fly the model properly, unless the propeller is badly oversize. The exception is the smaller glow motors (0.049cu.in and under) which have a relatively low power output and rely on high revs to produce enough power for a good flight performance.

With contest type models – where maximum flight performance is the aim – propeller selection can be very important. The best size, for top performance, can usually only be established by trial and error.

Manufacturers' recommendations usually give a range of propeller sizes as suitable for their engines as a general guide.

Propeller selection is further complicated by the fact that two propeller dimensions are involved – the diameter and pitch. Pitch is the theoretical advance of the propeller per rev, determined by the blade angle. In general, free flight models require propellers with a fairly generous diameter and a relatively low pitch. Control line models require propellers with a rather smaller diameter and higher pitch. Propellers for R/C models tend to be similar in diameter to free flight sizes (or very slightly less), with a little more pitch. These comparisons refer to the same size of engine.

As another general rule, because

tively weak. They are easily broken in a bad landing, and when used on high speed engines can shed a blade on starting. For most types of models a nylon propeller is probably the best answer.

## Fuel tanks

Only a few of the smaller engines are supplied with an integral fuel tank. The rest need a separate tank to be installed in the fuselage as close to the engine as possible with the top of the tank level with the spraybar of the engine. This position will ensure that there is minimum change of 'head' of fuel as the tank is emptied, or the model changes its attitude in flight. A marked change in 'head' can affect the amount of fuel drawn through the spraybar, and thus the fuel mixture even though the needle valve setting remains unchanged.

Tank shape is not important on a free flight model. Its size (capacity) is dependent on the type of model. Engine runs are usually short on free flight models, so the tank can be quite small (stopping the engine being achieved by a timer shutting off the fuel supply). Larger tanks are required on R/C models where engine runs of 10–15min may be required. There is a wide range of proprietary tanks available from which to choose.

Tanks normally have three metal tubes – a feed pipe, filler and vent. The feed pipe is horizontal (when the tank is mounted in position) with the inner end angled down to the bottom of the tank. In a metal tank, filler and vent are vertical pipes emerging from the top of the tank. In a 'plastic bottle' tank, all three tubes emerge from the bung. The klunk tank is similar except that the metal feed pipe is shorter and extended by a length of very flexible plastic (or neoprene rubber) tube with a weight attached at the far end. This weight makes the open end of the feed pipe follow any displacement of fuel in the tank if the model undergoes a marked change in attitude – e.g. this type of tank will continue to feed fuel even in inverted flight. Klunk tanks are not necessary on free flight models, but are the (almost) universal choice for R/C models, particularly aerobatic models.

A klunk tank is also suitable for use in a control line model. Other special tanks are also produced for this type of model, the main requirement being that since the model is flying continuously in a circle, centrifugal force tends to

they are slower revving diesels normally need propellers which have similar or slightly less diameter to a glow engine of the same size, but rather greater pitch in each of the above categories.

The best answer in any case is to start with a propeller size recommended by the engine manufacturer. This will be given in the operating instructions supplied with the engine. If not, enquire at the model shop from which the engine was bought. Performance will then usually be satisfactory, if not always the best the engine can give. If you are after the latter, then it will pay to experiment with slightly different propeller sizes – e.g. a slightly smaller diameter size to increase engine speed; or a smaller diameter and larger pitch

to increase model speed.

Bear in mind, too, that different makes of propellers of the same nominal size may well give different results. This is a matter of differences in blade shape and section, and how much the actual pitch may vary from the quoted nominal pitch.

Moulded nylon propellers are the most popular choice. These are tough and reasonably crashproof. Edges can be dangerously sharp, however, so for safety reasons round them off very slightly with fine glasspaper. Glass-reinforced nylon propellers are even stronger, designed particularly for use on speed models which use small diameter propellers on high revving engines. Wood propellers are probably the most efficient of them all (especially in larger sizes), but rela-

throw the fuel towards the outside of the tank, so the filler pipe must terminate on this side of the tank. If the tank design is symmetrical – e.g. a wedge or triangular section – with the feed pipe at the apex, such a tank will work equally well in inverted flight.

Special tanks are also made for control line models which are not aerobatic – e.g. team racers – where the aim is to produce a tank which not only feeds from the offside but maintains a constant supply or constant 'head' as the fuel level drops. Centrifugal force and fuel weight can cause mixture variations.

## Silencers

Model engines are inherently noisy, operating as they do at very high speeds with an open exhaust. The noise problem associated with model flying has for long been a source of complaint by neighbours and has resulted in the loss of many flying sites. Better public relations have been established by the insistence on the use of engine silencers (mufflers) on many sites, and pending legislation will make it illegal to operate any model engine which generates a noise in excess of 82 decibels, measured at a distance of 7m (22ft).

Silencers, therefore, are really an essential accessory, and most manufacturers now make matching silencers to suit their engine. If not, these are available from independent manufacturers to suit virtually every engine available. The majority are designed to clamp or bolt directly onto the stub exhaust of the engine, so are simple and easy to fit. Some engines may require an additional manifold, but again fitting is straightforward. The main thing is to ensure a tight fit with no leak paths through which noise can escape.

Silencers add bulk and weight to an engine installation, but that is unavoidable. The more usual objection is that they reduce engine power. This is true, but not to the extent that is commonly imagined. The power loss with many of the more modern types of silencers is quite moderate, and acceptable, for most types of model aircraft. For speed or similar contest models there is an alternative answer – the tuned pipe, as mentioned (see Chapter 7).

## Starting and adjusting glow engines

The best guide to starting and adjusting a new glow engine is the manufacturer's instructions. These will specify the approximate needle valve setting for starting (so many turns open), and the recommended fuel to use as well as a suitable propeller size. It is not common practice to supply glow engines complete with glow plug (except where this is an integral part of the head),

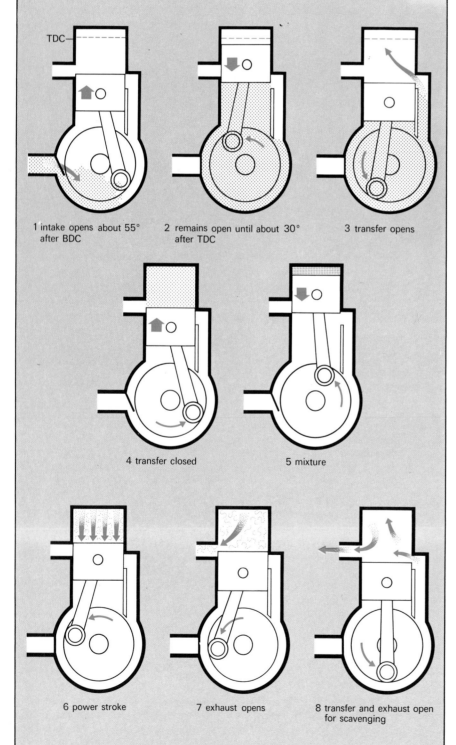

1 intake opens about 55° after BDC
2 remains open until about 30° after TDC
3 transfer opens
4 transfer closed
5 mixture
6 power stroke
7 exhaust opens
8 transfer and exhaust open for scavenging

*Opposite:* Rigid mounting enables an engine to deliver peak power, so cast metal 'pans' are used in C/L speed and team race models and, as here, in high performance competition free flight machines.
*Left and below:* The working cycle and timing of a glow engine.

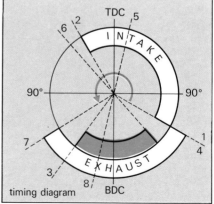

timing diagram

so this will have to be bought separately. A matching size of starter battery will also be required – e.g. a 2v accumulator for a 2v glow plug; or a large 1.5v bell battery for a 1.5v glow plug. Buy one or two extra glow plugs as spares.

The propeller should be tightened on the shaft so that it comes at 'ten-past-eight' when compression is felt as the propeller is rotated anti-clockwise (all model engines rotate in this direction). With the fuel tank full of fuel and the engine properly mounted (either installed in a model or on a bench rig), basic starting procedure is as follows:

1. Screw down the needle valve until resistance is felt (do not screw down too tight). Open the prescribed number of turns. If these are not known, open the needle valve two full turns.
2. Cover the top of the intake tube with a finger and turn the engine over until the fuel line to the spraybar is full of fuel. Turn over two or three more times to suck fuel into the engine.
3. Connect the battery to the glow plug, using a glow plug clip and leads.
4. Flip the propeller over *smartly* in an anti-clockwise direction. Repeat this about three or four times until the engine starts to run.
5. Adjust the needle valve for smooth running. If the engine runs roughly after starting, the fuel mixture is too rich, so screw the needle valve in to correct. If the engine starts and gives a

short burst of high speed running and stops, the fuel mixture is too lean. Screw the needle valve out a quarter of a turn or so to correct.
6. Remove the glow plug clip, disconnecting the battery.
7. Make final fine adjustments to the needle valve for smooth running.

If the engine does *not* start, there are four possible causes:

a. Not enough fuel. Open the needle valve another half turn and repeat 2, 3 and 4. Do not *overdo* 4, however, or the engine may become flooded, wetting the glow plug. In this state the engine will never start until the plug has been removed and dried out, and excess fuel blown out of the engine by spinning it over smartly with the plug removed.
b. Too much fuel. Close needle valve half a turn, remove plug and treat as above for a flooded engine. Then go through 2, 3 and 4 again.
Note: removal of the plug will show whether there is not enough fuel for starting (plug quite dry); or too much fuel (plug very wet).
c. Flat starter battery. This is a common cause of trouble when a 1.5v dry battery is used.
d. Glow plug element broken.
Note: c and d can be checked by removing the plug, connecting to the battery and observing the glow plug element. It

should glow a bright red. No glow indicates a flat battery or a broken element. A dull glow indicates a weak battery if the plug is dry.

As a general rule the running setting for a glow engine is the needle valve screwed in about one turn from the starting setting, but this can vary quite a bit with different engines. In other words, to re-start a cold engine, first open up the needle valve one turn and go through the starting procedure. If the engine is still hot from a previous run it is usually possible to start it with the needle valve at the running position after giving it one or two 'priming' turns – starting procedure stage (ii).

There are two ways to stop the engine:

Pinch the fuel line to shut off the fuel supply.
Place a finger over the top of the intake tube to 'choke' the engine.

**Starting and adjusting diesels**
The manufacturer's instructions should specify the needle valve setting for starting, but you will have to find the compression setting by trial and error. Set the propeller on the shaft in the same position as for glow engines, connect up the fuel line and proceed as follows.

1. Turn the engine over *gently* via the propeller and check that there is no undue resistance as

the piston reaches its TDC position. If there is, open the compression adjusting screw one to two turns, then spin the engine over rapidly to blow the contra-piston back against the screw.

2. Prime the engine as in stage (ii) for glow engines. Again if strong resistance is felt on turning the engine past TDC, back off the compression screw another turn.

3. Flip the engine over *smartly* several times. If it shows no signs of starting, open the needle valve a little, re-prime and try again.

4. Screw in the compression screw *a little at a time* until the engine fires and starts to run roughly.

5. Screw in the needle valve until the engine runs more smoothly but with some misfiring.

6. Screw in the compression screw *a little at a time* until the misfiring disappears.

7. Readjust needle valve by screwing in a little more, with further adjustment of the compression screw (downwards) as necessary to produce smooth running.

The aim should be to adjust for *minimum* compression which will give smooth running. If the engine labours or runs roughly, this can be the result of too much compression or too rich a mixture. Try reducing the compression a little first. If this produces misfiring, return compression setting to its original position and screw in the needle valve a little.

After a diesel has warmed up, some further adjustment may be necessary (particularly if the fuel used contains an anti-knock additive). Adjustment in this case should be confined to the compression.

The process of starting and adjusting diesels may seem rather complicated, but is easily mastered with a little practice. Once familiar with a particular diesel it can prove easier to start than a glow engine.

The chief cause of non-starting is a flooded engine, caused either by excessive choking (especially if the needle valve is too far open) or continuous flicking over with the compression backed off too much. If the engine starts but only runs in short bursts, open the needle valve a little. This should either cure the trouble or make the engine run continuously but roughly. In the latter case, return the needle valve to its original position and increase the compression a little.

Once you have established the correct settings for running a diesel, everything should be simple from then on. For starting from cold, back off the compression a quarter to half turn and unscrew the needle valve one half to one full turn. This should give more or less instant starting following a prime. For re-starting a warm engine, leave the settings at their running position and merely give the engine an initial prime.

## Running-in new engines

To ensure maximum performance and long life, every new engine should be run in before being used 'operationally' to fly a model. This is less important in the case of free flight models where normal engine running time is usually quite short, but very important for engines used on control line and R/C models where extended engine runs are required.

The amount of running-in required varies with engine size and type, and with different makes. The smaller sizes of engines with plain pistons normally need little running-in time. Larger engines, particularly those with plain bearings, may need up to an hour of actual running time before they are properly bedded-down and capable of delivering their rated performance without overheating.

Use only a standard fuel for running in – never a 'racing' fuel which has a lower lubricant content and could result in permanent damage through overheating. The only exception is small glow motors designed to run on fuels with a high nitro content. They need little running-in time and can be operated on their recommended fuel from the start.

The following abridged notes should serve as a useful guide for running-in new engines.

1. Fit a recommended size propeller – not an 'oversize' propeller to slow the engine down as this will not allow the engine to be run-in properly.

2. Give the engine runs of not more than two or three minutes at first, adjusting the needle valve so that the engine is four-stroking, then re-adjusting to give short bursts of two-stroke running. Stop and allow the engine to cool down between runs.

3. Gradually increase the length of two-stroke running but avoid *too lean* a setting (where the engine tends to speed up a little

and then stop). Err on the side of a *slightly rich* mixture for two-stroke running.

4. Finally check out with continuous two-stroke running, *re-adjusting immediately* to four-stroking should the engine show any signs of slowing down (overheating).

How and where to carry out running-in is another matter! If only a short running-in time is anticipated, then the engine can be fitted in the fuselage of the model prior to running-in. Where a longer running-in period is likely to be necessary it is better to mount the engine on a bench rig to save the model being liberally coated with oily exhaust waste. It also helps if running-in can be done in some isolated place where noise is not likely to be a problem (in which case you need to make a portable bench rig).

Do not run-in an engine in an enclosed space, such as a garage, even with a silencer, unless there is adequate provision to extract the exhaust fumes. Fitting a hose to the end of the silencer to take the exhaust fumes 'outside' is not recommended as this can aggravate any tendency for the engine to overheat – and that is something which must be avoided in running-in.

## Engines with throttles

The modern variable-speed carburettor used on R/C engines is based on the *barrel throttle* replacing the simple spraybar used on standard engines. A form of spraybar or equivalent jet with mixture control via a needle valve is still retained but the amount of air flowing through the carburettor is controlled by the position of the 'barrel'. In fact barrel movement controls both the air and mixture flow, so it acts as a true carburettor providing a range of speeds over which the engine will run.

Various refinements are also incorporated. The 'closed' position of the barrel is controlled by a stop which can be adjusted to provide a consistent idling speed, and a separate adjustment may provide automatic mixture control by reducing the quantity of fuel as the throttle is closed (a simple barrel throttle merely produces an increasingly rich mixture as it is closed).

Design and construction of automatic carburettors of this type is quite complex. They are capable of giving a consistent and progressive speed and power range from idling at about 2000rpm up to the peak rpm of the engine – and are an automatic choice for all of the larger sizes of R/C engines.

### Pressurized fuel systems

Mention should also be made of pressurized fuel systems as these are directly related to carburetion. The object is to make the fuel mixture, as set by the needle valve, independent of changes of 'head' or 'g' forces generated in manoeuvres. To do this, the filler pipe of the fuel tank is sealed off (after filling), and pressure fed to the vent pipe.

There are two simple sources of pressure which can be used – a tapping point on the engine crankcase, or one on the engine exhaust or silencer. Tapping the silencer is rather better since this provides automatic compensation for variations in mixture which tend to occur at different settings with simple barrel throttles. Crankcase pressure, on the other hand, tends to exaggerate this effect, but in this case a separate pressure regulator can be added to provide a constant pressure regardless of engine speed.

The other type of pressurization system used is a small air pump mounted on the back of the engine and driven by the crankshaft (the pump unit replaces the conventional backplate and is driven by the crankpin in a similar manner to a rear rotary valve). Again this may be used with a pressure regulator.

Another advantages of a pressurized fuel system is that it enables a larger choke area to be used in the carburettor without suffering from loss of suction effect on which the formation of a proper fuel/air mixture depends.

### Care and maintenance

Model aero engines need care in handling, installing and operation, but little or no maintenance, unless they are damaged in a crash. Normal maintenance requirements, in fact, consist of no more than wiping an engine clean after use (a sticky, oily surface attracts dust and grit which could get inside the engine and damage the working surfaces). After cleaning, a little light oil can be squirted into the carburettor or exhaust port and the engine turned over to spread this oil over the bearings and cylinder wall.

It is even more important to clean an engine after a crash (or if the model has landed upside down with the engine partly buried in dirt). In this case squirt fuel over the outside of the engine to wash, taking care not to wash any dirt down into the intake tube, then wipe dry with an oily rag. Never try to turn an engine over after a crash to check whether the crankshaft has been bent until dirt has been cleaned off.

The only tools required are a prop spanner (matching the propeller nut size), glow plug spanner, and a screwdriver to match the screws holding the cylinder head and backplate (if applicable). Never use pliers for tightening the prop nut, or removing or replacing a glow plug. Check head and backplate screws periodically, as these can work loose under vibration. Never overtighten these screws as this could strip the threads in light alloy castings.

Never grip an engine in a vice for working on it. This can cause serious damage – or at best, a badly marked engine.

Never put a screwdriver through the exhaust port to lock the piston in place to assist in disassembly of an engine. In fact, for the average modeller, it would be better if he never disassembled the engine at all for repair or replacement of parts. 'Repair' is virtually impossible, and damaged parts can only be treated by replacing them. This is best left to the professionals who specialize in engine repairs. Their service is usually quick and efficient, and not too costly. The inexperienced amateur can ruin a whole engine by attempting replacement work of major components.

### Field spares to carry

Prop spanner and plug spanner*.
Spare glow plugs*.
Spare propellers of matching size.
Spare starter battery if using a dry battery* (otherwise make sure the accumulator is fully charged)*.
At least one spare can of fuel.
Clean cloth or stockinette.
Filter for use in filling tank of R/C engines*.
Spare fuel line filter for R/C engines*.

\* Not necessary in the case of diesels.

An electric starter is an asset with multi-engine models such as this C/L Fortress B17G. The starter and its battery are by the modeller's right hand.

From the foregoing chapters, one particular point emerges clearly – for successful flight, some understanding of the basic principles of flight is necessary. Fortunately, the extent of the knowledge required is quite modest and to absorb it requires nothing more than a little common sense.

Flight is possible because of forces created when a fluid (in this case air) flows over a surface. It is explained by Bernoulli's Law which, reduced to its simplest, states that the energy of movement plus the energy of pressure plus the energy of density add up to a constant. Accepting that air density will not change significantly, this means that an increase in movement must create a decrease in pressure. This is the secret of flight, since to avoid an empty space, air must flow faster over the top of a cambered surface to rejoin air which has travelled a shorter dis-

tance across the bottom of the surface. Figure 1a shows an airfoil (or aerofoil) section in which the distance from A to B is obviously greater along the top surface than along the bottom.

Introducing something like a wing into a mass of air must displace a quantity of air equal to the volume of the wing, and since air shows some resistance to movement, instantaneous displacement cannot occur. There is thus a tiny increase in pressure in the vicinity of the wing, which must result in a small decrease in movement, and because of the shape of the airfoil

*Left:* Competitors at an all-helicopter event working on their models. Judging by the attention of the crowd, one of the entrants is putting his machine through its paces.
*Below:* Activity in the pits at a pylon race meeting. Major meetings attract crowds of well into five figures; naturally the exciting and the spectacular draw them, but the overall favourites for the general public seem to be the scale events.

and its angle, most of the increase in pressure occurs beneath the wing. It is usually accepted that of the lift from the wing, roughly two-thirds arises from the reduced pressure on the top surface and the other third from increased pressure beneath.

The curved shape of the airfoil is called 'camber' and the example in Figure 1a is a 'flat-bottomed airfoil'. Mention has been made of 'undercamber', and this refers to the undersurface of the airfoil having a camber in the same direction as the top surface camber, as in 1b. Faster-flying models normally use an airfoil with a convex under-surface (1c) conveniently referred to as bi-convex or sometimes semi-symmetrical; this may be taken to the extreme of a fully symmetrical section (1d), where the difference in length between upper and lower surfaces is created by only the tiny difference at the leading edge occasioned by the slight angle at which the airstream meets the airfoil.

This angle is termed the *angle of attack* and cannot really be measured accurately on an ordinary flying model. What can be established is the *angle of incidence*, which is the angle at which a flying surface is mounted in relation to the aircraft's datum line. In fact, what a modeller usually *measures* is the *rigging angle*, which is taken from a convenient line, possibly a tangent to the underside of the wing centre-section, which is physically easy to check. Incidence proper is measured to a mean line, roughly that connecting A and B in the sections sketched.

Just as all of an object has weight but it balances at one point, so all the lift forces acting on an airfoil can be considered to balance out at one point, called the *centre of pressure*. With conventional airfoil sections, a change of the angle at which the airflow meets the section (i.e. a change in angle of attack) causes a redistribution of the pressure pattern, which in turn means that the centre of pressure (CP) will move. For present purposes it is enough to say that the CP moves forward with increasing angles, and vice versa (Figure 2).

Now if at a given angle of attack a weight was to be hung immediately beneath the CP, a stable arrangement would be achieved, but only while there was no change of angle. As soon as a change occurred the CP would move and stability would be destroyed. Some automatic stabilizing system must

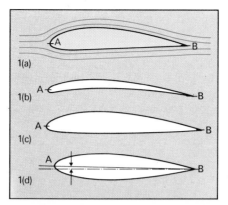

1(a)

1(b)

1(c)

1(d)

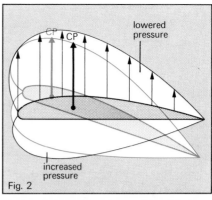

lowered pressure

CP

CP

increased pressure

Fig. 2

therefore be introduced, and this is the function of the tailplane, or stabilizer as it is called in the USA. At its simplest, it works by introducing a neutral (i.e. non-lifting) surface at a distance from the main wing so that when a change of attitude and hence angle of attack occurs, the surface (the tailplane) is itself presented to the air-flow at an angle of attack. Tailplane lift, either upward or downward, results, applying a force tending to return the aeroplane to its original attitude (Figure 3). Factors affecting the size and hence lift available from the tailplane include the moment through which it acts, the amount of movement of the CP (which varies with different airfoils) and the closeness of the centre of gravity (CG – the point through which the weight acts) to the CP *vertically*; a CG a long way beneath the CP will produce a greater relative displacement. Generally-speaking, therefore, a long and shallow model with an airfoil having small CP travel can use a much smaller tailplane than a short, deep model with a large CP travel airfoil.

The tailplane can be used to contribute to overall lift – a 'lifting tailplane' – so that in normal flight

the wing is contributing, say, 90% of the total lift and the tailplane the rest. This means that the CG must be further aft to balance the forces (Figure 4); examples are the towline glider and free-flight power model full-size plans in this book. Although more efficient, there is a danger that an increase in speed will cause a disproportionate increase of tailplane lift, forcing the nose down. This can be avoided by not straying too far from the designed rigging angles of the wing and tail; the more similar the angles are, the greater the chance of diving in, and a little nose ballast is a safer move than a large increase in tailplane angle in trimming an average model of this type.

All components of a model are bound to have some resistance to the passage of air, called drag, and the total of all drag components acts through a single point. Opposed to this force is the line of thrust, so to be in equilibrium a model must achieve a balance between four forces, lift, weight, thrust and drag (Figure 5). If thrust/drag produce a nose-up couple, lift/weight must balance it with a nose-down couple. When gliding, the weight factor can be separated into downward and forward com-

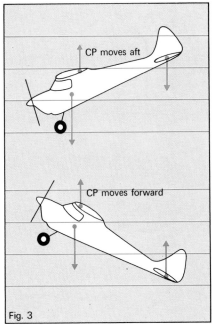

Fig. 3

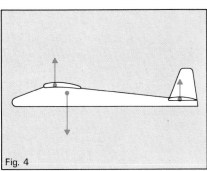

Fig. 4

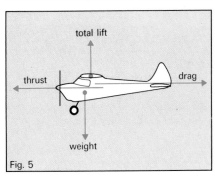

Fig. 5

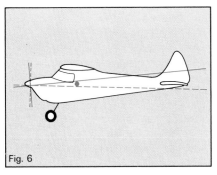

Fig. 6

The photograph opposite shows World Champion R/C aerobatic flier Hanno Prettner of Austria. With him is the model with which he won, for the fifth time, the Championship of Champions at Las Vegas, a huge scale Dalotel DM165 with 2,700sq.in of wing area and two 10cc engines geared together to drive a single 20in propeller.

ponents, and it is the forward component which replaces thrust. Drag is more or less fixed, so the first aim of trimming is to balance lift and weight to achieve a satisfactory glide. Once achieved, a glider model is trimmed, but a rubber or power model introduces thrust, and trimming must continue, to take this additional force into account. Since a satisfactory glide has been achieved, no change should be made to the basic trim, so that the only adjustment possible is to position the line of thrust to cancel out any nose-up or nose-down couple produced when power is applied. As a rule power (or thrust) will create a nose-up tendency, and by angling the propeller shaft line downward (downthrust) the corrective nose-down force is introduced. Figure 6 shows that downthrust has the effect of raising the line of thrust in relation to the CG of the model.

Application of power also introduces torque reaction, or the tendency of the aeroplane to rotate in the opposite direction to the airscrew, caused by the braking effect of the air on the airscrew. Torque will tend to make the model turn to the left, and can be cancelled out without affecting glide trim by giving right sidethrust, i.e. pointing the propeller shaft slightly to the right. There is also a precessional effect from the airscrew normally only evident in tight turns.

## Stalling

The airflow over a wing produces lift while it follows the airfoil shape, but, as is obvious from Figure 1a, the flow over the upper surface has to 'bend' to remain in contact with the surface. Too great a bend leads to the airflow beginning to separate towards the trailing edge, and the amount of bend, or change of direction of the airflow, required is obviously influenced by the angle at which the wing meets the airflow, the *angle of attack*. The greater the angle of attack, the more deflection is required of the airflow to remain attached to the wing. Above

perhaps 6 to 7°, slight separation begins to occur towards the trailing edge (Figure 7a), progressing with increasing angle of attack until at a critical angle, the whole of the upper airflow breaks down and becomes detached from the after two-thirds of the upper surface, destroying lift. This is the *stall*, and the critical angle at which it occurs, the *stalling angle*, differs with different airfoil sections; perhaps 12 to 15° is average.

Confusion is created by mention of stalling speed; there is a relationship between speed and angle of attack in that the slower the aircraft flies the greater the angle of attack needed to produce sufficient lift to maintain level flight. A particular speed will therefore be registered when the critical angle is reached and the stall occurs, and it is easier to read or gauge airspeed than angle of attack. Because of slight airflow differences and G forces, incidentally, the stalling speed is higher when the aircraft is turning, although the loss of lift occurs at the same stalling angle.

Since a stall is a breakaway of airflow from the wing, a sudden change of angle at any speed can cause separation and hence a stall. A R/C model with a level-flight stalling speed of, say, 50km/h (32mph) can quite easily be stalled at 150km/h (94mph) if it is pulled too sharply out of a dive. This is usually called a *high speed stall*, but with a sharp enough change of direction it can happen at any speed.

It is unusual for a wing to stall simultaneously over its whole area, but rather for the airflow separation to spread. A sharply tapered wing can be expected to stall at the tips first, while one of constant chord (width) will normally stall at the centre, which is preferable as the stall is gentler and the aeroplane likely to remain level. Tip stalling can lead to dropping one wing and thence to the machine flicking on to its back. Wash-out, the decrease of incidence angle towards the tips, helps to reduce the chances of tip-first stalling.

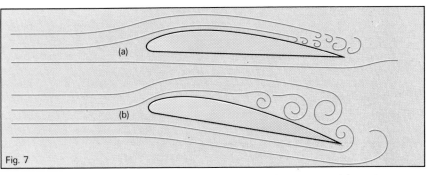

Fig. 7

## Aspect ratio

The aspect ratio, or chord to span relation, of a wing has an effect on its efficiency. Strictly, the ratio is defined by dividing span squared by area, but mean chord (i.e. average width) divided into span gives an approximation. As already mentioned, the pressure beneath a wing is increased and that above it decreased. At the wingtip air from beneath flows round to the lower pressure area above, forming a vortex; an effect of this is to cause the air beneath the wing to flow slightly outward and the air above to angle inward. Where these airstreams meet at the trailing edge the differing directions cause further small vortices; this is termed *induced drag*.

A broad, blunt wingtip will create a bigger vortex and hence a greater induced drag effect, which is why high performance machines such as soaring sailplanes have such long, narrow (high aspect ratio) wings. Tapering the wing reduces the effect, but brings the possibility of unwelcome tip stalling. At average model flying speeds, any chord of less than about 80mm (3in) is inefficient (the exceptions are small slow-flying models) and the structural weight of high aspect ratio wings to withstand flight loads can bring problems so, as in all aspects of design, compromise is necessary.

## Inherent stability

Free-flight models must be able to fly stably and possess the ability to return to stable flight if disturbed, in other words, they must possess inherent stability. A full-size aeroplane, or an advanced radio model, would find too much natural stability a handicap, but most incorporate the same stabilizing factors in some degree. A machine which will not to some extent fly itself is very tiring to control.

Stability is required in pitch, roll and yaw, the first of which has already been mentioned in connection with the tailplane. Roll is to some extent pendulum stability, that is, the centre of gravity below the centre of lift, but principally dihedral effect. Dihedral angle is the shallow V angle of the wings; it can be polyhedral, where the outboard wing panels make a second angle (Figure 8) or tip dihedral, where the centre panel of the wing is flat. If the aeroplane is tipped to one side, the projected area of the low wing is increased and that of the high wing decreased, the resultant difference in lift tending to

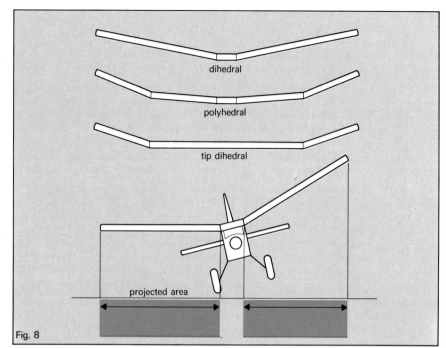

Fig. 8

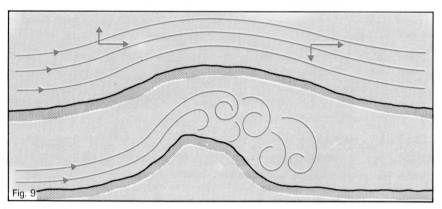

Fig. 9

return the aeroplane to level flight.

If the model turns, slip inwards or skid outwards is certain to occur, and stability in yaw requires that the fin/rudder area is sufficient to balance out the side area of the whole aircraft and produce just sufficient force to return the machine to straight flight. Fin area works with and is related to the amount of dihedral as well as the profile area of the fuselage and the moment through which it acts. Too much area may produce a diving turn into the ground, too little a condition known as 'Dutch Roll' where the model wallows along in a combination of roll and yaw recognizable by the wingtips describing circles rather like the shoulders of a racing walker.

Aerodynamicists may feel that some over-simplification has been made in this outline, or that it could have been taken further. If, however, a novice aeromodeller can relate the above description to his own model, he will be less likely to damage it, will fly it better because he has some glimmering of what is happening, and will consequently enjoy his new hobby.

## Thermals

It is a peculiarity of the atmosphere that sunshine passes through it without heating it. When the sun's rays strike something denser, it is warmed, and the air in contact with it is heated by conduction. The degree of warming is affected by the colour and texture of the object, so that sun striking a variety of surfaces leads to variation in the temperature of the air. If a mass of air is heated, it expands and becomes effectively lighter than surrounding unheated air, and it will therefore rise. Perhaps the largest scale illustration is the creation of onshore and off-shore winds; when the sun heats a land mass so that the air over it becomes warmer than that over the sea, it rises and air flows in from the sea to replace it. At night, as the land cools, the air over it becomes relatively cooler than that over the sea. Sea air rises and air flows off land to replace it.

On a smaller, local scale the air surrounding a building or over a road or runway will become warmer than that over, say, grass and will eventually break away and start to rise. This is a thermal. Someone standing facing a thermal source on a flat calm day will suddenly feel a gentle draught on the back of his head as air moves in to replace the rising air. It used to be thought that thermals were continuous streams of rising air, but subsequent experience and investigation has shown them to be a series of bubbles breaking away, the size and frequency of the bubbles relating basically to the area of heating surface and the temperature difference.

Thermals can form wherever there is a sufficient difference in temperature, and the ideal conditions are calm or light breeze, strong sun and a fair humidity level. Under such circumstances, when the thermal loses heat and pressure its water content becomes visible in the formation of a puffy white 'fair weather' cumulus cloud. In breezy conditions several thermal sources can produce rows of such

*Below:* The search for the unusual attracts many enthusiasts. This Firebird original design, with inverted gull wing and swept V-tail is perfectly practical, if a little too sharply tapered at the wingtips.

clouds drifting away downwind, forming 'cloud streets'. Although a strong breeze can reduce thermal activity over flattish country, it can also give rise to 'wind shadow thermals', where a sheltered ground depression, or a sunny area in the lee of trees or hills, creates a warm spot from which bubbles periodically break away.

The effect of a thermal on a model is sometimes misunderstood, although it is only common sense. If a model is gliding with a sink rate of 1m/sec (3ft per sec) and flies into a thermal bubble rising at 1.5m/sec, it will be rising *in relation to the ground* at 0.5m/sec, though of course it is still sinking through the thermal. How long it stays in the thermal depends on its glide circle diameter and sinking speed in relation to the diameter and depth of the thermal bubble. Ten minutes at 0.5m/sec will take it 300m (1,000ft) higher than the point at which it entered the lift and a distance of one-sixth of the wind speed (in km/h or mph) downwind. Hence dethermalizers!

Only in conditions of complete calm will a thermal rise vertically; it will naturally move downwind with any breeze as soon as it has broken free of the ground. Since air is invisible, knowing when a thermal has started to rise and

estimating its angle of ascent is difficult, so a number of artificial aids have been tried by competition fliers. The most successful is a bubble machine which emits a stream of soap bubbles indicating, by sudden deflections, the likelihood of a thermal. Launch of a model within a few seconds of such an indication gives a very good chance of connecting with the thermal.

Although air flowing in to replace a thermal appears to be travelling horizontally, it is drawn from air displaced by the upward rise of the thermal. In other words, when some air is rising, air from surrounding areas is sinking. Avoiding areas of sink is almost as important as catching a thermal, since if no competitor manages to find much thermal assistance, the one most successful in avoiding sink stands a good chance of winning. The predictability of sink areas is, however, much more hit and miss because of the space they can cover.

### Turbulence and wind gradient
It is to be expected that turbulence will be found to leeward of trees, hedges, hills, buildings and even parked cars. Wind striking such obstructions will roll for a considerable distance and a model flying into such turbulence will be thrown about, depending on wind speed and the height and steepness of the lee side of the obstruction. Launching a model in the 'shelter' of an obstruction is clearly not a very wise procedure.

Perhaps less realized is wind gradient effect, where the moving air in contact with the ground is slowed by friction. Depending on wind strength and the roughness of the ground, this effect can result in a gradual decrease in wind strength from possibly 3m (10ft) height to ground level. It can easily be recognized by standing, squatting, and lying and noting the feel of the wind at each position, and explains why a model gliding in to land into wind may suddenly drop the last two or three feet.

### Slope lift
Wind blowing across reasonably level ground and encountering a hill or slope will flow up the slope and over the top; if the slope is steep or the break at the top sharp the air may separate and the flow break up into considerable turbulence (Figure 9). The flow on the windward slope divides into hori-

zontal and vertical components, and if the upward component exceeds the sinking speed of a model, height can be maintained or gained. This is the principle used in slope soaring, as discussed in Chapter 9, but it is worth remembering that the same conditions apply on all small hills and slopes. If a slope faces into wind, there will be an upward component to the wind which, if it will not sustain a model, will delay its return to earth. More seriously, a slope facing downwind will have a downward component affecting the model's flight, and any obstruction will produce a greater area of turbulence on such a site than on level ground.

### Flying fields

The golden rule before flying anywhere is to secure permission from some responsible person. Public open spaces such as parks or commons are likely to have bye-laws prohibiting or limiting model flying, and private land is just that – private. Small rubber-powered and glider models are unlikely to cause too many problems and might reasonably be flown in a large park or recreation ground (unless there is a blanket ban on *all* model flying), but larger models and anything with an engine are likely to need space or distance from houses. One very good reason for joining a club is that a regular flying site will have been negotiated.

Control-line models need relatively little space but, even if silenced, should be flown well away from houses. Firms' car-parks on industrial estates at week-ends are a possibility, or school playing fields are worth investigating if they are on the outskirts of a town. Some local authorities have an area set aside for these models, and a few enquiries should turn up a site without too much difficulty. For beginners, short grass is probably best, resulting in less model damage, provided the area is smooth and level, away from power lines (this cannot be taken too seriously) and reasonably clear of pedestrians. Competition flying is better on smooth asphalt or concrete; favourite sites where possible are the huge aprons in front of hangars on aerodromes.

Free-flight models require a lot of space with a minimum of obstructions; if there is one tree a model will unerringly find it! Even a 2min flight in a 16km/h (10mph) breeze will take a model downwind some

500m (nearly 600yd). An upwind area reasonably clear of tall trees, to avoid turbulence, and as far as possible downwind clear of woods or standing crops are the ideals. A short DT setting is advisable when there is any wind, but in any event, ensure that your name and address are on the model, in non-fade ink; DTs can fail and models have been known to DT and still carry on upwards in a strong thermal. If a long chase is needed, take time to close all gates and walk round crops, not through them. Take a bearing on some distant point beyond the model so that even when it is down the right direction can still be maintained. Red, orange, and yellow are the best colours for visibility on the ground and are almost the best for airborne visibility.

Nowadays few FF models take off the ground, so the field surface is not too important. Rough ground makes towing up a glider in calm conditions a little hazardous, but long grass is kinder to models landing. If take-offs are fancied, a length of roofing felt or similar can be laid on the grass and is adequate for most FF take-offs.

Radio models need a relatively smaller area, something about football pitch size often being quoted. However, such an area must have reasonably clear approaches and preferably uncluttered surroundings; an expert can take-off and land in a confined space and is unlikely to suffer unexpected motor failure when the model is some distance away, but not everyone flying radio models is expert. A site well away from housing is desirable, since R/C models make quite lengthy flights fairly high, so that the cone of engine noise covers a wide area and can constitute a nuisance. Also, if fast and heavy models get out of control they can be dangerous both to people and property.

From a flying point of view, it is far safer for most R/C models to take-off rather than be hand-launched, and a suitable strip or area is needed for this and for landing. An aerodrome runway is ideal, but most clubs use a grass field and, with the consent of the owner, mow a take-off strip. Sometimes a footpath crossing a field or common will provide an adequate surface. An area of 25 × 5m, aligned with the prevailing wind, will suffice for most purposes.

Indoor models offer the greatest satisfaction in the largest (es-

pecially highest) hall possible. There are few airship hangars like those at Akron or Cardington, with ceilings over 40m (130ft), but models can be flown successfully in sports and civic halls, theatres and ballrooms. In most cases such buildings have to be hired, though school halls may be available providing some of the school's pupils are participating in the activity. Empty aeroplane hangars on some service aerodromes may also be worth investigation, and some church halls may be large enough, especially for electric RTP flying. As is often the case, activities must be tailored to suit available facilities.

### Clubs

Emerging from the flying site question is the clear advantage of joining a club, or even forming one if there are several like-minded enthusiasts and no established club within convenient reach. Use of a site is often more likely to be granted to a club, particularly when local authorities are involved, or, if a rental has to be paid, what might be excessive for an individual becomes practical when spread among a group.

There are many other benefits of club membership. Help is available in construction and learning to fly, lessons can be learned from other members' successes and failures, a knowledgeable assistant is likely to be at hand to help launch, or start an engine, sources of supply can be shared, and money can even be saved by bulk purchases of items such as fuel; many clubs carry a stock of basic materials. Good clubs run a year-round programme which encourages members to build, perhaps indoor or electric RTP models in the winter. Whatever your experience, flying with a club is enjoyable; watching other people's models or informal club or inter-club competitions add to one's pleasure.

To form a club notices should be displayed in the local model shop and library and sent to local newspapers and the model press notifying anyone interested of a meeting to be held at an easily accessible place at a convenient time. The model press require several weeks' notice, incidentally. At the meeting, depending on response, the decision to form a club will be made. A name should be chosen, preferably not too light-hearted a one, as it may affect future negotiations, and the objects of the club clearly defined. A chairman, secretary, treasurer and committee must be elected, if only temporarily while the club gets under way, further elections being held when membership has grown. Club fees should be decided, and a programme mapped out. Affiliation to a national body is desirable as soon as the club is settled, not least because in many cases insurance is part of the affiliation package.

Formality is not necessary, but notes should be taken of decisions made; experience shows that a club with conscientious officers working in a conventional framework will be happier and more successful, and hence longer lived, than too casual a group.

Flying, whether by an individual or a club, should always be carried out with care and consideration for people who may not share enthusiasm for models. Safety is a matter of common sense and awareness that spectators or passers-by do not know what the models might do; it has been known for people to walk or cycle into the path of a C/L model. Never show off with a R/C model by deliberately 'buzzing' people or houses or stunting over spectators' heads.

Noise is the most frequent complaint, and in Britain a formal Code of Practice has been agreed nationally. This includes such rules as no C/L model to be flown within 150m of occupied dwellings if muffled, 250m unmuffled. If total engine capacity exceeds 3.5cc these distances become 250m and 400m. Unmuffled FF models are limited to a 20sec engine run and no closer than 150m, and all R/C models must have effective mufflers. Ground running of engines must be kept to a minimum and never exceed one minute. Operating times are also

suggested. These and other simple rules show that model fliers are responsible people, anxious to avoid grounds for complaint. A ban imposed because of noise can often include *all* model flying.

One man's enjoyment should not be another's irritation. With a little care, courtesy, consideration and common sense we can all continue to derive pleasure and satisfaction from model flying.

*Below, centre:* Pulse jet engines for models have existed for over 30 years, but suffer from noise and fire hazard. This delta model was demonstrated at Las Vegas by a Dutch team, flying at over 320kph (200mph).
*Bottom:* There have been many models of Concorde, but this one is unique in having twin pulse jets and virtually scale supersonic speed! Built by the Dutch team in the previous picture.

# Glossary

## A

**Acetate** – a heat deformable transparent material, actually cellulose acetate.

**Aerodyne** – an aircraft supported dynamically by reaction of moving surfaces to air.

**Aerofoil** – surface designed to produce aerodynamic reaction normal to direction of motion.

**Aeroplane** – mechanically driven aerodyne supported by fixed wings.

**Aerostat** – an aircraft supported statically (e.g. balloon).

**Aileron** – hinged panel on fixed airfoil near tip providing lateral control.

**Air brake** – surface capable of presentation at 90° to motion to increase drag.

**Aircraft** – any vehicle deriving support from reaction of air.

**Airfoil** – alternative to 'aerofoil'.

**Anhedral** – inverted V angle, opposite to dihedral.

**Aspect ratio** – relationship of width to length; in wings, average chord to span.

**Attack, angle of** – the angle at which an airfoil meets the airflow.

**Autogiro** – aeroplane deriving lift from freely spinning rotor.

**Autorotation** – condition of continual rotation created by aerodynamic factors.

## B

**Banana oil** – form of thin cellulose lacquer.

**Barrel-roll** – complete roll in which axis of roll describes a circle.

**Bay** – space between bulkheads or between sets of interplane struts e.g. single bay biplane etc.

**BDC** – bottom dead centre (of a reciprocating piston).

**Beam mounting** – method of engine or accessory mounting on parallel beams.

**Bearer** – beam for engine or accessory mounting.

**Bell-crank** – triangular plate providing 90° change in direction of motion.

**Biplane** – aeroplane having two superimposed wings.

**Blimp** – form of frameless airship with propulsion and control.

**Body putty** – plastic filler which dries hard for filling cracks or adding protrusions.

**Boom** – exposed spar, often hollow, carrying additional structure.

**Boundary layer** – thin layer of fluid (e.g. air) immediately adjacent to surface of a body.

**Brace** – subsidiary reinforcement member.

**Bulkhead** – solid cross-member occupying total cross-section area of a structure.

**Bungee** – fabric-covered multistrand rubber rope used for catapult, shock absorption etc.

**Bunt** – first half of an inverted loop.

## C

**Cabane** – pyramid struts on fuselage for parasol or upper wing.

**Camber** – curvature of the surface of an airfoil.

**Cantilever** – without external support.

**Capping** – flat strips applied to the edges of narrow members (e.g. ribs).

**Carburettor** – engine fitting mixing fuel spray with air.

**Centre-section** – central part of wing.

**CG** – centre of gravity, effectively the object's balance point.

**Choke** – restriction on carburettor intake to reduce amount of air inducted.

**Chord** – fore and aft length of an airfoil, i.e. width of wing.

**CL** – centre of lift, the single point through which total lift acts.

**CLA** – centre of lateral area.

**Clevis** – adjustable fitting on end of control rod incorporating a pivot rod.

**Clock roll** – roll checked with wings at positions corresponding to hours on clock face.

**Collet** – cylindrical block capable of being locked on rod or wire by grub-screw etc.

**Compression ignition** – spontaneous combustion engine employing heat of compression.

**Condenser tissue** – lightest form of tissue, used for some indoor models.

**Contra-piston** – adjustable inverted piston giving variable compression ratio.

**Cowling** – covering enclosing an engine, usually thin metal or wood panels.

**CP** – centre of pressure, i.e. centre of lift of an aerofoil section.

**Crutch** – strong centrally-placed fuselage member round which lighter structure is assembled.

**Crystal** – piece of ground quartz used to control radio frequency.

## D

**Deac** – nickel-cadmium button cell (after the German company, DEAC).

**Decalage** – difference in incidence angles between superimposed wings.

**Decals** – US term for slide-on paint film transfers.

**Decking** – the light fairing on the upper side of a fuselage.

**Dethermalizer** – device for spoiling the trim and increasing sink on a model.

**Digital** – system of coding control pulses in radio transmissions.

**Dihedral** – the angle between the two halves (or outer sections) of a wing.

**Dope** – cellulose-based 'paint' to tauten and airproof covering.

**Dowel** – wood or metal rod of circular cross-section.

**Downthrust** – inclination of the thrust line to introduce a nose-down component.

**Downwash** – change of angle of airstream as it leaves an aerofoil or other body.

**Drag** – the resistance of an object to movement through a fluid.

**Dutch roll** – combination of yaw and roll to alternate sides due to instability.

# E

**Elevator** – surface hinged to tail-plane providing longitudinal (pitch) control.

**Empennage** – strictly, the basic frame of the undercarriage excluding wheels etc.

**Epoxy** – a resin adhesive of considerable strength.

# F

**FAI** – Federation Aeronautique Internationale, world controlling body.

**Fairing** – light structural addition to reduce head-resistance.

**Fin** – fixed vertical surface, usually at tail of aircraft.

**Firewall** – strong bulkhead to which engine is attached.

**Flaps** – surfaces at rear of wing used to increase lift at expense of increased drag.

**Flick roll** – sudden roll requiring one wing to be stalled.

**Folding propeller** – where the blades fold back at end of power run to reduce drag.

**Former** – a cross member giving shape to a fuselage or nacelle.

**Four-stroke** – cycle in an engine having combustion on alternate revolutions.

**Fuel-proofer** – type of varnish, usually resin-based, impervious to model fuels.

**Fuse** – usually dry cotton lamp-wick used to release a mechanism after a delay.

# G

**Glide** – descent in a flying attitude without applied power.

**Glider** – fixed wing aircraft, non-mechanically propelled.

**Glow-plug** – cylinder head plug equipped with constantly glowing element.

**GRP** – glass-reinforced plastic, commonly polyester resin.

**Gusset** – small triangular brace fitted in the angle between two members.

# H

**Hesitation roll** – a roll with periodic pauses.

**Horn** – projecting lever on a control surface through which control movement is applied.

**Hydraulic lock** – condition of engine when overflooded and unable to pass TDC.

# I

**Incidence** – angle of aerofoil to longitudinal axis of aircraft.

**Induction** – intake of air or fuel mixture in engine.

**Intake** – tube or aperture through which outside air is drawn.

# J

**Japanese tissue** – particular type of lightweight tissue for light outdoor models.

# K

**Keeper** – in models, a brace in intimate contact where a spar is angled.

**Kerosene** – paraffin, a petroleum product.

**Key** – small locating block to ensure correct assembly and alignment.

**Klunk tank** – type of fuel tank having a weighted movable pick-up tube.

**Knife-edge flight** – flying aircraft on side, wings vertical, using fuselage for lift.

# L

**Laminar flow** – steady airflow without tendency to turbulence or separation.

**Landing gear** – normally the complete undercarriage plus nose-wheel or tailskid etc.

**Leading edge** – forward edge of a body, also the forward structural member.

**Lift** – result of aerodynamic forces acting at right angles to direction of airflow.

**Longeron** – a main fore and aft member of a fuselage or nacelle.

**Loop scavenge** – design of gas flow in two-stroke engine to clear exhaust gases.

# M

**Methanol** – methyl alcohol, main constituent of glow-plug engine fuel.

**Microfilm** – cellulose preparation used for covering indoor models.

**Mid-wing** – wing mounted approximately on fuselage centre line.

**Monocoque** – type of construction in which most of the load is taken by the skin.

**Monoplane** – aeroplane with one main plane.

**Muffler** – silencer, a device for reducing emitted noise.

# N

**Nacelle** – a body enclosing an engine or, occasionally, crew.

**Needle-valve** – adjustable screwed valve regulating flow of fuel to carburettor.

**Neoprene** – a type of plastic, usually tubing for fuel feed.

**Nitro-methane** – hydrocarbon oxygen-releasing fuel additive.

**Nose-block** – detachable front fuselage plug carrying propeller bearing on rubber model.

# O

**Oleo leg** – undercarriage strut incorporating oil dashpot for shock absorption/damping.

**Ornithopter** – machine achieving flight by wing flapping.

# P

**Pan** – cast metal fuselage shape used in high performance C/L and FF models.

**Pants** – streamlining covers over wheels.

**Parasol** – layout in which fuselage is carried beneath wing by braces.

**Piano wire** – (music wire) tempered spring steel wire.

**Pitch** – movement about lateral axis, also distance travelled by propeller in one revolution.

**Pitot head** – small twin tubes for measuring pressures to show air speed.

**Polyhedral** – form of double dihedral angle.

**Pressure feed** – supply of fuel to carburettor at constant (above atmospheric) pressure.

**Pre-tensioning** – method of limiting unwinding of rubber motor to desired motor length.

**Priming** – injection of fuel direct into cylinder or air intake.

**Proportional** – in radio, control surface movement relating directly to transmitter stick movement.

**Pulse** – radio signal of very short duration.

**Pusher** – aeroplane with the propeller behind the main plane(s).

**Push-rod** – rigid rod transmitting push-pull motion to a control.

**PVA** – polyvinyl alcohol, commonly encountered as 'white glue'.

**Pylon** – a one-piece wing support for a parasol wing; turning point for models in one form of R/C racing; special yoke used in C/L speed flying.

# Q

**Quadruplane** – aeroplane with four superimposed wings.

**Quarter-grain** – cut of balsa giving maximum stiffness for minimum weight.

# R

**Radial mount** – method of mounting engine on flat firewall with fore and aft bolts.

**Reed induction** – type of engine using flat sprung metal valve intake operating on crankcase pressure.

**Reynolds number** – ratio of length × velocity of a body to kinematic viscosity of a fluid, used to express condition for similar motions in viscous fluids.

**Rib** – structural member giving required shape to covering of a plane.

**Riblet** – short additional rib extending over the leading 10–15% or so of a plane.

**Roll** – revolution about the longitudinal axis.

**Rotary induction** – fuel/air intake through a crankshaft valve or disc driven by the crankpin.

**RTP** – round-the-pole, a tethered flight about a fixed centre.

# S

**Sailplane** – high efficiency glider.

**Sanding sealer** – cellulose preparation with filler (e.g. talc) for grain-filling.

**Scale effect** – effect on absolute coefficients of a marked reduction in Reynolds number.

**Servo** – electro-mechanical relay producing control movement when switched by radio.

**Sesquiplane** – biplane with one wing markedly smaller in span/chord than the other.

**Sidethrust** – angular displacement of the engine to introduce a side (turning) force.

**Sideport** – a two-stroke engine where intake to crankcase is through cylinder wall.

**Slat** – an auxiliary airfoil sited on the leading edge to increase lift or delay a stall.

**Slipstream** – the wash from a propeller.

**Slope lift** – upward component of wind striking rising ground.

**Slope soaring** – gliding along face of hill or cliff making use of slope lift.

**Slot** – aperture through wing or between wing and slat to improve lift or delay stall.

**Slow roll** – a 360° rotation about the longitudinal axis at modest rate.

**Snap roll** – see flick roll.

**Soaring** – maintenance or gain of height by a glider in upcurrents.

**Spacer** – vertical or cross-strut in basic fuselage framework.

**Spar** – a principal structural member supporting subsidiary members.

**Spark ignition** – ignition of gases in an engine by generation of electrical spark.

**Spar model** – see stick model.

**Spat** – streamlined cover almost totally enclosing landing wheel.

**Spin** – downward spiral path with aeroplane in stalled condition.

**Spinner** – streamlined central boss cover on airscrew.

**Spiral dive** – downward spiral path in unstalled condition.

**Spoiler** – device exposable to reduce lift and increase sink.

**Spray bar** – drilled tube across engine intake allowing fuel to be drawn in as spray.

**Sprue** – the waste formed in the feed lines of a die in moulding or casting.

**Stabilizer** – normal US term for tailplane.

**Stagger** – vertical difference in positions of superimposed wings to reduce interference.

**Stall** – total loss of lift due to airflow breakdown over aerofoil.

**Stall turn** – 180° yaw at top of vertical climb.

**Standing wave** – deflection of airstream at considerable height above hills etc.

**Stick model** – model (usually rubber powered) employing a single spar as fuselage.

**Stringer** – light longitudinal structural member producing required shape.

**Sweep** – angle formed by a wing etc. in plan form to longitudinal centre line.

# T

**Tailplane** – small plane mounted (normally) behind main plane for stabilizing.

**Tail tilt** – inclination of tailplane to induce a turn.

**TDC** – top dead centre, of a reciprocating piston.

**Team racer** – type of C/L model raced three or four together in one circle.

**Template** – an actual size guide to cutting or sanding.

**Thermal** – rising air due to convection from unequal heat absorption.

**Thickness/chord ratio** – thickness of an aerofoil as a percentage of its chord.

**Thinners** – cellulose solvent.

**Three-port** – type of two-stroke engine with intake port in cylinder wall.

**Throttle** – control lever regulating speed of engine.

**Thrust** – force created by the propeller, drawing the aeroplane forward.

**Tongue and box** – method of mounting wings etc. with box in wing root engaging tongue on fuselage.

**Torque** – reaction of whole aeroplane to rotating airscrew, in opposite direction.

**Torsion bar** – use of twist resistance in steel wire etc. to provide springing.

**Tow-launch** – method of achieving height before release of a glider.

**Towline** – line used to kite up glider.

**Townend ring** – ring placed round radial engine to reduce drag.

**Track** – distance between wheels of undercarriage, also path of flight over ground.

**Tractor** – aeroplane with airscrew mounted ahead of main wing.

**Trailing edge** – the rearmost edge, the member forming the rearmost edge.

**Transfer port** – aperture through which fresh charge enters cylinder from crankcase in two-stroke engine.

**Transfers** – paint film decoration on gummed paper, soaked and slid into place.

**Trim** – the balance of aerodynamic forces leading to most efficient flight performance.

**Trim tab** – a small permanently-adjusted surface applying a correcting force.

**Triplane** – aeroplane with three superimposed wings.

**Turtle-back** – light fairing structure behind cockpit.

**Two-stroke** – cycle of engine operation with one power stroke per revolution.

# U

**Under camber** – concavity in the underside of an aerofoil.

**Undercarriage** – structure including main landing wheels and struts.

# V

**Valve, needle** – see needle-valve.

**Venturi** – a narrow-necked tube widening at each end employing Bernoulli's Law.

**VIT** – variable incidence tailplane, used to balance power on/power off trim in FF.

# W

**Warp** – twist or change of angle in a wing panel etc.

**Wash** – stream of air leaving a body.

**Wash-in** – increase of incidence towards a wingtip.

**Wash-out** – decrease of incidence towards a wingtip.

**Weather-cocking** – excess of vertical area aft leading to directional over-stability.

**Whipping** – leading or pulling control lines to increase speed of model.

**Wing-over** – path of C/L model in vertical half-circle over flier's head.

**Wing section** – cross-section of wing, often loosely called 'airfoil' or 'aerofoil'.

# Y

**Yaw** – rotation of the aircraft about its vertical axis, i.e. directionally.

# Index

To avoid constant repetition,
the first and/or most significant
references are listed. Page numbers
in *italic* denote an illustration.

**Acknowledgements**
We are indebted to Henry J. Nicholls and Sons for the equipment supplied on pages 120 and 121, and to A. Greenhalgh who supplied the models for Chapter One.

**Special Photography by:**
**Ian Dawson** 142 below, 143, 144, 147; **Paul Forrester** 67, 92, 93 (except for below right), 118, 119; **Mike Sheil** endpapers, title page, 74–75, 77, 78, 80, 81, 138, 158, 158–159, 160, 163, 166, 172, 173, 174, 175, 176, 177, 207, 209; **Terry Trott** contents, half title, 64–65 below, 93 below, 120–121, 131 above, 170 above, 170–171, 186–187, 196–197, 200–201; **John Wylie** 12, 13, 15 above, 16 above, 16–17 below, 24, 25, 26, 28, 30–31 above, 30 centre, 30–31 below, 31 centre, 33, 46 above, 46–47, 48–49 below, 49 above, 184 above.

The publishers would also like to thank the following individuals and organizations for their kind permission to reproduce the photographs in this book:
G. Alison 96–97, 98 above, 98–99 below, 99 right, 100, 101, 103, 104; John Barnard 148, 150, 184 below, 185; Bill Burkinshaw 131 centre and below; George Bushell 168; Ciba-Geigy (Ron Moulton) 52, 53; G. Dallimer 134, 137, 139; Mary Evans Picture Library 8 centre left and right; Mike Fantham 58 below, 89, 90; A. Greenhalgh 8–9 below, 10–11 below, 11 inset below; Irvine Engines 125 below; E. J. Johns 188, 189, 190–191 above, 191, 192, 193, 195 below; Dave Linstrum 58 above right, 65 above; MAP Ltd 34–35, 40 above, 112; Andrew Morland 151, 183 centre and below, 201 above; Ron Moulton 54, 55, 56 above left and right insets, 59, 64 above, 114, 122, 125 above, 132–133, 141, 194, 195 above, 200 above, 211, 212 above, 212–213, 214, 217, 219; John O'Donnell 58 above left, 83, 84, 85, 86, 87, 88, 109, 110, 179, 183 above; Jenny Potter 56–57, 68 below left and right, 69 below left and right, 70; R. L. Rimell 18, 19, 20–21, 22–23, 39 below, 42, 44, 45; Ripmax Models Ltd 204; Ann Ronan Picture Library 8 above; Vic Smeed 114 below; Mike Wells 14–15 below; Norman Witcomb 34 inset above, 39 above and centre, 40 below.

Illustrations by:
Brian Mayor, Technical Art Services and Studio Briggs.
Full colour cutaways by Tony Matthews.